The Post-Containment Handbook

An East-West Forum Publication

The Post-Containment Handbook

Key Issues in U.S.–Soviet Economic Relations

EDITED BY

Robert Cullen

Westview Press
BOULDER, SAN FRANCISCO, & OXFORD

Copyright © 1990 by The Samuel Bronfman Foundation, Inc.

Published in 1990 in the United States of America by Westview Press, Inc., 5500 Central Avenue, Boulder, Colorado 80301, and in the United Kingdom by Westview Press, Inc., 36 Lonsdale Road, Summertown, Oxford OX2 7EW

Library of Congress Cataloging-in-Publication Data
The Post-containment handbook: key issues in U.S.-Soviet economic
    relations/edited by Robert Cullen.
        p.   cm.
    ISBN 0-8133-7978-4
    1. United States—Foreign economic relations—Soviet Union.
2. Soviet Union—Foreign economic relations—United States.
3. United States—Commercial policy. I. Cullen, Robert.
HF1456.5.S624P67   1990
337.47073—dc20

90-12038
CIP

Printed and bound in the United States of America

The paper used in this publication meets the requirements
of the American National Standard for Permanence of Paper
for Printed Library Materials Z39.48-1984.

10   9   8   7   6   5   4   3   2   1

Contents

About the Contributors

Harry C. Blaney III is a former diplomat and member of the Policy Planning Staff at the U.S. Department of State. Mr. Blaney was also a senior visiting fellow at the Council on Foreign Relations and a Rusk Fellow at Georgetown University's Institute for the Study of Diplomacy. He writes frequently on international affairs, especially on problems of East-West relations.

Sarah C. Carey is a partner at the law firm of Heron, Burchette, Ruckert & Rothwell. She has represented numerous corporations involved in selling products and technology to the People's Republic of China, the Eastern bloc and the USSR.

Robert Cullen is the editor of *Soviet-American Trade*, a monthly newsletter.

Steve Dryden is a Washington journalist specializing in trade and foreign policy issues. He has written for *Business Week, The Washington Post* and the *International Herald Tribune*.

Joan Kloepfer is a graduate of the Johns Hopkins University Paul H. Nitze School of Advanced International Studies. She specializes in Soviet foreign economic relations.

Michael Mastanduno is an Assistant Professor in the Department of Government at Dartmouth College. He has published several articles on East-West trade and export controls, and is currently completing a manuscript on the coordination of alliance export control policy in COCOM.

James M. Montgomery was Deputy Assistant Secretary of State for Legislative Affairs from 1981 to 1986. He is now Executive Director of the East-West Forum.

Kevin L. Tritle is an economic analyst with the Central Intelligence Agency. He has been following developments in Soviet foreign economic relations for five years. The views expressed in his essay are his own and do not necessarily reflect the views of the Central Intelligence Agency.

Preface

The East-West Forum, located in Washington, D.C., and New York, is a research and policy analysis organization sponsored by the Samuel Bronfman Foundation. The Forum aims to build a bridge between scholarship and policymaking. It brings scholars and policymakers together in seminars, briefings, and conferences and in the production of books. Through this process it hopes to generate reliable information and high quality analyses that will prove useful to those engaged in the debates that shape and will shape U.S. policy during this period of dramatic changes in East-West relations.

The East-West Forum would like to extend its thanks to Stephen E. Herbits, Executive Vice President, Joseph E. Seagram & Sons, Inc.; William K Friedman, Trustee of the Samuel Bronfman Foundation; Seweryn Bialer, Chairman of the East-West Forum and David E. Morey. In addition to writing Chapter 7, Joan Kloepfer did invaluable work in locating documents and assembling material. Colleen Eller and Betty Katzner contributed valuable advice and careful proofreading. We also benefitted handsomely from the review and counsel of several experts; Robert Frowick, William Long, Theodore Papendorp, John Hardt and Robert Park.

The Forum plans to continue providing useful information and analyses. The continued participation and help of these individuals and others will be invaluable.

James M. Montgomery
Executive Director, East-West Forum

Introduction

President Bush has forced us to change the way we think about our economic relations with the Soviet Union. He said at Malta that he supported *perestroika* and would do everything possible to encourage Soviet entry into the world economy. Prior to Malta, U.S. policy tended to see Soviet economic achievements as a threat that could strengthen the Soviets' military potential, the sinew of Stalin's and Brezhnev's aggressive policies. The President has now accepted Mikhail Gorbachev's assurances that the Soviets no longer pursue policies aimed at imposing their economic order on the world by military force. In these circumstances, advances in the Soviet economy need no longer be viewed as a threat to the United States' or its allies' security; they can be viewed positively.

In response, the United States is going to have to review a large number of existing laws, regulations and bureaucratic practices. With this book, we have attempted to put in one volume all of the documents that those participating in this review will need. We have also tried to offer an analysis and explanation of the various issues these documents encompass.

The American policy review will address several issues:

- An export control regime appropriate to the new view of the Soviet economy;
- Cooperation with our allies in the creation and operation of such a regime;
- The relevance of legislation that has conditioned the economic relationship with the USSR on its emigration laws and practices and
- The institutional mechanisms best suited for encouraging rapid integration of the USSR into the larger economy.

The Export Administration Act has been the centerpiece of our effort to control the flow of technology to the Soviet Union and its allies. This act expires in 1990, and the President, at Malta, replaced the basic assumptions behind it. The Congress, the business community and the Administration will have to review it carefully and construct an export regime that is appropriate for a new member of the club—not a candidate who has been blackballed. This volume contains the sections of the Export Administration Act that go to the heart of many of the issues: How vigorously should the United States attempt to control the export of items available from other countries? What executive agencies should have the lead in administering an export regime? How much latitude should the President have to impose controls on items that pose no technological threat?

The Export Administration Act concerns unilateral U.S. efforts to control exports. The Coordinating Committee on Multilateral Export Controls (COCOM) is the means by which the United States has attempted to get other countries to cooperate with us in controlling the export of militarily threatening technology to the Soviet Union and Eastern Europe. Again, its practices and traditions are geared to deny goods and technologies to potential adversaries. These practices are already under considerable pressure, particularly from our European friends, and they too will have to be reviewed in light of the new realities. In addition to an essay by Michael Mastanduno, which endeavors to explain the workings of COCOM, we have included samples of the materials from which COCOM makes it decisions. Steven Dryden's chapter covers efforts by both the United States and the Europeans to control the Soviets' access to credit.

Another feature of the export control regime has been the efforts of the United States government to restrict Soviet access to the vast store of technological information in this country. This has had repercussions, not only for industry, but also for the government and academia. Joan Kloepfer's essay traces the development of these practices. This chapter also includes a number of the administrative and legal documents designed to restrict Soviet access to sensitive technological information.

In addition to the restrictions the United States has put on strategically significant trade with the USSR, it has also restricted its trading relationship because of the USSR's emigration practices. The best known of these restrictions are embodied in the Jackson-Vanik Amendment to the 1974 Trade Act. Basically, these provisions prohibit normal tariff treatment for Soviet exports as long as the Soviet government restricts its citizens' freedom of emigration. This and other legislation will clearly be part of the review. Robert Cullen's chapter provides the background and the text of these provisions. His prologue gives us even more perspective with its examination of earlier clashes with the Soviets and their predecessors concerning trade and human rights.

The integration of the Soviet Union into the world economy will not happen automatically. Kevin Tritle's chapter discusses the Soviet economy in considerable detail, and from it we get some idea of how far it has to go. Sarah Carey's discussion of the Soviets' first efforts to open their economy to Western ideas and capital also underlines the difficulties ahead.

The bilateral U.S.-Soviet relationship will significantly influence the movement toward integration, but ultimate success will depend on the actions and initiatives of all the members of the economic community, particularly the Europeans. This will require close coordination between the United States and Europe. The management of the emergence of the Soviet Union and Eastern Europe as serious economic players would be demanding in its own right. It will, however, have to be combined with the longer-standing but equally important task of managing the United States' evolving relationship with Western Europe as it moves toward its own integrated market in 1992.

The East-West Forum believes that the economic provisions in the Helsinki Act of 1975 could provide the United States with the institutional mechanisms it needs to stay engaged in Europe's economic evolution, particularly as it reaches out to the East. The Helsinki process has served the United States effectively in both the security and human rights areas, or "Baskets" I and III. The Forum believes it is now time to turn to Basket II, the one on economic cooperation. Both President Bush and Secretary of State James Baker have made it clear that the Administration views Basket II as an appropriate means of arriving at conclusions and agreements about economic integration. The most immediate application of this will be the conference in Bonn in March of 1990 on economic cooperation in Europe. We have included all of the background documents, not only on the conference but also on Basket II as well as an explanatory essay by Harry Blaney.

With President Bush's statements, this country has clearly moved beyond viewing trade with the USSR as the grudging exchange of goods between hostile nations. President Bush has foreseen a day when the USSR is a full participant in the market economy which has served the world so well since 1945. The Soviet Union has been left out of the process, as have been the other members of the Warsaw Pact. Eastern European countries are almost desperate to become participants. The same probably holds true of the Soviet Union, although President Gorbachev keeps insisting he is a dedicated Communist. The United States now supports the possibility of Soviet participation. The East-West Forum hopes that this volume will be useful to those engaged in making the necessary changes in the way in which the United States has done business with this part of the world for the last four decades.

Edgar M. Bronfman
President, East-West Forum

1

Prologue

Robert Cullen

Modern chronicles of Soviet-American trade, and the human rights disputes that often accompany it, are apt to begin sometime in the late 1960s. That was when Soviet Jews, exhilarated by Israel's triumph in the Six Day War, began demanding the right to emigrate. It was when the Nixon administration began exploring the possibility of détente with Moscow, including the extension of most-favored nation tariff status to the Soviets. The two issues, emigration and trade, inextricably entwined themselves a couple of years later in the Jackson-Vanik Amendment to the 1974 Trade Act.

But, in fact, the issues and the linkage between them go back much further into history. The first Russian-American treaty on trade was signed in 1832 by a future president, James Buchanan, on behalf of the administration of Andrew Jackson. It gave both countries most-favored nation status (MFN). **(Document 1.1)**

The treaty was born of mutual interest: the Russians and the Americans needed each other to combat British efforts to dominate maritime trade. Buchanan had arrived in St. Petersburg in the summer of 1832. His negotiations were strictly secret. In December, when the treaty was about ready for signature, Emperor Nicholas I could not resist rubbing the British nose in it. Buchanan found himself at a court reception with the rest of the diplomatic corps, standing next to the British minister, a Mr. Bligh. "You may judge of my astonishment," Buchanan wrote home, "when the Emperor, accosting me in French, in a tone of voice which could be heard by all around, said, 'I signed the order yesterday that the Treaty should be executed according to your wishes,' and then immediately turning to Mr. Bligh, asked him to become the interpreter of the information. [Buchanan did not speak French, the court language in St. Petersburg.] He is a most amiable man, and his astonishment and embarrassment were so striking that I felt for him most sincerely."

United by their mutual fear of British domination, the two countries got along well for some thirty years. But the 1832 treaty, like the 1972 U.S.-Soviet trade agreement, was destined to be scrapped. And the reason, in both cases, was American insistence on the rights of Jews in Russia.

The 1911 Abrogation

The precursor of Anatoly Shcharansky, Vladimir Slepak, Andrei Sakharov, and all the dissidents and refuseniks of the 1970s and 1980s was a man named Bernhard Bernstein, who emigrated to the United States from Russia in 1845 and became a naturalized American citizen. In 1864, Bernstein found himself visiting Russia. He was arrested by the Tsar's police, who told him that he had not fulfilled his military service obligation to the Russian Empire. **(Document 1.2)** The United States protested, and the vehicle for the protest was the 1832 commercial treaty.

Article I of that treaty provided that Americans in Russia should have all the rights and privileges of Russian citizens. But beginning with the Bernstein case, the Russian authorities periodically refused to grant those rights to Jewish Americans. Sometimes, American Jewish businessmen were denied the right to buy property. Sometimes they were told they could not live in St. Petersburg, which was not in the "Pale of Settlement," to which Russian Jews were confined.

The State Department's response to these episodes was an offer to negotiate an agreement clarifying Article I of the 1832 treaty. Russia refused, saying that as long as the United States refused to treat blacks and Orientals as equals, it should not tell Russia how to treat Jews. The dispute simmered for 40 years, until 1903. That year witnessed the horrible Kishinev pogrom, an Easter attack on Russian Jews that left 47 people dead, hundreds injured, and thousands homeless. The Russian government's attitude toward the event was one of callous indifference.

The pogrom further soured the general American attitude toward the Russian autocracy, an attitude

1

which had been growing steadily worse for years. In 1891, George Kennan (a distant relative of the 20th Century diplomat and historian) had written a book about the depredations of Russian prisons called "Siberia and the Exile System." He toured the country lecturing about it, sometimes appearing on stage in prison garb and irons. At about the same time, the Russian government had adopted the insulting policy of refusing to give visas to American Jews.

The American Jewish community, by the time of the Kishinev pogrom, was politically much more powerful than it had been at the time of Bernhard Bernstein's troubles. Its leaders, such as Jacob H. Schiff, Oscar S. Straus and Louis Marshall, were men of wealth and influence. When they asked the State Department to lodge a protest with Russia, they first encountered the traditional American diplomatic attitude toward such matters from Secretary of State John Hay. "What possible advantage would it be to the United States, and what possible advantage to the Jews of Russia, if we should make a protest against these fiendish cruelties and be told it was none of our business?" Hay wrote to Schiff. But the Jewish leaders were not to be denied. With an election coming up in 1904, President Theodore Roosevelt soon yielded. In July, he accepted a petition to the Tsar complaining about the pogrom and ordered the State Department to forward it to the court in St. Petersburg. **(Document 1.3)**

As Hay had predicted, however, the Russians replied that it was none of America's business. The Tsar's government refused to receive the petition. **(Document 1.4)** But the issue was joined.

Just as it would some 65 years later, the American Jewish community launched a campaign to force Washington to link human rights and trade. Although persecution of Russian Jews was the real motivating issue, the campaign focused on the Russian government's abuse of American Jews, insisting that it violated the 1832 treaty. By 1904, the Jewish community had managed to persuade both the Republicans and Democrats to put a plank in their campaign platforms insisting on equal treatment abroad for all Americans, regardless of their religion. In 1905, Schiff used his influence in the New York financial community to help deny loans to Russia for its war with Japan. By 1908, when conditions in Russia seemed to be getting only worse, the Jewish community began to seek abrogation of the treaty.

"There rests a stain on the honor of our nation and on the integrity of American citizenship, for the passport issued by the State Department of the United States, bearing the great seal of our country, and which vouches for the citizenship of him to whom it is issued, is dishonored, rejected, and arbitrarily disregarded by the Russian government whenever the citizen by whom it is presented happens to be a Jew," said Louis Marshall at the height of the abrogation campaign. "And unless the virtue of manhood has deserted this Republic, its citizens will no longer patiently witness the mockery of diplomatic procedure, but will insist on a complete abrogation of every treaty now existing between the United States and Russia."

It was a winning argument. On December 13, 1911, the House passed, by a vote of 301–1, a resolution calling for abrogation. **(Document 1.5)** The Taft Administration, certain that the resolution would also pass the Senate, went ahead and abrogated the treaty before the Congress forced the action.

There is, however, no evidence that this first use of an American economic sanction improved the lot of Russian Jews. To the contrary, their plight grew worse, according to contemporary reports by the American Ambassador in St. Petersburg, Curtis Guild. **(Document 1.6)** As late as 1913, the Tsar's Minister of Justice, at a celebrated murder trial in Kiev, based the prosecution's case on the ancient libel that Jews murdered Christian children to use their blood in devilish rituals. Only war and revolution ended the anti-Semitic policies of the Romanovs.

Geopolitical Concerns

The war and the Russian Revolution, for a time, changed the American approach to economic relations with Russia. Questions of human rights became secondary to geopolitical concerns. In the immediate aftermath of the October Revolution, the principal concern of the Wilson Administration and its allies was finding a way to keep Russia in the war. After the new Soviet government frustrated the West by concluding its separate peace with Germany, the allies opted to intervene on the side of the anticommunist White Army, first with covert assistance and then, in the middle of 1918, with troops.

From the outset, the Bolsheviks displayed a cynical, and fundamentally flawed, conception of the role that trade might play in the overall Soviet-American relationship. Trotsky, in his maiden speech as the Bolsheviks' Foreign Minister, portrayed the United States as a nation totally dominated by its financiers, a country which would scrap any scruple in the pursuit of profits, including profits from Russia. **(Document 1.7)** Lenin and his cohorts believed that the Allies' rhetoric about solidarity and the fight for democracy was only rhetoric. They believed they could play one Allied nation off against others by tempting it with offers of trade concessions and profit. That picture of the capitalist world still resonated more than 60 years later in the belief of the Brezhnev government that the West should, and would, pursue trade with the Soviet Union regardless of its internal human rights policies or its Third World interventions.

And the Bolsheviks put their theories into practice. In February, they formally repudiated the debts of both the Tsarist and the Provisional governments. **(Document 1.8)** Only three months later, Lenin had a remarkable interview with Raymond Robins, who was about to end a tour in Russia as chief of the American Red Cross Mission. Robins had been sympathetic to the Revolution. Not being a government employee, he had not been bound by the State Department's policy of forbidding official contacts with the Bolsheviks, and he had developed friendly relations with both Lenin and Trotsky.

Lenin handed Robins a proposal for major Soviet-American economic cooperation. He asked the United States, implicitly and explicitly, to ignore the recent debt repudiation and the treaty the Soviets had just concluded with Germany, giving that nation and its allies most-favored nation trade status with Russia. The United States could have the preeminent share of the profits from Russia's foreign trade, he suggested, since Germany and its allies would be exhausted by the war.

Robins delivered Lenin's proposal to the Secretary of State, Robert Lansing. But if Lenin had really expected the United States to pounce greedily on his offer, he badly miscalculated. Wilson refused even to see Robins. There was never a reply to Lenin's offer, and within two months, American troops had joined in the Allied intervention. It would take Washington and Moscow 17 more years to reach a trade agreement.

The Roosevelt administration signed that agreement **(Document 1.9)** on July 13, 1935. In exchange for most-favored nation status, the Soviets agreed to buy at least $30 million worth of American goods each year. The two sides renewed the agreement each summer until 1942, when the Lend Lease Agreement superseded it. After World War II, however, the Cold War set in, and there were no more trade agreements. In 1951, Congress enacted a trade law **(Document 1.10)** that revoked MFN status for imports from the Soviet Union and any other country "dominated or controlled by...the world Communist movement." It was another 20 years before economic relations began to thaw.

Document 1.1

Russo-American Trade Agreement of 1832

(From Hunter Miller, ed., *Treaties and Other International Acts of the United States of America*, Volume 3, Document No. 75, Washington, D.C.: U.S. Government Printing Office, 1933.)

In the name of the most Holy and indivisible Trinity

The United States of America, and his Majesty the Emperor of all the Russias, equally animated with the desire of maintaining the relations of good understanding, which have hitherto so happily subsisted between their respective States, and of extending, and consolidating the commercial intercourse between them, have agreed to enter into negotiations for the conclusion of a Treaty of navigation and commerce. For which purpose the President of the United States has conferred full powers on James Buchanan their Envoy Extraordinary and Minister Plenipotentiary near His Imperial Majesty; and his Majesty the Emperor of all the Russias has conferred like powers on the Sieur Charles Robert Count de Nesselrode, His Vice-Chancellor, Knight of the orders of Russia and of many others &c: and the said Plenipotentiaries having exchanged their full powers, found in good and due form, have concluded and signed the following Articles:

ARTICLE I.

There shall be between the territories of the high contracting parties, a reciprocal liberty of commerce and navigation. The inhabitants of their respective States shall, mutually, have liberty to enter the ports, places, and rivers of the territories of each party, wherever foreign commerce is permitted. They shall be at liberty to sojourn and reside in all parts whatsoever of said territories, in order to attend to their affairs, and they shall enjoy, to that effect, the same security and protection as natives of the country wherein they reside, on condition of their submitting to the laws and ordinances there prevailing, and particularly to the regulations in force concerning commerce.

ARTICLE II.

Russian vessels arriving either laden or in ballast, in the ports of the United States of America; and, reciprocally, vessels of the United States arriving either laden, or in ballast, in the ports of the Empire of Russia, shall be treated, on their entrance, during their stay, and at their departure, upon the same footing as national vessels, coming from the same place, with respect to the duties of tonnage. In regard to light house duties, pilotage, and port charges, as well as to the fees and perquisites of public officers, and all other duties and charges, of whatever kind or denomination, levied upon vessels of commerce, in the name or to the profit of the Government, the local authorities, or of any private establishments whatsoever, the high contracting parties shall reciprocally treat each other, upon the footing of the most favored nations, with whom they have not Treaties now actually in force, regulating the said duties and charges on the basis of an entire reciprocity.

ARTICLE III.

All kind of merchandise and articles of commerce, which may be lawfully imported into the ports of the Empire of Russia in Russian vessels, may, also, be so imported in vessels of the United States of America, without paying other or higher duties or charges, of whatever kind or denomination, levied in the name, or to the profit of the Government, the local authorities, or of any private establishments whatsoever, than if the same merchandise or articles of commerce had been imported in Russian vessels. And, reciprocally, all kind of merchandise and articles of commerce, which may be lawfully imported into the ports of the United States of America, in vessels of the said States, may, also, be so imported in Russian vessels, without paying other or higher duties or charges, of whatever kind or denomination, levied in the name, or to the profit of the Government, the local authorities, or of any private establishments whatsoever, than if the same merchandise or articles of commerce had been imported in vessels of the United States of America.

ARTICLE IV.

It is understood that the stipulations contained in the two preceding Articles, are to their full extent, applicable to Russian vessels, and their cargoes, arriving in the ports of the United States of America; and, reciprocally, to vessels of the said States and their cargoes, arriving in the ports of the Empire of Russia, whether the said vessels clear directly from the ports of the country to which they respectively belong, or from the ports of any other foreign country.

ARTICLE V.

All kind of merchandise and articles of commerce, which may be lawfully exported from the ports of the United States of America in national vessels may, also, be exported therefrom in Russian vessels, without paying other or higher duties or charges, of whatever kind or denomination, levied in the name, or to the profit of the Government, the local authorities, or of any private establishments whatsoever, than if the same merchandise or articles of commerce had been exported in vessels of the United States of America. And, reciprocally, all kind of merchandise and articles of commerce, which may be lawfully exported from the ports of the Empire of Russia in national vessels, may also be exported therefrom in vessels of the United States of America, without paying other or higher duties or charges of whatever kind or denomination, levied in the name, or to the profit of the Government, the local authorities, or of any private establishments whatsoever, than if the same merchandise or articles of commerce had been exported in Russian vessels.

ARTICLE VI.

No higher or other duties shall be imposed on the importation into the United States, of any article, the produce or manufacture of Russia; and no higher or other duties shall be imposed on the importation into the Empire of Russia, of any article, the produce or manufacture of the United States, than are, or shall be, payable on the like article, being the produce or manufacture of any other foreign country. Nor shall any prohibition be imposed on the importation or exportation of any article the produce or manufacture of the United States, or of Russia, to, or from the ports of the Russian Empire, which shall not equally extend to all other nations.

ARTICLE VII.

It is expressly understood that the preceding Articles II, III, IV, V, and VI shall not be applicable to the coastwise navigation of either of the two countries, which each of the high contracting parties reserves exclusively to itself.

ARTICLE VIII.

The two contracting parties shall have the liberty of having, in their respective ports, Consuls, Vice-Consuls, Agents and Commissaries of their own appointment, who shall enjoy the same privileges and powers, as those of the most favored nations; but if any such Consul shall exercise commerce, they shall be submitted to the same laws and usages to which the private individuals of their nation are submitted, in the same place.

The Consuls, Vice-Consuls, and Commercial Agents shall have the right, as such, to sit as judges and arbitrators in such differences as may arise between the Captains and crews of the vessels belonging to the nation whose interests are committed to their charge, without the interference of the local authorities, unless the conduct of the crews, or of the captain, should disturb the order or the tranquillity of the Country; or the said Consuls, Vice-Consuls, or Commercial Agents should require their assistance to cause their decisions to be carried into effect or supported. It is, however, understood, that this species of judgment or arbitration shall not deprive the contending parties of the right they have to resort, on their return, to the judicial authority of their Country.

ARTICLE IX.

The said Consuls, Vice-Consuls, and Commercial Agents, are authorised to require the assistance of the local authorities, for the search, arrest, detention and imprisonment of the deserters from the ships of war and merchant vessels of their country. For this purpose they shall apply to the competent tribunals, judges, and officers, and shall, in writing, demand said deserters, proving by the exhibition of the registers of the vessels, the rolls of the crews, or by other official documents that such individuals formed part of the crews; and, this reclamation being thus substantiated, the surrender shall not be refused.

Such deserters, when arrested, shall be placed at the disposal of the said Consuls, Vice Consuls, or Commercial Agents, and may be confined in the public prisons, at the request and cost of those who shall claim them, in order to be detained until the time when they shall be restored to the vessels to which they belonged, or sent back to their own country by a vessel of the same nation or any other vessel whatsoever. But if not sent back within four months, from the day of their arrest, they shall be set at liberty, and shall not be again arrested for the same cause.

However, if the deserter should be found to have committed any crime or offense, his surrender may be delayed until the tribunal before which his case shall be depending shall have pronounced its sentence, and such sentence shall have been carried into effect.

ARTICLE X.

The citizens and subjects of each of the high contracting parties shall have power to dispose of their personal goods within the jurisdiction of the other, by testament, donation, or otherwise, and their representatives, being citizens or subjects of the other party, shall succeed to their said personal goods, whether by testament or *ab intestato*, and may take possession thereof, either by themselves, or by others acting for them, and dispose of the same, at will, paying to the profit of the respective Governments, such dues only as the inhabitants of the country wherein the said goods are, shall be subject to pay in like cases. And in case of the absence of the representative, such care shall be taken of the said goods, as would be taken of the goods of a native of the same country, in like case, until the lawful owner may take measures for receiving them. And if a question should arise among several claimants, as to which of them said goods belong, the same shall be decided finally by the laws and judges of the land wherein the said goods are. And where, on the death of any person holding real estate, within the territories of one of the high contracting parties, such real estate would, by the laws of the land, descend on a citizen or subject of the other party, who by reason of alienage may be incapable of holding it, he shall be allowed the time fixed by the laws of the country, and in case the laws of the country, actually in force, may not have fixed any such time, he shall then be allowed a reasonable time to sell such real estate and to withdraw and export the proceeds without molestation, and without paying to the profit of the respective Governments, any other dues than those to which the inhabitants of the country wherein said real estate is situated, shall be subject to pay, in like cases. But this Article shall not derogate, in any manner, from the force of the laws already published, or which may hereafter be published by His Majesty the Emperor of all the Russias: to prevent the emigration of his subjects.

ARTICLE XI.

If either party shall, hereafter, grant to any other nation, any particular favor in navigation or commerce, it shall, immediately, become common to the other party, freely, where it is freely granted to such other nation, or on yielding the same compensation, when the grant is conditional.

ARTICLE XII.

The present treaty, of which the effect shall extend, in like manner, to the Kingdom of Poland, so far as the same may be applicable thereto, shall continue in force until the first day of January, in the year of our Lord one thousand Eight hundred and Thirty nine, and if, one year before that day, one of the high contracting parties, shall not have announced to the other, by an official notification, its intention to arrest the operation thereof, this treaty shall remain obligatory one year beyond that day, and so on, until the expiration of the year which shall commence after the date of a similar notification.

ARTICLE XIII.

The present Treaty shall be approved and ratified by the President of the United States of America, by and with the advice and consent of the Senate of the said States, and by His Majesty the Emperor of all the Russias; and the ratifications shall be exchanged in the City of Washington within the space of one year, or sooner if possible.

In faith whereof, the respective Plenipotentiaries have signed the present treaty in duplicate and affixed thereto the seal of their arms. Done at St. Petersburg the sixth/Eighteenth December, in the year of Grace, One thousand Eight hundred and thirty two.

JAMES BUCHANAN [Seal]

[Seal] **CHARLES COMTE DE NESSELRODE**

SEPERATE ARTICLE

Certain relations of proximity and anterior engagements, having rendered it necessary for the Imperial Government to regulate the commercial relations of Russia with Prussia and the Kingdoms of Sweden and Norway by special stipulations, now actually in force, and which may be renewed hereafter; which stipulations are, in no manner, connected with the existing regulations for foreign commerce in general: the two high contracting parties, wishing to remove from their commercial relations every kind of ambiguity or subject of discussion, have agreed, that the special stipulations granted to the commerce of Prussia, and of Sweden and Norway, in consideration of equivalent advantages granted in these countries, by the one to the commerce of the Kingdom of Poland, and by the other

to that of the Grand Dutchy of Finland, shall not, in any case, be invoked in favor of the relations of commerce and navigation, sanctioned between the two high contracting parties by the present Treaty.

The present Seperate Article shall have the same force & value as if it were inserted, word for word, in the Treaty signed this day, and shall be ratified at the same time.

In faith whereof, we, the undersigned, by virtue of our respective full powers, have signed the present Seperate Article, and affixed thereto the seals of our arms.

Done at St. Petersburg, the 6/18 of December, in the year of Grace, one Thousand Eight hundred & thirty Two.

JAMES BUCHANAN [seal]

[seal] CHARLES COMTE DE NESSELRODE

[Original in English and French. Submitted to the Senate February 22, 1833. Resolution of advice and consent February 27, 1833. Ratified by the United States April 8, 1833. Ratified by Russia January 8, 1833 (December 27, 1832, Old Style). Ratifications exchanged at Washington May 11, 1833. Proclaimed May 11, 1833.]

Document 1.2

Documents Pertaining to Bernhard Bernstein

(Ex. Doc. No. 197, House of Representatives, 42nd Congress, 3rd Session.)

Mr. Bernstein to Mr. Seward

ISBICA, RUSSIA POLEN, October 31, 1864
(Received 18th November)

SIR: I am a naturalized citizen of the United States of America. In the month of January last I got granted a pass in your honory office, signed by your honor, William H. Seward, and sealed with the great seal of the United States of America. I took my departure from the Empire city, New York, in the month of May. June 22 I came through Berlin, Prussia, got my pass indorsed by his honor H. Kreismann, and in due form, came hereto, this day, my native place of birth, on no other business but to pay a visit to an old father of mine now living, thank God, aged eighty-three years. I staid here all the time without any molestation until Tuesday last, the 25th instant, when I was arrested, on what charge I know not. I was kidnaped, sent under a military escort to Wloclawek; there I was thrown in prison, kept as a common outlaw; but, fortunately, my friends got me out of prison on bail; my pass, together with the charges they brought against me, which charge never was read to me, they sent off to Warsaw, to headquarters. What the orders from there will be I can't tell.

But, as a citizen of the United States of America, I apply to your honor for protection, and, sir, I rely upon you that your honor will attend to it at once. As a citizen of the United States of America I appeal to the Government under which I have lived this last fourteen years, and under which I shelter myself, and which Government I expect to live the remainder of my days, to protect me. God bless the President, his cabinet, and the people at large.

I am, &c.,

BERNHARD BERNSTEIN,
A citizen of the United States of America

Mr. Seward to Mr. Clay

DEPARTMENT OF STATE
Washington, November 20, 1864

SIR: I transmit herewith a copy of a letter addressed to this Department by Mr. Bernhard Bernstein, who claims the protection of this Government, and who states that having visited Isbica, Russia, for no other purpose than to see his aged father, he was arrested, and is now confined in that place. You are instructed to ascertain the circumstances attending the arrest and imprisonment of Mr. Bernstein, and if his statement shall prove to be well founded, to do what you properly can toward procuring his release.

I am, &c.,

WILLIAM H. SEWARD.

Document 1.3

Letter from Secretary of State John Hay to Ambassador Riddle Including the Text of the Petition to be Presented to the Tsar of Russia.

(Reprinted from Cyrus Adler, *With Firmness in the Right; American Diplomatic Action Affecting Jews 1840–1945*, New York: Arno Press, 1977.)

Department of State
Washington, D.C., July 15, 1903

RIDDLE, St. Petersburg:

You are instructed to ask an audience of the Minister of Foreign Affairs and to make him the following communication:

EXCELLENCY: The Secretary of State instructs me to inform you that the President has received from a large number of citizens of the United States, of all religious affiliations and occupying the highest positions in both public and private life, a respectful Petition relating to the Jews and running as follows:

To His Imperial Majesty the Emperor of Russia

The cruel outrages perpetrated at Kishineff during Easter of 1903, have excited horror and reprobation throughout the world. Until your Majesty gave special and personal directions, the local authorities failed to maintain order or suppress the rioting. The victims were Jews and the assault was the result of race and religious prejudice. The rioters violated the laws of Russia.

The local officials were derelict in the performance of their duty.

The Jews were the victims of indefensible lawlessness.

These facts are made plain by the official reports of, and by the official acts following, the riot.

Under ordinary conditions the awful calamity would be deplored without undue fear of a recurrence, but such is not the case in the present instance. Your petitioners are advised that millions of Jews, Russian subjects, dwelling in Southwestern Russia, are in constant dread of fresh outbreaks.

They feel that ignorance, superstition and bigotry, as exemplified by the rioters, are ever ready to persecute them; that the local officials, unless thereunto specially admonished, cannot be relied on as strenuous protectors of their peace and security; that a public sentiment of hostility has been engendered against them and hangs over them as a continuing menace.

Even if it be conceded that these fears are to some extent exaggerated, it is unquestionably true that they exist, that they are not groundless, and that they produce effects of great importance.

The westward migration of Russian Jews, which has proceeded for over twenty years, is being stimulated by these fears, and already that movement has become so great as to overshadow in magnitude the expulsion of the Jews from Spain and to rank with the exodus from Egypt.

No estimate is possible of the misery suffered by the hapless Jews who feel driven to forsake their native land, to sever the most sacred ties, and to wander forth to strange countries.

Neither is it possible to estimate the misery suffered by those who are unwilling or unable to leave the land of their birth; who must part from friends and relatives, who emigrate; who remain in never-ending terror.

Religious persecution is more sinful and more fatuous than war. War is sometimes necessary, honorable and just; religious persecution is never defensible.

The sinfulness and folly which give impulse to unnecessary war received their greatest check when your Majesty's initiative resulted in an International Court of Peace.

With such an example before it, the civilized world cherishes the hope that upon the same initiative there shall be fixed in the early days of the twentieth century, the enduring principle of religious liberty; that by a gracious and convincing expression your Majesty will proclaim, not only for the government of your own subjects, but also for the guidance of all civilized men, that none shall suffer in person, property, liberty, honor or life, because of his religious belief; that the humblest subject or citizen may worship according to the dictates of his own conscience, and that government, whatever its form or agencies, must safeguard these rights and immunities by the exercise of all its powers.

Far removed from your Majesty's dominions, living under different conditions, and owing allegiance to another Government, your petitioners yet venture, in the name of civilization, to plead for religious liberty and tolerance; to plead that he who led his own people and all others to the shrine of peace, will add new luster to his reign and fame by leading a new movement that shall commit the whole world in opposition to religious persecution.

I am instructed to ask whether the Petition will be received by your Excellency to be submitted to the gracious consideration of his Majesty. In that case the Petition will be at once forwarded to St. Petersburg.

I avail myself, etc.,

You will report at the earliest possible moment your execution of this instruction.

HAY

Document 1.4

Telegram from Ambassador Riddle to Secretary of State Hay

(State Department File #711.612)

from: PETERSBURG
July 16, 1903

Secretary of State,
    Washington.

Minister for Foreign Affairs after returning yesterday afternoon from seeing the Emperor summer place of Peterhoff sent for me and said that he wished to speak confidentially and in a friendly way on subject which has lately filled the newspapers. He said he had seen that a Jewish petition addressed to the Emperor of Russia was about to be forwarded to the Embassy under the auspices of the Government of the United States. As he wished to avoid all friction, and did not wish to be under the necessity of offering the least discourtesy to me personally, he thought it would be better to notify me informally that such a petition would not be received; if I delivered it to him in person he would at once hand it back without looking at it. If I sent it accompanied by an official note would at once place it in an envelope and return it to me unopened, unread; that the Emperor whose will is the sole law of this Land had no need of information from outside sources as to what is taking place within his dominions; and that even a respectful petition or prayer relating to internal matters could not be received from foreigners. The Emperor's kindly feeling toward America, and the Minister's own esteem for the Embassy, made them desirous of avoiding the smallest diplomatic incident. This prompted his present conversation, but the Russian Government did not think that any Sovereign State whether big and powerful, or little and weak, could permit observations on the management of its internal affairs to reach it officially from outside.

Your cipher telegram just received this morning. Foregoing statement of Minister for Foreign Affairs for Russia I shall consider your instructions as already carried out by the present report unless I am ordered to take further steps.

RIDDLE

Document 1.5

Resolution Providing for the Termination of the Treaty of 1832 Between the United States and Russia

(House Joint Resolution 166, 62nd Congress, 2nd Session, December 13, 1911)

Resolved, etc., That the people of the United States assert as a fundamental principle that the rights of its citizens shall not be impaired at home or abroad because of race or religion; that the Government of the United States concludes its treaties for the equal protection of all classes of its citizens, without regard to race or religion; that the Government of the United States will not be a party to any treaty which discriminates, or which by one of the parties thereto is so construed as to discriminate, between American citizens on the ground of race or religion; that the Government of Russia has violated the treaty between the United States and Russia, concluded at St. Petersburg December 18, 1832, refusing to honor American passports duly issued to American citizens, on account of race and religion; that in the judgment of the Congress the said treaty, for the reasons aforesaid, ought to be terminated at the earliest possible time; that for the aforesaid reasons the said treaty is hereby declared to be terminated and of no further force and effect from the expiration of one year after the date of notification to the Government of Russia of the terms of this resolution, and that to this end the President is hereby charged with the duty of communicating such notice to the Government of Russia.

Document 1.6

Letter From Curtis Guild Reporting on the Effect of the Treaty Abrogation on Jews in Russia

(From State Department File #711.612.)

St. Petersburg, January 28, 1913

The Honorable
     The Secretary of State,
          Washington.

SIR:

In accordance with standing instructions to report to the Department from time to time any events or expressions of public opinion which directly or indirectly have any bearing on the abrogation of the treaty of 1832, I have the honor to enclose a letter from the American Consul at Odessa.

This letter, it will be seen, bears out earlier testimony in regard to the increased bitterness between Slavs and Jews in Russia since the abrogation of the Treaty.

It will be remembered that at the time of the public meetings held to protest against the action of the United States about a year since, attention was constantly called to the fact that the numerous restrictive laws against Jews had in many localities been relaxed. Instead of encouraging a more lenient treatment of Jews it would appear that the abrogation of the treaty, by causing a stricter enforcement of all these repressive laws, has actually if anything made the condition of the Jew in Russia distinctly worse than it was before, which naturally was the exact opposite of the effect which the prime movers of the bill for the abrogation of the treaty expected would be the case.

In this connection the Department may be interested to know that the authorities of New Bokhara have begun expelling Jews from that district on the ground that they are getting control of the new cotton fields.

The bitterness of the feeling in Poland against the Jews is the more remarkable as in times past there has been something like sympathy between the Jews and the Poles in their common hostility to the Russian Government. Now, however, the Poles are if anything more hostile than the Russians themselves. The enclosed article from the Commercial & Industrial Gazette, which is not a political paper but devoted to business matters, under date of 16/29 January is in regard to the commercial boycott of Jewish merchants by Poles. As will be seen the Christian inhabitants of Poland are banding themselves together and refuse to purchase anything from Jews.

I enclose another corroborative extract to show that in Warsaw merely for the publication of one of Max Nordau's essays a Jewish publisher was sent to prison.

In previous despatches I have noted the very common practice of Jews in Russia to seek baptism from Christian clergymen. Dr. G. Symons who has been with me here this morning tells me that this pressure is more constant than ever, the Jews seeking baptism that the word Methodist may be written on their passport. In several cases he and other Protestant clergymen here take the ground that unless evidence is produced of a genuine change of religious conviction baptism is refused.

The Holy Synod, as will be seen by another extract, which I enclose, is now taking up the question whether persons of the Hebrew race shall be allowed to adopt Christian names, as is so frequently the practice in the United States. The question was introduced into the Senate, but as will be seen by another extract, the long process of submission to the Duma and the usual legislative course was adopted.

As an exception to the general rule of increasing severity towards the Jews, I have the honor to enclose evidence showing that a new ruling depriving Jews of the privilege of leasing vineyards was rejected by the Senate. Furthermore, a trivial privilege allowing Jewish delegates to appear at the Congress of Commerce and Agriculture is granted.

I have the honor to be,
          Sir,
     Your obedient Servant,
          Curtis Guild

Document 1.7

Excerpt From Speech by Leon Trotsky at the Central Executive Committee, November 21, 1917

(Reprinted with permission from Jane Degras, ed., *Soviet Documents on Foreign Policy*, New York, N.Y.: Volume 1, 1978, pp. 6–7, Published by Octagon Books, a division of Hippocrene Books, Inc.)

The United States began to intervene in the war after three years, under the influence of the sober calculations of the American Stock Exchange. America could not tolerate the victory of one coalition over the other. America is interested in the weakening of both coalitions and in the consolidation of the hegemony of American capital. Apart from that, American war industry is interested in the war. During the war American exports have more than doubled and have reached a figure not reached by any other capitalist State. Exports go almost entirely to the Allied countries. When in January Germany came out for unrestricted U-boat warfare, all railway stations and harbours in the United States were overloaded with the output of war industries. Transport was disorganized and New York witnessed food riots such as we ourselves have never seen here. Then the finance capitalists sent an ultimatum to Wilson: to secure the sale of the output of the war industries within the country. Wilson accepted the ultimatum, and hence the preparations for war and war itself. America does not aim at territorial conquests; America can be tolerant with regard to the existence of the Soviet Government, since it is satisfied with the exhaustion of the Allied countries and Germany. Apart from that America is interested in investing its capital in Russia.

Document 1.8

Text of Decree Repudiating Russia's Debts, February 8, 1918

(Reprinted with permission from C.K. Cumming and Walter Pettit eds., *Russian-American Relations, March 1917–March 1920 Documents and Papers*, New York: Harcourt, Brace & Howe, 1920, pp. 77–78.)

1. All loans contracted by former Russian Governments which are specified in a special list are canceled as from December 1, 1917. The December coupons of these loans will not be paid.

2. All the guarantees for these loans are canceled.

3. All loans made from abroad are canceled without exception and unconditionally.

4. The short-term series of State Treasury bonds retain their validity. The interest on them will not be payable, but they will circulate on a par with paper money.

5. Indigent persons who hold stock not exceeding 10,000 rubles in internal loans will receive in exchange, according to the nominal value of their holdings, certificates in their own name for a new loan of the Russian Socialist Federal Republic of Soviets for an amount not exceeding that of their previous holding. The conditions of this loan are specially defined.

6. Deposits in the State savings banks and the interest upon them are not to be touched. All holdings in the canceled loans belonging to these banks will be replaced by debt entered to their credit in the Great Book of the Russian Socialist Republic.

7. Co-operative and other institutions of general or democratic utility, and possessing holdings in the canceled loans, will be indemnified in accordance with the special regulations laid down by the Supreme Council of Political Economy, in agreement with their representatives, if it is proved that the holdings were acquired before the publication of the present decree.

8. The State Bank is charged with the complete liquidation of loans and the immediate registration of all holders of bonds in the State loans and other funds, whether annulled or not.

9. The Soviet of the Workmen's, Soldiers', and Peasants' Deputies, in accord with the local economic councils, will form committees for the purpose of deciding whether a citizen is to be classed as "indigent." These committees will be competent to cancel entirely all savings acquired without working for them, even in the case of sums below 5,000 rubles.

Document 1.9

U.S.-Soviet Trade Agreement of 1935

(U.S. Statutes at Large, Volume 49, Part 2, 74th Congress, pp. 3805–3806)

EMBASSY OF THE UNITED STATES OF AMERICA,
Moscow, July 13, 1935

EXCELLENCY:

I have the honor to refer to recent conversations in regard to commerce between the United States of America and the Union of Soviet Socialist Republics and to the trade agreements program of the United States of America, and to confirm and to make of record by this note the following agreement which has been reached between the Governments of our respective countries:

1. The duties proclaimed by the President of the United States of America pursuant to trade agreements entered into with foreign governments or instrumentalities thereof under the authority of the Act entitled, "An Act to Amend the Tariff Act of 1930," approved June 12, 1934, shall be applied to articles the growth, produce, or manufacture of the Union of Soviet Socialist Republics as long as this Agreement remains in force. It is understood that nothing in this Agreement shall be construed to require the application to articles the growth, produce, or manufacture of the Union of Soviet Socialist Republics of duties or exemptions from duties proclaimed pursuant to any trade agreement between the United States of America and the Republic of Cuba, which has been or may hereafter be concluded.

2. On its part, the Government of the Union of Soviet Socialist Republics will take steps to increase substantially the amount of purchases in the United States of America for export to the Union of Soviet Socialist Republics of articles the growth, produce, or manufacture of the United States of America.

3. This Agreement shall come into force on the date of signature thereof. It shall continue in effect for 12 months. Both parties agree that not less than 30 days prior to the expiration of the aforesaid period of 12 months, they shall start negotiations regarding the extension of the period during which the present Agreement shall continue in force.

Accept, Excellency, the renewed assurances of my highest consideration.

WILLIAM C. BULLITT

His Excellency
MAXIM M. LITVINOV,
People's Commissar for Foreign Affairs,
Moscow.

MOSCOW, July 13, 1935.

MR. AMBASSADOR,

I have the honour to refer to recent conversations in regard to commerce between the Union of Soviet Socialist Republics and the United States of America and to the trade agreements program of the United States of America, and to confirm and to make of record by this note the following agreement which has been reached between the Governments of our respective countries:

1. The duties proclaimed by the President of the United States of America pursuant to trade agreements entered into with foreign governments or instrumentalities thereof under the authority of the Act entitled, "An Act to Amend the Tariff Act of 1930," approved June 12, 1934, shall be applied to articles the growth, produce, or manufacture of the Union

of Soviet Socialist Republics as long as this Agreement remains in force. It is understood that nothing in this Agreement shall be construed to require the application to articles the growth, produce or manufacture of the Union of Soviet Socialist Republics of duties or exemptions from duties proclaimed pursuant to any trade agreement between the United States of America and the Republic of Cuba, which has been or may hereafter be concluded.

2. On its part, the Government of the Union of Soviet Socialist Republics will take steps to increase substantially the amount of purchases in the United States of America for export to the Union of Soviet Socialist Republics of articles the growth, produce, or manufacture of the United States of America.

3. This Agreement shall come into force on the date of signature thereof. It shall continue in effect for 12 months. Both parties agree that not less than 30 days prior to the expiration of the aforesaid period of 12 months, they shall start negotiations regarding the extension of the period during which the present Agreement shall continue in force.

Accept, Mr. Ambassador, the renewed assurances of my highest consideration.

MAXIM LITVINOFF

MR. WILLIAM C. BULLITT,
  Ambassador of the United States of America,
   Moscow.

EMBASSY OF THE UNITED STATES OF AMERICA
Moscow, July 11, 1935.

EXCELLENCY:
  I have the honor to refer to our recent conversations in regard to commerce between the United States of America and the Union of Soviet Socialist Republics and to ask you to let me know the value of articles the growth, produce, or manufacture of the United States of America which the Government of the Union of Soviet Socialist Republics intends to purchase in the United States of America during the next twelve months for export to the Union of Soviet Socialist Republics.

  Accept, Excellency, the renewed assurances of my highest consideration.

WILLIAM C. BULLITT

His Excellency
  MAXIM M. LITVINOV,
   People's Commissar for Foreign Affairs,
   Moscow.

MOSCOW, July 15, 1935.

MR. AMBASSADOR,
  In reply to your inquiry regarding the intended purchases by the Union of Soviet Socialist Republics in the United States of America within the next twelve months, I have the honour to bring to your knowledge that according to information received from the People's Commissariat for Foreign Trade it is intended to purchase in the United States of America during the above mentioned period American goods to the value of thirty million dollars.

  Accept, Mr. Ambassador, the renewed assurances of my highest consideration.

MAXIM LITVINOFF

MR. WILLIAM C. BULLITT,
  Ambassador of the United States of America,
   Moscow.

Document 1.10

Excerpts from Law Revoking Most-Favored Nation Status for Imports from the U.S.S.R.

(U.S. Statutes at Large, Volume 65, 82nd Congress, 1st Session, Public Law 50, June 16, 1951)

Be it enacted by the Senate and House of Representatives of the United States of America in Congress assembled, That this Act may be cited as the "Trade Agreements Extension Act of 1951."

SEC. 5. As soon as practicable, the President shall take such action as is necessary to suspend, withdraw or prevent the application of any reduction in any rate of duty, or binding of any existing customs or excise treatment, or other concession contained in any trade agreement entered into under authority of section 350 of the Tariff Act of 1930, as amended and extended, to imports from the Union of Soviet Socialist Republics and to imports from any nation or area dominated or controlled by the foreign government or foreign organization controlling the world Communist movement.

SEC. 11. The President shall, as soon as practicable, take such measures as may be necessary to prevent the importation of ermine, fox, kolinsky, marten, mink, muskrat, and weasel furs and skins, dressed or undressed, which are the product of the Union of Soviet Socialist Republics or of Communist China.

Approved June 16, 1951.

2

Banking and Credit

Steve Dryden

When Franklin D. Roosevelt was elected President in 1932, the United States had withheld diplomatic recognition from the Soviet government for 15 years. American business contacts with the Soviets, however, had become extensive since the Bolshevik Revolution, even without government support in the form of loans or credits to back exports. Roosevelt established relations with the Soviet Union in his first year in office. He also set up an Export-Import Bank to finance trade. As part of the recognition accord, the Soviet Union pledged to negotiate the repayment of the Tsarist debt.

But the Soviet promise did not satisfy Congress. In April of 1934, shortly after Roosevelt's recognition of Moscow, Congress passed a law, known as the Johnson Debt Default Act, prohibiting loans to countries in default to the United States, or the buying or selling of bonds of countries in default. **(Document 2.1)**

U.S.-Soviet negotiations over the debt in 1934 and 1935 failed to produce an agreement. The Soviets requested a new $200 million credit, but as long as the two sides could not resolve the Tsarist debt problem, the Roosevelt Administration refused to consider fresh loans or credits by the Export-Import Bank or other agencies.

Although the debt issue has never been settled, several opinions by the Justice Department interpreting the Johnson Act have narrowed the applicability of the law and opened up opportunities for American banks. In 1939, the department ruled that foreign branches of American banks were not covered by the act. Opinions issued by the Attorney General in 1963 and 1967 allowed domestic American bank branches to make loans to finance sales of goods and services to the Soviet Union as long as the loan was tied to a particular transaction. The Johnson Act also affected loans to several East European countries, but Congress amended the Act in 1948 to exclude countries that had joined the International Monetary Fund and the World Bank. Currently, the only Warsaw Pact countries covered by the Act are the Soviet Union, East Germany and Czechoslovakia.

Efforts In The OECD

The restrictive U.S. policy towards bank loans to the Soviet Union has been accompanied in the postwar period by efforts to deny the Soviets access to favorable credit terms for purchases of Western goods. Here, the goal of U.S. policy was to force the Soviet Union to make up for this loss of favorable credit by spending less on the military sector. The initial American efforts on this front during the 1950s and 1960s, however, were largely unsuccessful. The United States tried to get its European allies to maintain a limit of five years on maturities for government credits and guarantees to the Soviets (which was U.S. policy), but as competition for sales heated up the allies extended loans with maturities up to 14 years.

In the mid-1970s, the United States re-launched its efforts on the export credit issue, this time within the Organization for Economic Cooperation and Development. Discussions were already underway in this group regarding overall guidelines for export credits, sparked by the realization that the oil crisis of 1973 could set off a destructive race for export sales to finance oil needs. The United States used the discussions to campaign for a reduction in the amount of credits, and an increase in the low interest rates made available to the Soviets. But the other OECD countries would only support a policy that applied to all recipients of credits. The result was a 1978 agreement, since amended several times, called the Arrangement on Guidelines for Officially Supported Export Credits. **(Document 2.2)** Known as the "consensus," the agreement was not binding and provided only for consultation among the members. It did not single out the Soviets, or the Soviet Bloc, and did not affect private bank credits. The arrangement specified that interest rates would vary according to whether the recipient countries were wealthy, middle income or poor. The United States wanted the Soviet Bloc nations put in the wealthy category, which would have given them the least favorable interest rates, but at the insistence of Western European governments, the bloc nations were put in the middle income group.

The credit issue surfaced again in 1982 when the United States criticized the low interest rates that Western European countries were granting for Soviet purchases of equipment for the Siberian pipeline. While the Europeans resisted American pressure on this point, negotiations underway on the export credit arrangement led to an agreement in May 1982 that reclassified countries' eligibility for interest rates according to standard economic criteria. This put the Soviet Union into the wealthy category (countries with a GNP per capita of over $4,000 annually). Interest rates were raised for those nations in the wealthy category, maximum maturities were set at five years, and members of the arrangement agreed to follow the guidelines explicitly.

At the Versailles summit the next month, the United States unsuccessfully tried to persuade the allies to go one step further and cut the volume of credits granted to the Soviet Union, and shorten the repayment period again. The allies, who were dependent on trade with the East, would not agree to a policy of overt economic warfare. The United States had to settle for a vague final communique in which the summit participants acknowledged the "need for commercial prudence in limiting export credits." **(Document 2.3)** The next year, at their annual meeting, OECD ministers agreed to a slightly stronger statement that said "East-West trade and credit flows should be guided by the indications of the market," and opposed "preferential treatment" for East Bloc nations. **(Document 2.4)**

The United States won a partial victory on the export credit issue in March 1987, when OECD members agreed to amend their agreement to forbid subsidized interest rates for loans to the wealthiest category of nations, which included the Soviet Union. This amendment specified that these nations should only receive commercial interest rates. But the amendment's effect was limited because it did not cover private banks, which were a fast-growing source of credit for the Soviets.

Indeed, as the United States campaigned in the 1970s against favorable official credits for the Soviets, total Western lending to Moscow for all purposes was also increasing steadily. But the involvement of private U.S. banks was limited. In 1980, U.S. bank loans were only about eight percent of the estimated $60 billion in total Western loans to Comecon countries. The U.S. share remained small in the early 1980s as U.S.-Soviet ties worsened and Poland's ability to meet its debt payments collapsed. From 1980 to 1985, total borrowing from U.S. banks by East Bloc countries declined from $5.5 billion to $1.9 billion.

Congressional Concern

But as relations between Washington and Moscow began to thaw out in the mid-1980s, U.S. banks participated in new lending to the East Bloc. This helped spur legislation on the lending issue by Sen. Jake Garn (R-Utah), the chairman of the Committee on Banking, Housing and Urban Affairs, along with the ranking Democrat of the committee, Sen. William Proxmire of Wisconsin. The "Financial Export Control Act" (S.812), introduced in March of 1985, attempted to amend the Export Administration Act (EAA) of 1979. The changes would have empowered the President to regulate the export or transfer of money or other financial assets, including the making of a loan or the extension of credit, to the Soviet Union and its allies, and other countries covered by the EAA, including the Peoples' Republic of China.

In one sense, S.812 was redundant. Under an existing statute, the International Emergency Economic Powers Act, the President can declare a national emergency and restrict exports, imports and lending activities. But Garn intended the amendments as a message to the banks that Congress was not pleased with their East Bloc loans. He also wanted to signal congressional unhappiness with the hesitancy of the Reagan Administration to restrict such lending.

Garn expressed a number of specific objections to the loans:

—The Soviet Union was using dollars and other hard currencies to illegally acquire Western technology for the buildup of the Soviet military. While U.S. loans, both government and commercial, were often made to finance Soviet purchases of U.S. commodities, such as grain, Garn argued that the availability of Western capital enabled the Soviets to use scarce foreign currency for their technology acquisition program.

—The Western funds added to the resources available to the Soviets to back their foreign activities—such as the occupation of Afghanistan—and support client states such as Cuba.

—The weak economies of the East Bloc could cause those countries to fail to repay their loans, leading to a debt crisis similar to that of Latin America.

—The interest rates paid by the Soviets to American and other Western banks were often lower than those charged by the banks for loans in the United

States. Although the interest rates charged to the Soviets were determined by international market conditions (and not the result of bank favoritism), Garn saw the difference as a fundamental inequity that made the loans even more objectionable.

The Reagan Administration was divided over how to respond to the Garn bill. The Pentagon favored the legislation, but following months of internal debate the opponents of the bill (among them the Treasury, State and Commerce Departments) prevailed. Assistant Treasury Secretary David Mulford, in testimony before Garn's committee in December 1985, presented the administration position. He pointed out that the U.S. supported non-strategic trade with the Soviet Bloc, and that to deny financing for this trade would require a major reversal of U.S. policy. In addition, U.S. allies were unlikely to go along with an American effort to restrict lending to the Bloc. Denial of U.S. funds would have little effect because they represented such a small (at that time, six to seven percent) share of Western exposure to Bloc nations. Finally, the administration was unhappy with the prospect of the Garn bill because the United States was carefully rebuilding its relations with Moscow and believed the legislation would send the wrong signal to the Soviets.

Facing administration opposition, Garn's committee never took action on his bill. (There also was apparently no agreement within the committee on whether the President should indeed restrict American banks' lending activities.) The bill was reintroduced in 1987 but it again died without Banking committee action.

On the House side, Rep. Jack Kemp (R-N.Y.) and Rep. Toby Roth (R-Wisc.) introduced a bill in 1987 (H.R. 3095, the International Financial Security Act of 1987) that, in addition to authorizing the President to control the export of U.S. capital, required that banks and other financial institutions report to the government and make public the number and amount of "untied loans" made to countries subject to U.S. export controls.

"Untied loans"—loans not made for a particular purchase of goods or other purpose—had in the mid-1980s become a more popular form of lending by Western banks to the Soviet Union. Sponsors of H.R. 3095 said that this trend, combined with increased lending by private commercial banks, which was not as easy to track as government loans, amounted to a situation in which the West was giving the Soviets billions of dollars in a virtual carte blanche fashion.

"What if a Soviet official asked to borrow the money in your savings account, offered you interest that was well below the prime rate and then refused to tell you what the money would be used for?" Kemp asked at a November 1987 hearing on his bill. "I think most of us would say no to such a deal and unfortunately, many Western banks see this sort of lending as somehow good for the bank and good for the West."

Soviet Debt

The Kemp-Roth bill also died in committee, and the Reagan Administration left office maintaining its hands-off policy toward lending to the East Bloc. A rationale for the administration's position on the lending issue can be found in the November 1988 report of an interagency task force created to examine the issue. (Document 2.5) The report said the debt of the Soviet Union and its allies had increased little in real terms in recent years, and that most of the increase was due to the dollar's depreciation against other major currencies since 1985. While the Soviet Bloc's gross debt to the West had increased by 14 percent between 1981 and 1986, the net debt (gross debt minus deposits in Western banks) had fallen when that sum was adjusted for exchange rate changes.

In addition, the task force report said "there is no clear parallel between the growth of exposure to the Soviet Bloc and the origins of the Latin America debt situation," particularly in the case of U.S. banks, since their claims were small and on the decline. The report also found that the large-scale extension of credits to the Soviets by Western sources in 1988 (which could amount to as much as $5 billion to $6 billion and were tied to specific equipment and consumer goods) did not appear to violate the OECD arrangement restricting the use of subsidies with export credits.

Critics of Western lending to the Soviet Bloc have continued to campaign on the issue. In addition to legislation providing for Presidential restrictions on lending, the critics have made increasing use of non-binding resolutions, and letters to the President and organizations like the International Monetary Fund. While most of the non-binding resolutions have passed unanimously, indicating support across the political spectrum, there are discernible differences in members' positions.

One approach is exemplified by the sense of the Senate resolution (Document 2.6) passed on June 15, 1988, which was offered by Sen. Bill Bradley (D-N.J.) and Sen. Jim Sasser (D-Tenn.). The resolution asked that the President consult with the allies at the upcoming Toronto summit on the impact on Western security of loans to the Soviet Union and its allies. Bradley, in testimony before the House Banking Committee in September 1988, said Western governments should end ''all types of loan subsidies, guarantees and other indirect means of reducing the costs of borrowing'' by the Soviets. He also said there appeared to be a need to upgrade the collection and disclosure of data on Soviet financial flows. But Bradley did not support efforts to cut off Soviet access to Western capital.

A different kind of initiative was seen in the legislation introduced by Rep. John Miller (R-Wash) and Rep. Larry Smith (D-Fla.) in May 1989, aimed at creating a voluntary code of conduct for American companies doing business in the Soviet Union (the so-called Slepak Principles). The code included a pledge not to extend untied loans to the Soviets.

A more restrictive measure, introduced by Sen. Steve Symms (R-Idaho) in May 1989 as a sense of the Senate resolution, called for the United States to work for a multilateral initiative to end untied loans. In his remarks introducing the resolution, Symms said ''it is high time the United States exert its influence to stop financing the hungry bear... after all Mr. President, where are Soviet missiles aimed?''

The efforts of Garn, Kemp and Roth have been relaunched in the new Congress. In March 1989, Rep. Stan Parris (R-Va.) introduced a modified version of the Kemp-Roth bill. Separately, Garn has indicated to his staff that he wants to re-introduce his legislation.

Critics of Western lending to the East Bloc said the Bush Administration took a step in the right direction by stating that its aid package for Poland (announced in April 1989) included no untied aid or unconditional credits. But there are no signs that Bush has relaxed the previous administration's opposition to legislation providing additional powers to restrict lending to the East Bloc. And there apparently is no consensus in Congress to take more forceful action on the issue.

Document 2.1

Johnson Debt Default Act

(73rd Congress, 2nd Session, Chapter 112, April 13, 1934)

AN ACT

To prohibit financial transactions with any foreign government in default on its obligations to the United States.

Be it enacted by the Senate and House of Representatives of the United States of America in Congress assembled, That hereafter it shall be unlawful within the United States or any place subject to the jurisdiction of the United States for any person to purchase or sell the bonds, securities, or other obligations of, any foreign government or political subdivision thereof or any organization or association acting for or on behalf of a foreign government or political subdivision thereof, issued after the passage of this Act, or to make any loan to such foreign government, political subdivision, organization, or association, except a renewal or adjustment of existing indebtedness while such government, political subdivision, organization, or association, is in default in the payment of its obligations, or any part thereof, to the Government of the United States. Any person violating the provisions of this Act shall upon conviction thereof be fined not more than $10,000 or imprisoned for not more than five years, or both.

SEC. 2. As used in this Act the term ''person'' includes individual, partnership, corporation, or association other than a public corporation created by or pursuant to special authorization of Congress, or a corporation in which the Government of the United States has or exercises a controlling interest through stock ownership or otherwise.

Approved, April 13, 1934.

Document 2.2

Arrangement on Guidelines for Officially Supported Export Credits

(Reprinted with permission from the Organisation for Economic Cooperation and Development, ''Arrangement On Guidelines for Officially Supported Export Credits,'' Paris, June 1988. This latest version of the Arrangement will appear in OECD, *The Export Credit Financing Systems in OECD Member Countries*, fourth edition, 1988, which was due to appear in late 1989.)

I. FORM AND SCOPE OF THE ARRANGEMENT

1. EXPORT CREDIT TRANSACTIONS COVERED

a) Participants shall apply the guidelines contained in this informal Arrangement to officially supported (*) export credits with a repayment term (*) of two years or more relating to contracts for sales of goods and/or services or to leases equivalent in effect to such sales contracts.

b) Special Guidelines apply to the following sectors in accordance with the provisions of paragraph 9:
1) Ships
2) Nuclear Power Plants
3) Power Plants other than Nuclear Power Plants
4) Aircraft

c) This Arrangement does not apply to export credits relating to exports of:
1) Military Equipment
2) Agricultural Commodities

2. PARTICIPATION

Present participants are listed in Annex I to this Arrangement. Countries willing to apply these Guidelines may become participants upon the prior invitation of the then existing Participants.

II. GUIDELINES FOR BASIC EXPORT CREDIT TERMS AND CONDITIONS

3. CASH PAYMENTS

Participants shall require purchasers of exported goods and services receiving officially supported export credits to make cash payments (*) at or before the starting point (*) equal to a minimum of 15 per cent of the export contract value (*). Participants shall not provide official support for such cash payments other than insurance and guarantees against the usual pre-credit risks.

4. REPAYMENT

Participants shall apply the following Guidelines for the repayment of export credits that are officially supported by way of direct credit, refinancing, eligibility for an interest subsidy, guarantee or insurance.

a) Maximum Repayment Term

For the three categories of countries (*) of destination, the following maximum repayment terms shall apply. The export credit agreement and ancillary documents shall not permit the extension of the relevant repayment term.

Countries of destination	Maximum repayment terms
Category I: relatively rich	= five years, but after prior notification in accordance with paragraph 14 b) 1) eight and a half years;
Category II: intermediate	= eight and a half years (1)
Category III: relatively poor	= ten years

b) Repayment of Principal and Payment of Interest

1) Principal of an export credit shall normally be repaid in equal and regular instalments not less frequently than every six months commencing not later than six months after the starting point. In the case of leases, this repayment procedure may be applied either for the amount of principal only or else for the amount of principal and interest combined.

2) Interest (*) as set forth in paragraph 5 below shall normally not be capitalised during the repayment term but shall be payable not less frequently than every six months commencing not later than six months after the starting point.

3) If a participant intends not to follow the normal practices or repayment of principal or for

payment of interest set forth in 1) and 2) above, the participant shall give prior notification in accordance with the procedure set forth in paragraph 14 b) 1).

5. MINIMUM INTEREST RATES

Participants providing official financing support by way of direct credit, refinancing or interest rate subsidy shall apply the following minimum rates of interest:

a) Matrix rates

1) Without prejudice to b) below, the following minimum annual interest rates (matrix rates) shall apply:

Countries of destination	Repayment periods	
	2–5 years	over 5 years
Category II	SDR(2) + 105 bp	SDR(2) + 155 bp
Category III	SDR(2) + 20 bp	SDR(2) + 20 bp

2) SDR base rates for the above matrix interest rates are reviewed semi-annually and subject to the following method:

i) An adjustment is made if the SDR-weighted average of the monthly interest rates referred to in footnote (2) for the immediately preceding December or June respectively differs by 50 basis points or more from the SDR-weighted average interest rate underlying the preceding adjustment in matrix rates. When such a change occurs, the levels of the matrix rates set out above shall be adjusted by the same number of basis points as the difference in the SDR-weighted averages, the recalculated matrix rates being rounded off to the nearest five basis points (3).

ii) The interest rates for the currencies constituting the SDR-weighted average are the secondary market yields of financing instruments reported to the OECD pursuant to paragraph 18 a) i).

b) Commercial Interest Reference Rates (*)

For countries of destination in Category I, participants shall apply the relevant commercial interest reference rate. Notwithstanding a) above, participants may also choose to apply these commercial interest reference rates for countries of destination in Categories II and III. If the terms of such official financing support are fixed before the date of contract, a premium of 20 basis points is added to the commercial interest reference rate (4). This commercial interest reference rate is also used to compute the discount rate to be used in the calculation of the concessionality level of tied and partially untied aid financing in accordance with paragraph 22 m).

c) Interest Rate System Choice

Participants are prohibited from taking any action that allows banks to offer throughout the life of a floating rate loan the option of either 1) the matrix rate, 2) the CIRR (at time of the original contract) or 3) the short-term market rate, whichever is lower.

6. LOCAL COSTS (*)

a) Category II or Category III Countries

Participants shall not finance, guarantee or insure credit for more than 100 per cent of the value of the goods and services exported, including goods and services supplied by third countries. Thus, the amount of local costs supported on credit terms and conditions will not exceed the amount of the cash payment. They shall not grant such support for local costs financed on conditions more favourable than those supported for the exports to which such local costs are related.

b) Category I Countries

The provisions of a) above shall apply, provided that any official support is confined to insurance or guarantees.

7. MAXIMUM PERIOD OF VALIDITY OF COMMITMENTS (*) AND PRIOR COMMITMENTS

Participants shall not fix credit terms and conditions for an individual export credit or of a credit line (*), whether new or one that is being renewed or prolonged, for a period exceeding six months (5). Commitments in effect prior to a modification of the Guidelines of this Arrangement and that become non-conforming because of this modification may not remain in effect for more than six months following the date of modification. Aid protocols, aid credit lines or similar agreements shall not be valid for more than two years after their signature.

8. TIED AND PARTIALLY UNTIED AID FINANCING (*)

If a participant intends to support tied or partially untied aid financing, the participant shall, without prejudice to official development assistance procedures administered by the Development Assistance Committee, give notification in accordance with the procedures set forth in paragraphs:

a) 14 c) 1), if the grant element is less than 50 per cent

b) 14 d), if the grant element is 50 per cent or more.

9. SPECIAL SECTORS

Participants shall apply the following special Guidelines to the sectors listed below:

a) Ships

The Guidelines of this Arrangement shall apply to ships not covered by the OECD Understanding on Export Credits for Ships (Annex II to this Arrangement). Efforts shall be pursued to arrive at common provisions for all ships. Until common provisions for all ships are agreed upon, if for any type of ship that is covered by that Understanding and therefore not by the Guidelines of the Arrangement, a participant intends to support terms that would be more favourable than those terms permitted by this Arrangement, the participant shall notify all other participants of such terms in accordance with the procedure set forth in paragraph 14 b) 1).

b) Nuclear Power Plants

This Arrangement shall apply; except that where relevant, the provisions of the Sector Understanding on Export Credits for Nuclear Power Plants (Annex III to this Arrangement), which complements this Arrangement, shall apply in lieu of the corresponding provisions of the Arrangement.

c) Power Plants other than Nuclear Power Plants

This Arrangement shall apply; except that the maximum repayment term shall be twelve years. If a participant intends to support a repayment term longer than five years in transactions with Category I countries or a repayment term longer than the relevant maximum term set forth in paragraph 4 a) for Category II and III countries, the participant will give prior notification in accordance with the procedure set forth in paragraph 14 b) 1).

d) Aircraft

This Arrangement shall apply; except that where relevant, the provisions of the Sector Understanding on Export Credits for Civil Aircraft (Annex IV to this Arrangement), which complements this Arrangement, shall apply in lieu of the corresponding provisions of the Arrangement.

10. BEST ENDEAVOURS

a) Objectives

1) The Guidelines set out in this Arrangement represent the most generous credit terms and conditions that participants may offer when giving official support. All participants recognise the risk that in the course of time these Guidelines may come to be regarded as the normal terms and conditions. They therefore undertake to take the necessary steps to prevent this risk from materialising.

2) In particular, if in an individual branch of trade or industrial sector to which this Arrangement applies, credit terms and conditions less generous to buyers than those set forth above in the Arrangement are customary, participants shall continue to respect such customary terms and conditions and shall do everything in their power to prevent these from being eroded as a result of recourse to the credit terms and conditions set forth in this Arrangement.

b) Firm Undertaking

In keeping with the objectives in a) above, the Participants, recognising the advantage which can accrue if a clearly defined common attitude toward the credit terms and conditions for a particular transaction can be achieved, firmly undertake:

1) to respect strictly the existing procedures for notification and in particular to give prior notification at the latest at the stipulated moment before commitment as well as to supply all the information in the detail called for in the form set forth in Annex V;

2) to make maximum use of existing arrangements for exchanging information at an early stage with a view of forming a common line towards credit terms and conditions for particular transactions;

3) to consider favourable face to face consultations if a participant so requests in the case of important transactions as set out in the protocol to this Arrangement.

c) Maximum Delays for Replies

If in an exchange of information referred to under b) above, a participant informs another participant of the credit terms and conditions that it envisages supporting for a particular transaction and requests similar information from the other participant, then, in the absence of a satisfactory reply within seven calendar days, the enquiring participant may assume that the other will support the transaction on the most favourable credit terms and conditions permitted by these Guidelines. In cases of particular urgency, the enquiring participant may request a more rapid reply.

11. MATCHING

A participant has the right to match credit terms and conditions notifiable under paragraph 14, as well as credit terms and conditions offered by a non-participant. Participants shall match by offering terms that comply with this Arrangement unless the initiating offer does not comply with this Arrangement (6). A participant intending to match credit terms and conditions:

a) notified by another participant shall follow the procedures set forth in paragraph 15 a) or c) as appropriate;

b) offered by a non-participant shall follow the procedures set forth in paragraph 15 b).

12. NO-DEROGATION ENGAGEMENT

Participants shall not:

a) derogate with respect to maximum repayment terms (whatever the form of support), to minimum interest rates or to the limitation of the validity of commitments to a maximum of six months or extend the relevant repayment term through an extension of the grace period before the start of the repayment beyond the normal practice of six months after the starting point; or

b) avail themselves of the possibilities provided under paragraph 14 c) 1) of this Arrangement to support tied or partially untied aid financing having a concessionality level of less than 35 per cent, or 50 per cent if the beneficiary country is a least developed country (LLDC) as defined by the United Nations.

13. ACTION TO AVOID OR MINIMISE LOSSES

The provisions of this Arrangement are without prejudice to the right of the export credit or insurance authority to take appropriate action after the export credit agreement and ancillary documents become effective to avoid or minimise losses.

III. PROCEDURES

14. PRIOR AND PROMPT NOTIFICATIONS

a) Derogations: Procedure for Prior Notification and Discussion

1) If a participant intends to take the initiative to support terms and conditions not in conformity with this Arrangement, the participant shall notify all other participants of the terms and conditions it intends to support at least ten calendar days before issuing any commitment. If any other participant requests a discussion during this period, the initiating participant shall delay an additional ten calendar days before issuing any commitment on such terms. Normally this discussion will be by telex.

2) If the initiating participant moderates or withdraws its intention to support the notified nonconforming terms and conditions, it must immediately inform all other participants accordingly.

3) A participant intending to match notified derogating terms and conditions shall follow the procedure set forth in paragraph 15 a) 1).

b) Deviations: Procedure for Prior Notification without Discussion

1) A participant shall notify, at least ten calendar days before issuing any commitment, all other participants of the terms and conditions if it intends:

i) to support a credit with a repayment term of more than 5 but not exceeding eight and a half years to a relatively rich country,

ii) not to follow normal payment practices with respect to principal or interest referred to in paragraph 4 b), or

iii) to support a credit for a power plant other than a nuclear power plant with a repayment term longer than the relevant maximum set forth in paragraph 4 a), but not exceeding twelve years, or

iv) to support for any kind of ships to which the OECD Understanding on export credits for ships applies, credit terms and conditions that would be more favourable than those credit terms and conditions permitted by this Arrangement.

2) If the initiating participant moderates or withdraws its intention to give such support to the notified deviating credit conditions, it must immediately inform all other participants accordingly.

3) A participant intending to match notified deviating terms and conditions shall follow the procedure set forth in paragraph 15 a) 2).

c) Procedures for Prior Notification of Aid Financing

1) The procedures set out in paragraph 14 b) shall apply where a participant intends to provide or support tied aid or partially untied aid financing involving a concessionality level of less than 50 per cent; except that wherever paragraph 14 b) refers to a period of ten calendar days, a period of twenty working days shall apply and that participants intending to match shall use the procedures of paragraph 15 a) 3).

2) A participant shall notify all other participants of the terms it intends to support at least twenty working days before issuing any commitment if the participant intends to provide or support trade related aid financing transactions involving a concessionality level of less than 50 per cent that are fully and freely available to finance procurement from the recipient country, from substantially all other developing countries and from participating countries. Participants intending to match such financing shall use the procedures of paragraph 15 a) 3).

d) Procedure for Prompt Notification (*)

As soon as a participant commits itself to support a tied or partially untied aid financing transaction having a grant element of 50 per cent or more, the participant will promptly notify all other participants accordingly.

e) Exception for Small Projects and Technical Assistance

The reporting requirements of paragraphs 12 b) and 14 c) and d) do not apply to the following transactions:

1) Aid financing where the official development aid component consists solely of technical cooperation that is less than either 3 per cent of the total value of the transaction or one million US dollars, whichever is lower, and

2) Capital projects of less than one million US dollars that are funded entirely by development assistance grants.

15. PROCEDURES FOR MATCHING

a) Matching Terms and Conditions Notified in Accordance with Paragraph 14

1) Matching of notified derogations: On and after the expiry of the first ten calendar day period referred to in paragraph 14 a) 1) if no discussion is requested (or on and after the expiry of the second ten calendar day period if discussion is requested) and unless the participant intending to match has received notice from the initiating participant that the latter has withdrawn its intention to support non-conforming terms and conditions, any participant will have the right to support:

i) in a case of "identical matching," terms and conditions that include the identical non-conforming element but that otherwise conform to the Guidelines; provided that the matching participant gives as early as possible notification of its intention to match; or

ii) in a case of "other support" prompted by the initial derogation, any other non-conforming element of the terms subject to the restrictions of paragraph 11; provided that the responding participant introducing a fresh derogation, initiated a five calendar day prior notification and five calendar day discussion procedure and awaits its completion. This period can run concurrently with that of the prior notification and discussion procedure initiated by the originally derogating participant but cannot elapse before the end of the applicable ten or twenty calendar day period referred to under paragraph 14 a) 1).

2) Matching of notified deviations: On and after the expiry of the ten calendar day period referred to in paragraph 14 b) 1) and unless the matching participant has received notice from the initiating participant that the latter has withdrawn its intention to support the terms and conditions notified in accordance with paragraph 14 b) 1), any participant will have the right to support:

i) in a case of "identical matching," terms and conditions that include the identical element notified in accordance with paragraph 14 b) 1) but that otherwise conform to the Guidelines; provided that the matching participant gives notification as early as possible of its intention to match.

ii) in a case of "other support," any other element of the terms which does not conform to the Guidelines subject to the restrictions of paragraph 11; provided that the responding participant initiates a five calendar day prior notification procedure without discussion and awaits its completion. This period may run concurrently with that of the prior notification procedure started by the initiating participant, but may not elapse before the end of the ten calendar day period referred to under paragraph 14 b) 1).

3) Matching of a prior notification of aid financing: The procedures set out in paragraph 15 a) 2) shall apply where a participant intends to match aid financing; except that where paragraph 15 a) 2) refers to a period of ten calendar days, a period of twenty working days shall apply.

4) Matching of a prompt notification: No prior notification need be given if a participant intends to match terms and conditions that were subject to a prompt notification according to paragraph 14 d).

b) Matching Export Terms and Conditions Offered by a non-Participant

1) Before considering meeting non-conforming terms and conditions assumed to be offered by a non-participant, a participant shall make every effort to verify that these terms are receiving official support. The participant shall inform all other participants of the nature and outcome of these efforts.

2) A participant that intends to match non-conforming terms offered by a non-participant shall follow the prior notification and discussion procedure under paragraph 14 a) 1).

c) Matching non-Conforming Prior Commitments

1) A participant intending to match a prior commitment shall make reasonable efforts to determine whether the non-conforming terms and conditions of the individual transaction or credit line in question will be used to support a particular transaction. This participant shall be considered to have made such reasonable efforts if it has informed by telex the participant assumed to offer such non-conforming terms and conditions of its intention to match but in reply to the telex has not been informed within three working days, exclusive the day of reception, that this prior commitment will not be used to support the transaction in question.

2) A prior credit line may be matched by an individual transaction or by means of a credit line. In both cases, the dates of expiry of the matching offer shall not be later than that of the credit line being matched.

3) A participant intending to match another participant's non-conforming prior commitment shall, in the case of:

i) "identical matching," follow the procedure set forth in paragraph 15 a) 1) i) when matching a derogation and paragraph 15 a) 2) i) when matching a deviation;

ii) "other support," follow the procedure set forth in paragraph 15 a) 1) ii) when matching a derogating prior commitment and the procedure set forth in paragraph 15 a) 2) ii) when matching a deviating prior commitment.

16. INFORMATION ON COMMITMENT

As soon as a participant commits credit terms and conditions it had notified in accordance with paragraph 14 or 15, it shall, in all cases, inform all other participants accordingly by including the notification reference number on the relevant Berne Union 1c form.

17. INFORMATION TO BE SUPPLIED UNDER THE NOTIFICATION AND MATCHING PROCEDURES

The notifications called for by the above procedures shall be made in accordance with and contain the information set out in the "standard form" in Annex V and be copied to the Secretariat of the OECD.

IV. OPERATIONAL PROVISIONS

18. REGULAR NOTIFICATION AND CIRCULATION OF INFORMATION ON SELECTED INTEREST RATES

a) Yields on Government or Public Sector Bonds

1) Participants shall notify by telex each month to the Secretariat for distribution to all participants the monthly information on yields of government or public sector bonds as described in the Annex VI to this Arrangement. This information shall reach the Secretariat at the latest five days after the end of the month covered by this information.

2) Upon receipt of this information from the five countries whose currencies constitute the IMF's Special Drawing Right, the Secretariat shall calculate the SDR-weighted average of interest rates for immediate circulation to all participants.

3) At the beginning of July and of January, the Secretariat will in accordance with the method set forth in paragraph 5 a) 2), calculate on the basis of the SDR-weighted averages the semi-annual adjustments to be made to the minimum interest rates set forth in paragraph 5 a) 1).

b) Commercial Interest Reference Rates

1) Commercial interest reference rates for currencies that are subject to the provisions of paragraph

5 b) shall be telexed at least monthly to the Secretariat for circulation to all participants.

2) Such notification shall reach the Secretariat not later than five days after the end of each month covered by this information. The Secretariat shall then inform immediately all participants of the applicable rates. Any changes in these rates shall enter into effect on the fifteenth day after the end of each month.

3) When market developments require the notification of a change in a commercial interest reference rate in the course of a month, the changed rate shall be implemented ten days after the date of receipt of the notification of this change.

19. REVIEWS

a) Annual Review

1) The Participants shall review at least annually the functioning of the Arrangement. The reviews will normally take place in the northern Spring of each year. In the review, they shall examine inter alia notification procedures, derogations, implementation and operation of the differentiated discount rate system, questions of matching, prior commitments, practices on credits for agricultural commodities and possibilities of wider participation in this Arrangement. They shall also review possible modifications of the matrix rates, notably with the aim to bring them closer to market interest rates.

2) These reviews shall be based on information on participants' experience and on their suggestions for improving the operation and efficacy of the Arrangement and shall take account of the objectives of the Arrangement and the prevailing economic and monetary situation. The information and suggestions that participants wish to put forward to this end shall reach the Secretariat not later than forty-five days before the date of review.

b) Review of Commercial Interest Reference Rates

1) The Participants shall review periodically the operation in practice of the commercial interest reference rates with a view to ensuring that the notified rates reflect current market conditions and meet the aims underlying the establishing of the rates in operation. Such reviews shall also cover the premium to be added when these rates are applied.

2) Any participant may submit to the Chairman a substantiated request for an extraordinary review in case this participant considers that the commercial interest reference rates for one or more currencies no longer reflect current market conditions.

20. VALIDITY AND DURATION

The provisions of this Arrangement are applicable without time limit, unless revised as a result of the review referred to in paragraph 19.

21. WITHDRAWAL

Any participant may withdraw from this Arrangement upon not less than sixty calendar days prior written notice to the other participants.

V. DEFINITIONS AND INTERPRETATIONS

22. For the purposes of this Arrangement, the Participants agreed to the following definitions and interpretations:

a) Cash Payments means payments to be received for goods and services exported by the completion of the exporter's contractual obligations, the date of completion being determined by the starting point.

The quantum of the minimum cash payments is established by reference to the total export contract value; except that in the case of a transaction involving some goods or services supplied from outside the exporter's country, the total export contract value may be reduced proportionally if the official support from which the exporter benefits does not cover those goods and services.

Retention payments due after the latest appropriate starting point referred to under k) below do not count as cash payments for the purpose of conformity with the Guidelines.

b) Export Contract Value means the total amount to be paid by the buyer; exclusive of interest in the case of an export sale of goods and/or services or to be paid by the lessee, exclusive of the portion of the lease payment equivalent to interest in the case of a cross border lease.

c) The Classification of Countries into categories in paragraph 4 a) and 5 a) is based on the following criteria:

Cat I: Countries with a GNP per capita income of over $4,000 p.a. according to the definite 1979 figures shown in the 1981 World Bank Atlas.

Cat. II: Countries not classified with Categories I or III.

Cat. III: Countries eligible for IDA credits plus any other low income countries or territories, the GNP per capita of which would not exceed the IDA eligibility level.

d) Repayment term and interest rates

1) Repayment Term means the period of time commencing at the starting point and terminating on the contractual date of the final payment.

2) Interest excludes:

i) any payment by way of premium or other charge for insuring or guaranteeing supplier credits or financial credits;

ii) any other payment by way of banking fees or commissions associated with the export credit, other than annual or semi-annual bank charges payable throughout the repayment term; and

iii) withholding taxes imposed by the importing country;

3) in the case of an export through a relay country, the relevant interest rate and repayment term set out in paragraphs 4 and 5 are those corresponding to the country of final destination in cases:

i) where the "relay country" makes payment, if and when received from the country of final destination, to the exporting country on the basis of the latter's portion in the total export value; or

ii) where there is security or payment by the country of final destination.

e) Commercial Interest Reference Rate means an interest rate established in accordance with Annex VII to this Arrangement.

f) Local Costs means expenditure, excluding commissions payable to the exporter's agent in the buying country, for the supply from the buyer's country of goods and services, that are necessary either for executing the exporter's contract or for completing the project of which the exporter's contract forms part.

g) Commitment means any arrangement for or declaration on credit conditions, in whatever form, by means of which the intention or willingness to refinance, insure or guarantee supplier credits or to grant, refinance, insure or guarantee financial

credits is brought to the attention of the recipient country, the buyer or the borrower, the exporter, or the financial institution.

h) Line of Credit means any understanding or statement, in whatever form, whereby the intention to grant credit benefiting from official support up to a ceiling and in respect of a series of transactions, linked or not to a specific project, is brought to the attention of the recipient country, the buyer or the borrower, or the financial institution.

i) Tied aid financing (7) is defined as loans or grants or associated financing packages involving a concessionality level greater than zero per cent that is in effect tied to procurement of goods and services from the donor country. Partially untied aid financing (7) is defined as loans or grants or associated financing packages involving a concessionality level greater than zero per cent that is in effect tied to procurement of goods and services from the donor country and from a restricted number of countries. (8)

1) Such financing can take the form of either:

i) Official Development Assistance loans;

ii) Official Development Assistance grants;

iii) Other Official Flows (including grants and loans but excluding officially supported export credits that are in conformity with this Arrangement); or

iv) Any association in law or in fact (6) either in the hands of the donor, lender or borrower among two or more of the following:

—Official Development Assistance loans;

—Official Development Assistance grants;

—Other Official Flows (including grants and loans but excluding officially supported export credits that are in conformity with this Arrangement);

—An export credit that is officially supported by way of direct credit, refinancing, eligibility for an interest subsidy, guarantee or insurance to which this Arrangement applies, other funds at or near market terms or cash payments from the buyer's own resources.

2) Such financing is defined to be in effect tied to procurement of goods and services from one or a restricted number of countries as soon as:

i) one of the financial components listed above is not freely and fully available to finance procurement from the recipient country, substantially all other developing countries and from participating countries, whether by a formal or informal understanding to that effect between the recipient and the donor country, or

ii) it involves practices that the Development Assistance Committee of the OECD or the Participants may determine to result in such tying. (10)

3) The definition of "Official Development Assistance" is identical to that in the "DAC Guiding Principles for Associated Financing and Tied and Partially Untied Official Development Assistance."

j) Prompt Notification means a maximum delay of two working days following the date of commitment within which notification is to be given.

k) Starting Point is the same as the Berne Union definition currently in use and is as follows:

1) In the case of a contract for the sale of capital goods consisting of individual items usable in themselves (e.g. locomotives), the starting point is the mean date or actual date when the buyer takes physical possession of the goods in his own country.

2) In the case of a contract for the sale of capital equipment for complete plant or factories where the supplier has no responsibility for commissioning, the starting point is the date when the buyer is to take physical possession of the entire equipment (excluding spare parts) supplied under the contract.

3) In the case of construction contracts where the contractor has no responsibility for commissioning, the starting point is the date when construction has been completed.

4) In the case of any contract where the supplier or contractor has a contractual responsibility for commissioning, the starting point is the date when he has completed installation or construction and preliminary tests to ensure that it is ready for operation. This applies whether or not it is handed over to the buyer at that time in accordance with the terms of the contract and irrespective of any continuing commitment which the supplier or contractor may have, e.g. for guaranteeing its effective functioning or for training local personnel.

5) In the case of paragraphs 2), 3) and 4) above where the contract involves the separate execution of individual parts of a project, the date of

the starting point is the date of the starting point for each separate part, or the mean date of those starting points or, where the supplier has a contract, not for the whole project but for an essential part of it, the starting point may be that appropriate to the project as a whole.

l) Interest Rate and Official Support: Apart from agreement on the definition of interest set forth in paragraph 22 d) 2) it has not proved possible to establish common definitions of interest rate and official support in the light of differences between long-established national systems of export credit and export credit insurance now in operation in the participating countries. Efforts shall be pursued to elaborate solutions for these definitions. While such definitions are being elaborated, these guidelines do not prejudice present interpretations. In order to facilitate these efforts, notes concerning actual practices in this area, including information on annual or semi-annual bank charges payable throughout the repayment term and considered as part of interest, as they result from the different national systems, were transmitted to the Secretariat of the OECD and distributed to all participants in document TD/CSUS/78.12 and Addenda.

m) 1) Concessionality level is very similar in concept to the "grant element" used by the Development Aid Committee (DAC) of the OECD. In the case of grants, it is 100 per cent. In the case of loans, it is the difference between the nominal value of the loan and the discounted present value of the future debt service payments to be made by the borrower, expressed as a percentage of the nominal value of the loan, and is calculated in accordance with the method of calculating the grant element used by the DAC, except that: i) The discount rate used in calculating the concessionality level of a loan in a given currency is subject to change on an annual basis on the 15th of January and calculated as follows:

CIRR + 1/4 (10 − CIRR). In this formula, CIRR is the average of the monthly CIRRs valid during the six-month period extending from the 15th of August of the previous year through the 14th of February of the current year. The calculated rate is rounded to the nearest 10 basis points.

ii) The base date for the calculation of the concessionality level is the starting point as defined in paragraph 22 k).

2) For the purpose of calculating the overall concessionality level of an associated financing

package, the concessionality levels i) of export credits that are in conformity with this Arrangement, ii) of other funds at or near market rates, iii) of other official funds with a concessionality level of less than the minimum permitted by paragraph 12 b) above, except in cases of matching (11), or iv) of cash payments that are from the buyer's own resources, are considered to be zero. The overall concessionality level of a package is determined by dividing i) the sum of the results obtained by multiplying the nominal value of each component of the package by the respective concessionality level of each component by ii) the aggregate nominal value of the components.

3) The discount rate for a given aid loan is the rate that is in effect at the time of notification (12), except in cases of prompt notification, where the discount rate is the rate in effect at the time of commitment. A change in the discount rate during the life of a loan does not change its concessionality level.

4) Without prejudice to 3) above, when calculating the concessionality level of individual transactions initiated under an aid credit line, the discount rate is the rate that was originally notified for the credit line.

n) Power plants other than nuclear power plants are complete power stations not fueled by nuclear power or parts thereof, comprising all components, equipment, materials and services, including the training of personnel, directly required for the construction and commissioning of such non-nuclear power stations. Not included are items for which the buyer is usually responsible, in particular, cost associated with land development, roads, construction village, power lines, switchyard and water supply, as well as costs arising in the buyer's country from official approval procedures (e.g. site permit, construction permit, fuel loading permit).

NOTES AND REFERENCES

(*)   The asterisk refers to the relevant definitions or interpretations set forth in paragraph 22.

1. For countries in Category II that were classified in Category III before 6th July 1982, the maximum repayment term shall be ten years; the minimum interest rate applicable for repayment term of over eight and a half to ten years being the same as that for repayment terms of over five to eight and a half years.

2. SDR means the IMF Special Drawing Right weighted average of the interest rates notified pursuant to paragraph 18 a). These currencies are the US dollar, Deutsche mark, Japanese yen, French franc and pound Sterling. In the calculation of the average interest rate, each currency shall be given the weight set by the IMF for the valuation of the Special Drawing Right.

3. After any semi-annual period, a change in the SDR-weighted average interest rate shall be computed only on the basis of the IMF weightings of the SDR valuation basket in effect at the end of the semi-annual period.

4. For the US dollar, this premium shall be increased to 40 basis points if the pre-contract period exceeds three months. For the Swiss franc, this premium shall be added whenever official financing support is provided.

5. The validity of all commitments or offers of aid with a concessionality level of less than 35 per cent that are notified between the 1st of May 1987 and the 15th of July 1988 shall be limited to one year.

6. However, participants may match an offer of aid financing that complies with the Arrangement with one that does not if the initiating offer had a concessionality level of less than 30 per cent.

7. It is understood that the terms "tied aid financing" and "partially untied aid financing" exclude aid programmes of multilateral or regional institutions.

8. These definitions do not prejudge the distinctions made in the DAC on the quality of aid as concerns tied, partially untied and untied aid.

9. Associated financing transactions may take various forms—such as "mixed credit," "mixed financing," "joint financing," "parallel financing" or single integrated transactions. Their main characteristic is that the concessional component is linked in law or in fact to the non-concessional component, that either the package is in effect tied or partially untied and that the availability of concessional funds is conditional upon accepting the linked non-concessional component.

Association or linkage "in fact" is determined by such factors as the existence of informal understandings between the recipient and the donor authority, the intention by the donor through the use of ODA to facilitate the acceptability of a financing package, the effective tying of the whole financing package to procurement in the donor country, the tying status of ODA and the modality of tender and/or of the contract of each financing transaction or any other practice, identified by the DAC or the Participants in which a de facto liaison exists between two or more financing components.

None of the following practices shall prevent the determination that an association or linkage "in fact" exists: contract splitting through the separate notification of component parts of one contract; splitting of contracts financed in several stages; non-notification of interdependent parts of a contract; non-notification arising from the partial untying of a financing package.

10. In cases of uncertainty as to whether a certain financing practice falls within the scope of the above definition, the donor country shall furnish evidence in support of any claim to the effect that such a practice is untied.

11. In identical matching, the concessionality level of any OOF in the initiating participant's offer shall be included in the calculation of the initial offer's concessionality level if the matching offer contains an OOF that is included in its concessionality level, even if the OOF in the initial offer has a concessionality level below the minimum permissible concessionality level.

12. If a change of currency is made before the contract is concluded, a revision of the notification is required. The discount rate used to calculate the concessionality level will be the one applicable at the time of the revision. However, if the alternative currency is indicated in the original notification and all necessary information is provided, a revision is not necessary.

Document 2.3

Excerpt from the Communique Issued after the Versailles Conference June 6, 1982

(From the *New York Times*, June 7, 1982.)

We will cooperate with the developing countries to strengthen and improve the multilateral system, and to expand trading opportunities in particular with the newly industrialized countries. We shall participate fully in the forthcoming GATT ministerial conference in order to take concrete steps toward these ends. We shall work for early agreement on the renewal of the O.E.C.D. export credit consensus.

We agree to pursue a prudent and diversified economic approach to the U.S.S.R. and Eastern Europe, consistent with our political and security interests. This includes actions in three key areas:

First, following international discussions in January, our representatives will work together to improve the international system for controlling exports of strategic goods to these countries and national arrangements for the enforcement of security controls.

Second, we will exchange information in the O.E.C.D. on all aspects of our economic, commercial and financial relations with the Soviet Union and Eastern Europe.

Third, taking into account existing economic and financial considerations, we have agreed to handle cautiously financial relations with the U.S.S.R. and other Eastern European countries, in such a way as to insure that they are conducted on a sound economic basis, including also the need for commercial prudence in limiting export credits. The development of economic and financial relations will be subject to periodic ex-post review.

Document 2.4

Excerpt from the OECD Communique of May 10, 1983

(From an OECD press release.)

EAST-WEST ECONOMIC RELATIONS

Following a decision taken by Ministers last year, the Organisation has carried out a thorough economic analysis of the evolution of trade and financial relations with the USSR and other Eastern European countries. Ministers noted that these relations have, with some exceptions, evolved in a less dynamic way than those with more market-oriented economies and not met earlier expectations.

This purely economic analysis demonstrates that East-West trade and credit flows should be guided by the indications of the market. In the light of these indications, Governments should exercise financial prudence without granting preferential treatment. Ministers recognised, moreover, that practices connected with the state-trading system of centrally planned economies can create problems which need to be kept under close examination within the Organisation. More generally, they agreed that, in the light of changing circumstances, the Organisation should continue to review East-West economic relations.

Document 2.5

Excerpts from the Report of the Special Interagency Task Force on Western Lending to the Soviet Bloc, Vietnam, Libya, Cuba and Nicaragua

(Report Released by the U.S. Department of the Treasury, November 8, 1988.)

Summary and Conclusions

—In recent years the debt of the Soviet Union and its Eastern European allies has risen in nominal (unadjusted) terms. However, when looked at in real terms the increase in debt is much less.

—Most of the increase in claims by the West has been due to the dollar's substantial depreciation against other major currencies since 1985, and not new lending. This depreciation has increased Soviet Bloc debt when expressed in dollars.

—A more accurate picture of the level of Soviet Bloc debt should take into account exchange rate changes, as well as Soviet Bloc redeposits in Western banks which have, to a large extent, offset new borrowing.

—Soviet Bloc *gross* debt to Western banks and other lenders at constant exchange rates increased by only 14 percent or $13 billion during the period between end-1981 and end-1986. *Net* debt (gross debt less deposits) adjusted for exchange rate changes had actually fallen.

—The Bank for International Settlements (BIS) estimates that gross borrowing by the Soviet Union from BIS-reporting banks (adjusted for exchange rate changes) has been $8.4 billion in the period 1985–1987 (Q3) compared to official creditors and for officially guaranteed non-bank credits were $2.9 billion, according to BIS/OECD estimates.

—Each of the countries discussed in this report differs substantially in terms of debt levels, borrowing potential, and debt servicing capabilities.

—Poland, for example, is an extremely weak credit and is, therefore, generally unable to obtain new financing. The Soviet Union's external financial position appears adequate and is likely to remain so during the foreseeable future, in the absence of severe external shocks and/or unexpected sharp changes in Soviet policy.

—Eighty-five percent of the claims of banks reported to the BIS on the Soviet Bloc are on four countries. Eighty-eight percent of the increase in such claims since 1983 is accounted for by the USSR, Hungary and the GDR.

—New borrowing by the Soviet Union in 1988 has been largely tied. In contrast, borrowing from 1983 through 1987 had been largely untied (general purpose) borrowing.

—Historically, the Soviet Union has maintained a close relationship with certain Western commercial banks, many of which feel comfortable in assessing the creditworthiness of the Soviet Union. Western banks' positive assessment of the Soviet Union stems in part from that country's gold reserves, currently valued at over $30 billion.

—There is no clear parallel between the growth of exposure to the Soviet Bloc and the origins of the Latin American debt situation.

—The Soviet Union has recently negotiated several lines of credit from Western sources. These credit lines, amounting to as much as $5 billion to $6 billion, appear to be tied to Soviet purchases of Western equipment and consumer goods. It is not possible to determine whether and/or to what extent these credit lines will be utilized and over what period of time. We have no evidence of Western government involvement that violates the OECD Arrangement on export credits.

—The future holds many uncertainties for each Soviet Bloc country. The U.S. Government will continue to monitor and review Western lending to the Soviet Union and Soviet Bloc countries and will continue to consult with our allies on this issue.

37

Document 2.6

Sense of the Senate Resolution sponsored by Bill Bradley (D-N.J.) and Jim Sasser (D-Tenn.)

(*Congressional Record*, June 15, 1988, S 7849)

It is the sense of the Senate that during the Toronto Economic Summit, the President of the United States should consult with the leaders of allied countries on the impact on Western Security of tied and untied loans, trade credits, direct investments, joint ventures, lines of credit, and guarantees or other subsidies to the Soviet Union, Warsaw Pact countries, Cuba, Vietnam, Libya, or Nicaragua.

3

The "Cumbersome...Apparatus"

James M. Montgomery

The Export Administration Act (EAA) has been the U.S. Government's principal tool in its unilateral and multilateral efforts to control exports to the Soviet Union and its allies. The EAA expires at the end of September 1990. The renewal debate in Congress may become a pivotal battle over the ambiguities that have marked this facet of American policy for more than 40 years—ambiguities created by the desire to promote exports and the fear that the Soviets might benefit from such trade.

If there is a major debate, several issues will stand out:
—Foreign policy controls;
—Foreign availability;
—Extraterritoriality;
—The interagency balance of power;
—Effectiveness and cost.

Background

The early versions of the EAA and its predecessors in the 1940s waged economic warfare, aimed at restraining Soviet military power by inhibiting the USSR's overall economic growth. Congress has since tried to reorient the law. Today, the ethos of economic warfare lingers, faintly in the law itself, and quite markedly in the way it is administered. The government—principally the Department of Commerce—now concentrates more narrowly on restricting the flow of civilian technology that can also have military applications that threaten national security (i.e., "dual-use" technology). However, under the broader "foreign policy" authorities also in the EAA, the President can, in addition, restrict the export of any items to any country for any purpose. Overall, Congress has advocated a more liberal approach to exports than the executive branch. But it has never taken away the President's authority to bar exports at his own discretion. The opening sections of the present EAA illuminate this Congressional ambivalence. **(Document 3.1)**

President Bush has also helped set the debate stage. In his May 1989 Texas A&M speech he said the time had come to move "beyond containment" and help the Soviets join the world economy. Thus, the executive branch must also grapple with the EAA's conflicting goals as it considers export restrictions appropriate for the years beyond containment. Equally important, if less visible, will be the Administration's political guidance to the bureaucracies that daily enforce the legislation.

Forces beyond U.S.-Soviet export questions will also shape the coming debate: (1) the increasing importance of commercial openness in maintaining America's technological edge; (2) global manufacturing and technological diffusion which make it difficult to control technology's spread, particularly unilaterally; (3) the diminished capacity of the United States to dictate allied export control policies; and (4) the changing perception of the Soviet threat and the potential of Eastern markets.

Controls: National Security or Foreign Policy?

The EAA gives the President broad authorities to control exports primarily for two reasons: 1) to protect our national security and 2) "...to further significantly the foreign policy of the United States." Under the national security rationale the President can "restrict the export of goods and technology which would make a significant contribution to the military potential of any other country or combination of countries which would prove detrimental to the U.S." This is more narrow than the foreign policy rationale which allows the President to restrict the export of just about anything to any country. **(Document 3.2)**

The Paris-based Coordinating Committee for Multilateral Export Controls (COCOM) is the mechanism through which the United States cooperates with its allies in the multilateral enforcement of national security controls. (See Chapter 4 for a fuller discussion of COCOM.) The allies, however, have not agreed to cooperate with the U.S. on foreign policy controls. The American exercise of these controls is essentially unilateral, although the United

States does seek allied cooperation in specific instances.

Until 1988, the United States, in addition to restricting the exportation of items on a list agreed to with our allies in COCOM, also imposed additional and unilateral national security controls on U.S. exports. Congress, in 1988, eliminated these unilateral controls, unless the United States is the sole manufacturer of the item in question. However, since the President still has the authority to restrict the export of any item for foreign policy purposes, the practical difference can be academic.

Congress has been most concerned—and frustrated—by the President's exercise of foreign policy powers. Unlike national security controls coordinated through COCOM, foreign policy export controls—such as President Carter's grain embargo against the Soviet Union—are nearly always unilateral and rarely supported by other countries, even by America's allies. The targeted country can easily find other sources. Many in Congress, and elsewhere, believe such foreign policy controls harm only U.S. exporters and also undermine the allied cooperation necessary for the effective enforcement of the more narrow, multilateral national security controls.

Congress did not attempt to constrain the President's foreign policy export control authority until the 1970s. Indeed, it was not until the 1969 EAA that Congress even drew a distinction between foreign policy and national security controls. In the 1979 EAA, Congress began to try to limit this authority. In the 1985 version and in the amendments to the 1988 Trade Act, Congress continued this process, seeking to ensure that the President's use of foreign policy export controls was more deliberative. **(Document 3.3)** Furthermore, under the 1985 EAA, the President may only impose foreign policy controls if he makes an extensive set of determinations. The President, in addition, is required to consult with Congress and submit a detailed justification. The Commerce Department must "in every possible instance" solicit advice from affected industries. COCOM members and other pertinent countries must also be consulted "at the earliest appropriate opportunity." The 1988 Trade Act further establishes that the President should not impose unilateral foreign policy controls if they inflict little or no economic cost on the target country, but should instead pursue diplomatic efforts and such alternatives as withdrawal of ambassadors and reduction in the target country's diplomatic staff in the United States. Despite these highly detailed restrictions on the use of this authority and equally detailed suggestions

on how to avoid using it, the Congress in the final analysis gives the President the ultimate authority to do what he wishes. (See particularly: (o) "Expanded authority to impose controls" in **Document 3.3**.)

Congress and the U.S. business community have been particularly concerned about "contract sanctity," i.e., that the President not use foreign policy controls to rescind existing contracts, as President Reagan did in the Soviet gas pipeline affair. In a 1985 post-pipeline amendment, Congress restricts the President in this regard, but—as with other restrictions—it also provides a loophole via Presidential determination. (See (m), **Document 3.3**.)

Perhaps as a consequence of these procedural restrictions, Presidents have recently made increasing use of an alternative statute, the International Emergency Economic Powers Act (IEEPA) of 1977 to impose *de facto* foreign policy controls. IEEPA gives the President broad powers to control foreign trade whenever he determines that there is an extraordinary threat to the national security, foreign policy, or economy of the United States. By declaring an emergency, the President can embargo any financial transaction, import or export to or from the countries posing the threat without the consultations and tests the EAA requires. Most recently, President Reagan used this emergency power against Panama, Libya and Nicaragua. He also used the IEEPA to keep all the EAA's provisions in use during the 1983–1985 debate when the EAA actually expired for a time.

Foreign Availability

Congress generally does not believe U.S. exporters should be kept from selling items that are readily available from other countries, particularly if the other countries do not impose restrictions on the export of the items in question. As with foreign policy controls, Congress has written detailed, legislated instructions on this issue of "foreign availability," in a generally futile effort to get the executive branch to administer the law in accordance with these views. **(Document 3.4)** For instance, a 1985 amendment to decontrol certain goods with embedded and non-reprogrammable microprocessors was only implemented in October 1989. Two years ago the President determined that a certain type of wire binders were readily available to the Soviets from other countries, but they are still on the control list. On October 5, 1989 Undersecretary of Commerce Dennis Kloske told the House Foreign Affairs Committee that the issue was still "under review."

Multilateral Cooperation and Extraterritoriality

From the outset, the U.S. has sought allied cooperation. For instance, the European allies had to join the embargo to qualify for Marshall Plan aid. **(Document 3.5)** That pressure is now gone, but the allies continue to cooperate through COCOM. Despite persistent frustration over the scope of controls, the allies still agree that the West should not export those items that do make a significant contribution to Soviet military capability.

The United States has long maintained the right to control the reexport of restricted American items and technologies that are purchased originally by buyers in COCOM countries. The United States has applied these controls to reexports from these COCOM countries to both non-COCOM and other COCOM countries. The United States has eased these demands marginally, but it still maintains the basic principle. This posture will have to be examined as the COCOM partners who also belong to the European Community also become members of Europe's integrated 1992 market. With the disappearance of border controls, EC/COCOM countries may not be inclined to maintain a system solely to control the reexport of U.S.-origin items to other COCOM countries. There may be no practical internal EC barriers to the reexport of sensitive items; thus technology could flow to the most "leaky" COCOM member. Therefore, if the United States wishes to maintain the strength of COCOM's present barriers, it will soon have to consider getting all COCOM members to agree to common enforcement standards. This could be the next major issue in COCOM.

COCOM partners at the governmental level have generally accepted American desires to control reexports—if they also agree that the items in question should be restricted on the basis of national security. COCOM members, however, have rebuffed U.S. attempts to impose foreign policy controls. The Reagan Administration's 1981 attempt to persuade the COCOM partners to cancel plans to supply the Soviets with equipment to build a natural gas pipeline was driven by what the Europeans saw as foreign policy reasons. The United States forced several participating American firms to cancel their contracts to provide equipment, but U.S. subsidiaries in Europe and foreign firms with U.S. licenses continued to participate. The United States then announced that its restrictions also applied to these firms, notwithstanding the fact they were under the jurisdiction of other countries. This was the United States' most aggressive assertion of extraterritoriality

and it failed. The Europeans unanimously defied it, U.S. businesses and Congress protested vociferously and the administration backed down.

The Cumbersome Apparatus

The House-Senate conferees on the 1988 Trade Act agreed on the following description of the export control system: "...the current export administration system, ...is burdened by ambiguous criteria, overlapping jurisdictions, and a cumbersome decision- and policy-making apparatus." **(Document 3.6)**

These administrators, however, play on a field marked-off by Congress' own ambivalent views. In its decades of tinkering, Congress has created overlapping responsibilities and ambiguous authorities within the executive branch—fertile ground for time-consuming, bureaucratic wrangles that frustrate would-be exporters. The primary wrangle is between the Departments of Commerce and Defense over "primacy" in administering the EAA. With its 1974 amendments to the EAA, Congress gave DoD a significant role in determining the nature and scope of national security controls and in reviewing individual license applications.

According to the law, it is the Department of Commerce that is responsible for the actual administration of both national security and foreign policy controls on the export of dual-use goods and technical data. It does this through the approval of licenses for certain items prior to shipment. It creates and maintains a Commodity Control List (CCL) of these restricted items. The CCL also contains items restricted for nuclear non-proliferation purposes.

Congress, however, has also authorized DoD to review exports and reexports to Communist destinations subject to national security controls, and under a 1985 executive order, DoD is also authorized to review licenses for certain categories of exports and reexports to some non-Communist destinations. The executive order led to an increase in the number of license applications reviewed by DoD from 2,250 in 1980 to 18,951 in 1986. DoD personnel engaged in export control activities increased more than tenfold during this period from 12 in 1981 to 150 in 1987.

Section 5(a) of the EAA gives the Secretary of Commerce the authority to carry out the act, but only in "consultation with the Secretary of Defense, and such other departments and agencies as the Secretary considers appropriate." **(Document 3.2)** More specifically, 5(c) gives the Secretary of Commerce the authority to make and keep the U.S. Commodity Control List (CCL), but says the Secretary of Defense shall "identify goods and technology for inclusion on the list.'' If the two Secretaries cannot agree on particular items, the matter is to be referred to the President—by the Secretary of Defense. **(Document 3.7)** Prior to 1988, this gave DoD the power to stall indefinitely on changes to the list. In 1988 Congress put a limit on this by stating that if the Secretary of Commerce had not heard an objection within 20 days from DoD, the Secretary could assume concurrence. **(Document 3.7)**

The by-play in the House-Senate conference on the 1988 changes to administration of the CCL offered a clear demonstration of Congressional ambivalence. The Senate version of these changes re-enforced the power of the Secretary of Commerce to make reviews on his own authority. The conferees, however, rejected this statutory language and settled instead for vague report language reaffirming the ''primacy'' of the Department of Commerce in administering the export control system and stating their hope that the Secretary ''. . .fulfill all of his responsibilities in accordance with the statute of and intent of Congress.'' **(Document 3.8)** The Secretary of Commerce recently exercised this ''primacy'' by deciding to ease the controls on personal computers to the Soviet Union on foreign availability grounds. The Secretary of Defense criticized the decision sharply and publicly.

Congress also gave the Secretary of Commerce the responsibility to consult with the Secretary of Defense in ensuring that the U.S. control list is consonant with a separate list of ''militarily critical technologies'' (MCTL) which Congress has also directed that the Secretary of Defense draw up. Congress further directs that the Secretaries of Commerce and Defense shall together integrate items on the MCTL into the CCL. The President, again, is directed to resolve any disputes. **(Document 3.9)**

Congress originally created the MCTL in an attempt to reduce the scope of U.S. controls. In mandating it, Congress tried to implement a 1976 Pentagon report recommending that the U.S. concentrate on controlling particular technologies and ideas rather than a broad range of products. This idea is the basis of the oft' quoted phrase, ''Higher fences around fewer products.'' **(Document 3.10)** DoD, however, has produced an eight hundred-page classified list and has used it in efforts to expand the CCL, which remains separate from the MCTL. Thane Gustafson in a 1981 Rand Corporation study observed that were DoD successful, ''the entire Department of Commerce would not have been large enough to administer the export control program.''

Congress in the 1988 Trade Act also adjusted the extraordinary degree of influence it had earlier given

DoD over the actual issuance of specific licenses. Section 10(g) of the EAA gave the Secretary of Defense the authority ''to review any proposed export of any goods or technology to any country to which exports are controlled for national security purposes and, whenever the Secretary of Defense determines that the export of such goods or technology will make a significant contribution, which would prove detrimental to the national security of the United States, to the military potential of any such country, to recommend to the President that such export be disapproved.'' The EAA required that the Secretary of Defense, after consultation with the Secretary of Commerce, spell out in writing what types of transactions he wanted to review. It then required the Secretary of Commerce to refer any such transaction to the Secretary of Defense. This provision, as with the one on deletions from the CCL, gave DoD a practical veto, by delay. Furthermore, should the Secretary of Defense decide to refer an issue to the President, paragraph 10(g)(4) in the 1985 law required the President to notify Congress should he rule against the Secretary of Defense. The President was not required to notify Congress should he rule against the Secretary of Commerce. In the 1988 Trade Act, Congress deleted the requirement that the President report his rejection of DoD recommendations. It also imposed the same 20-day rule on DoD that it had put on the CCL process. **(Document 3.11)** In doing this, the conferees said, ''Ensuring a final resolution of disputed issues is an important goal; once the President has reviewed and decided an issue, that decision should be implemented.'' **(Document 3.12)**

In the same amendment, the Congress also required the Secretaries of Commerce and Defense to report to Congress within six months on their joint process for reviewing license applications. The conferees said that they intended that ''such a report compel the Administration to review the functioning of such concurrent review, and to provide a factual basis in order to evaluate the effect of such a joint review.'' **(Document 3.12)** On a more general note, the conferees also expressed concern that ''. . .DoD's objections have been based on foreign policy grounds rather than. . .national security grounds.'' **(Document 3.12)**

This running argument between DoD and the Department of Commerce is not the only reason the apparatus is ''cumbersome.'' The Department of State is also generally involved and specifically charged with managing the COCOM relationship. State also conducts the many bilateral negotiations these matters entail. Furthermore, munitions exports are placed under the Department of State. The State Department's controls on arms, ammunition, and implements of war on the United States Munitions List (USML) derive from the Arms Export Control Act (AECA) of 1968, as amended. The AECA also enables the Department of State to determine if an article is within its jurisdiction or that of the Department of Commerce. The Department of State has successfully and contentiously asserted jurisdiction over many civilian items that are based on military technology. The Department of the Treasury and the Bureau of Customs are engaged on the enforcement side. And the staff of the National Security Council is often, for all practical purposes, the arbiter of issues referred to the President.

Finally, there is the role of the Judiciary, or lack of one. Disappointed exporters have no recourse to the courts should they be denied a license for an item that they believe should not be on the list. **(Document 3.13)**

These interagency disputes are at the heart of many of the delays, which frustrate the U.S. exporting community. They will be at the heart, too, of any serious debate over the Act's renewal.

Effectiveness and Cost

Does this "cumbersome apparatus" actually restrain Soviet military capabilities? Does it further U.S. foreign policy interests? Is it worth the cost it imposes on U.S. business? Does it not only keep U.S. firms from trading with the Soviet bloc, but also inhibit trade with the West because potential Western purchasers do not want to get involved in U.S. controls? Do efforts to control the flow of existing technology actually inhibit the development of new technology?

In January 1987, the National Academy of Sciences produced a report addressing some of these questions entitled, *Balancing the National Interest: U.S. National Security Export Controls and Global Economic Competition.* The report reaffirmed the genuine need for focused controls, but questioned the effectiveness and cost of the present system, particularly to U.S. competitiveness and technological innovation. The report generated much debate within the export control community and a specific reaction in Congress in 1988.

The Academy report emphasized that the control regime's complex and cumbersome nature put U.S. exporters at a serious competitive disadvantage, not just in Communist markets, but in the entire world market. The report made it clear that while the regime is aimed at the Soviet Union, it is U.S. trade with the non-Communist world that bears, by far, most of the cost.

East-West trade (especially Soviet-American trade) is relatively insignificant commercially. As a practical matter, the U.S. export control system is focused predominantly on the possible diversion of goods and technology to the Soviets by companies resident in allied and neutral countries. Thus, the Commerce Department and the other players spend most of their effort controlling trade, not with the Communists, but with these non-Communist countries—so-called "West-West" trade. Specifically, the Academy report noted that the Department of Commerce processed 104,320 licenses in 1987, involving more than $80 billion, more than one-third of U.S. exports. Furthermore, nearly 90 percent of these licenses governed the export or reexport of items, not to the Communists, but to friendly Western nations. Most important, the Academy estimated the direct cost of the export control system to the U.S. economy was between $7–10 billion per year (total direct and indirect costs were roughly twice as much) and resulted in the annual loss of 188,000 jobs.

Accepting the proposition that the current system is excessively burdensome on West-West trade, Congress in the 1988 Trade Act directed the Secretaries of Commerce and Defense to make arrangements with the National Academy to conduct a follow-up study of the "adequacy of the current export administration system in safeguarding United States national security while maintaining United States international competitiveness and Western technological preeminence." Congress, furthermore, asked that the report contain recommendations for legislative and regulatory reforms. Congress also asked that it receive the report eighteen months after the two Secretaries and the Academy make their arrangements. The Secretaries were given sixty days from enactment (August 23, 1988) to make these arrangements. **(Document 3.14)**

In their report, the House-Senate conferees elaborated their thinking. They said they were "...seeking more than another study on export controls; instead [they] seek a detailed road map which provides specific and long-term solutions to the dilemmas of administering the export control program." The conferees went on to say that it was "...not enough to examine and make judgments on which technologies should be controlled. [They] also want the Academies to examine the administration of the export control program." **(Document 3.6)**

The Congress in the 1988 Trade Act extended the life of the EAA from 1989 to 1990. Clearly looking to use the new report in the 1990 renewal debate, the Trade Act conferees said, "The answers to these and other questions should give the Congress and the President the information necessary to structure a vigorous and credible export control program that balances the objectives of both U.S. competitiveness and U.S. national security." **(Document 3.6)**

Due to the delays of the 1988 Presidential transition, the Secretaries of Defense and Commerce were not able to meet the sixty-day Congressional deadline in making their arrangements with the National Academy. As of mid-October 1989, however, the project was underway. The Academy expects to publish its report in early 1991. Therefore, if Congress indeed wishes to use this report and the occasion of the EAA's expiration as the basis for a thorough reconsideration of the "cumbersome apparatus," it will have to consider extending the EAA's expiration deadline beyond its present date of September 30, 1990.

Document 3.1

Excerpt from the Export Administration Act

(Public Law 96-72, Sept. 29, 1979, 93 Stat. 503 As Amended)

SECTION 2401. Congressional findings

The Congress makes the following findings:

(1) The ability of United States citizens to engage in international commerce is a fundamental concern of United States policy.

(2) Exports contribute significantly to the world economic well-being of the United States and the stability of the world economy by increasing employment and production in the United States, and by earning foreign exchange, thereby contributing favorably to the trade balance. The restriction of exports from the United States can have serious adverse effects on the balance of payments and on domestic employment, particularly when restrictions applied by the United States are more extensive than those imposed by other countries.

(3) It is important for the national interest of the United States that both the private sector and the Federal Government place a high priority on exports, consistent with the economic, security, and foreign policy objectives of the United States.

(4) The availability of certain materials at home and abroad varies so that the quantity and composition of United States exports and their distribution among importing countries may affect the welfare of the domestic economy and may have an important bearing upon fulfillment of the foreign policy of the United States.

(5) Exports of goods or technology without regard to whether they make a significant contribution to the military potential of individual countries or combinations of countries may adversely affect the national security of the United States.

(6) Uncertainty of export control policy can inhibit the efforts of United States business and work to the detriment of the overall attempt to improve the trade balance of the United States.

(7) Unreasonable restrictions on access to world supplies can cause worldwide political and economic instability, interfere with free international trade, and retard the growth and development of nations.

(8) It is important that the administration of export controls imposed for national security purposes give special emphasis to the need to control exports of technology (and goods which contribute significantly to the transfer of such technology) which could make a significant contribution to the military potential of any country or combination of countries which would be detrimental to the national security of the United States.

(9) Minimization of restrictions on exports of agricultural commodities and products is of critical importance to the maintenance of a sound agricultural sector, to a positive contribution to the balance of payments, to reducing the level of Federal expenditures for agricultural support programs, and to United States cooperation in efforts to eliminate malnutrition and world hunger.

(10) It is important that the administration of export controls imposed for foreign policy purposes give special emphasis to the need to control exports of goods and substances hazardous to the public health and the environment which are banned or severely restricted for use in the United States, and which, if exported, could affect the international reputation of the United States as a responsible trading partner.

(11) The acquisition of national security sensitive goods and technology by the Soviet Union and other countries, the actions or policies of which run counter to the national security interests of the United States, has led to the significant enhancement of Soviet bloc military-industrial capabilities. This enhancement poses a threat to the security of the United States, its allies, and other friendly nations, and places additional demands on the defense budget of the United States.

(12) Availability to controlled countries of goods and technology from foreign sources is a fundamental concern of the United States and should be eliminated through negotiations and other appropriate means whenever possible.

(13) Excessive dependence of the United States, its allies, or countries sharing common strategic objectives with the United States, on energy and other

critical resources from potential adversaries can be harmful to the mutual and individual security of all those countries.

SECTION 2402. Congressional declaration of policy

The Congress makes the following declarations:

(1) It is the policy of the United States to minimize uncertainties in export control policy and to encourage trade with all countries with which the United States has diplomatic or trading relations, except those countries with which such trade has been determined by the President to be against the national interest.

(2) It is the policy of the United States to use export controls only after full consideration of the impact on the economy of the United States and only to the extent necessary—

(A) to restrict the export of goods and technology which would make a significant contribution to the military potential of any other country or combination of countries which would prove detrimental to the national security of the United States;

(B) to restrict the export of goods and technology where necessary to further significantly the foreign policy of the United States or to fulfill its declared international obligations; and

(C) to restrict the export of goods where necessary to protect the domestic economy from the excessive drain of scarce materials and to reduce the serious inflationary impact of foreign demand.

(3) It is the policy of the United States (A) to apply any necessary controls to the maximum extent possible in cooperation with all nations, and (B) to encourage observance of a uniform export control policy by all nations with which the United States has defense treaty commitments or common strategic objectives.

(4) It is the policy of the United States to use its economic resources and trade potential to further the sound growth and stability of its economy as well as to further its national security and foreign policy objectives.

(5) It is the policy of the United States—

(A) to oppose restrictive trade practices or boycotts fostered or imposed by foreign countries against other countries friendly to the United States or against any United States person;

(B) to encourage and, in specified cases, require United States persons engaged in the export of goods or technology or other information to refuse to take actions, including furnishing information or entering into or implementing agreements, which have the effect of furthering or supporting the restrictive trade practices or boycotts fostered or imposed by any foreign country against a country friendly to the United States or against any United States person; and

(C) to foster international cooperation and the development of international rules and institutions to assure reasonable access to world supplies.

(6) It is the policy of the United States that the desirability of subjecting, or continuing to subject, particular goods or technology or other information to United States export controls should be subjected to review by and consultation with representatives of appropriate United States Government agencies and private industry.

(7) It is the policy of the United States to use export controls, including license fees, to secure the removal by foreign countries of restrictions on access to supplies where such restrictions have or may have a serious domestic inflationary impact, have caused or may cause a serious domestic shortage, or have been imposed for purposes of influencing the foreign policy of the United States. In effecting this policy, the President shall make reasonable and prompt efforts to secure the removal or reduction of such restrictions, policies, or actions through international cooperation and agreement before imposing export controls. No action taken in fulfillment of the policy set forth in this paragraph shall apply to the export of medicine or medical supplies.

(8) It is the policy of the United States to use export controls to encourage other countries to take immediate steps to prevent the use of their territories or resources to aid, encourage, or give sanctuary to those persons involved in directing, supporting, or participating in acts of international terrorism. To achieve this objective, the President shall make reasonable and prompt efforts to secure the removal or reduction of such assistance to international terrorists through international cooperation and agreement before imposing export controls.

(9) It is the policy of the United States to cooperate with other countries with which the United States has defense treaty commitments or common strategic objectives in restricting the export of goods

and technology which would make a significant contribution to the military potential of any country or combination of countries which would prove detrimental to the security of the United States and of those countries with which the United States has defense treaty commitments or common strategic objectives, and to encourage other friendly countries to cooperate in restricting the sale of goods and technology that can harm the security of the United States.

(10) It is the policy of the United States that export trade by United States citizens be given a high priority and not be controlled except when such controls (A) are necessary to further fundamental national security, foreign policy, or short supply objectives, (B) will clearly further such objectives, and (C) are administered consistent with basic standards of due process.

(11) It is the policy of the United States to minimize restrictions on the export of agricultural commodities and products.

(12) It is the policy of the United States to sustain vigorous scientific enterprise. To do so involves sustaining the ability of scientists and other scholars freely to communicate research findings, in accordance with applicable provisions of law, by means of publication, teaching, conferences, and other forms of scholarly exchange.

(13) It is the policy of the United States to control the export of goods and substances banned or severely restricted for use in the United States in order to foster public health and safety and to prevent injury to the foreign policy of the United States as well as to the credibility of the United States as a responsible trading partner.

(14) It is the policy of the United States to cooperate with countries which are allies of the United States and countries which share common strategic objectives with the United States in minimizing dependence on imports of energy and other critical resources from potential adversaries and in developing alternative supplies of such resources in order to minimize strategic threats posed by excessive hard currency earnings derived from such resource exports by countries with policies adverse to the security interests of the United States.

(15) It is the policy of the United States, particularly in light of the Soviet massacre of innocent men, women, and children aboard Korean Air Lines flight 7, to continue to object to exceptions to the International Control list for the Union of Soviet Socialist Republics, subject to periodic review by the President.

Document 3.2

Excerpt from the Export Administration Act

(Public Law 96-72, Sept. 29, 1979, 93 Stat. 503 As Amended)

SECTION 2404. National security controls

(a) Authority

(1) In order to carry out the policy set forth in section 3(2)(A) of this Act [section 2402(2)(A) of this Appendix], the President may, in accordance with the provisions of this section, prohibit or curtail the export of any goods or technology subject to the jurisdiction of the United States or exported by any person subject to the jurisdiction of the United States. The authority contained in this subsection includes the authority to prohibit or curtail the transfer of goods or technology within the United States to embassies and affiliates of controlled countries. For purposes of the preceding sentence, the term "affiliates" includes both governmental entities and commercial entities that are controlled in fact by controlled countries. The authority contained in this subsection shall be exercised by the Secretary, in consultation with the Secretary of Defense, and such other departments and agencies as the Secretary considers appropriate, and shall be implemented by means of export licenses described in section 4(a) of this Act [section 2403(a) of this Appendix].

(2) Whenever the Secretary makes any revision with respect to any goods or technology, or with respect to the countries or destinations, affected by export controls imposed under this section, the Secretary shall publish in the Federal Register a notice of such revision and shall specify in such notice that the revision relates to controls imposed under the authority contained in this section.

(3) In issuing regulations to carry out this section, particular attention shall be given to the difficulty of devising effective safeguards to prevent a country that poses a threat to the security of the United States from diverting critical technologies to military use, the difficulty of devising effective safeguards to protect critical goods, and the need to take effective measures to prevent the reexport of critical technologies from other countries to countries that pose a threat to the security of the United States.

(4)(A) No authority or permission may be required under this section to reexport any goods or technology subject to the jurisdiction of the United States to any country which maintains export controls on such goods or technology cooperatively with the United States pursuant to the agreement of the group known as the Coordinating Committee, or pursuant to an agreement described in subsection (k) of this section. The Secretary may require any person reexporting any goods or technology under this subparagraph to notify the Secretary of such reexports.

(B) Notwithstanding subparagraph (A), the Secretary may require authority or permission to reexport the following:

(i) supercomputers;

(ii) goods or technology for sensitive nuclear uses (as defined by the Secretary);

(iii) devices for surreptitious interception of wire or oral communications; and

(iv) goods or technology intended for such end users as the Secretary may specify by regulation.

(5)(A) Except as provided in subparagraph (B), no authority or permission may be required under this section to reexport any goods or technology subject to the jurisdiction of the United States from any country when the goods or technology to be reexported are incorporated in another good and—

(i) the value of the controlled United States content of that other good is 25 percent or less of the total value of the good; or

(ii) the export of the goods or technology to a controlled country would require only notification of the participating governments of the Coordinating Committee.

For purposes of this paragraph, the "controlled United States content" of a good means those goods or technology subject to the jurisdiction of the United States which are incorporated in the good, if the export of those goods or technology from the United States to a country, at the time that the good is exported to that country, would require a validated license.

(B) The Secretary may by regulation provide that subparagraph (A) does not apply to the reexport of a supercomputer which contains goods or technology subject to the jurisdiction of the United States.

(6) Not later than 90 days after the date of the enactment of this paragraph [Aug. 23, 1988], the Secretary shall issue regulations to carry out paragraphs (4) and (5). Such regulations shall define the term "supercomputer" for purposes of those paragraphs.

SECTION 2405. Foreign policy controls

(a) Authority

(1) In order to carry out the policy set forth in paragraph (2)(B), (7), or (8) of section 3 of this Act [section 2402(2)(B), (7), (8), or (13) of this Appendix], the President may prohibit or curtail the exportation of any goods, technology, or other information subject to the jurisdiction of the United States or exported by any person subject to the jurisdiction of the United States, to the extent necessary to further significantly the foreign policy of the United States or to fulfill its declared international obligations. The authority granted by this subsection shall be exercised by the Secretary, in consultation with the Secretary of State, the Secretary of Defense, the Secretary of Agriculture, the Secretary of the Treasury, the United States Trade Representative, and such other departments and agencies as the Secretary considers appropriate, and shall be implemented by means of export licenses issued by the Secretary.

(2) Any export control imposed under this section shall apply to any transaction or activity undertaken with the intent to evade that export control, even if that export control would not otherwise apply to that transaction or activity.

(3) Export controls maintained for foreign policy purposes shall expire on December 31, 1979, or one year after imposition, whichever is later, unless extended by the President in accordance with subsections (b) and (f). Any such extension and any subsequent extension shall not be for a period of more than one year.

(4) Whenever the Secretary denies any export license under this subsection, the Secretary shall specify in the notice to the applicant of the denial of such license that the license was denied under the authority contained in this subsection, and the reasons for such denial, with reference to the criteria set forth in subsection (b) of this section. The Secretary shall also include in such notice what, if any, modifications in or restrictions on the goods or technology for which the license was sought would allow such export to be compatible with controls implemented under this section, or the Secretary shall indicate in such notice which officers and employees of the Department of Commerce who are familiar with the application will be made reasonably available to the applicant for consultation with regard to such modifications or restrictions, if appropriate.

(5) In accordance with the provisions of section 10 of this Act [section 2409 of this Appendix], the Secretary of State shall have the right to review any export license application under this section which the Secretary of State requests to review.

(6) Before imposing, expanding, or extending export controls under this section on exports to a country which can use goods, technology, or information available from foreign sources and so incur little or no economic costs as a result of the controls, the President should, through diplomatic means, employ alternatives to export controls which offer opportunities of distinguishing the United States from, and expressing the displeasure of the United States with, the specific actions of that country in response to which the controls are proposed. Such alternatives include private discussions with foreign leaders, public statements in situations where private diplomacy is unavailable or not effective, withdrawal of ambassadors, and reduction of the size of the diplomatic staff that the country involved is permitted to have in the United States.

Document 3.3

Excerpt from the Export Administration Act

(Public Law 96-72, Sept. 29, 1979, 93 Stat. 503 As Amended)

SECTION 2405. Foreign policy controls (cont'd)

(b) Criteria

(1) Subject to paragraph (2) of this subsection, the President may impose, extend, or expand controls under this section only if the President determines that—

(A) such controls are likely to achieve the intended foreign policy purpose, in light of other factors, including the availability from other countries of the goods or technology proposed for such controls, and that foreign policy purpose cannot be achieved through negotiations or other alternative means;

(B) the proposed controls are compatible with the foreign policy objectives of the United States and with overall United States policy toward the country to which exports are to be subject to the proposed controls;

(C) the reaction of other countries to the imposition, extension, or expansion of such export controls by the United States is not likely to render the controls ineffective in achieving the intended foreign policy purpose or to be counterproductive to United States foreign policy interests;

(D) the effect of the proposed controls on the export performance of the United States, the competitive position of the United States in the international economy, the international reputation of the United States as a supplier of goods and technology, or on the economic well-being of individual United States companies and their employees and communities does not exceed the benefit to United States foreign policy objectives; and

(E) the United States has the ability to enforce the proposed controls effectively.

(2) With respect to those export controls in effect under this section on the date of the enactment of the Export Administration Amendments Act of 1985 [July 12, 1985], the President, in determining whether to extend those controls, as required by subsection (a)(3) of this section, shall consider the criteria set forth in paragraph (1) of this subsection

and shall consider the foreign policy consequences of modifying the export controls.

(c) Consultation with industry

The Secretary in every possible instance shall consult with and seek advice from affected United States industries and appropriate advisory committees established under section 135 of the Trade Act of 1974 [19 U.S.C.A. sec. 2155] before imposing any export control under this section. Such consultation and advice shall be with respect to the criteria set forth in subsection (b)(1) and such other matters as the Secretary considers appropriate.

(d) Consultation with other countries

When imposing export controls under this section, the President shall, at the earliest appropriate opportunity, consult with the countries with which the United States maintains export controls cooperatively, and with such other countries as the President considers appropriate, with respect to the criteria set forth in subsection (b)(1) and such other matters as the President considers appropriate.

(e) Alternative means

Before resorting to the imposition of export controls under this section, the President shall determine that reasonable efforts have been made to achieve the purposes of the controls through negotiations or other alternative means.

(f) Consultation with the Congress

(1) The President may impose or expand export controls under this section, or extend such controls as required by subsection (a)(3) of this section, only after consultation with the Congress, including the Committee on Foreign Affairs of the House of Representatives and the Committee on Banking, Housing, and Urban Affairs of the Senate.

(2) The President may not impose, expand, or extend export controls under this section until the President has submitted to the Congress a report—

(A) specifying the purpose of the controls;

(B) specifying the determinations of the President (or, in the case of those export controls described in subsection (b)(2), the considerations of the President) with respect to each of the criteria set forth in subsection (b)(1), the bases for such determinations (or considerations), and any possible adverse foreign policy consequences of the controls;

(C) describing the nature, the subjects, and the results of, or the plans for, the consultation with industry pursuant to subsection (c) and with other countries pursuant to subsection (d);

(D) specifying the nature and results of any alternative means attempted under subsection (e), or the reasons for imposing, expanding, or extending the controls without attempting any such alternative means; and

(E) describing the availability from other countries of goods or technology comparable to the goods or technology subject to the proposed export controls, and describing the nature and results of the efforts made pursuant to subsection (h) to secure the cooperation of foreign governments in controlling the foreign availability of such comparable goods or technology.

Such report shall also indicate how such controls will further significantly the foreign policy of the United States or will further its declared international obligations.

(3) To the extent necessary to further the effectiveness of the export controls, portions of a report required by paragraph (2) may be submitted to the Congress on a classified basis, and shall be subject to the provisions of section 12(c) of this Act [section 2411(c) of this Appendix]. Each such report shall, at the same time it is submitted to the Congress, also be submitted to the General Accounting Office for the purpose of assessing the report's full compliance with the intent of this subsection.

(4) In the case of export controls under this section which prohibit or curtail the export of any agricultural commodity, a report submitted pursuant to paragraph (2) shall be deemed to be the report required by section 7(g)(3)(A) of this Act [section 2406(g)(3)(A) of this Appendix].

(5) In addition to any written report required under this section, the Secretary, not less frequently than annually, shall present in oral testimony before the Committee on Banking, Housing, and Urban Affairs of the Senate and the Committee on Foreign Affairs of the House of Representatives a report on policies and actions taken by the Government to carry out the provisions of this section.

(g) Exclusion for medicine and medical supplies and for certain food exports

This section does not authorize export controls on medicine or medical supplies. This section also does not authorize export controls on donations of goods (including, but not limited to, food, educational materials, seeds and hand tools, medicines and medical supplies, water resources equipment, clothing and shelter materials, and basic household supplies) that are intended to meet basic human needs. Before export controls on food are imposed, expanded, or extended under this section, the Secretary shall notify the Secretary of State in the case of export controls applicable with respect to any developed country and shall notify the Director of the United States International Development Cooperation Agency in the case of export controls applicable with respect to any developing country. The Secretary of State with respect to developed countries, and the Director with respect to developing countries, shall determine whether the proposed export controls on food would cause measurable malnutrition and shall inform the Secretary of that determination. If the Secretary is informed that the proposed export controls on food would cause measurable malnutrition, then those controls may not be imposed, expanded, or extended, as the case may be, unless the President determines that those controls are necessary to protect the national security interests of the United States, or unless the President determines that arrangements are insufficient to ensure that the food will reach those most in need. Each such determination by the Secretary of State or the Director of the United States International Development Cooperation Agency, and any such determination by the President, shall be reported to the Congress, together with a statement of the reasons for that determination. It is the intent of Congress that the President not impose export controls under this section on any goods or technology if he determines that the principal effect of the export of such goods or technology would be to help meet basic human needs. This subsection shall not be construed to prohibit the President from imposing restrictions on the export of medicine or medical supplies or of food under the International Emergency Economic Powers Act. This subsection shall not apply to any export control on medicine, medical supplies, or food, except for donations, which is in effect on the date of the enactment of the Export Administration Amendments Act of 1985

[July 12, 1985]. Notwithstanding the preceding provisions of this subsection, the President may impose export controls under this section on medicine, medical supplies, food, and donations of goods in order to carry out the policy set forth in paragraph (13) of section 3 of this Act [section 2402(13) of this Appendix].

(h) Foreign availability

(1) In applying export controls under this section, the President shall take all feasible steps to initiate and conclude negotiations with appropriate foreign governments for the purpose of securing the cooperation of such foreign governments in controlling the export to countries and consignees to which the United States export controls apply of any goods or technology comparable to goods or technology controlled under this section.

(2) Before extending any export control pursuant to subsection (a)(3) of this section, the President shall evaluate the results of his actions under paragraph (1) of this subsection and shall include the results of that evaluation in his report to the Congress pursuant to subsection (f) of this section.

(3) If, within 6 months after the date on which export controls under this section are imposed or expanded, or within 6 months after the date of the enactment of the Export Administration Amendments Act of 1985 [July 12, 1985] in the case of export controls in effect on such date of enactment, the President's efforts under paragraph (1) are not successful in securing the cooperation of foreign governments described in paragraph (1) with respect to those export controls, the Secretary shall thereafter take into account the foreign availability of the goods or technology subject to the export controls. If the Secretary affirmatively determines that a good or technology subject to the export controls is available in sufficient quantity and comparable quality from sources outside the United States to countries subject to the export controls so that denial of an export license would be ineffective in achieving the purposes of the controls, then the Secretary shall, during the period of such foreign availability, approve any license application which is required for the export of the good or technology and which meets all requirements for such a license. The Secretary shall remove the good or technology from the list established pursuant to subsection (1) of this section if the Secretary determines that such action is appropriate.

(4) In making a determination of foreign availability under paragraph (3) of this subsection, the

Secretary shall follow the procedures set forth in section 5(f)(3) of this Act [section 2404(f)(3) of this Appendix].

(i) International obligations

The provisions of subsections (b), (c), (d), (e), (g), and (h) shall not apply in any case in which the President exercises the authority contained in this section to impose export controls, or to approve or deny export license applications, in order to fulfill obligations of the United States pursuant to treaties to which the United States is a party or pursuant to other international agreements.

(j) Countries supporting international terrorism

(1) The Secretary and the Secretary of State shall notify the Committee on Foreign Affairs of the House of Representatives and the Committee on Banking, Housing, and Urban Affairs and the Committee on Foreign Relations of the Senate at least 30 days before any license is approved for the export of goods or technology valued at more than $1,000,000 to any country concerning which the Secretary of State has made the following determinations:

(A) Such country has repeatedly provided support for acts of international terrorism.

(B) Such exports would make a significant contribution to the military potential of such country, including its military logistics capability, or would enhance the ability of such country to support acts of international terrorism.

(2) Any determination which has been made with respect to a country under paragraph (1) of this subsection may not be rescinded unless the President, at least 30 days before the proposed rescission would take effect, submits to the Congress a report justifying the rescission and certifying that—

(A) the country concerned has not provided support for international terrorism, including support or sanctuary for any major terrorist or terrorist group in its territory, during the preceding 6-month period; and

(B) the country concerned has provided assurances that it will not support acts of international terrorism in the future.

(k) Crime control instruments

(1) Crime control and detection instruments and equipment shall be approved for export by the Secretary only pursuant to a validated export

license. Notwithstanding any other provision of this Act [sections 2401 to 2420 of this Appendix]—

(A) any determination of the Secretary of what goods or technology shall be included on the list established pursuant to subsection (1) of this section as a result of the export restrictions imposed by this subsection shall be made with the concurrence of the Secretary of State, and

(B) any determination of the Secretary to approve or deny an export license application to export crime control or detection instruments or equipment shall be made in concurrence with the recommendations of the Secretary of State submitted to the Secretary with respect to the application pursuant to section 10(e) of the Act [section 2409(e) of this Appendix].

except that, if the Secretary does not agree with the Secretary of State with respect to any determination under subparagraph (A) or (B), the matter shall be referred to the President for resolution.

(2) The provisions of this subsection shall not apply with respect to exports to countries which are members of the North Atlantic Treaty Organization or to Japan, Australia, or New Zealand, or to such other countries as the President shall designate consistent with the purposes of this subsection and section 502B of the Foreign Assistance Act of 1961 [22 U.S.C. sec. 2304].

(l) Control list

The Secretary shall establish and maintain, as part of the control list, a list of any goods or technology subject to export controls under this section, and the countries to which such controls apply. The Secretary shall clearly identify on the control list which goods or technology, and which countries or destinations, are subject to which types of controls under this section. Such list shall consist of goods and technology identified by the Secretary of State, with the concurrence of the Secretary. If the Secretary and the Secretary of State are unable to agree on the list, the matter shall be referred to the President. Such list shall be reviewed not less frequently than every three years in the case of controls maintained cooperatively with other countries, and annually in the case of all other controls, for the purpose of making such revisions as are necessary in order to carry out this section. During the course of such review, an assessment shall be made periodically of the availability from sources outside the United States, or any of its territories or possessions, of goods and technology comparable to those

controlled for export from the United States under this section.

(m) Effect on existing contracts and licenses

The President may not, under this section, prohibit or curtail the export or reexport of goods, technology, or other information—

(1) in performance of a contract or agreement entered into before the date on which the President reports to the Congress, pursuant to subsection (f) of this section, his intention to impose controls on the export or reexport of such goods, technology, or other information, or

(2) under a validated license or other authorization issued under this Act [sections 2401 to 2420 of this Appendix].

unless and until the President determines and certifies to the Congress that—

(A) a breach of the peace poses a serious and direct threat to the strategic interest of the United States,

(B) the prohibition or curtailment of such contracts, agreements, licenses, or authorizations will be instrumental in remedying the situation posing the direct threat, and

(C) the export controls will continue only so long as the direct threat persists.

(n) Extension of certain controls

Those export controls imposed under this section with respect to South Africa which were in effect on February 28, 1982, and ceased to be effective on March 1, 1982, September 15, 1982, or January 20, 1983, shall become effective on the date of the enactment of this subsection [July 12, 1985], and shall remain in effect until 1 year after such date of enactment. At the end of that 1-year period, any of those controls made effective by this subsection may be extended by the President in accordance with subsections (b) and (f) of this section.

(o) Expanded authority to impose controls

(1) In any case in which the President determines that it is necessary to impose controls under this section without any limitation contained in subsection (c), (d), (e), (g), (h), or (m) of this section, the President may impose those controls only if the President submits that determination to the Congress, together with a report pursuant to subsection (f) of this section with respect to the proposed controls,

and only if a law is enacted authorizing the imposition of those controls. If a joint resolution authorizing the imposition of those controls is introduced in either House of Congress within 30 days after the Congress receives the determination and report of the President, that joint resolution shall be referred to the Committee on Banking, Housing, and Urban Affairs of the Senate and to the appropriate committee of the House of Representatives. If either such committee has not reported the joint resolution at the end of 30 days after its referral, the committee shall be discharged from further consideration of the joint resolution.

(2) For purposes of this subsection, the term ''joint resolution'' means a joint resolution of the matter after the resolving clause which is as follows: ''That the Congress, having received on
a determination of the President under section 6(o)(1) of the Export Administration Act of 1979 with respect to the export controls which are set forth in the report submitted to the Congress with that determination, authorizes the President to impose those export controls.'', with the date of the receipt of the determination and report inserted in the blank.

(3) In the computation of the periods of 30 days referred to in paragraph (1), there shall be excluded the days on which either House of Congress is not in session because of an adjournment of more than 3 days to a day certain or because of an adjournment of the Congress sine die.

(p) Spare parts

(1) At the same time as the President imposes or expands export controls under this section, the President shall determine whether such export controls will apply to replacement parts for parts in goods subject to such export controls.

(2) With respect to export controls imposed under this section before the date of the enactment of this subsection [Aug. 23, 1988], an individual validated export license shall not be required for replacement parts which are exported to replace on a one-for-one basis parts that were in a good that was lawfully exported from the United States, unless the President determines that such a license should be required for such parts.

Document 3.4

Excerpt from the Export Administration Act

(Public Law 96-72, Sept. 29, 1979, 93 Stat. 503 As Amended)

SECTION 2404. National security controls (cont'd)

(f) Foreign availability

(1) Foreign availability to controlled countries

(A) The Secretary, in consultation with the Secretary of Defense and other appropriate Government agencies and with appropriate technical advisory committees established pursuant to subsection (h) of this section, shall review, on a continuing basis, the availability to controlled countries, from sources outside the United States, including countries which participate with the United States in multilateral export controls, of any goods or technology the export of which requires a validated license under this section. In any case in which the Secretary determines, in accordance with procedures and criteria which the Secretary shall by regulation establish, that any such goods or technology are available in fact to controlled countries from such sources in sufficient quantity and of comparable quality so that the requirement of a validated license for the export of such goods or technology is or would be ineffective in achieving the purpose set forth in subsection (a) of this section, the Secretary may not, after the determination is made, require a validated license for the export of such goods or technology during the period of such foreign availability, unless the President determines that the absence of export controls under this section on the goods or technology would prove detrimental to the national security of the United States. In any case in which the President determines under this paragraph that export controls under this section must be maintained notwithstanding foreign availability, the Secretary shall publish that determination, together with a concise statement of its basis and the estimated economic impact of the decision.

(B) The Secretary shall approve any application for a validated license which is required under this section for the export of any goods or technology to a controlled country and which meets all other requirements for such an application, if the Secretary determines that such goods or technology will, if the license is denied, be available in fact to such country from sources outside the United States, including countries which participate with the United States in multilateral export controls, in sufficient quantity and of comparable quality so that denial of the license would be ineffective in achieving the purpose set forth in subsection (a) of this section, unless the President determines that approving the license application would prove detrimental to the national security of the United States. In any case in which the Secretary makes a determination of foreign availability under this subparagraph with respect to any goods or technology, the Secretary shall determine whether a determination of foreign availability under subparagraph (A) with respect to such goods or technology is warranted.

(2) Foreign availability to other than controlled countries

(A) The Secretary shall review, on a continuing basis the availability to countries other than controlled countries, from sources outside the United States, of any goods or technology the export of which requires a validated license under this section. If the Secretary determines, in accordance with procedures which the Secretary shall establish, that any goods or technology in sufficient quantity and of comparable quality are available in fact from sources outside the United States (other than availability under license from a country which maintains export controls on such goods or technology cooperatively with the United States pursuant to the agreement of the group known as the Coordinating Committee or pursuant to an agreement described in subsection (k) of this section), the Secretary may not, after the determination is made and during the period of such foreign availability, require a validated license for the export of such goods or technology to any country (other than a controlled country) to which the country from which the goods or technology is available does not place controls on the export of such goods or technology. The requirement with respect to a validated license in the preceding sentence shall not apply if the President determines that the absence of export controls under this section on the goods or technology would prove detrimental to the national security of the United States. In any case in which the President determines under this paragraph that export controls under this section must be maintained notwithstanding foreign availability, the Secretary shall publish that determination, together with a concise statement of its basis and the estimated economic impact of the decision.

(B) The Secretary shall approve any application for a validated license which is required under this section for the export of any goods or technology to a country (other than a controlled country) and which meets all other requirements for such an application, if the Secretary determines that such goods or technology are available from foreign sources to that country under the criteria established in subparagraph (A), unless the President determines that approving the license application would prove detrimental to the national security of the United States. In any case in which the Secretary makes a determination of foreign availability under this subparagraph with respect to any goods or technology, the Secretary shall determine whether a determination of foreign availability under subparagraph (A) with respect to such goods or technology is warranted.

(3) Procedures for making determinations

(A) The Secretary shall make a foreign availability determination under paragraph (1) or (2) on the Secretary's own initiative or upon receipt of an allegation from an export license applicant that such availability exists. In making any such determination, the Secretary shall accept the representations of applicants made in writing and supported by reasonable evidence, unless such representations are contradicted by reliable evidence, including scientific or physical examination, expert opinion based upon adequate factual information, or intelligence information. In making determinations of foreign availability, the Secretary may consider such factors as cost, reliability, the availability and reliability of spare parts and the cost and quality thereof, maintenance programs, durability, quality of end products produced by the item proposed for export, and scale of production. For purposes of this subparagraph, "evidence" may include

such items as foreign manufacturers' catalogues, brochures, or operations or maintenance manuals, articles from reputable trade publications, photographs, and depositions based upon eyewitness accounts.

(B) In a case in which an allegation is received from an export license applicant, the Secretary shall, upon receipt of the allegation, submit for publication in the Federal Register notice of such receipt. Within 4 months after receipt of the allegation, the Secretary shall determine whether the foreign availability exists, and shall so notify the applicant. If the Secretary has determined that the foreign availability exists, the Secretary shall, upon making such determination, submit the determination for review to other departments and agencies as the Secretary considers appropriate. The Secretary's determination of foreign availability does not require the concurrence or approval of any official, department, or agency to which such a determination is submitted. Not later than 1 month after the Secretary makes the determination, the Secretary shall respond in writing to the applicant and submit for publication in the Federal Register, that—

(i) the foreign availability does exist and—

(I) the requirement of a validated license has been removed,

(II) the President has determined that export controls under this section must be maintained notwithstanding the foreign availability and the applicable steps are being taken under paragraph (4), or

(III) in the case of a foreign availability determination under paragraph (1), the foreign availability determination will be submitted to a multilateral review process in accordance with the agreement of the Coordinating Committee for a period of not more than 4 months beginning on the date of the publication; or

(ii) the foreign availability does not exist.

In any case in which the submission for publication is not made within the time period specified in the preceding sentence, the Secretary may not thereafter require a license for the export of the goods or technology with respect to which the foreign availability allegation was made. In the case of a foreign availability determination under paragraph (1) to which clause (i)(III) applies, no license for such export may be required after the end of the 9-month period beginning on the date on which the allegation is received.

(4) Negotiations to eliminate foreign availability

(A) In any case in which export controls are maintained under this section notwithstanding foreign availability, on account of a determination by the President that the absence of the controls would prove detrimental to the national security of the United States, the President shall actively pursue negotiations with the governments of the appropriate foreign countries for the purpose of eliminating such availability. No later than the commencement of such negotiations, the President shall notify in writing the Committee on Banking, Housing, and Urban Affairs of the Senate and the Committee on Foreign Affairs of the House of Representatives that he has begun such negotiations and why he believes it is important to national security that export controls on the goods or technology involved be maintained.

(B) If, within 6 months after the President's determination that export controls be maintained, the foreign availability has not been eliminated, the Secretary may not, after the end of that 6-month period, require a validated license for the export of the goods or technology involved. The President may extend the 6-month period described in the preceding sentence for an additional period of 12 months if the President certifies to the Congress that the negotiations involved are progressing and that the absence of the export controls involved would prove detrimental to the national security of the United States. Whenever the President has reason to believe that goods or technology subject to export controls for national security purposes by the United States may become available from other countries to controlled countries and that such availability can be prevented or eliminated by means of negotiations with such other countries, the President shall promptly initiate negotiations with the governments of such other countries to prevent such foreign availability.

(C) After an agreement is reached with a country pursuant to negotiations under this paragraph to eliminate or prevent foreign availability of goods or technology, the Secretary may not require a validated license for the export of such goods or technology to that country.

(5) Expedited licenses for items available to countries other than controlled countries

(A) In any case in which the Secretary finds that any goods or technology from foreign sources is of similar quality to goods or technology the export of which requires a validated license under this section and is available to a country other than a controlled country without effective restrictions, the Secretary shall designate such goods or technology as eligible for export to such country under this paragraph.

(B) In the case of goods or technology designated under subparagraph (A), then 20 working days after the date of formal filing with the Secretary of an individual validated license application for the export of those goods or technology to an eligible country, a license for the transaction specified in the application shall become valid and effective and the goods or technology are authorized for export pursuant to such license unless the license has been denied by the Secretary on account of an inappropriate end user. The Secretary may extend the 20-day period provided in the preceding sentence for an additional period of 15 days if the Secretary requires additional time to consider the application and so notifies the applicant.

(C) The Secretary may make a foreign availability determination under subparagraph (A) on the Secretary's own initiative, upon receipt of an allegation from an export license applicant that such availability exists, or upon the submission of a certification by a technical advisory committee of appropriate jurisdiction that such availability exists. Upon receipt of such an allegation or certification, the Secretary shall publish notice of such allegation or certification in the Federal Register and shall make the foreign availability determination within 30 days after such receipt and publish the determination in the Federal Register. In the case of the failure of the Secretary to make and publish such determination within that 30-day period, the goods or technology involved shall be deemed to be designated as eligible for export to the country or countries involved, for purposes of subparagraph (B).

(D) The provisions of paragraphs (1), (2), (3), and (4) do not apply with respect to determinations of foreign availability under this paragraph.

(6) Office of foreign availability

The Secretary shall establish in the Department of Commerce an Office of Foreign Availability, which shall be under the direction of the Under Secretary of Commerce for Export Administration. The Office shall be responsible for gathering and analyzing all the necessary information in order for the Secretary to make determinations of foreign availability under this Act [sections 2401 to 2420 of this Appendix]. The Secretary shall make available to the Committee on Foreign Affairs of the House of Representatives and the Committee on Banking, Housing, and Urban Affairs of the Senate at the end of each 6-month period during a fiscal year information on the operations of the Office, and on improvements in the Government's ability to assess foreign availability, during that 6-month period, including information on the training of personnel, the use of computers, and the use of Commercial Service Officers of the United States and Foreign Commercial Service. Such information shall also include a description of representative determinations made under this Act [sections 2401 to 2420 of this Appendix] during that 6-month period that foreign availability did or did not exist (as the case may be), together with an explanation of such determinations.

(7) Sharing of information

Each department or agency of the United States, including any intelligence agency, and all contractors with any such department or agency, shall, upon the request of the Secretary and consistent with the protection of intelligence sources and methods, furnish information to the Office of Foreign Availability concerning foreign availability of goods and technology subject to export controls under this Act [sections 2402 to 2420 of this Appendix]. Each such department or agency shall allow the Office of Foreign Availability access to any information from a laboratory or other facility within such department or agency.

(8) Removal of controls on less sophisticated goods or technology

In any case in which Secretary may not, pursuant to paragraph (1), (2), (3), or (4) of this subsection or paragraph (6) of subsection (h) of this section, require a validated license for the export of goods or technology, then the Secretary may not require a validated license for the export of any similar goods or technology whose function, technological approach, performance thresholds, and other attributes that form the basis for export controls

under this section do not exceed the technical parameters of the goods or technology from which the validated license requirement is removed under the applicable paragraph.

(9) Notice of all foreign availability assessments

Whenever the Secretary undertakes a foreign availability assessment under this subsection or subsection (h)(6), the Secretary shall publish notice of such assessment in the Federal Register.

(10) Availability defined

For purposes of this subsection and subsections (f) and (h), the term "available in fact to controlled countries" includes production or availability of any goods or technology in any country—

(A) from which the goods or technology is not restricted for export to any controlled country; or

(B) in which such export restrictions are determined by the Secretary to be ineffective.

For purposes of subparagraph (B), the mere inclusion of goods or technology on a list of goods or technology subject to bilateral or multilateral national security export controls shall not alone constitute credible evidence that a country provides an effective means of controlling the export of such goods or technology to controlled countries.

(g) Indexing

(1) In order to ensure that requirements for validated licenses and other licenses authorizing multiple exports are periodically removed as goods or technology subject to such requirements becomes obsolete with respect to the national security of the United States, regulations issued by the Secretary may, where appropriate, provide for annual increases in the performance levels of goods or technology subject to any such licensing requirement. The regulations issued by the Secretary shall establish as one criterion for the removal of goods or technology from such license requirements the anticipated needs of the military of controlled countries. Any such goods or technology which no longer meets the performance levels established by the regulations shall be removed from the list established pursuant to subsection (c) of this section unless, under such exceptions and under such procedures as the Secretary shall prescribe, any other department or agency of the United States objects to such removal and the Secretary determines, on the basis of such objection, that the goods or technology shall not be removed from the list. The

Secretary shall also consider, where appropriate, removing site visitation requirements for goods and technology which are removed from the list unless objections described in this subsection are raised.

(2)(A) In carrying out this subsection, the Secretary shall conduct annual reviews of the performance levels of goods or technology—

(i) which are eligible for export under a distribution license,

(ii) below which exports to the People's Republic of China require only notification of the governments participating in the group known as the Coordinating Committee, and

(iii) below which no authority or permission to export may be required under subsection (b)(2) or (b)(3) of this section.

The Secretary shall make appropriate adjustments to such performance levels based on these reviews.

(B) In any case in which the Secretary receives a request which—

(i) is to revise the qualification requirements or minimum thresholds of any goods eligible for export under a distribution license, and

(ii) is made by an exporter of such goods, representatives of an industry which produces such goods, or a technical advisory committee established under subsection (h) of this section.

the Secretary, after consulting with other appropriate Government agencies and technical advisory committees established under subsection (h) of this section, shall determine whether to make such revision, or some other appropriate revision, in such qualification requirements or minimum thresholds. In making this determination, the Secretary shall take into account the availability of the goods from sources outside the United States. The Secretary shall make a determination on a request made under this subparagraph within 90 days after the date on which the request is filed. If the Secretary's determination pursuant to such a request is to make a revision, such revision shall be implemented within 120 days after the date on which the request is filed and shall be published in the Federal Register.

(h) Technical advisory committees

(1) Upon written request by representatives of a substantial segment of any industry which produces any goods or technology subject to export controls under this section or being considered for such controls because of their significance to the national security of the United States, the Secretary shall appoint a technical advisory committee for any such goods or technology which the Secretary determines are difficult to evaluate because of questions concerning technical matters, worldwide availability, and actual utilization of production and technology, or licensing procedures. Each such committee shall consist of representatives of United States industry and Government, including the Departments of Commerce, Defense, and State, the intelligence community, and, in the discretion of the Secretary, other Government departments and agencies. No person serving on any such committee who is representative of industry shall serve on such committee for more than four consecutive years.

(2) Technical advisory committees established under paragraph (1) shall advise and assist the Secretary, the Secretary of Defense, and any other department, agency, or official of the Government of the United States to which the President delegates authority under this Act [sections 2401 to 2420 of this Appendix], with respect to actions designed to carry out the policy set forth in section 3(2)(A) of this Act [section 2402(2)(A) of this Appendix]. Such committees, where they have expertise in such matters, shall be consulted with respect to questions involving (A) technical matters, (B) worldwide availability and actual utilization of production technology, (C) licensing procedures which affect the level of export controls applicable to any goods or technology, (D) revisions of the control list (as provided in subsection (c)(4)), including proposed revisions of multilateral controls in which the United States participates, (E) the issuance of regulations, (F) any other questions relating to actions designed to carry out the policy set forth in section 3(2)(A) of this Act. [Section 2402(2)(A) of this Appendix]. Nothing in this subsection shall prevent the Secretary or the Secretary of Defense from consulting, at any time, with any person representing industry or the general public, regardless of whether such person is a member of a technical advisory committee. Members of the public shall be given a reasonable opportunity, pursuant to regulations prescribed by the Secretary, to present evidence to such committees.

(3) Upon request of any member of any such committee, the Secretary may, if the Secretary determines it appropriate, reimburse such member for

travel, subsistence, and other necessary expenses incurred by such member in connection with the duties of such member.

(4) Each such committee shall elect a chairman, and shall meet at least every three months at the call of the chairman, unless the chairman determines, in consultation with the other members of the committee, that such a meeting is not necessary to achieve the purposes of this subsection. Each such committee shall be terminated after a period of 2 years, unless extended by the Secretary for additional periods of 2 years. The Secretary shall consult each such committee with respect to such termination or extension of that committee.

(5) To facilitate the work of the technical advisory committees, the Secretary, in conjunction with other departments and agencies participating in the administration of this Act [sections 2401 to 2420 of this Appendix], shall disclose to each such committee adequate information, consistent with national security, pertaining to the reasons for the export controls which are in effect or contemplated for the goods or technology with respect to which that committee furnishes advice.

(6) Whenever a technical advisory committee certifies to the Secretary that goods or technology with respect to which such committee was appointed have become available in fact, to controlled countries, from sources outside the United States, including countries which participate with the United States in multilateral export controls, in sufficient quantity and of comparable quality so that requiring a validated license for the export of such goods or technology would be ineffective in achieving the purpose set forth in subsection (a) of this section, the technical advisory committee shall submit that certification to the Congress at the same time the certification is made to the Secretary, together with the documentation for the certification. The Secretary shall investigate the foreign availability so certified and, not later than 90 days after the certification is made, shall submit a report to the technical advisory committee and the Congress stating that—

(A) the Secretary has removed the requirement of a validated license for the export of the goods or technology, on account of the foreign availability,

(B) the Secretary has recommended to the President that negotiations be conducted to eliminate the foreign availability, or

(C) the Secretary has determined on the basis of the investigation that the foreign availability does not exist.

To the extent necessary, the report may be submitted on a classified basis. In any case in which the Secretary has recommended to the President that negotiations be conducted to eliminate the foreign availability, the President shall actively pursue such negotiations with the governments of the appropriate foreign countries. If, within 6 months after the Secretary submits such report to the Congress, the foreign availability has not been eliminated, the Secretary may not, after the end of that 6-month period, require a validated license for the export of the goods or technology involved. The President may extend the 6-month period described in the preceding sentence for an additional period of 12 months if the President certifies to the Congress that the negotiations involved are progressing and that the absence of the export control involved would prove detrimental to the national security of the United States. After an agreement is reached with a country pursuant to negotiations under this paragraph to eliminate foreign availability of goods or technology, the Secretary may not require a validated license for the export of such goods or technology to that country.

(i) Multilateral export controls

Recognizing the ineffectiveness of unilateral controls and the importance of uniform enforcement measures to the effectiveness of multilateral controls, the President shall enter into negotiations with the governments participating in the group known as the Coordinating Committee (hereinafter in this subsection referred to as the "Committee") with a view toward accomplishing the following objectives:

(1) Enhanced public understanding of the Committee's purpose and procedures, including publication of the list of items controlled for export by agreement of the Committee, together with all notes, understandings, and other aspects of such agreement of the Committee, and all changes thereto.

(2) Periodic meetings of high-level representatives of participating governments for the purpose of coordinating export control policies and issuing policy guidance to the Committee.

(3) Strengthened legal basis for each government's export control system, including, as appropriate, increased penalties and statutes of limitations.

(4) Harmonization of export control documentation by the participating governments to verify the movement of goods and technology subject to controls by the Committee.

(5) Improved procedures for coordination and exchange of information concerning violations of the agreement of the Committee.

(6) Procedures for effective implementation of the agreement through uniform and consistent interpretations of export controls agreed to by the governments participating in the Committee.

(7) Coordination of national licensing and enforcement efforts by governments participating in the Committee, including sufficient technical expertise to assess the licensing status of exports and to ensure end-use verification.

(8) More effective procedures for enforcing export controls, including adequate training, resources, and authority for enforcement officers to investigate and prevent illegal exports.

(9) Agreement to provide adequate resources to enhance the functioning of individual national export control systems and of the Committee.

(10) Improved enforcement and compliance with the agreement through elimination of unnecessary export controls and maintenance of an effective control list.

(11) Agreement to enhance cooperation, among members of the Committee in obtaining the agreement of governments outside the Committee to restrict the export of goods and technology on the International Control List, to establish an ongoing mechanism in the Committee to coordinate planning and implementation of export control measures related to such agreements, and to remove items from the International Control List if such items continue to be available to controlled countries or if the control of the items no longer serves the common strategic objectives of the members of the Committee.

For purposes of reviews of the International Control List, the President may include as advisors to the United States delegation to the Committee representatives of industry who are knowledgeable with respect to the items being reviewed.

(j) Commercial agreements with certain countries

(1) Any United States firm, enterprise or other nongovernmental entity which enters into an agreement with any agency of the government of a controlled country, that calls for the encouragement of technical cooperation and that is intended to result in the export from the United States to the other party of unpublished technical data of United States origin, shall report to the Secretary the agreement with such agency in sufficient detail.

(2) The provisions of paragraph (1) shall not apply to colleges, universities, or other educational institutions.

(k) Negotiations with other countries

The Secretary of State, in consultation with the Secretary of Defense, the Secretary of Commerce, and the heads of other appropriate departments and agencies, shall be responsible for conducting negotiations with other countries, including those countries not participating in the group known as the Coordinating Committee, regarding their cooperation in restricting the export of goods and technology in order to carry out the policy set forth in section 3(9) of this Act [section 2402(9) of this Appendix], as authorized by subsection (a) of this section, including negotiations with respect to which goods and technology should be subject to multilaterally agreed export restrictions and what conditions should apply for exceptions from those restrictions. In cases where such negotiations produce agreements on export restrictions comparable in practice to those maintained by the Coordinating Committee, the Secretary shall treat exports, whether by individual or multiple licenses, to countries party to such agreements in the same manner as exports to members of the Coordinating Committee are treated, including the same manner as exports are treated under subsection (b)(2) of this section and section 10(o) of this Act [section 2409(o) of this Appendix].

(l) Diversion of controlled goods or technology

(1) Whenever there is reliable evidence, as determined by the Secretary, that goods or technology which were exported subject to national security controls under this section to a controlled country have been diverted to an unauthorized use or consignee in violation of the conditions of an export license, the Secretary for as long as that diversion continues—

(A) shall deny all further exports, to or by the party or parties responsible for that diversion or who conspired in that diversion, of any goods or technology subject to national security controls under this section, regardless of whether

61

such goods or technology are available from sources outside the United States; and

(B) may take such additional actions under this Act [sections 2401 to 2420 of this Appendix] with respect to the party or parties referred to in subparagraph (A) as the Secretary determines are appropriate in the circumstances to deter the further unauthorized use of the previously exported goods or technology.

(2) As used in this subsection, the term "unauthorized use" means the use of United States goods or technology in the design, production, or maintenance of any item on the United States Munitions List, or the military use of any item on the International Control List of the Coordinating Committee.

(m) Goods containing controlled parts and components

Export controls may not be imposed under this section, or under any other provision of law, on a good solely on the basis that the good contains parts or components subject to export controls under this section if such parts or components—

(1) are essential to the functioning of the good,

(2) are customarily included in sales of the good in countries other than controlled countries, and

(3) comprise 25 percent or less of the total value of the good, unless the good itself, if exported, would by virtue of the functional characteristics of the good as a whole make a significant contribution to the military potential of a controlled country which would prove detrimental to the national security of the United States.

(n) Security measures

The Secretary and the Commissioner of Customs, consistent with their authorities under section 12(a) of this Act [section 2411(a) of this Appendix], and in consultation with the Director of the Federal Bureau of Investigation, shall provide advice and technical assistance to persons engaged in the manufacture or handling of goods or technology subject to export controls under this section to develop security systems to prevent violations or evasions of those export controls.

(o) Recordkeeping

The Secretary, the Secretary of Defense, and any other department or agency consulted in connection with a license application under this Act [sections 2401 to 2420 of this Appendix] or a revision of a list of goods or technology subject to export controls under this Act [sections 2401 to 2420 of this Appendix], shall make and keep records of their respective advice, recommendations, or decisions in connection with any such license application or revision, including the factual and analytical basis of the advice, recommendations, or decisions.

(p) National Security Control Office

To assist in carrying out the policy and other authorities and responsibilities of the Secretary of Defense under this section, there is established in the Department of Defense a National Security Control Office under the direction of the Under Secretary of Defense for Policy. The Secretary of Defense may delegate to that office such of those authorities and responsibilities, together with such ancillary functions, as the Secretary of Defense considers appropriate.

(q) Exclusion for agricultural commodities

This section does not authorize export controls on agricultural commodities, including fats, oils, and animal hides and skins.

Document 3.5

Excerpt from the Mutual Defense Assistance Control Act of 1951

(Public Law 213 October 26, 1951)

Be it enacted by the Senate and House of Representatives of the United States of America in Congress assembled, That this Act may be cited as the "Mutual Defense Assistance Control Act of 1951."

TITLE I—WAR MATERIALS

SEC. 101 The Congress of the United States, recognizing that in a world threatened by aggression the United States can best preserve and maintain peace by developing maximum national strength and by utilizing all of its resources in cooperation with other free nations, hereby declares it to be the policy of the United States to apply an embargo on the shipment of arms, ammunition, and implements of war, atomic energy materials, petroleum, transportation materials of strategic value, and items of primary strategic significance used in the production of arms, ammunition, and implements of war to any nation or combination of nations threatening the security of the United States, including the Union of Soviet Socialist Republics and all countries under its domination, in order to (1) increase the national strength of the United States and of the cooperating nations; (2) impede the ability of nations threatening the security of the United States to conduct military operations; and (3) to assist the people of the nations under the domination of foreign aggressors to reestablish their freedom.

It is further declared to be the policy of the United States that no military, economic, or financial assistance shall be supplied to any nation unless it applies an embargo on such shipments to any nation or combination of nations threatening the security of the United States, including the Union of Soviet Socialist Republics and all countries under its domination.

Document 3.6

Excerpt from Conference Report to Accompany H.R. 3 Omnibus Trade and Competitiveness Act of 1988

(Report 100-576, 100th Congress, 2nd Session, April 20, 1988)

Conference agreement

The conference agreement directs the Secretaries of Commerce and Defense to enter into appropriate arrangements with the National Academy of Sciences to conduct a study of national security export controls.

The agreement reflects concerns by the conferees that national security, U.S. competitiveness, and Western technological preeminence are not well-served by the current export administration system, which is burdened by ambiguous criteria, overlapping jurisdictions, and a cumbersome decision- and policy-making apparatus.

The conferees recognize that regulating exports of U.S. goods and technology is an exceedingly difficult and costly task. A poorly administered and cumbersome program can undermine America's competitiveness, and can lead to reduced R & D funding and a decline in the rate of technological innovation in key sectors of the economy, thereby endangering U.S. national security. Conversely, serious breaches of the export control program can do severe harm to national security, especially in the near-term. In this regard, the conferees are seeking more than another study on export controls; instead, the conferees seek a detailed roadmap which provides specific and long-term solutions to the dilemmas of administering the export control program.

The conferees note that certain aspects of the study may parallel recent efforts by the CIA in assessing Soviet technology requirements for new weapons systems. This is important since criteria for establishing national security controls on U.S. technology and products should consider their potential contribution to Soviet military capabilities. Once the Academies have an inventory of the technologies that make crucial differences to Soviet military capabilities, a comprehensive set of criteria can aid in evaluating which of these technologies should be controlled and which technologies should no longer be controlled. It is not enough to examine and make judgements on which technologies should be controlled. The conferees also want the Academies to examine the administration of the export control program. Can decision-making be made more timely and efficient? How can the information base of the relevant industries be more effectively integrated into the policy process? What are the appropriate administrative measures to deal with decision-making when questions of competitiveness and national security cannot be answered with certainty? The answers to these and other questions should give the Congress and the President the information necessary to structure a vigorous and credible export control program that balances the objectives of both U.S. competitiveness and U.S. national security.

Document 3.7

Excerpt from the Export Administration Act

(Public Law 96-72, Sept. 29, 1979, 93 Stat. 503 As Amended)

SECTION 2404. National security controls (Cont'd)

(c) Control list

(1) The Secretary shall establish and maintain, as part of the control list, a list of all goods and technology subject to export control under this section. Such goods and technology shall be clearly identified as being subject to controls under this section.

(2) The Secretary of Defense and other appropriate departments and agencies shall identify goods and technology for inclusion on the list referred to in paragraph (1). Those items which the Secretary and the Secretary of Defense concur shall be subject to export controls under this section shall comprise such list. If the Secretary and the Secretary of Defense are unable to concur on such items, as determined by the Secretary, the Secretary of Defense may, within 20 days after receiving notification of the Secretary's determination, refer the matter to the President for resolution. The Secretary of Defense shall notify the Secretary of any such referral. The President shall, not later than 20 days after such referral, notify the Secretary of his determination with respect to the inclusion of such items on the list. Failure of the Secretary of Defense to notify the President or the Secretary, or failure of the President to notify the Secretary, in accordance with this paragraph, shall be deemed by the Secretary to constitute concurrence in the implementation of the actions proposed by the Secretary regarding the inclusion of such items on the list.

(3) The Secretary shall conduct partial reviews of the list established pursuant to this subsection at least once each calendar quarter in order to carry out the policy set forth in section 3(2)(A) of this Act [section 2402(2)(A) of this Appendix] and the provisions of this section, and shall promptly make such revisions of the list as may be necessary after each such review. Before beginning each quarterly review, the Secretary shall publish notice of that review in the Federal Register. The Secretary shall provide a 30-day period during each review for comment and the submission of data, with or without oral presentation, by interested Government agencies and other affected or potentially affected parties. After consultation with appropriate Government agencies, the Secretary shall make a determination of any revisions in the list within 30 days after the end of the review period. The concurrence or approval of any other department or agency is not required before any such revision is made. The Secretary shall publish in the Federal Register any revisions in the list, with an explanation of the reasons for the revisions. The Secretary shall use the data developed from each review in formulating United States proposals relating to multilateral export controls in the group known as the Coordinating Committee. The Secretary shall further assess, as part of each review, the availability from sources outside the United States of goods and technology comparable to those subject to export controls imposed under this section. All goods and technology on the list shall be reviewed at least once each year. The provisions of this paragraph apply to revisions of the list which consist of removing items from the list or making changes in categories of, or other specifications in, items on the list.

Document 3.8

Excerpt from Conference Report to Accompany H.R. 3 Omnibus Trade and Competitiveness Act of 1988

(Report 100–576, 100th Congress, 2nd Session, April 20, 1988)

Responsibilities of Secretary of Commerce (sec. 1008 of
Senate amendment; section 2416 of Conference agreement)

Present law

The EAA provides general authority to the Secretary of Commerce to carry out all functions under the Act, unless specifically delegated to another agency.

House bill

No provision.

Senate amendment

The Senate amendment reinforces the authority of the Secretary of Commerce to formulate list review proposals; review other COCOM countries' license applications; and determine comparability of third countries' export systems.

Conference agreement

The Conference agreement is the House position.

In agreeing to delete the Senate provision, the conferees do so in the belief that such amendments are unnecessary because the Export Administration Act already specifies the Department of Commerce as the primary agency responsible for all functions under the Act except those expressly delegated to another agency.

The Department of State has primary responsibility, pursuant to section 5(k) of the Act, to conduct negotiations with other countries. Section 5(c) of the Act explicitly charges the Secretary of Commerce with responsibility of revisions to the control list, which are the basis for U.S. proposals for the COCOM list review process. Technical expertise regarding revisions of the control list, as well as evaluations of license applications by foreign countries, reside with the Commerce Department. Commerce review of foreign cases submitted to COCOM is important to assure uniformity of licensing decisions and that U.S. exporters are not disadvantaged vis-a-vis their COCOM competitors, since cases often involve foreign products similar to, and in competition with U.S. exports licensed by the Secretary. Furthermore, section 2415 of this bill explicitly invests in the Secretary of Commerce the responsibility for determining which COCOM countries have effective systems.

In reaffirming the primacy of the Department of Commerce in administering the export control system, the conferees expect the Secretary to fulfill all of his responsibilities in accordance with the statute and the intent of Congress.

Document 3.9

Excerpt from the Export Administration Act

(Public Law 96-72, Sept. 29, 1979, 93 Stat. 503 As Amended)

SECTION 2404. National security controls (Cont'd)

(d) Militarily critical technologies

(1) The Secretary, in consultation with the Secretary of Defense, shall review and revise the list established pursuant to subsection (c), as prescribed in paragraph (3) of such subsection, for the purpose of insuring that export controls imposed under this section cover and (to the maximum extent consistent with the purposes of this Act [sections 2401 to 2420 of this Appendix]) are limited to militarily critical goods and technologies and the mechanisms through which such goods and technologies may be effectively transferred.

(2) The Secretary of Defense shall bear primary responsibility for developing a list of militarily critical technologies. In developing such list, primary emphasis shall be given to—

(A) arrays of design and manufacturing know-how,

(B) keystone manufacturing, inspection, and test equipment,

(C) goods accompanied by sophisticated operation, application, or maintenance know-how, and

(D) keystone equipment which would reveal or give insight into the design and manufacture of a United States military system,

which are not possessed by, or available in fact from sources outside the United States to, controlled countries and which, if exported, would permit a significant advance in a military system of any such country.

(3) The list referred to in paragraph (2) shall be sufficiently specific to guide the determinations of any official exercising export licensing responsibilities under this Act [sections 2401 to 2420 of this Appendix].

(4) The Secretary and the Secretary of Defense shall integrate items on the list of militarily critical technologies into the control list in accordance with the requirements of subsection (c) of this section. The integration of items on the list of militarily critical technologies into the control list shall proceed with all deliberate speed. Any disagreement between the Secretary and the Secretary of Defense regarding the integration of an item on the list of militarily critical technologies into the control list shall be resolved by the President. Except in the case of a good or technology for which a validated license may be required under subsection (f)(4) or (h)(6) of this section, a good or technology shall be included on the control list only if the Secretary finds that controlled countries do not possess that good or technology, or a functionally equivalent good or technology, and the good or technology or functionally equivalent good or technology is not available in fact to a controlled country from sources outside the United States in sufficient quantity and of comparable quality so that the requirement of a validated license for the export of such good or technology is or would be ineffective in achieving the purpose set forth in subsection (a) of this section. The Secretary and the Secretary of Defense shall jointly submit a report to the Congress, not later than 1 year after the date of the enactment of the Export Administration Amendments Act of 1985 [July 12, 1985], on actions taken to carry out this paragraph. For the purposes of this paragraph, assessment of whether a good or technology is functionally equivalent shall include consideration of the factors described in subsection (f)(3) of this section.

(5) The Secretary of Defense shall establish a procedure for reviewing the goods and technology on the list of militarily critical technologies on an ongoing basis for the purpose of removing from the list of militarily critical technologies any goods or technology that are no longer militarily critical. The Secretary of Defense may add to the list of militarily critical technologies any good or technology that the Secretary of Defense determines is militarily critical, consistent with the provisions of paragraph (2) of this subsection. If the Secretary and the Secretary of Defense disagree as to whether any change in the list of militarily critical technologies by the addition or removal of a good or technology should also be made in the control list, consistent with the provisions of the fourth sentence of paragraph (4) of this subsection, the President shall resolve the disagreement.

(6) The establishment of adequate export controls for militarily critical technology and keystone equipment shall be accompanied by suitable reductions in the controls on the products of that technology and equipment.

(7) The Secretary of Defense shall, not later than 1 year after the date of the enactment of the Export Administration Amendments Act of 1985 [July 12, 1985], report to the Congress on efforts by the Department of Defense to assess the impact that the transfer of goods or technology on the list of militarily critical technologies to controlled countries has had or will have on the military capabilities of those countries.

Document 3.10

The Bucy Report

(Excerpt from the U.S. Department of Defense, Office of the Director of Defense Research and Engineering, Report of the Defense Science Board Task Force on Export of U.S. Technology, *An Analysis of Export Control of U.S. Technology—A DoD Perspective*, 1976.)

After examining the entire technology spectrum from basic research through maintenance of the finished product, the subcommittees concurred that the transfer of design and manufacturing know-how is of overwhelming importance to our national security. It is mastery of design and manufacturing that increases a nation's capability, and it is in this area that the U.S. maintains its technological leadership.

These elements of technology are transferred through the following export categories:

1. Export of an array of design and manufacturing information plus significant teaching assistance which provides technical capability to design, optimize, and produce a broad spectrum of products in a technical field.

This is the highest and most effective level of technology transfer. It effects virtually total transfer of current U.S. practice in a relatively short time. Moreover, it provides a basis on which the receiving nation can build further advances in technology.

2. Export of manufacturing equipment required to produce, inspect, or test strategically related products, with only the necessary "point design" information. In this category, none of the design and manufacturing background, rationale, or alternatives is transferred.

This export category provides incremental gains to a national capability by improving existing manufacturing capabilities or supporting infrastructure. Such equipment does not in itself transfer product design technology, nor does it give the receiving country comprehensive insight to the entire manufacturing process. But added to an already developed technology base, specific manufacturing equipment may give a country the only means of rapid product proliferation.

"Keystone" equipment that completes a process line and allows it to be fully utilized is especially critical. The strategic significance of keystone equipment derives from its uniqueness when compared to the other process and test equipment required to produce a strategic product. If it is the only unique equipment required and all the remaining equipment is general or multipurpose, then its significance is evident. In this regard, computer-controlled process, inspection, and test equipment is often "keystone" equipment. It provides not only the capability of high throughput and improved precision, but also great flexibility in fulfilling unique and multiproduct manufacturing requirements. Moreover, it provides a growth capability on which advanced new production skills can be built.

3. Export of products with technological know-how supplied in the form of extensive operating information, application information, or sophisticated maintenance procedures.

Elements of design or manufacturing know-how are embodied in this type of information, which is often included in sales of such complex high-technology products as electronic computers and jet engines. However, this know-how is usually dated as it accrues to the product's development and design-time period. The significance of older technology is discussed in a subsequent finding.

Each of the industries studied has a different "technology profile." The critical portion of jet engine technology lies in the design and development phase of a program's life—the fundamental science and user know-how are largely in the public domain. On the other hand, the semiconductor industry emphasizes manufacturing know-how as uniquely central to their technology. The airframe and instrumentation subcommittees use the phrases "corporate memory" and "engineering-manufacturing-marketing establishment" to reflect the importance of group experience and organization in the embodiment of their technology.

Yet among these diverse industries, there is unanimous agreement that the *detail of how to do things* is the essence of the technologies. This body of detail is hard earned and hard learned. It is not likely to be transferred inadvertently. But it can be taught and learned.

RECOMMENDATIONS:

Three categories of export should receive primary emphasis in control efforts, since they transfer vital design and manufacturing know-how most effectively:

1. Arrays of design and manufacturing information that include detailed "how to" instructions on design and manufacturing processes.

2. "Keystone" manufacturing, inspection, or automatic test equipment.

3. Products accompanied by sophisticated operation, application, or maintenance, information.

Document 3.11

Excerpt from the Export Administration Act

(Public Law 96-72, Sept. 29, 1979, 93 Stat. 503 As Amended)

SECTION 2409. Procedures for processing export license applications; other inquiries

(g) Special procedures for Secretary of Defense

(1) Notwithstanding any other provision of this section, the Secretary of Defense is authorized to review any proposed export of any goods or technology to any country to which exports are controlled for national security purposes and, whenever the Secretary of Defense determines that the export of such goods or technology will make a significant contribution, which would prove detrimental to the national security of the United States, to the military potential of any such country, to recommend to the President that such export be disapproved.

(2) Notwithstanding any other provision of law, the Secretary of Defense shall determine, in consultation with the Secretary, and confirm in writing the types and categories of transactions which should be reviewed by the Secretary of Defense in order to make a determination referred to in paragraph (1). Whenever a license or other authority is requested for the export to any country to which exports are controlled for national security purposes of goods or technology within any such type or category, the Secretary shall notify the Secretary of Defense of such request, and the Secretary may not issue any license or other authority pursuant to such request before the expiration of the period within which the President may disapprove such export. The Secretary of Defense shall carefully consider any notification submitted by the Secretary pursuant to this paragraph and, not later than 20 days after notification of the request, shall—

(A) recommend to the President and the Secretary that he disapprove any request for the export of the goods or technology involved to the particular country if the Secretary of Defense determines that the export of such goods or technology will make a significant contribution, which would prove detrimental to the national security of the United States, to the military potential of such country or any other country;

(B) notify the Secretary that he would recommend approval subject to specified conditions; or

(C) recommend to the Secretary that the export of goods or technology be approved.

Whenever the Secretary of Defense makes a recommendation to the President pursuant to paragraph (2)(A), the Secretary shall also submit his recommendation to the President on the request to export if the Secretary differs with the Secretary of Defense.

If the President notifies the Secretary, within 30 days after receiving a recommendation from the Secretary of Defense, that he disapproves such export, no license or other authority may be issued for the export of such goods or technology to such country. If the Secretary of Defense fails to make a recommendation or notification under this paragraph within the 20-day period specified in the third sentence, or if the President, within 20 days after receiving a recommendation from the Secretary of Defense with respect to an export, fails to notify the Secretary that he approves or disapproves the export, the Secretary shall approve or deny the request for a license or other authority to export without such recommendation or notification.

(3) The Secretary shall approve or disapprove a license application, and issue or deny a license, in accordance with the provisions of this subsection, and, to the extent applicable, in accordance with the time periods and procedures otherwise set forth in this section.

(4) Repealed. Pub. L. 100-418, Title II, sec. 2425(a)(4), Aug. 28, 1988, 102 Stat. 1360.

Document 3.12

Excerpt from Conference Report to Accompany H.R. 3 Omnibus Trade and Competitiveness Act of 1988

(Report 100-576, 100th Congress, 2nd Session, April 20, 1988)

Conference agreement

(1) The conference agreement deletes the House provision clarifying the authority of the Defense Department to review exports to countries to which exports are controlled for national security purposes. The conferees do so without prejudice to different interpretations of the statutory authority for DoD to review exports to countries other than controlled countries.

The conferees concurred that whenever the Department of Defense reviews any license application, the nature and extent of such review shall be limited to national security, not foreign policy, considerations. Since the 1985 Memorandum of Understanding between DoD and DoC regarding review of Free World license applications, concern has been expressed that DoD's objections have been based on foreign policy grounds, rather than on [whether proposed exports would contribute to the military potential of a controlled country] national security grounds.

(2) To address the continuing problem of timely resolution of disputes, the conferees agreed to place time limits on all parties for decisions on export license applications. The amendment provides that if the Secretary of Defense fails to make a recommendation or notification within the 20 day period specified, or if the President fails to notify the Secretary that he approves or disapproves the export, the Secretary shall then act upon the license application.

(3) The conferees agreed to eliminate the Presidential reporting requirement when overruling

DoD. Ensuring a final resolution of disputed issues is an important goal; once the President has reviewed and decided an issue, that decision should be implemented.

(b) Report by the Secretaries of Commerce & Defense

The conferees agreed to require the Secretaries of Commerce and Defense, within 6 months of enactment, to evaluate and jointly report to the Congress on the process for reviewing, for national security reasons, export license applications to destinations other than controlled countries, and the role played by the Department of Defense in such review.

While the EAA clearly states that to the maximum extent possible, the Commerce Department should make licensing decisions without referral to other agencies, there are situations when other departments are included in specific licensing decisions. Under a Memorandum of Understanding between the Departments of Commerce and Defense of January 1985, and subsequent related documents, the Commerce Department refers to DoD applications for certain exports to a list of specified Free World countries. In order to evaluate the effect of such concurrent review from the standpoint of redundancy and effectiveness, the conferees have directed the two agencies, in consultation with the Secretary of State as appropriate, to evaluate and provide a detailed report to the Congress. The conferees intend such report to compel the Administration to review the functioning of such concurrent review, and to provide a factual basis in order to evaluate the effect of such joint review.

Document 3.13

Excerpt from the Export Administration Act

(Public Law 96-72, Sept. 29, 1979, 93 Stat. 503 As Amended)

SECTION 2412. Administrative procedure and judicial review

(e) Appeals from license denials

A determination of the Secretary, under section 10(f) of this Act [section 2409(f) of this Appendix], to deny a license may be appealed by the applicant to an administrative law judge who shall have the authority to conduct proceedings to determine only whether the item sought to be exported is in fact on the control list. Such proceedings shall be conducted within 90 days after the appeal is filed. Any determination by an administrative law judge under this subsection and all materials filed before such judge in the proceedings shall be reviewed by the Secretary, who shall either affirm or vacate the determination in a written decision within 30 days after receiving the determination. The Secretary's written decision shall be final and is not subject to judicial review. Subject to the limitations provided in section 12(c) of this Act [section 2411(c) of this Appendix], the Secretary's decision shall be published in the Federal Register.

Document 3.14

Excerpt from the Omnibus Trade and Competitiveness Act of 1988

(Public Law 100-418, August 23, 1988)

SECTION 2433. Study on National Security Export Controls

(a) Arrangements for and Contents of Study—

(1) Arrangements for Conducting Study—The Secretary of Commerce and the Secretary of Defense, not later than 60 days after the date of the enactment of this Act, shall enter into appropriate arrangements with the National Academy of Sciences and the National Academy of Engineering (hereafter in this section referred to as the "Academies") to conduct a comprehensive study of the adequacy of the current export administration system in safeguarding United States national security while maintaining United States international competitiveness and Western technological preeminence.

(2) Requirements of Study—Recognizing the need to minimize the disruption of United States trading interests while preventing Western technology from enhancing the development of the military capabilities of controlled countries, the study shall—

(A) identify those goods and technologies which are likely to make crucial differences in the military capabilities of controlled countries, and identify which of those goods and technologies controlled countries already possess or are available to controlled countries from other sources;

(B) develop implementable criteria by which to define those goods and technologies;

(C) demonstrate how such criteria would be applied to the control list by the relevant agencies to revise the list, eliminate ineffective controls, and strengthen controls;

(D) develop proposals to improve United States and multilateral assessments of foreign availability of goods and technology subject to export controls; and

(E) develop proposals to improve the administration of the export control program, including procedures to ensure timely, predictable, and effective decision-making.

(b) Advisory Panel—

In conducting the study under subsection (a), the Academies shall appoint an Advisory Panel of not more than 24 members who shall be selected from among individuals in private life who, by virtue of their experience and expertise, are knowledgeable in relevant scientific, business, legal, or administrative matters. No individual may be selected as a member who, at the time of his or her appointment, is an elected or appointed official or employee in the executive, legislative, or judicial branch of the Government. In selecting members of the Advisory Panel, the Academies shall seek suggestions from the President, the Congress, and representatives of industry and the academic community.

(c) Executive Branch Cooperation—

The Secretary of Commerce, the Secretary of Defense, the Secretary of State, the Director of the Central Intelligence Agency, and the head of any department or agency that exercises authority in export administration—

(1) shall furnish to the Academies, upon request and under appropriate safeguards, classified or unclassified information which the Academies determine to be necessary for the purposes of conducting the study required by this section; and

(2) shall work with the Academies on such problems related to the study as the Academies consider necessary.

(d) Report—

Under the direction of the Advisory Panel, the Academies shall prepare and submit to the President and the Congress, not later than 18 months after entering into the arrangements referred to in subsection (a), a report which contains a detailed statement of the findings and conclusions of the Academies pursuant to the study conducted under subsection (a), together with their recommendations for such legislative or regulatory reforms as they consider appropriate.

(e) Authorization of Appropriations—

There are authorized to be appropriated $900,000 to carry out this section.

4

What Is COCOM and How Does It Work?

Michael Mastanduno

COCOM, the Coordinating Committee on Multilateral Export Controls, is the export control arrangement of the United States and its Western allies. It was created in 1949 and has been functioning since January 1950. Its membership includes the NATO countries (minus Iceland), plus Japan and most recently Australia, which joined in April 1989.

COCOM does not have treaty status or a charter. It is a "gentlemen's agreement" with a modest institutional presence. It operates from an annex to the U.S. Embassy in Paris (set back from the street at 58 Rue La Boetie), with a small secretariat that handles records and translations. It has a budget estimated during the mid-1980s at approximately $500,000. The budget is financed by contributions from member states, with the United States contributing the largest share, approximately twenty-five per cent. COCOM has also maintained a tradition of confidentiality. The deliberations of its member governments and the decisions they make are not, as a matter of course, made public.

Informality and confidentiality are a legacy of the early cold war compromise that created COCOM. Some West European states (e.g., France and the Netherlands) were willing to participate in a multilateral control system, yet preferred that cooperation be discreet and informal so that if politically necessary they could deny—to the Soviet Union or to their domestic political opponents—that they were in fact participating. The United States preferred a more formal and politically prominent arrangement, with COCOM perhaps subsumed under NATO, in order to assure that defense as opposed to commercial considerations were granted sufficient emphasis in the control process. In the interest of creating and maintaining a viable export control system the United States deferred to the sentiments of the West Europeans, and accepted the institutional arrangements that have characterized COCOM during its forty-year existence.

COCOM's primary activity is to have its national delegations agree on a list of technologies and products that they as individual nations will control in their trade to certain countries for reasons of national security. Proscribed destinations include the Warsaw Pact members, the People's Republic of China, Albania, Mongolia, Vietnam, and North Korea.

Administration of Controls

While the construction of the control lists is a multilateral exercise, the administration and enforcement of agreed-upon controls is ultimately left to the discretion of member states. COCOM itself has no formal enforcement mechanism, and does not impose sanctions against violators of its controls. Instead, national governments (which formally accept COCOM controls as "guidance") administer and enforce agreed-upon restrictions through their national laws and procedures. This, not surprisingly, has created tension among COCOM members, since some member states interpret the control lists more restrictively and enforce them more diligently than others.

COCOM member governments actually draw up three embargo lists. They cover: 1) munitions, 2) atomic energy items, and 3) industrial or "dual use" items. The third list, civilian items with potential military applications (e.g., computers, machine tools, scientific instruments), has proven historically to be the most controversial, since it raises most starkly the trade-off between economic benefits and security risks inherent in trade with potential adversaries.

The COCOM lists themselves are not made public. Member governments, however, publicize their own national lists in order to guide firms that seek to export items to controlled destinations. Following this chapter are excerpts from a recent version of the British control list, which closely resembles the COCOM list, for purposes of illustration. **(Document 4.1)**

The three lists cited in the Table of Contents of this British version contain 168 items, with the industrial list accounting for 120 of the total. As the contents indicate, the industrial list is divided into eight broad groups. A review of industrial list category 1565 (computers and related electronic equipment) in Groups F and G suggests the density and complexity of the list, which assures that the task of interpreting controls as they apply to specific export license requests is left to technical specialists (as opposed to policy-level officials) in the member states.

List Review

From 1969 through 1984, COCOM members would review the control lists about every three or four years. Members agreed in 1985 to conduct a continuous or rolling review (i.e., every year some segments of the lists are reviewed), in the interest of keeping the controls more up-to-date in the face of rapidly changing technologies. In the list review process, officials from each member government develop proposals for list additions and deletions, and then forward instructions to their respective national delegations in Paris, who conduct negotiations on an item-by-item basis. The addition, deletion, or revision of list items requires the unanimous consent of member states. In practice, the United States makes the majority of proposals for additions to the lists; the other members make the most proposals for deletions.

Several criteria are relevant in this review process, including military utility and significance, and the availability of the item in question from non-COCOM countries. In a typical bargaining sequence the United States might provide an assessment of a particular item's military utility (e.g., "these machine tools are used in the following way by our Air Force"), while other members might produce evidence that the item can be readily purchased in non-COCOM countries or can be produced by controlled destinations themselves. The review process is tedious and time-consuming. It usually involves a series of proposals and counterproposals based on technical assessments colored by bureaucratic or economic interests. Delegations in Paris frequently must refer back to their home governments for guidance and negotiating instructions. Some of the technologically less advanced members do not participate actively in list reviews, and instead rely on the technical judgments of others. The United States will frequently seek bilateral agreement with certain key member states as a means to facilitate reaching multilateral agreement.

Exceptions

The presence of an item on a COCOM control list does not mean it is unconditionally embargoed.

Under certain circumstances items on these lists may be exported to proscribed destinations as "exceptions."

There are several varieties of exceptions, but the distinction between "general" and "administrative" exceptions is crucial. Administrative exceptions may be exported to proscribed destinations at the national discretion of member governments, who must only report the export to COCOM, usually after the fact. In contrast, a general exception request by one member state requires the formal consent of other members prior to being exported. The unanimity principle applies here as well—each COCOM member has the right to object to the exception requests of others. (Occasionally, extremely contentious exception cases are settled by the concerned national governments outside of COCOM, at higher policy levels.) The United States exercises its veto in COCOM more than any other member. This has been a subject of some controversy, since during the 1970s and 1980s the United States was also the COCOM member that most frequently requested general exceptions.

Whether an exception request falls under the general or administrative category usually depends on the technological parameters of the item in question. At higher levels of technological sophistication (e.g., a supercomputer), general exceptions are required. Firms requesting general exceptions first approach their national governments. If national licensing authorities are satisfied that a proposed export meets the criteria for a general exception (i.e. that the commodity is necessary and appropriate for civil purposes and is unlikely to be diverted to military use) they may submit an exception request to COCOM. At lower levels (e.g., some personal computers that remain under COCOM control), member states may license at national discretion without going in advance to COCOM. The threshold or "line" separating general from administrative exceptions varies across items and with regard to the same item over time. In Document 4.1, items requiring administrative exceptions are in bold face.

Members of the national COCOM delegations meet at the working or staff level weekly (recently, on Tuesdays) to consider exception requests, clarify positions on items under review, and discuss miscellaneous issues (e.g., budget or staffing). An Executive Committee of political level officials from the member states meets twice yearly to consider broad policy issues and to establish or review the progress of COCOM's ad hoc working groups. Current working groups consider issues such as trade among COCOM members, the streamlining of the control list, and the harmonization of national enforcement procedures.

Since 1982 COCOM has held a series of High Level Meetings (HLMs), in which member states are represented at the sub-Cabinet level. Such meetings have been intended to inject political vigor into and develop political support for the multilateral control process. In the HLM of January 1988, members agreed to streamline the control list and simultaneously improve and harmonize enforcement efforts.

Certain developments stand out in COCOM's forty-year history. During the Korean War the industrial embargo was broadened beyond items of direct military utility to include items of general economic significance, on the grounds that Soviet economic and military power were synonymous. This policy of economic warfare was short-lived, despite an American desire to maintain it after the war ended. Major list reviews took place in 1954 and 1958, resulting in sharp reductions in the lists. After 1958 COCOM controls focused more narrowly on civilian items of direct military utility, as preferred by West European governments.

Member governments also agreed during the Korean War to apply more restrictive controls on trade with China than with the European Soviet bloc. This so-called "China differential" was administered by a separate China Committee, abbreviated ChinCom. The differential was abandoned in 1957 when West European members and Japan refused any longer to acknowledge it. Great Britain took the initiative, arguing that China no longer represented an exceptional threat to the West, and that, in any event, items covered by the differential controls could be transshipped to China through the European Soviet bloc.

While no major changes took place in the structure of COCOM controls during the 1960s and 1970s, the system became increasingly controversial, as Western trade competition intensified and general exception requests mounted. The growth in requests for exceptions and the ensuing controversy reflected, in part, the fact that the list review process was not keeping pace with rapid changes in technology, most strikingly in the electronics sector. Political disagreements between the United States and its major Western allies prevented agreement on comprehensive revisions to the all-important computer category (IL 1565) on the industrial list for almost an entire decade. IL 1565 was revised during the 1974–75 list review and not again until 1984, leaving Western firms in the interim to adhere to outdated control parameters in perhaps the most dynamic sector technologically.

The decade of the 1980s witnessed changes both in the attention devoted to COCOM controls and in the organization's political salience. The United States turned high-level attention to an effort to strengthen COCOM, seeking support from member governments for an expanded control list, improved enforcement, and the creation of a permanent military subcommittee. The latter was intended to rectify what United States officials saw as a bias in many COCOM member delegations in favor of commercial interests.

The response of the other COCOM states was mixed. There was some agreement on list expansion, and some members (e.g., Great Britain and France) devoted more attention to administration and enforcement. The military subcommittee was rejected; as a compromise, COCOM members agreed to the formation of STEM (Science and Technology Experts' Meeting). STEM, comprised of military and technology specialists from member states, is not involved in COCOM's routine activities but advises COCOM periodically on the military utility of advanced technologies. STEM meets in Paris, and is organized into working groups which cover and report to COCOM on specific technologies or sets of technologies.

Following the invasion of Afghanistan and at the behest of the United States, in 1980 COCOM adopted a "no exceptions" policy on trade with the Soviet Union. The practice applied to general exception requests (excluding a narrow category related to health and safety, or which involved spare parts or services for previously exported items), but not to administrative exceptions. The policy in effect sought to deny the export of advanced Western technology to the Soviet Union, even for civilian applications. A similar policy was applied to Poland in 1982, following the imposition of martial law. The no exceptions policy for Poland was lifted by 1987. The Soviet policy was lifted in June 1989, in the wake of the Soviet decision to withdraw from Afghanistan and in the context of considerable political pressure on the United States by other COCOM members.

While COCOM tightened Soviet controls in the 1980s, it liberalized those on trade with China. The United States took the initiative, announcing in 1981 that China could purchase American technology at "twice the level of sophistication" of that normally allowed for the Soviet Union, and later moving China into control destination category "V," which includes NATO states and Japan. The United States also established a "green zone" in its national control list to facilitate trade; for items falling within it there was a presumption of quick license approval. The green zone concept was subsequently adopted in COCOM in 1985, allowing members to license at national discretion many items previously requiring full COCOM approval. The special provisions for exports to China are in italics in Document 4.1.

The COCOM green zone was intended not only to facilitate China trade but also to relieve growing administrative bottlenecks in COCOM; for instance the United States requested about 500 general exceptions for China in 1982 but about 4000 in 1985. Until the tragic events in Tienanmen Square in June, 1989, COCOM members were exploring whether to liberalize China controls even further.

By the end of the 1980s it was apparent that COCOM faced significant problems in the related areas of streamlining and enforcement. Enforcement, of particular concern to the United States, was dramatized by evidence of a systematic Soviet campaign to acquire Western technology illegally, and of complicity by some firms in COCOM countries (e.g., Japan's Toshiba Machine and France's Forest Line). To other COCOM members, an even more pressing problem was the need to reduce and streamline COCOM controls, the comprehensiveness of which strained the credibility of the embargo and hampered enforcement efforts. Both streamlining and enforcement are high on COCOM's agenda as it approaches the 1990s.

The existing COCOM consensus will face new pressures over the next decade. First, in light of Soviet and Eastern European reform efforts, member governments will find it more difficult to justify to their constituencies the economic sacrifices and political frictions that come with maintaining export controls for national security reasons. Soviet leader Mikhail Gorbachev is combining an increased demand for controlled technology with domestic political liberalization. He has succeeded in diminishing the military threat, in the minds of many in COCOM countries. Gorbachev's policies pose obvious problems for the cohesion of COCOM. This dilemma is all the more pressing since some members (though clearly not all) are convinced that the increased transfer of Western technology could promote, and even render irreversible, desirable changes in Soviet foreign and domestic policy.

1992 is a second challenge. This could force COCOM members to reconsider the principle of national discretion in enforcement, since if the European market is truly integrated technology will find its way through the weakest national link in the enforcement chain. COCOM's challenge will be to assure that the formal or de facto common European enforcement standard reflects the practices of the more vigilant rather than of the more lax. If internal liberalization outpaces the adoption of uniformly strict enforcement standards, the United States might feel compelled to resort to intra-Western technology restrictions to protect the integrity of its own controls. That, in turn, would likely result in a serious intra-alliance confrontation.

The world-wide diffusion of advanced technology is a third challenge. COCOM members no longer have complete control over the production and dissemination of militarily significant technologies. The United States worked hard during the 1980s to convince non-COCOM suppliers to observe COCOM comparable controls. It had mixed success. The U.S. will probably continue these efforts since more and more militarily significant technology will be produced in non-member countries.

Document 4.1

Excerpts from Great Britain's Export Control Regulations

(COCOM as such does not publish export control regulations; they are issued by the member countries. The following are excerpts from the British regulations of March 1989 governing computer sales. Items requiring only an administrative exception are in bold face. Items approved for sale to the People's Republic of China are in italics. Reprinted with permission.)

CONTENTS

INDUSTRIAL LIST—GROUP 3

A   Metal-working machinery
       IL 1001–1093

B   Chemical and petroleum equipment
       IL 1110–1145

C   Electrical and power-generating
       equipment
       IL 1203–1206

D   General industrial equipment
       IL 1301–1399

E   Transportation equipment
       IL 1401–1485

F and G Electronic equipment including
       communications, radar, computer
       hardware and software
       IL 1501–1595

H   Metals, minerals and their
       manufactures
       IL 1601–1675

I   Chemicals, mettaloids and petroleum
       products
       IL 1702–1781

MUNITIONS LIST—GROUP 1

ML1–ML24

ATOMIC ENERGY LIST—GROUP 2

A.   Nuclear materials
       A1–A14

B.   Nuclear facilities
       B1–B6

C.   Nuclear-related equipment
       C1–C6

* * * * *

BOLD TYPE: Goods described can be licensed at national discretion for export to the proscribed countries.

ITALICIZED TYPE: Goods described can be licenced for export to the People's Republic of China only, either at national discretion or under the 'favourable consideration' conditions indicated.

IL 1565

Electronic computers, "related equipment," equipment or systems containing electronic computers, and technology therefor, as follows; and specially designed components and accessories for these electronic computers and "related equipment": (For the embargo status of "software," see Item IL 1566)

TECHNICAL NOTES:

1. Electronic computers and "related equipment" are categorised as follows:

"analogue computer"—

Equipment which can, in the form of one or more continuous variables:

(a) Accept data;
(b) Process data; and
(c) Provide output of data.

"digital computer"—

Equipment which can, in the form of one or more discrete variables:

(a) Accept data;
(b) Store data or instructions in fixed or alterable (writable) storage devices;
(c) Process data by means of a stored sequence of instructions which is modifiable; and
(d) Provide output of data.

NOTE:

Modifications of a stored sequence of instructions include replacement of fixed storage devices, but not a physical change in wiring or interconnections.

"hybrid computer"—

Equipment which can:

(a) Accept data;
(b) Process data in both analogue and digital representations, and
(c) Provide output of data.

"related equipment"—

Equipment "embedded" in, "incorporated" in, or "associated" with electronic computers, as follows:

(a) Equipment for interconnecting "analogue computers" with "digital computers";
(b) Equipment for interconnecting "digital computers";
(c) Equipment for interfacing electronic computers to "local area networks" or to "wide area networks";
(d) Communication control units;
(e) Other input/output (I/O) control units;
(f) Recording or reproducing equipment referred to this Item by Item IL 1572;
(g) Displays; or
(h) Other peripheral equipment.

NOTE:

"Related equipment" which contains an "embedded" or "incorporated" electronic computer, but which lacks "user-accessible programmability," does not thereby fall within the definition of an electronic computer.

2. This Item includes:

(a) "Assemblies," "modules," or printed circuit boards with mounted components referred to this Item by Item IL 1564;
(b) Assemblies of materials or thin film devices or devices containing them referred to this Item by Item IL 1588;
(c) Central processing unit—"main storage" combinations;
(d) Digital differential analyzers (incremental computers); and
(e) Processors for stored-programme control.

(This ends the Technical Notes. For a complete list of definitions of terms used in this Item, see Note 16 below.)

Listed as follows:

(a) "Analogue computers" and "related equipment" therefor, which are designed or modified for use in airborne vehicles, missiles or space vehicles and rated for continuous operation at temperatures from below 228 K (−45 degrees C) to above 328 K (+55 degrees C);
(b) Equipment or systems containing "analogue computers" embargoed by sub-item (a);
(c) "Analogue computers" and "related equipment" therefor, other than those embargoed by sub-item (a), except:
(i) Those which neither:
(a) Are capable of containing more than 20 summers, integrators, multipliers or function generators; nor
(b) Have facilities for readily varying the interconnections of such components; or
(ii) Those which are limited as follows:
(a) They use neither:
(1) Optical computation devices; nor
(2) Acoustic wave devices embargoed by Item IL 1586 other than those exportable at National Discretion pursuant to Note 1 to Item IL 1586:
(b) The rated errors for summers, inverters and integrators are not less than:
(1) Static   :0.01%;

(2) Total at 1 kHz   :0.15%;
(c) The rated errors for multipliers are not less than:
(1) Static   :0.025%;
(2) Total at 1 kHz   :0.25%;
(d) The rated errors for fixed function generators (log and sine/cosine) are not less than:
Static   :0.1%;
(e) No more than 350 operational amplifiers; and
(f) No more than four integrator time scales switchable during one programme.

TECHNICAL NOTES:
1. The percentage to (b)(1) above applies to the actual output voltage; all the other percentages apply to full scale, that is from maximum negative to maximum positive reference voltages.
2. Total errors at 1 kHz to (b)(2) and (c)(2) above are to be measured with those resistors incorporated in the inverter summer or integrator which provide the last error.
3. Total error measurements include all errors of the unit resulting from, for example, tolerances of resistors and capacitors, tolerances of input and output impedances of amplifiers, the effects of loading, the effects of phase shift or the generating of functions.
(d) "Hybrid computers" and related equipment" therefor, with all the following characteristics:
(1) The analogue section is embargoed by sub-item (c);
(2) The digital section has an internal fixed or alterable storage of more than 2,048 bit; and
(3) Facilities are included for processing numerical data from the analogue section in the digital section or vice versa;
(e) "Digital computers" or embargoed "analogue computers" containing equipment for interconnecting "analogue computers" with "digital computers";
(f) "Digital computers" and "related equipment" therefor, with any of the following characteristics:
(1) Designed or modified for use in airborne vehicles, missiles or spacer vehicles and rated for continuous operation at temperatures from below 228 K (−45 degrees C) to above 328 K (+55 degrees C);
(2) Designed or modified to limit electromagnetic radiation to levels much less than

those required by government civil interference specifications;
(3) Designed as ruggedized or radiation-hardened equipment and capable of meeting military specifications for ruggedized or radiation-hardened equipment;
(4) Modified for military use; or
(5) Designed or modified for certifiable multi-level security or certifiable user isolation applicable to government classified material or to applications requiring an equivalent level of security;
(g) Equipment or systems containing "digital computers" embargoed by sub-item (f);
(h) "Digital computers" and "related equipment" therefor, other than those embargoed by sub-items (e) or (f), even when "embedded" in, "incorporated" in, or "associated" with equipment or systems;

NOTE:
The embargo status of these "digital computers" and "related equipment" therefor is governed by the appropriate Item provided that:
(a) They are "embedded" in other equipment or systems;
(b) The other equipment or systems are described in other Items in these Lists; and
(c) the technology for these "digital computers" and "related equipment" is governed by sub-item (j) below.
(1) Including "digital computers" and "related equipment," as follows:
(i) Designed or modified for:

NOTE:
"Digital computers" and "related equipment" containing equipment, devices or logic control for the following functions are also included.
(a) "Signal processing";
(b) "Image enhancement";
(c) "Local area networks";

NOTE:
For the purpose of this sub-item, data communication systems when located within a single piece of equipment (e.g. television set, car) are not considered to be designed or modified for "local area networks."
(d) "Multi-data-stream processing";

NOTE:

For the purpose of this sub-item, "digital computers" and "related equipment" are not considered to be designed or modified for "multi-data-stream processing" if they:

(a) Utilize staged (pipelined) instruction interpretation for conventional single instruction—single data sequence processing; or

(b) Have an arithmetic unit implemented with bit-slice microprocessor microcircuits.

(e) Combined recognition, understanding and interpretation of image, continuous (connected) speech or connected word text other than "signal processing" or "image enhancement" described in sub-item (h)(1)(i)(a) or (b);

(f) "Real time processing" of sensor data:

(1) Concerning events occurring outside the "computer using facility"; and

(2) Provided by equipment embargoed by Items IL 1501, IL 1502, IL 1510 or IL 1518;

NOTE:

This does not include digital radar signal processing by equipment which is:

(a) Embargoed by Item IL 1501(c)(2)(vi) only, for which the conditions of Item IL 1501 apply; or

(b) Freed from embargo by the two-year limit in Item IL 1501(c)(2)(vii).

(g) Microprocessor or microcomputer development systems;

NOTE:

For microprocessor or microcomputer development systems, see Item IL 1529(b)(6);

(h) "Fault tolerance";

NOTE:

For the purpose of this sub-item, "digital computers" and "related equipment" are not considered to be designed or modified for "fault tolerance," if they utilize:

(a) Error detection or correction algorithms in "main storage";

(b) The interconnection of two "digital computers" so that, if the active central processing unit fails, an idling but mirroring central processing unit can continue the system's functioning;

(c) The interconnection of two central processing units by data channels or by use of shared storage to permit one central processing unit to perform other work until the second central processing unit fails, at which time the first central processing unit takes over in order to continue the system's functioning; or

(d) The synchronization of two central processing units by "software" so that one central processing unit recognizes when the other central processing unit fails and recovers tasks from the failing unit.

(i) Not used;

(j) "User-accessible microprogrammability";

NOTE:

For the purpose of this sub-item, "digital computers" and "related equipment" are not considered to be designed or modified for "user-accessible microprogrammability," if this facility is limited to:

(a) Loading, reloading or inserting of "microprogrammes," provided by the supplier; or

(b) Simple loading of "microprogrammes," which may or may not be provided by the supplier, but which are neither designed to be accessible to the user nor accompanied by training or "software" for user accessibility.

(k) "Data (message) switching";

(l) "Stored programme controlled circuit switching"; or

(m) "Wide area networks";
(ii) Having the following characteristics:
(a) Size, weight, power consumption and reliability or other characteristics (e.g. bubble memory), which allow easy application in mobile tactical military systems; and
(b) Ruggedised above the level required for a normal commercial office environment but not necessarily up to levels specified in sub-item (f);

(2) Except:
(i) "Digital computers" or "related equipment" therefor, provided:
(a) They are "embedded" in other equipment or systems;

NOTE:
This does not preclude: Input/output control unit—disk drive combinations having all of the following characteristics:
(1) "Total transfer rate" not exceeding 5.5 million bit per second;
(2) Total connected "net capacity" not exceeding 320 million bit;
(3) no more than two independent drives; and
(4) "Total access rate" not exceeding 80 accesses per second with a maximum "access rate" of 40 accesses per second per drive;
(b) They are not the "principal element" of the other equipment or systems in which they are "embedded";
(c) The other equipment or systems are not described by other Items in these Lists;
(d) They have been designed and used for non-strategic applications;
(e) They are by nature of design or performance restricted to the particular application for which they have been designed;
(f) The "total processing data rate" of any one "embedded" "digital computer" does not exceed 54 million bit per second;
(g) The sum of the "total processing data rate" of each "embedded"

"digital computer" does not exceed 100 million bit per second;
(h) They do not include equipment or systems embargoed by sub-item IL 1519 (a)(2) or by Item IL 1567;
(i) Not used; and
(j) They do not include equipment described in sub-item (h)(1)(i)(a) to (m), other than for:
(1) "signal processing" or "image enhancement" when lacking "user-accessible programmability" and when "embedded" in medical imaging equipment; or
(2) "local area networks" which are excluded from embargo;
(ii) "Digital computers" or "related equipment" therefor, provided:
(a) They are "incorporated" in other equipment or systems;
(b) They are not the "principal element" of the other equipment or systems in which they are "incorporated";
(c) The other equipment or systems are not embargoed by other Items in these Lists;
(d) The "total processing data rate" of any one "incorporated" "digital computer" does not exceed 15 million bit per second;
(e) The "total internal storage available to the user" does not exceed 9.8 million bit;
(f) They do not include embargoed "related equipment" other than input/output control unit—disk drive combinations having all of the following characteristics:
(1) "Total transfer rate" not exceeding 5.5 million bit per second;
(2) Total connected "net capacity" not exceeding 320 million bit;
(3) No more than two independent drives; and
(4) "Total access rate" not exceeding 80 accesses per second with a maximum "access rate" of 40 accesses per second per drive;
(g) They do not include equipment or systems embargoed by sub-item IL 1519(a)(2) or by Item IL 1567;
(h) They do not include equipment described in sub-item (h)(1)(ii);

83

(i) Not used;

(j) They do not include equipment described in sub-item (h)(1)(i)(a) to (m), other than for:

(1) "Signal processing' or "image enhancement" when lacking "user-accessible programmability" and when "embedded" in medical imaging equipment; or

(2) "Local area networks" which are excluded from embargo;

NOTE:
"Digital computers" or "related equipment" "incorporated" in equipment exportable under the provisions of Items IL 1501, IL 1502, IL 1510 or IL 1518, which are for internal functions which incidentally might be considered to be described by sub-item (h)(1)(i)(f), are exportable as part of that equipment. "Digital computers" or "related equipment" for the "real-time processing" of the outputs of the equipment embargoed by Items IL 1501, IL 1502, IL 1510 or IL 1518 and for Air Traffic Control systems are covered by this Item.

(iii) "Digital computers" other than those described in sub-item (h)(1) above, and "related equipment," having all the following characteristics:

(a) Shipped as complete systems;

(b) Designed and announced by the manufacturer for identifiable civil use

(c) Not specially designed for any equipment embargoed by any other Item in these Lists;

(d) "Total processing data rate" not exceeding 6.5 million bit per second;

(e) "Total internal storage available to the user" not exceeding 6.2 million bit; and

(f) They do not include a central processing unit implemented with more than two microprocessor or microcomputer microcircuits;

NOTE:
This limit does not include any dedicated microprocessor or microcomputer microcircuit used solely for display, keyboard or input/output control, or any bit-slice microprocessor microcircuit.

(g) They do not include a microprocessor or microcomputer microcircuit with more than 16-bit word length or a bus architecture with more than 16 bit;

(h) They do not include analogue-to-digital or digital-to-analogue converter microcircuits exceeding the limits of Item IL 1568;

NOTE:
This does not apply in the case of direct driven video monitors for normal commercial television;

(i) Not used;

(j) They do not include embargoed "related equipment" other than input/output control unit—disk drive combinations having all of the following characteristics;

(1) "Total transfer rate" not exceeding 5.5 million bit per second;

(2) Total connected "net capacity" not exceeding 200 million bit;

(3) No more than one independent drive, and

(4) "Total access rate" not exceeding 40 accesses per second; and

(k) They do not include equipment embargoed by sub-item IL 1519(a)(2) or by Item IL 1567;

(iv) Peripheral equipment, as follows, provided it lacks "user-accessible programmability";

(a) Card punches and readers;

(b) Paper tape punches and readers;

(c) Manually operated keyboards and teletype devices;

(d) Manually operated graphic tablets not having more than 1,024 resolvable points along any axis;

(e) Impact printers;

(f) Non-impact printers not embargoed by Item IL 1572(b) or (c), which do not exceed:

(1) 2,000 lines (30 pages) per minute; or

(2) 600 characters per second;

(g) Plotting equipment, not embargoed by Item IL 1572(b) or (c), producing a physical record by ink, photographic, thermal, or electrostatic techniques, which has:

   (1) A linear accuracy worse than or equal to +0.004%; and

   (2) An active plotting area less than or equal to 1,700 mm (66.9 inch) by 1,300 mm (51.2 inch);

(h) Digitising equipment, generating rectilinear coordinate data by manual or semi-automatic tracing of physical records, which has:

   (1) A linear accuracy worse than or equal to + 0.004 per cent; and

   (2) An active digitising area less than or equal to 1,700 mm (66.9 inch) by 1,300 mm (51.2 inch);

(i) Not used;

(j) Optical mark recognition (OMR) equipment:

(k) Optical character recognition (OCR) equipment which:

   (1) Does not contain "signal processing" or "image enhancement" equipment; and

   (2) Is only for:

      (i) Stylised OCR characters;

      (ii) Other internationally standardised stylized character fonts; or

      (iii) Other characters limited to non-stylised or hand printed numerics and up to 10 hand printed alphabetic or other characters;

(l) Displays or monitors having all of the following characteristics:

   (1) Not including equipment described in sub-item (h)(1)(ii) above;

   (2) Not containing cathode ray tubes embargoed by Item IL 1541;

   (3) If capable of other than alphanumeric characters, graphs and symbols, in fixed formats:

      (i) Not more than 1,024 resolvable elements along any axis;

      (ii) Not more than 16 shades of grey or colour; and

      (iii) The maximum bit transfer rate from the electronic computer to the display does not exceed 19,200 bit per second;

   NOTE:
   (ii) and (iii) above do not apply in the case of direct driven video monitors.

(m) Displays or monitors having all of the following characteristics:

   (1) They do not contain cathode ray tubes;

   (2) They are not capable of displaying more than 3 levels (i.e. off, intermediate and full on); and

   (3) They do not have as an integral part of the display device:

      (a) circuitry; or

      (b) non-mechanical character generation devices;

(n) Displays having all of the following characteristics;

   (1) Not containing cathode ray tubes embargoed by Item IL 1541;

   (2) Being part of industrial or medical equipment; and

   (3) Not specially designed for use with electronic computers;

(o) Graphic displays specially designed for signature or security checking having an active display area not exceeding 150 sq. cm (23.25 sq. inch); display area not exceeding 150 sq. cm (23.25 sq. inch);

(p) Not used;

(q) Light gun devices or other manual graphic input devices which are;

   (1) Part of unembargoed displays; and

   (2) Limited to 1,024 resolvable elements along any axis;

(r) Disk drives for non-rigid magnetic media (floppy disks) which do not exceed;

   (1) A "gross capacity" of 17 million bit;

   (2) A "maximum bit transfer rate" of 0.52 million bit per second; or

(3) An "access rate" of 12 access-es per second; or

(s) Cassette/cartridge tape drives or magnetic tape drives which do not exceed:

(1) A "maximum bit packing density" of 131 bit per mm (3,300 bit per inch) per track; or

(2) A "maximum bit transfer rate" of 2.66 million bit per second;

(v) Input/output interface or control units, as follows, provided they lack "user-accessible programmability":

(a) Designed for use with peripheral equipment free from embargo under sub-item (h)(2)(iv) above;

(b) Designed for use with digital recording or reproducing equipment specially designed to use magnetic card, tag, label or bank cheque recording media, free from embargo according to Item IL 1572 (a)(ii); or

(c) Designed to meet ANSI/IEEE Standard 488–1978 or IEC Publication 625–1;

(vi) "Equipment for "local area networks" which do not exceed any of the following characteristics:

(a) Interfaces and protocols up to or including Layer 2 of the Open System Interconnection (OSI) reference model, that is ISO logical link control Draft International Standard (DIS) 8802/2, IEEE 802.2, 802.3, 802.4, 802.5, or equivalents;

(b) Implementations that contain functions of, or equivalent to those provided by, CCITT X.25. Level 3, protocols—none;

(c) Maximum "data signalling rate" on the common transmission medium—2 million bit per second; or

(d) "Internetwork gateways"—none;

(i) Not used;

(j) Technology, as follows:

(1) Technology applicable to the:

(i) Development, production or use (i.e. installation, operation and maintenance of electronic computers or "related equipment," even if these electronic computers or "related equipment" are not embargoed by this Item; except

(a) Technology which is unique to "related equipment" free from embargo under sub-item (h)(2)(iv)(a) to (c), (e), (f), (m), (n), or (q) and which is not otherwise embargoed by any other Item in these Lists; or

(b) The minimum technical information necessary for the use of electronic computers or "related equipment" free from embargo; or

(ii) Development, production or use of equipment or systems embargoed by sub-item (b) or (g); or

(2) Technology for the integration of:

(i) Embargoed electronic computers or embargoed "related equipment" into other equipment or systems whether or not the other equipment or systems are embargoed; or

NOTE:
Nothing in the above should be construed to embargo technology for the integration which is unique to the other equipment or systems if they are free from embargo.

(ii) Unembargoed "related equipment" into embargoed equipment or systems.

NOTE: This does not, however, release from embargo technology for the integration of electronic computers or "related equipment" which are freed from embargo only by sub-item (h)(2)(i) or only by sub-item (h)(2)(ii).

NOTES:

1. **"Digital computers" or "related equipment" therefor embargoed by sub-item (h), provided:**

(a) **They are "incorporated" in other equipment or systems;**

(b) **They are not the "principal element" of the equipment or systems in which they are "incorporated";**

(c) **The other equipment or systems are embargoed by other Items in these Lists, and they are permitted for export according to the provisions of the appropriate Item:**

(d) **The "total processing data rate" of any "incorporated" "digital computer" does not exceed 28 million bit per second;**

(e) All other parameters do not exceed the relevant limits of Note 9(b)(1)(ii) to (iv) and (b)(2) to (9) to this Item; and

(f) The "incorporated" "digital computers" or "related equipment" therefor do not include:

    (1) Equipment embargoed by sub-item IL 1519 (a)(2) or by Item IL 1567;

    (2) Equipment described in sub-item (h)(1)(ii); or

    (3) Equipment described in sub-item (h)(1)(i)(a) to (m), other than for;

      (i) "Signal processing" or "image enhancement" when lacking "user-accessible programmability" and being "embedded" in medical imaging equipment; or

      (ii) "local area networks" which are excluded from embargo;

NB:

"Digital computers" or "related equipment" "incorporated" in equipment exportable under the provisions of Items IL 1501, IL 1502, IL 1510 or IL 1518, which are for internal functions which incidentally might be considered to be described by sub-item (h)(1)(i)(f), are exportable as part of that equipment. "Digital computers" or "related equipment" for the "real-time processing" of the outputs of the equipment embargoed by Items IL 1501, IL 1502, IL 1510 or IL 1518 and for Air Traffic Control systems are covered by this Item.

2. The minimum technical information for the use (i.e. installation, operation and maintenance) of electronic computers or "related equipment" authorized for export, when shipped together with or solely for use with these electronic computers or "related equipment."

3. Not used.

4. Not used.

5. "Digital computers" or "related equipment" therefor, embargoed by sub-item (h), provided:

(a) The "digital computers" or the "related equipment":

    (1) Have been designed and announced by a manufacturer for identifiable and dedicated medical applications:

    (2) Are substantially restricted to the area of medical applications by nature of design and performance;

    (3) Are the equipment necessary for the medical application;

    (4) Are exported as complete systems;

    (5) Will be located within one "computer using facility"; and

    (6) Do not include communication control unit—"communication channel" combinations;

(b) Equipment for "signal processing," "image enhancement," or "multi-data-stream processing":

    (1) Is "embedded";

    (2) Is designed or modified specially for the identifiable and dedicated medical applications;

    (3) Does not have "user-accessible micro-programmability"; and

    (4) Does not have "user-accessible programmability" other than allowing for insertion of the original or modified "programmes" supplied by the original manufacturer;

(c) The "total processing data rate" of any one "incorporated" "digital computer" does not exceed 43 million bit per second;

(d) The "digital computers" or "related equipment" therefor do not include:

    (1) Equipment or systems embargoed by sub-Item IL 1519(a)(2) or Item IL 1567; or

    (2) Equipment described in sub-item (h)(1)(i)(c) or (e) to (m).

6. "Digital computers" or "related equipment" therefor, embargoed by sub-item (h), provided that:

(a) They have been approved by the Department of Trade and Industry as eligible for export under the conditions of this Note;

(b) They are described in sub-item (h)(1) only by an accident of definition; and

(c) They fulfil any one of the following conditions:

    (1) They are shipped as complete systems and do not exceed:

      (i) A "total processing data rate" of 43 million bit per second; and

(ii) Any of the limits for parameters in Note 9(b)(1)(ii) to (iv) and (b)(2) to (9) to this Item;

(2) They fail to meet the conditions of sub-items (h)(2)(iii),(iv) or (v) only by an accident of definition; or

(3) They:

   (i) Are designed for identifiable commercial office or personal use and substantially restricted to the particular application for which they have been designed by nature of design and performance;

   (ii) Are of a type generally available to the public in non-proscribed areas; and

NB:

For the purpose of this Note "generally available to the public" means:

(a) Also available at retail selling points, other than those specialized in selling electronic computers to the general public in model series exceeding the limits in (1) above; and

(b) Selling from stock by means of:

   (1) Over-the-counter transactions;

   (2) Mail order transactions;

   (3) Telephone call transactions;

   (iii) Fulfil the conditions of (c)(1) above.

7. Spare parts for exported electronic computers or "related equipment," provided:

(a) The parts are:

   (1) "Related equipment" or specially designed components embargoed by this Item; or

   (2) Equipment or components embargoed by other Items in this List;

(b) The parts:

   (1) Are destined for embargoed equipment previously authorized for export under a National Discretion note or under note 12 to this Item or for equipment free from embargo;

   (2) Are shipped in the minimum quantities necessary for the types and quantities of exported equipment being serviced; and

(3) Do not upgrade the performance of the exported equipment beyond the level:

   (i) Specified in the relevant National Discretion note or Note 12 to this Item or

   (ii) Specified as free from embargo;

(c) If the parts are advanced technology parts and not eligible for export at National Discretion under another Item in this List, the Western supplier's organisation must:

   (1) Guarantee that parts will be replaced on a one-for-one basis;

   (2) Take measures to obtain custody of the defective parts; and

   (3) If custody is not obtained, certify that the defective parts are destroyed;

TECHNICAL NOTE:

For the purpose of this sub-paragraph, "advanced technology parts" are either:

(a) Parts embargoed by Item IL 1564 (c)(2);

(b) Microprocessor, microcomputer, storage, programmed logic array or arithmetic logic unit microcircuits embargoed by Item IL 1564 (d);

(c) Magnetic tape heads, magnetic disk heads, magnetic drum heads, or non-exchangeable magnetic disk or drum recording media, embargoed by Item IL 1572; or

(d) Acoustic wave devices embargoed by Item IL 1586, other than those exportable at National Discretion pursuant to the Note 1 to Item IL 1586.

8. Not used.

9. "Digital computers" or "related equipment" therefor embargoed by sub-item (h), provided that:

(a) The "digital computers" or "related equipment" therefor:

   (1) Are not described in sub-items (h)(1)(i)(d) to (m);

   (2) Are not used with "digital computers" produced in proscribed areas;

NB:

This does not preclude the exchange of data media.

   (3) Are exported as:

(i) Complete systems; or

(ii) Enhancements to a previously exported system provided that the enhanced system does not exceed the limits of paragraph (b) of this Note;

(4) Have not been designed for any equipment:

(i) Embargoed by any other Item in this List; and

(ii) Not eligible for consideration for export at National Discretion to such an Item;

(5) Have been primarily designed and used for non-strategic applications;

(6) Do not have any of the following characteristics:

(i) They fall within the scope of both sub-items (h)(1)(ii)(a) and (b); or

(ii) They fall within the scope of sub-item (h)(1)(ii)(a) and are microprocessor-based systems having a word length of more than 8 bit; or

(iii) They are ruggedized above the level required for a normal commercial/civil environment, but not necessarily up to the levels specified in sub-item (f), and are microprocessor-based systems having a word length of more than 8 bit; and

NB:
Microprocessor based systems with 8-bit word length and not more than a 16-bit architecture are regarded as 8-bit systems for the purpose of this sub-paragraph.

(7) Do not have all of the following characteristics:

NB:
This sub-paragraph does not apply to workstations designed for and limited to graphic arts (e.g. printing, publishing).

(i) They are stand-alone graphics work stations designed or modified for the generation, transformation, and display of 2 or 3 dimensional vectors;

(ii) They have a "total processing data rate" of the central processing unit exceeding 28 million bit per second;

(iii) They have a central processing unit with a word length exceeding 16 bit; and

NB:
Microprocessor based systems with 16-bit word-length and not more than a 32-bit architecture are regarded as 16-bit systems for the purpose of this sub-paragraph.

(iv) They exceed either of the following limits:

(a) "Block move data rate"—800,000 pixels/sec; or

(b) Maximum bit transfer rate of the channel for direct access to the "main storage" (Direct Memory Access or DMA channel)—11 million bit per second;

(b) The "digital computers" or "related equipment" therefor do not exceed any of the following limits:

(1) Central processing unit—"main storage" combinations:

(i) "Total processing data rate"—43 million bit per second;

(ii) "Total connected capacity" of "main storage"—39 million bit;

(iii) "Non-volatile storage" with "user-accessible programmability" including bubble memory—none;

NB:
Magnetic core "main storage" may however be included.

(iv) Number of microprocessor or microcomputer microcircuits implementing the central processing unit—three:

NB:
This limit does not include any dedicated microprocessor or microcomputer microcircuit used solely for display, keyboard or input/output control, or any bit-slice microprocessor microcircuit.

(v) "Virtual storage" capability—512 MByte.

NB:
1. Supermini "digital computers" with a "virtual storage" capability exceeding the level

89

in this sub-paragraph will not be eligible for consideration under this Note. It is recognized, however, that other "digital computers" (e.g. main frames) may have a "virtual storage" capability exceeding this limit and in such cases they may be considered under this Note.

2. If the "total processing data rate" does not exceed 28 million bit per second this sub-paragraph will not apply.

(2) Input/output control unit—drum or disk drive combinations:

(i) "Total transfer rate"—16 million bit per second;

(ii) "Total access rate"—200 accesses per second;

(iii) Total connected "net capacity"—5.120 million bit;

(iv) "Maximum bit transfer rate" of any drum or disk drive—16 million bit per second.

(v) Number of independent drum or disk drives—six, of which five must not exceed a "maximum bit transfer rate" of 10.3 million bit per second.

(vi) Exchangeable disk packs which contain magnetic heads;

(a) "Access rate" of an independent seek mechanism—20 accesses per second;

(b) "Net capacity"—240 million bit;

(3) Input/output control unit—bubble memory combinations:

(i) Total connected "net capacity" for point of sale devices used by cashiers—9.8 million bit;

(ii) Total connected "net capacity" for "digital computers" or "related equipment" other than those in (i) above—2.1 million bit;

(4) Input output control unit—magnetic tape or cartridge-type streamer tape drive combinations:

(i) Magnetic tape drives:

(a) "Maximum bit packing density"—246 bit per mm (6.250 bpi);

(b) Maximum read/write speed—508 cm per second (200 ips);

(c) "Maximum bit transfer rate"—10 million bit per second;

(d) Number exceeding 131 bit/mm (3,300 bpi)—four;

(ii) Cartridge-type streamer tape drives:

(a) Maximum "total transfer rate"—16 million bit/s;

(b) Number—two;

(5) Communication control unit—"communication channel" combinations;

(i) "Total data signalling rate" of all "communication channels" terminating remote from the "computer using facility"—19,200 bit/s;

(ii) Maximum "data signalling rate" of any "communication channel"—9,600 bit/s;

(iii) Number of "communication channels" not dedicated full time to the given application—three, provided:

(a) They are connected to the public switched network;

(b) They have a "data signalling rate" not exceeding 1,200 bit/s at the interface between the "digital computer" and the public switched network; and

(c) Number of "communication channels" not limited to Telex interfaces for services conforming to CCITT recommendations F60 to F79—one;

(6) Input/output or communication control unit—directly connected data channel combinations:

(i) "Total transfer rate"—1.6 million bit/s;

(ii) "Transfer rate of any date channel"—1.6 million bit/s;

(iii) Terminations of such combinations or any extensions thereto outside the "computer using facility"—none;

(7) Communication control unit—"local area network" combinations;

NB:
For the purpose this sub-paragraph all "local area networks" interconnected within a "computer using facility" are considered as a single "local area network":

(i) Maximum "data signalling rate" on the common transmission medium—10 million bit/s;

(ii) Interfaces and protocols up to and including Layer 2 of the Open System Interconnection (OSI) reference model, i.e. logical link control Draft International Standard (DIS) 8802/2, IEEE 802.2, 802.3, 802.4, 802.5 or equivalents;

(iii) Implementations that contain functions of, or equivalent to those provided by, CCITT X.25, Level 3, protocols—none;

(iv) "Internetwork gateways"—none;

(v) "Communications channels" from such combinations to one "digital computer" located outside the "computer using facility"—one, provided that:

(a) the "communication channel" is dedicated full time to the given application;

(b) the maximum "data signalling rate" does not exceed 9,600 bit/s; and

(c) the "digital computer" is not designed or modified for "local area networks";

(vi) The sum of the "total processing data rate" of all embargoed "digital computers" directly connected to a "local area network"—285 million bit/s.

NB:

If the maximum "data signalling rate" on the common transmission medium does not exceed 2 million bit per second, this sub-paragraph will not apply.

(8) "Other peripheral devices";

(i) Maximum bit transfer rate of any "terminal device" located remote from the "computer using facility"—19,200 bit/s;

(ii) Displays or graphic input devices;

(a) Resolvable elements along any axis—1,024, and shades of grey or colour—64; or

(b) Resolvable elements along any axis—320, and shades of grey or colour—256;

(9) "Equivalent multiply rate" for "signal processing" or "image enhancement" equipment—800,000 operations per second;

(c) Exports covered by this Note are subject to the following conditions:

(1) The number, type and characteristics of the equipment are reasonable for the application;

(2) When the parameters of the equipment do not exceed:

(i) "Total processing data rate"—20 million bit/s; and

(ii) "Maximum bit transfer rate" of any independent drum or disk drive—10.3 million bit per second; Then, subject to the equipment not being destined for military end-use, there are no limitations on number of systems which may be licensed per transaction;

(3) When the parameters of any equipment involved in one transaction exceed any limit of (2) above;

(i) The "cumulative total processing data rate" must not exceed 285 million bit/s; and

NB:

When calculating the "cumulative total processing data rate," the "total processing data rates" of any stand-alone microcomputers are not to be included.

(ii) The Department of Trade and Industry shall:

(a) Be reasonably satisfied that:

(1) The equipment will be used primarily for the specific non-strategic application for which the export would be approved; and

(2) The equipment will not be used for the design, development or production of embargoed items, especially not in microelectronics; and

(b) Be supplied with the full name and address of the end-user and details of the end-use of the equipment.

NB:

Special consideration will be given to the activities of proposed end users of "digital

computers'' which have a ''total processing data rate'' exceeding 28 million bit per second.

10. Not used.

11. Not used.

12. Favourable consideration will be given to the export of ''digital computers'' or ''related equipment'' therefor embargoed by sub-item (h), provided that:
   (a) The ''digital computers'' or ''related equipment'' therefor:
      (1) Are not described in sub-items (h)(1)(i)(d) to (m);
      (2) Are not used with ''digital computers'' produced in proscribed areas;

      NB:
      This does not preclude the exchange of data media.
      (3) Are exported as:
         (i) Complete systems; or
         (ii) Enhancements to a previously exported system provided that the enhanced system does not exceed the limits of paragraph (b) of this Note;
      (4) Have not been designed for any equipment:
         (i) Embargoed by any other Item in this List; and
         (ii) Not eligible for export at National Discretion to such an Item;
      (5) Have been primarily designed and used for non strategic applications;
      (6) Do not have any of the following characteristics:
         (i) They fall within the scope of both sub-items (h)(1)(ii)(a) and (b); or
         (ii) They fall within the scope of sub-item (h)(1)(ii)(a) and are microprocessor-based systems having a word length of more than 16 bit; or
         (iii) They are ruggedized above the level required for a normal commercial/civil environment, but not necessarily up to the levels specified in sub-item (f) and are microprocessor-based systems having a word length of more than 16 bit; and

      NB:
      Microprocessor-based systems with 16-bit word-length and not more than 32-bit architecture are regarded as 16-bit systems for the purpose of this sub-paragraph.
      (7) Do not have all the following characteristics:

      NB:
      This paragraph does not apply to workstations designed for and limited to graphic arts (e.g. printing, publishing).
         (i) They are stand-alone graphics work stations designed or modified for the generation, transformation and display of 2 or 3 dimensional vectors;
         (ii) They have a ''total processing data rate'' of the central processing unit exceeding 48 million bit per second;
         (iii) They have a central processing unit, with a word-length exceeding 16-bit; and

      NB:
      Microprocessor based systems with 16-bit word-length and not more than a 32-bit architecture are regarded as 16-bit systems for the purpose of this sub-paragraph.
         (iv) They exceed either of the follow limits:
            (a) ''Block move data rate''—1,500,000 pixels/sec; or
            (b) Maximum bit transfer rate of the channel for direct access to the ''main storage'' (Direct Memory Access or DMA channel)—15 million bit/s;
   (b) The ''digital computers'' or ''related equipment'' therefor do not exceed any of the following limits:
      (1) Central processing unit—''main storage'' combinations:
         (i) ''Total processing data rate''—78 million bit/s;
         (ii) ''Total connected capacity'' of ''main storage''—76.7 million bit;
         (iii) ''Non-volatile storage'' with ''useraccessible programmability'' including bubble memory—none;

      NB:
      Magnetic core ''main storage'' may however be included.

(iv) "Virtual storage" capability—512 MByte;

NB:
Supermini "digital computers" with a "virtual storage" capability exceeding the level in this sub-paragraph will not be eligible for consideration under this Note. It is recognized, however, that other "digital computers" (e.g. mainframes) may have a "virtual storage" capability exceeding this limit and in such cases they may be considered under this Note.

(2) Input/output control unit—drum or disk drive combinations:
  (i) "Total transfer rate"—22 million bit/s;
  (ii) "Total access rate"—360 accesses per second;
  (iii) Total connected "net capacity"—14,000 million bit;
  (iv) "Maximum bit transfer rate" of any drum or disk drive—20.6 million bit/s;
  (v) Number of drum or disk drives exceeding a "maximum bit transfer rate" of 10.3 million bit/s—four;
  (vi) Exchangeable disk packs which contain magnetic heads:
    (a) "Access rate" of an independent seek mechanism—29 accesses per second;
    (b) "Net capacity"—640 million bit;

(3) Input/output control unit—bubble memory combinations:
  (i) Total connected "net capacity" for point of sale devices used by cashiers—9.8 million bit;
  (ii) Total connected "net capacity" for "digital computers" or "related equipment" other than those in (i) above—2.1 million bit;

(4) Input/output control unit—magnetic tape or cartridge-type streamer tape drive combinations:
  (i) Magnetic tape drives:
    (a) "Maximum bit packing density"—246 bit per mm (6,250 bpi);
    (b) Maximum read/write speed—508 cm/s (200 ips);
    (c) "Maximum bit transfer rate"—10 million bit/s;

    (d) Number exceeding 131 bit/s (3,300 bpi)—four;
  (ii) Cartridge-type streamer tape drives;
    (a) Maximum "total transfer rate"—16 million bit/s;
    (b) Number—two;

(5) Communication control unit—"communication channel" combinations:
  (i) "Total data signalling rate" of all "communication channels" terminating remote from the "computer using facility"—38,400 bit/s;
  (ii) Maximum "data signalling rate" of any "communication channel"—19,200 bit/s;
  (iii) Number of "communication channels" not dedicated full time to the given application—six, provided that:
    (a) They are connected to the public switched network;
    (b) They have a "data signalling rate" not exceeding 1200 bit per second at the interface between the "digital computer" and the public switched network; and
    (c) Number of "communication channels" not limited to telex interfaces for services conforming to CCITT recommendations F60 to F79—two.

(6) Input/output or communication control unit—directly connected data channel combinations;
  (i) "Total transfer rate"—3.6 million bit/s;
  (ii) "Transfer rate of any data channel"—3.6 million bit/s;
  (iii) Terminations of such combinations or of any extensions thereto outside the "computer using facility"—none;

(7) Communication control unit—"local area network" combinations:

NB:
For the purpose of this sub-paragraph all "local area networks" interconnected within a "computer using facility" are considered as a single "local area network."
  (i) Maximum "data signalling rate" on the common transmission medium—10 million bit/s;

(ii) Interfaces and protocols up to and including Layer 2 of the Open System Interconnection (OSI) reference model, that is ISO logical link control Draft International Standard (DIS) 8802/2, IEEE 802.2, 802.3, 802.4, 802.5 or equivalent;

(iii) Implementations that contain functions of, or equivalent to those provided by, CCITT X.25, Level 3 protocols—none;

(iv) Internetwork gateways—none;

(v) "Communications channels" from such combinations to one "digital computer" located outside the "computer using facility"—one, provided that:

(a) the "communication channel" is dedicated full time to the given application;

(b) the maximum "data signalling rate" is 19,200 b/s; and

(c) the "digital computer" is not designed or modified for "local area networks";

(vi) The sum of the "total processing data rate" of all embargoed "digital computers" directly connected to a "local area network"—285 million bit per second.

NB:

1. Only one "digital computer" may exceed 54 million bit per second.

2. If the maximum "data signalling rate" on the common transmission medium does not exceed 2 million bit/s, this sub-paragraph does not apply.

(8) "Other peripheral devices":

(i) "Maximum bit transfer rate" of any "terminal device" located remote from the "computer using facility"—19,200 bit/s:

(ii) Displays or graphic input devices:

(a) Resolvable elements—512 × 640, and shades of grey or colour—256; or

NB:

Paragraph (a) does not prohibit the export under this Note of displays for systems specially designed for and limited to graphic arts (e.g. printing, publishing) which have displays not exceeding 576 × 900 resolvable elements and 256 shades of grey or colour.

(b) Resolvable elements—1024 × 1280, and shades of grey or colour—64;

NB:

Paragraph (b) does not prohibit the export under this Note of displays for systems specially designed for and limited to graphic arts (e.g. printing, publishing) which have displays not exceeding 1560 × 1024 resolvable elements and 64 shades of grey or colour.

(9) "Signal processing or "image enhancement" equipment:

(i) "Equivalent multiply rate"—1,500,000 operations per second;

(ii) Output—10 million image elements per second;

(c) Applications under this Note must comply with the following:

(1) Provide information which includes:

(i) A signed statement by a responsible representative of the end-user(s) or the importing agency describing the end-use and certifying that:

(a) The "digital computers" or "related equipment" will:

(1) Be used only for civil applications; and

(2) Not be reexported or otherwise disposed of without permission from the Department of Trade and Industry;

(b) Responsible Western representatives of the supplier will:

(1) Have the right of access to the "computer using facility" and all equipment, wherever located, during normal working hours and at any other time the equipment is operating; and

(2) Be furnished information demonstrating continued authorized application of the equipment; and

(c) These Western representatives will be notified of any significant change of application or of other facts, on which the licence was based;

(ii) A full description of:

(a) The equipment; and

(b) Intended application and workload; and

(iii) A complete identification of all end-users and their activities;

(2) Not used.

(3) When the parameters of the equipment do not exceed:

(i) "Total processing data rate"—54 million bit per second; and

(ii) "Total connected capacity" of "main storage"—39 million bit; Then there is no visitation requirement;

(4) When the parameters of the equipment exceed either limit in (3) above, the supplier will:

(i) Have a responsible Western representative visit and inspect the "computer using facility" and all equipment, wherever located, at least quarterly for three years; and

(ii) Report periodically to the licensing authorities whether the "digital computers" and "related equipment" therefor are still being used for the approved purposes at the authorized location;

NB:

The visitation requirements of this sub-paragraph will be waived for remote "terminal devices" if they consist only of peripheral equipment freed from embargo by sub-item (h)(2)(iv) above.

13. Not used.

14. A limited range of equipment covered by Item IL 1565 for use with "digital computers" or "related equipment" produced in proscribed areas, or the export of minimum technology, including the transfer of skills and data necessary for fabrication, assembly and checkout of equipment, but excluding design technology, which is necessary to manufacture such equipment in those areas.

15. Not used.

16. Definitions of terms used in this Item "access rate"—

(a) Of an input/output control unit—drum or disk drive combination (R_{ad})—Either the "access rate" of an input/output control unit (R_{ac}) or the sum of the individual "access rates" of all independent seek mechanisms (R_{as}), whichever is smaller.

$$R_{ad} = \min (R_{ac}; \text{SUM } R_{as})$$

(b) Of an input/output control unit (R_{ac})—

(1) With rotational position sensing (rps), the sum of the individual "access rates" of all independent seek mechanisms (R_{as}) connected to the control unit.

Thus: $R_{ac} = \text{SUM } R_{as}$ (with rps); or

(2) Without rotational position sensing (rps), the number (C) of independent read/write channels connected to the control unit divided by the least "latency time" (t_{lmin}) of any connected independent seek mechanism.

Thus: $R_{ac} = \dfrac{C}{t_{lmin}}$ (without rps)

(c) Of a seek mechanism (R_{as})

The reciprocal of the "average access time" (t_{aa}) of the seek mechanism.

Thus: $R_{as} = \dfrac{1}{t_{aa}}$

"average access time" of a seek mechanism (t_{aa})—The sum of the "average seek time" (t_{sa}) and the "latency time" (t_l).

Thus: $t_{aa} = t_{sa} + t_l$

"average seek time" (t_{sa})—

The sum of the "maximum seek time" (t_{smax}) and twice the "minimum seek time" (t_{smin}), divided by three.

Thus: $t_{sa} = \dfrac{t_{smax} + 2t_{smin}}{3}$

"maximum seek time" (t_{smax})—

(1) For fixed head devices, it is zero; or

(2) For moving head or moving media devices, the rated time to move

between the two most widely separated tracks.

"minimum seek time" (t_{smin})—
(1) For fixed head devices, it is zero; or
(2) For moving head or moving media devices, the rated time to move from one track to an adjacent track.

"latency time" (t_l)—
The rotational period divided by twice the number of independent read/write heads per track.

"analogue computer"—
Equipment which can, in the form of one or more continuous variables:
(a) Accept data;
(b) Process data; and
(c) Provide output of data.

"associated" with equipment or systems—
(a) Can feasibly be either:
    (i)   Removed from such equipment or systems; or
    (ii) Used for other purposes; and
(b) Is not essential to the operation of such equipment or systems.

"block move data rate"—
The maximum number of pixels which can be moved per second from one location to another in the storage which functions as the frame buffer.

"communication channel"—
The transmission path or circuit including the terminating transmission and receiving equipment (modems) for transferring digital information between distant locations.

"computer operating area"—
The immediate contiguous and accessible area around the electronic computer, where the normal operating, support and service functions take place.

"computer using facility"—
The end-users contiguous and accessible facilities:
(a) Housing the "computer operating area" and those end-user functions which are being supported by the stated application of the electronic computer and its "related equipment"; and
(b) Not extending beyond 1,500 meters in any direction from the centre of the "computer operating area."

"cumulative total processing data rate"—

The sum of all "total processing data rates" in a given transaction.

"data device"—
Equipment capable of transmitting or receiving sequences of digital information.

"data (message) switching"—
The technique, including but not limited to store-and forward or packet switching, for:
(a) Accepting data groups (including messages, packets, or other digital or telegraphic information groups which are transmitted as a composite whole);
(b) Storing (buffering) data groups as necessary;
(c) Processing part or all of the data groups, as necessary, for the purpose of:
    (1)   Control (routing, priority, formatting, code conversion, error control, retransmission or journaling);
    (2)   Transmission; or
    (3)   Multiplexing; and
(d) Retransmitting (processed) data groups when transmission or receiving facilities are available.

"data signalling rate"—
The rate as defined in ITU Recommendation 53-36, taking into account that, for non-binary modulation, baud and bit per second are not equal. Binary digits for coding, checking, and synchronization functions are included.

NB:
It is the maximum one-way rate, i.e., the maximum rate in either transmission or reception.

"digital computer"—
Equipment which can, in the form of one or more discrete variables:
(a) Accept data;
(b) Store data or instructions in fixed or alterable (writable) storage devices;
(c) Process data by means of a stored sequence of instructions which is modifiable; and
(d) Provide output of data.

NB:
Modifications of a stored sequence of instructions include replacement of fixed storage devices, but not a physical change in wiring or interconnections.

"embedded" in equipment or systems—Can feasibly be neither:

(a) Removed from such equipment or systems; nor

(b) Used for other purposes.

"equivalent multiply rate"—

The maximally achievable number of multiplication operations which can be performed per second considering that, in the case of simultaneous multiplication operations, all multiplication rates have to be summed in order to arrive at the "equivalent multiply rate":

(a) Assuming
  (1) Optimal operand locations in the "most immediate storage"; and
  (2) Operand lengths at least 16 bit, or more if this allows for faster operation; and

(b) Neglecting
  (1) Set-up operations;
  (2) Pipeline filling operations;
  (3) Initialization;
  (4) Interrupts; and
  (5) Data reordering times.

NB:

Simultaneous multiplication operations can occur because of:

(a) Multiple arithmetic units for operations such as complex multiplication, convolution or recursive filtering;

(b) Parallel pipelining;

(c) More than one arithmetic unit in one data processing unit; or

(d) More than one data processing unit in one system.

"fault tolerance"—

The capability to perform correctly without human intervention after failure of any "assembly," so that there is no single point in the system the failure of which could cause catastrophic failure of the system's functioning.

  "assembly"—

  A number of components (i.e. circuit elements, discrete components, microcircuits) connected together to perform a specific function or functions, replaceable as an entity and normally capable of being disassembled.

"firmware"—

See "microprogramme."

"gateway"—

The function, realised by any combination of equipment and "software," to carry out the conversion of conventions for representing, processing or communicating information used in one system into the corresponding but different conventions used in another system.

"gross capacity"—

The product of:

(a) The maximum number of binary digit (bit) positions per unformatted track; and

(b) The total number of tracks including spare tracks and tracks not accessible to the user.

"hybrid computer"—

Equipment which can:

(a) Accept data;

(b) Process data, in both analogue and digital representations; and

(c) Provide output of data.

"image digitiser"—

A device for directly converting an analogue representation of an image into a digital representation.

"image enhancement"—

The processing of externally derived information-bearing images by algorithms such as time compression, filtering, extraction, selection, correlation, convolution or transformations between domains (e.g. Fast Fourier Transform or Walsh Transform). This does not include algorithms using only linear or rotational transformation of a single image, such as translation, feature extraction, registration or false colouration.

"incorporated" in equipment or systems—

(a) Can feasibly be either;
  (i) Removed from such equipment or systems; or
  (ii) Used for other purposes; and

(b) Is essential to the operation of such equipment or systems.

"internetwork gateway"—

A "gateway" for two systems which are themselves "local area networks," "wide area networks" or both.

"local area network"—

A data communication system which:

(a) Allows an arbitrary number of independent "data devices" to communicate directly with each other; and

(b) Is confined to a geographical area of moderate size (e.g. office building, plant, campus, warehouse).

"main storage"—

The primary storage for data or instructions for rapid access by a central processing unit. It consists of the internal storage of a "digital computer" and any hierarchical extension thereto, such as cache storage or non-sequentially accessed extended storage.

"maximum bit packing density"—

The density of recording specified in accordance with the appropriate ANSI or ISO Standard (e.g. ANSI X3.14-1979, ISO 1863–1975; ANSI X3.22-1973; ISO 1873–1976; ANSI X3.39-1973; ISO 3788–1976; ANSI X3.48-1977; ISO 3407–1976; ANSI X3.56-1977; ISO 4057–1979; ANSI X3.54-1976).

"maximum bit transfer rate"—

(a) Of a drum or disk drive (R_{tdmax}) is the product of:

  (1) The maximum number of binary digit (bit) positions per unformatted track; and

  (2) The number of tracks which simultaneously can be read or written, divided by the rotational period;

(b) Of a magnetic tape drive (R_{ttmax}) is the product of:

  (1) The "maximum bit packing density";

  (2) The number of data bits per character (ANSI) or per row (ISO); and

  (3) The maximum tape read/write speed.

"microprogramme"—

A sequence of elementary instructions, maintained in a special storage, the execution of which is initiated by the introduction of its reference instruction into an instruction register.

"most immediate storage"—

The portion of the "main storage" most directly accessible by the central processing unit:

(a) For single level "main storage" this is:

  (1) The cache storage;

  (2) The instruction stack; or

  (3) The data stack.

"multi-data-stream processing"—

The "microprogramme" or equipment architecture technique which permits processing two or more data sequences under the control of one or more instruction sequences by means such as;

(a) Parallel processing;

(b) Structured arrays of processing elements;

(c) Single Instruction Multiple Data (SIMD) operations; or

(d) Multiple Instruction Multiple Data (MIMD) operations;

"net capacity"—

Of a drum, disk nor cartridge-type streamer tape drive, or a bubble memory: The total capacity designed to be accessible to the "digital computer" excluding error control bits;

"non-volatile storage"—

A storage device the contents of which are not lost when power is removed.

"other peripheral device"—

A "data device" which is:

(a) Peripheral to a central processing unit—"main storage" combination; and

(b) Not an input/output control unit—drum, disk or magnetic tape drive or bubble memory combination.

"principal element"—

A "digital computer" or "related equipment" which is:

(a) Either "embedded" or "incorporated" in another equipment or system; and

(b) In replacement value more than 35% of the replacement value of the total equipment or system, i.e. including the "digital computer" or "related equipment."

"programme"—

A sequence of instructions to carry out a process in, or convertible into, a form executable by an electronic computer.

"real time processing"—

Processing of data by an electronic computer in response to an external event according to time requirements imposed by the external event.

"related equipment"—

Equipment "embedded" in, "incorporated" in, or "associated" with electronic computers, as follows:

(a) Equipment for interconnecting "analogue computers" with "digital computers";

(b) Equipment for interconnecting "digital computers";

(c) Equipment for interfacing electronic computers to "local area networks" or to "wide area networks";

(d) Communication control units;

(e) Other input/output (I/O) control units;

(f) Recording or reproducing equipment referred to Item IL 1565 by Item IL 1572;

(g) Displays; or

(h) Other peripheral equipment.

NB:

"Related equipment" which contains an "embedded" or "incorporated" electronic computer, but which lacks "user-accessible programmability," does not thereby fall within the definition of an electronic computer.

"signal processing"—

The processing of externally derived information-bearing signals by algorithms such as time compression, filtering, extraction, selection, correlation, convolution or transformations between domains (e.g. Fast Fourier Transform or Walsh Transform).

"software"—

A collection of one or more "programmes" or "microprogrammes" fixed in any tangible medium of expression.

"stored-programme-controlled circuit switching"—

The technique for establishing, on demand and until released, a direct (space-division switching) or logical (time-division switching) connection between circuits based on switching control information derived from any source or circuit and processed according to the stored "programme" by one or more electronic computers.

"terminal device"—

A "data device" which:

(a) Does not include process control sensing and actuating devices; and

(b) Is capable of:

(1) Accepting or producing a physical record;

(2) Accepting a manual input; or

(3) Producing a visual output.

NB:

Normal groupings of such equipment (e.g. a combination of paper tape punch/reader and printer), connected to a single data channel or "communication channel," shall be considered as a single "terminal device."

"total access rate" (R_{atot})—

The sum of the individual "access rates" of all input/output control unit—drum or disk drive combinations (R_{ad}) provided with the system which can be sustained simultaneously assuming the configuration of equipment which would maximize this "total access rate."

Thus: $R_{atot} + SUM\ R_{ad}$

"total connected capacity"—

The storage capacity excluding error control bits, word marker bits, and flag bits.

"total data signalling rate"—

The sum of the individual "data signalling rates" of all "communication channels" which:

(a) Have been provided with the system; and

(b) Can be sustained simultaneously assuming the configuration of the equipment which would maximize this sum of rates.

"total internal storage available to the user"—

The sum of the individual capacities of all internal user-alterable or user-replaceable storage devices, which may be:

(a) Included in the equipment at the same time; and

(b) Used to store "software" instructions or data.

"total processing data rate"—

(a) Of a single central processing unit, is its "processing data rate";

(b) Of multiple central processing units which do not share direct access to a common "main storage," is: The individual "processing data rate" of each central processing unit, i.e., each unit is separately treated as a single central processing unit as in (a) above; or

(c) Of multiple central processing units, which partially or fully share direct access to a common "main storage" at any level, is the sum of:

(1) The highest of the individual "processing data rates" of all central processing units; and

(2) 0.75 times the "processing data rate" of each remaining central processing unit, sharing the same "main storage"; assuming the configuration of equipment, which would maximize this sum of rates.

"processing data rate"—

The maximum of either:
(a) the "floating point processing data rate" (R_f); or
(b) The "fixed point processing data rate" (R_x).

NB:
The "processing data rate" of a central processing unit implemented with two or more microprocessor microcircuits, not including any dedicated microprocessor microcircuit used solely for display, keyboard or input/output control, is the sum of the individual "processing data rates" of all these microprocessor microcircuits.
"floating point processing data rate" (R_f)—
The sum of:
(1) 0.85 times the "number of bits in a fixed point instruction" (n_{ix}) or 0.85 times the "number of bits in a floating point instruction" (n_{if}), if no fixed point instructions are implemented;
(2) 0.15 times the "number of bits in a floating point instruction" (n_{if});
(3) 0.40 times the "number of bits in a fixed point operand" (n_{ox}) or 0.40 times the "number of bits in a floating point operand" (n_{of}), if no fixed point instructions are implemented; and
(4) 0.15 times the "number of bits in a floating point operand" (n_{of});
Divided by the sum of:
(1) 0.85 times the 'execution time' for a fixed point addition (t_{ax}) or for a floating point addition (t_{af}), if no fixed point instructions are implemented;
(2) 0.09 times the 'execution time' for a floating point addition (t_{af}); and
(3) 0.06 times the 'execution time' for a floating point multiplication (t_{mf}) or for the fastest available subroutine (t_{msub}) to simulate a floating point multiplication instruction, if no floating point multiplication instructions are implemented.
Thus:

$$R_f = \frac{(0.85)n_{ix} + (0.15)n_{if} + (0.40)n_{ox} + (0.15)n_{of}}{(0.85)t_{ax} + (0.09)t_{af} + (0.06)t_{mf}}$$

or if no fixed point instructions are implemented, then:

$$R_f = \frac{(1.00)n_{if} + (0.55)n_{of}}{(0.94)t_{af} + (0.06)t_{mf}}$$

or if no floating point multiplication instructions are implemented ($t_{mf} = t_{msub}$) then:

$$R_f = \frac{(0.85)n_{ix} + (0.15)n_{imf} + (0.40)n_{ox} + (0.15)n_{of}}{(0.85)t_{ax} + (0.09)t_{af} + (0.06)t_{msub}}$$

NB:
If a "digital computer" has neither floating point addition nor floating point multiplication instructions, then its "floating point processing data rate" is equal to zero.
"fixed point processing data rate" (R_x)
The sum of:
(1) 0.85 times the "number of bits in a fixed point addition instruction" (n_{iax});
(2) 0.15 times the "number of bits in a fixed point multiplication instruction" (n_{imx}); and
(3) 0.55 times the "number of bits in a fixed point operand" (n_{ox});
divided by the sum of:
(1) 0.85 times the "execution time" for a fixed point addition (t_{ax}); and
(2) 0.15 times the "execution time" for a fixed point multiplication (t_{mx}) or for the fastest available subroutine (t_{msub}) to simulate a fixed point multiplication instruction if no fixed point multiplication instructions are implemented.
Thus:

$$R_x = \frac{(0.85)n_{iax} + (0.15)n_{imx} + (0.55)n_{ox}}{(0.85)t_{ax} + (0.15)t_{mx}}$$

or if no fixed point multiplication instructions are implemented ($t_{mx} = t_{msub}$), then:

$$R_x = \frac{(0.85)n_{iax} + (0.15)n_{imx} + (0.55)n_{ox}}{(0.85)t_{ax} + (0.15)t_{msub}}$$

NB:

If a "digital computer" has neither fixed point addition nor fixed point multiplication instructions, then its "fixed point processing data rate" is equal to zero.

"number of bits in a:

Fixed point addition instruction" (n_{iax})—
Fixed point multiplication instruction" (n_{imx})—
Floating point addition instruction" (n_{iaf})—
Floating point multiplication instruction (n_{imf})—

The appropriate shortest single fixed or floating point instruction length which permits full direct addressing of the "main storage."

NB:

1. When multiple instructions are required to simulate an appropriate single instruction, the number of bits in the above instructions is defined as 16 bits plus the number of bits (b_{iax}, b_{imx}, b_{iaf}, b_{imf}) which permits full direct addressing of the "main storage."

Thus:

$$n_{iax} = 16 + b_{iax};$$
$$n_{imx} = 16 + b_{imx};$$
$$n_{iaf} = 16 + b_{iaf};$$
$$n_{imf} = 16 + b_{imf};$$

2. If the addressing capability of an instruction is expanded by using a base register, then the "number of bits in an instruction, fixed or floating point, addition or multiplication" is the number of bits in the instruction with the standard address length including the number of bits necessary to use the base register.

"Number of bits in a fixed point operand" (n_{ox})—

(a) The shortest fixed point operand length; or
(b) 16 bit; whichever is greater.

"number of bits in a floating point operand" (n_{of})—

(a) The shortest floating point operand length: or
(b) 30 bit; whichever is greater.

"execution time"

(a) The time certified or openly published by the manufacturer for the execution of the fastest appropriate instruction, under the following conditions:

(1) No indexing or indirect operations are included;
(2) The instruction is in the "most immediate storage";
(3) One operand is in the accumulator or in a location of the "most immediate storage" which is acting as the accumulator;
(4) The second operand is in the "most immediate storage"; and
(5) The result is left in the accumulator or the same location in the "most immediate storage" which is acting as the accumulator;

(b) If only the maximum and minimum execution times of the instructions are published, the sum of:

(1) The maximum execution time of an instruction (t_{max}); and
(2) Twice the minimum execution time of this instruction (t_{min});

Divided by three

Thus: $$t = \frac{t_{max} + 2t_{min}}{3}$$

(t stands for any of the values t_{ax}, t_{af}, t_{mx}, or t_{mf});

(c) For central processing units which simultaneously fetch more than one instruction from one storage location: The average of the "execution times" when executing instructions fetched from all possible locations within the stored word.

(d) If the longest fixed point operand length is smaller than 16-bit, then use the time required for the fastest available subroutine to simulate a 16 bit fixed point operation.

NB:

1. If the addressing capability of an instruction is expanded by using a base register, then the 'execution time' shall include the time for adding the content of the base register to the address part of the instruction.

2. When calculating 'processing data rate' for computers with cache sizes smaller then 64 K Bytes, the 'execution time' of the appropriate instructions will be calculated as follows:

(cache hit rate) × ('execution time' when both instruction and operand are in cache storage + (1 − cache hit rate) × ('execution time' when neither instruction nor operand are in cache storage),

The cache hit rate being:

1.00 for cache size of 64 K Byte
0.95 for cache size of 32 K Byte
0.90 for cache size of 16 K Byte
0.85 for cache size of 8 K Byte
0.75 for cache size of 4 K Byte

"total transfer rate"—

(a) Of the input/output control unit—drum, disk or cartridge-type streamer tape drive combinations (R_{tdtot}): The sum of the individual 'transfer rates' of all input/output control unit—drum, disk or cartridge-type streamer tape drive combinations (R_{td}) provided with the system which can be sustained simultaneously assuming the configuration of equipment which would maximize this sum of rates.

Thus: $R_{tdtot} = SUM\ R_{td}$;

'transfer rate'—

(1) Of an input/output control unit—drum or disk drive combination (R_{td}), the smaller of either:

NB:

For the 'transfer rate' of an input/output control unit—cartridge-type streamer tape drive combination, see (b) below.

(i) The input/output control unit "transfer rate" (R_{tc}); or

(ii) The sum of the individual "transfer rates" of all independent seek mechanisms (R_{ts}).

Thus: $R_{td} = min\ (R_{tc};\ SUM\ R_{ts})$;

(2) Of an input/output control unit (R_{tc});

(i) With rotational position sensing (rps), is the product of:

(a) The number of independent read/write channels (C); and

(b) The greatest "maximum bit transfer rate" ($R_{tsmaxmax}$) of all independent seek mechanisms; or

(ii) Without rotational position sensing (rps), is two-thirds of this product.

Thus:

$R_{tc} = C.R_{tsmaxmax}$ (with rps); or

$R_{tc}\ \dfrac{2C.}{3} = R_{tsmaxmax}$ (without rps);

(3) Of an independent seek mechanism (R_{ts}):

The product of:

(i) The "maximum bit transfer rate" (R_{tsmax}); and

(ii) The rotational period (t_r);

Divided by the sum of:

(i) The rotational period (t_r);

(ii) The 'minimum seek time' (t_{smin}); and

(iii) The 'latency time' (t_1);

Thus: $R_{ts} = \dfrac{R_{tsmax} \times t_r}{t_r + t_{smin} + t_1}$;

'minimum seek time' (t_{smin})—

(1) For fixed head devices, it is zero; or

(2) For moving head or moving media devices, the rated time to move from one track to an adjacent track.

'latency time' (t_1)—

The rotational period divided by twice the number of independent read/write heads per track.

(b) Of the input/output control unit—magnetic tape drive combinations (R_{tttot}):

The sum of the individual 'transfer rates' of all input/output control unit—magnetic tape drive combinations (R_{tt}) provided with the system which can be sustained simultaneously assuming the configuration of equipment which would maximize this sum of rates.

Thus: $R_{tttot} = SUM\ R_{tt}$;

'transfer rate'—

Of an input/output control unit—cartridge-type streamer or magnetic tape drive combination (R_{tt}):

The product of:

(1) The number of independent read/write channels (C); and

(2) The greatest "maximum bit transfer rate" ($R_{ttmaxmax}$) of all tape drives.

Thus: $R_{tt} = C.R_{ttmaxmax}$.

(c) Of the input/output or communication control unit—directly connected data channel combinations: The sum of the individual "transfer rates of all data channels" provided with the system which can be sustained simultaneously assuming the configuration of equipment which would maximize this sum of rates.

"transfer rate of any data channel"—

The sum of the individual bit transfer rates of all the "other peripheral devices," excluding "terminal devices," which can be sustained simultaneously on the data channel.

"user-accessible microprogrammability"—

The facility allowing a user to insert, modify or replace "microprogrammes."

"user-accessible programmability"—

The facility allowing a user to insert, modify or replace "programmes" by means other than:

(a) A physical change in wiring or interconnections; or

(b) The setting of function controls including entry of parameters.

"virtual storage"—

The storage space that may be regarded as addressable "main storage" by the user of a computer system in which virtual addresses are mapped into real addresses.

NB:

The size of "virtual storage" is limited by the addressing scheme of the computer system and not by the actual number of "main storage" locations.

"wide area network"—

A data communication system which:

(a) Allows an arbitrary number of independent "data devices" to communicate with each other;

(b) May include "local area networks"; and

(c) Is designed to interconnect geographically dispersed facilities.

FOR THE PEOPLE'S REPUBLIC OF CHINA ONLY:

17. "Digital computers" or "related equipment" therefor embargoed by sub-item (h) provided that:

(a) The "digital computers" or "related equipment" therefor:

(1) Will be operated by civil end-users for civil applications;

(2) Are exported as complete systems or enhancements to previously exported systems up to the limits of sub-paragraph (b) of this Note;

(3) Have been primarily designed and used for non-strategic applications; and

(4) Do not fall within the scope of both sub-items (h)(1)(ii)(a) and (b);

(b) The "digital computers" or "related equipment" therefor do not exceed any of the following limits:

(1) Central processing unit—"main storage" combinations with a "total processing data rate" of 550 million bit/s.

(2) Array transform processors:

(i) "Equivalent multiply rate"—800,000 operations per second;

(ii) Fast Fourier Transform of 1,024 complex points—40 ms;

(c) The "digital computers" or "related equipment" therefor do not have the following characteristics:

(1) Those identified in sub-items (h)(1)(i)(d) to (h) and (m);

(2) Those identified in sub-item (h)(1)(i)(b) having an "equivalent multiply rate" of more than 2 million operations per second;

NB:

Equipment which exceeds this limit may qualify for export under the conditions of this Note if approved by the Department of Trade and Industry.

18. "Digital computers" or "related equipment" therefor in accordance with Note 5 above, on the understanding that:

(a) sub-para (b)(1) of Note 5 does not apply;

(b) the "total processing data rate" under Note 5(c) does not exceed 155 million bit/s.

19. Individual or bulk shipments of peripheral equipment as follows, and input/output interfaces or control units therefor:

(a) Cathode ray tube graphic displays, which do not exceed

(1) 1,024 resolvable elements along one axis and 1,280 resolvable elements along the perpendicular axis; or

(2) 256 shades of grey or colour (8 bit per pixel);

(b) Plotting equipment and digitizing equipment

which has an accuracy of 0.002% or worse, and an active area of 254 cm × 254 cm or smaller.

(c) *Disk drives which do not exceed:*
   (1) *"Maximum bit transfer rate"—10.3 million bit/s; or*
   (2) *"Net capacity"—1,227 million bit.*

(d) *Non-impact type printers and laser printers having a resolution not exceeding 300 dots per inch;*

(e) *Optical character recognition (OCR) equipment;*

(f) *Light gun devices or other manual graphic input devices.*

20. *Bulk shipments of personal computers and small business computer systems embargoed by sub-item (h) which do not exceed any of the following parameters:*

NB:

This Note may not be used for graphic workstations exceeding the limits of Note 9 (a)(7):

(a) *"Total processing data rate"—136 million bit per second;*

(b) *"Virtual storage" capability—512 MByte;*

NB:

Supermini "digital computers" with a "virtual storage" capability exceeding the level in this sub-paragraph will not be eligible for consideration under this Note. It is recognized, however, that other "digital computers" (e.g. mainframes and microcomputers) may have a "virtual storage" capability exceeding this limit and in such cases they may be considered under this Note.

(c) *The other technical parameters of the system—the limits contained in Note 9 (b) above without taking into account Note 9(b)(ii)(b).*

21. *The shipment of spare parts in accordance with Note 7(a) and (b) to this Item.*

EXPLANATORY NOTES

A. Conversion of Byte to bit in computing storage limits:
   (a) 1 MByte = $(1024)^2$ Byte = 1,048,576 Byte
   (b) 1 KByte = 1,024 Byte
   (c) 1 Byte: usually equals 8 bit or 9 bit.

B. Limits on "total connected capacity" of "main storage": The limits in the various Notes to Item 1565 assume a 9-bit Byte and an appropriate amount of cache storage (16, 32, 48 or 64 kByte), as follows (although other combinations within these limits would be permissible):

Internal Storage (MByte)	Cache Storage (KByte)	"Total Connected Capacity" (million bit)
0.25	16	2.5
0.5	16	4.9
0.75	32	7.4
1.0	32	9.8
1.5	48	14.6
2.0	48	19.4
2.5	64	24.2
4.0	64	39.0
8.0	128	76.7

C. Total Processing Data Rate:
   Two examples of applying the Note 16 definition of "fixed point processing data rate" and "floating point processing date rate"
   1. Z80 at 8 MHz clock frequency:
   (i) Instruction lengths and cycles

Operation	Instruction(s)	Instr. Length (Bytes)	Cycles
Add	LHD HE, MEM	3	16
	DAD	1	11
Totals		4	27
Multiply	(Emulation routine)	—	747

   (ii) Execution Times
   Add   27 cycles divided by 8 MHz = 3.37 microseconds

   Multiply 747 cycles divided by 8 MHz = 93.37 microseconds

   (iii) Fixed Point PDR (XPDR)
   $$XPDR = \frac{.85(32) + .15(16+16) + .55(16)}{.85(3.37) + .15(93.37)}$$
   = 2.42 million bits per second

   NOTE:
   Direct addressing capability of the Z80 is 16 bit, which means 65,536 addresses of storage.

   (iv) Floating Point PDR (FP PDR)
   FP PDR = 0 million bits per second (no floating point addition nor multiplication instruction).

(v) "Total PDR"
"Total PDR" (Z80 at 8 MHz) = 2.42
million bits per second.

2. 8088/8087 at 4.77 MHz clock frequency
(i) Instruction lengths and cycles

Operation	Instruction(s)	Instr. Length (bytes)	Cycles (OPN + EA + BUS)
Fixed point:			
Add	ADD	4	9 + 5 + 4 = 18
Multiply	MUL	4	129 + 5 + 4 = 138
Floating point:			
Add	FADD	4	100 + 5 + 16 = 121
Multiply	FMUL	4	115 + 5 + 16 = 136

(ii) Execution times
Fixed point:
ADD 18 cycles divided by 4.77 MHz = 3.77 microseconds
MUL 138 cycles divided by 4.77 MHz = 28.93 microseconds
Floating point:
FADD 121 cycles divided by 4.77 MHz = 25.37 microseconds
FMUL 136 cycles divided by 4.77 MHz = 28.51 microseconds

(iii) "Fixed point PDR (XPDR)

$$XPDR = \frac{.85(32) + .15(32) + .55(16)}{.85(3.77) + .15(28.93)}$$

= 5.41 million bits per second

(iv) Floating point PDR (FP PDR)

$$FP\ PDR = \frac{.85(32) + .15(32) + .4(16) + .15(32)}{.85(3.77) + .09(25.37) + .06(28.51)}$$

= 6.01 million bits per second.

(v) "Total PDR"
"Total PDR" (8088/8087 at 4.77 MHx) =
6.01 million bits per second.

5

Détente and Trade

Robert Cullen

In the late 1960s, three events, seemingly unrelated, began to shape the Soviet-American economic relationship. In 1967, Israel won a resounding victory over a coalition of Arab states in the Six-Day War. At about the same time, in Moscow, Leonid Brezhnev was consolidating his power and looking for ways to push the Soviet economy forward after the fizzling of a mid-1960s reform effort. In the United States, Richard Nixon became president and brought Henry Kissinger to Washington with him.

By the time of the Six-Day War, Israeli diplomats had for years been crisscrossing the Soviet Union, meeting with their fellow Jews and planting the idea of *aliyah*, or emigration to Israel. But they had found a traumatized community, discouraged and disorganized after years of Stalinist terror, war, and campaigns against religion. There was no great pressure for emigration until Israel's victory electrified and emboldened Soviet Jewry. Within a couple of years, the Jews' campaign for emigration rights had begun.

Meanwhile, Brezhnev faced an economic dilemma. Shortly after Nikita Khruschev's ouster in 1964, the Kremlin had launched a major economic reform; its political sponsor was Alexei Kosygin, the prime minister whose influence initially rivaled Brezhnev's in the coalition that overthrew Khrushchev. The reform was an early effort to reduce the government's role in the economy, but the tenacious Moscow bureaucracy, by the end of the decade, had squelched it.

That same bureaucracy formed Brezhnev's political base. He had promised "stability of cadres," in contrast to Khrushchev's capricious personnel policies. Brezhnev could hardly opt to push the reform program further, for risk of alienating the bureaucrats. Instead, as Raymond Garthoff recounts in *Détente and Confrontation*, he challenged the autarkic economic policies of Stalin and Khrushchev. Trade with the West, Brezhnev said, could give the Soviet economy a fresh infusion of capital and technology.

At the same time, Nixon and Kissinger faced the problems of extricating the United States from Vietnam and repairing a Soviet-American relationship badly bruised by both America's Southeast Asian imbroglio and the Soviet invasion of Czechoslovakia. The two problems, Kissinger believed, were not unrelated: better relations with Moscow might lead to pressure on North Vietnam to negotiate an end to the war. The requisite leverage, he thought, lay in the Soviet desire for trade. "Our strategy was to use trade concessions as a political instrument, withholding them when Soviet conduct was adventurous and granting them in measured doses when the Soviets behaved cooperatively," he wrote in his memoirs. Kissinger indeed presided over the enshrinement of linkage between Soviet-American trade and Soviet political behavior. But, it was not the kind of linkage he originally had in mind.

Trade Agreement

As the 1970s began, there was no trade agreement between the United States and the Soviet Union, and not much trade. As noted in Chapter One, the 1935 Roosevelt administration decision to extend most-favored nation status to Moscow was reversed in 1951 when Congress, during the Korean War, placed all communist countries in a high-tariff category. In the late 1940s, export control legislation had launched a continuing American effort to deny advanced technology to the Soviets. There was not even much grain trade, partly because American longshoremen refused to load grain bound for the Soviets.

Nixon and Kissinger began their stewardship of the Soviet-American trade issue with what Kissinger later acknowledged was a mistake. The export control laws were up for renewal in 1969. The administration, Kissinger recalled, could have asked that the bill include a provision superseding the 1951 legislation and giving the president authority to extend most-favored nation status to the Soviet Union and Eastern Europe. It did not. "We could have gotten it if we had asked for it," he wrote in his memoirs.

''This came back to haunt us a few years later, when we sought this authority, and the Congressional mood had meanwhile shifted 180 degrees.'' As a result, in 1972, extending MFN treatment to the Soviets would require Congressional approval.

Still, that seemed like a surmountable problem as negotiations for a trade agreement opened shortly after the Soviet-American summit meeting in May, 1972. Grain sales were a natural place to start improving commercial relations. In July, 1972, the Department of Agriculture granted the Soviets $750 million in credits to buy American grain. The Soviets quietly used the credit to buy up nearly the entire American surplus, causing a furor when domestic prices rose sharply in 1973. In 1975, the two countries signed a long-term grain agreement that set minimum annual purchase requirements and required the Soviets to notify the United States if they wanted to buy more than a stipulated amount. After the 1980 grain embargo due to the Soviet invasion of Afghanistan was lifted, the Reagan administration negotiated a new grain agreement in 1983 **(Document 5.1)** and extended it in 1988. The Bush Administration scheduled negotiations for a new agreement in December, 1989.

In the summer of 1972, the most difficult trade barrier, in the minds of the officials who handled the negotiations, was settling the Soviets' Lend Lease debt from World War II. Kissinger himself handled that issue. On October 18, 1972, the two sides unveiled two agreements. In the first, the Soviets agreed to pay $722 million over 28 years to wipe out the World War II debt. **(Document 5.2)** In the second, each side agreed to extend MFN to the other. **(Document 5.3)** The agreement was hedged, however. It would ''enter into force upon the exchange of written notice of acceptance.'' In the case of the United States, that meant after Congress had approved the requisite legislation. In addition, Nixon signed a presidential determination permitting the Export-Import Bank to finance or guarantee Soviet-American transactions **(Document 5.4)**.

Linkage was implied, rather than specified, in these agreements. They committed the Soviets, in vague terms, to order substantial amounts of machinery, agricultural products, and other goods from the United States. The agreements, further, envisioned tripling the volume of U.S.-Soviet trade, which traditionally had favored the United States. But there was no single political hurdle the Soviets had to jump in return for MFN. Kissinger envisioned trade as a flexible lever, that could be used in a multitude of ways in reaction to a variety of potential Soviet policies.

The Jackson-Vanik Amendment

Sen. Henry Jackson had another vision. Jackson disagreed with the course of détente. During the ratification process for the SALT I Treaty, he attached an amendment demanding that future treaties bind each side to equal levels in each weapon category. After it became clear that the Nixon Administration intended to extend détente to include MFN status for the Soviets, Jackson prepared an amendment that made MFN status conditional on emigration rights in the Soviet Union. The amendment withheld MFN status and U.S. government credits from communist countries that denied their citizens free emigration.

A serious blunder in Moscow made Jackson's job much easier. Beginning in 1969, the Soviets had begun to open the door somewhat to Jewish emigration. In 1971, 13,022 had left; in 1972, the figure would be 31,681. But in August, 1972, Soviet officials began demanding a heavy ''exit tax'' from each prospective emigrant, supposedly in return for the cost of his or her public education. The tax struck most Americans as a kind of extortion. Although the collection of the tax was later suspended, it galvanized Congressional support for Jackson's approach. When he introduced his amendment, on October 4, 1972, he had 71 co-sponsors. When the new Congress convened in 1973, Jackson reintroduced the legislation as an amendment to an omnibus trade reform bill. In the House, Rep. Charles Vanik of Ohio introduced the same measure. Three quarters of both houses endorsed it.

Nixon, by then in the throes of Watergate, could not squelch the Jackson-Vanik Amendment. Nor did he choose to withdraw the section of the trade legislation to which the Jackson-Vanik Amendment was attached, a step which might have preserved the opportunity to extend MFN to the Soviets at a later date. The idea of linking trade and emigration had forged a broad political coalition. Traditionally liberal American Jews, anxious to help their brethren in Russia, joined with conservative anti-Communists eager to stop and reverse détente. Organized labor signed on. Its leadership was profoundly anticommunist and looking for a way to torpedo the whole trade bill, which it feared would promote foreign manufacturing and cost American jobs. In August, 1974, the next president, Gerald Ford, inherited the problem.

In the summer and fall of that year, Ford and Kissinger conducted a triangular negotiation in an effort to save the 1972 Trade Agreement. Jackson and two Senate colleagues, Jacob Javits and Abraham

Ribicoff, comprised the second side. The Soviets, represented by Foreign Minister Andrei Gromyko and Ambassador Anatoly Dobrynin, were the third. The administration tried to obtain, at least tacitly, a Soviet promise to allow a high level of emigration each year. It hoped to persuade the Senate to accept such a promise and, in return, to modify the Jackson-Vanik Amendment and deliver MFN status to the Soviets.

The negotiations lurched from public pronouncements to secret understandings. The Soviets publicly insisted that the number of emigrants was none of the Americans' business, but Gromyko apparently led Kissinger to believe that he might wink and nod at a figure of 45,000 annually. Once that was in hand, Jackson insisted on 60,000. The Soviets told Kissinger that they might be willing to settle the issue if they were confident that there would be no public embarrassment. Jackson periodically went on television to proclaim Soviet concessions. In the end, the negotiations produced three conflicting letters: one from Kissinger (**Document 5.5**), one from Jackson (**Document 5.6**), and one from Gromyko (**Document 5.7**). Gromyko's, which was publicly released by the Soviets, returned to the position that emigration "is entirely within the internal competence of our state."

The failure of the negotiations meant that the Jackson-Vanik Amendment (**Document 5.8**) was enacted into law as part of the 1974 Trade Act. The amendment denies normal tariffs (most-favored nation status), or any government credits or credit guarantees, to countries without market economies—if they deny their citizens the right to emigrate. The president may waive the amendment if he has "received assurances that the emigration practices of the country will henceforth lead substantially to the achievement of the objectives" of the amendment. The amendment contains a complicated congressional review process under which either the House or the Senate could veto a waiver. A subsequent Supreme Court decision in an unrelated case (INS vs. Chada), nullified the one-house veto. So it is unclear exactly what procedure Congress would have to follow to overturn a presidential decision. It is clear, however, that the law requires the president to conclude a trade agreement with a country before he extends normal tariffs. Therefore, waiving Jackson-Vanik would not, in itself, give the Soviet Union MFN status. The two countries would also have to either agree to return to the 1972 trade agreement or negotiate a new one.

Before it was done in 1974, the Congress compounded the impact of the Jackson-Vanik Amendment with the Stevenson Amendment, which was sponsored by Sen. Adlai Stevenson Jr. of Illinois. The Stevenson Amendment (**Document 5.9**) limits the Soviets to $300 million in credits from the Export-Import Bank over a four-year period. A third amendment, sponsored by Sen. Harry Byrd of Virginia, (**Document 5.10**) extended that limit to all government credit programs, except for the Commodity Credit Corp. Both amendments are moot as long as Jackson-Vanik denies the Soviets access to any credits. At the time, though, the Stevenson Amendment meant that even if the Soviets met the emigration test in Jackson-Vanik, they would get far less Export-Import Bank credit than they had been receiving since 1972. In the years since 1974, the effect of the Stevenson Amendment has been blunted because the Export-Import Bank has stopped making direct loans to industrialized countries. The Export-Import Bank still has loan guarantee and insurance programs the Soviets might be eligible for, which would marginally lower the commercial interest rates available to them.

Jackson and his allies succeeded in ending the economic phase of détente. The absence of normal tariff rates probably had only a marginal economic impact on potential trade. Tariffs affect manufactured goods more than the fuels and raw materials which comprise the bulk of Soviet exports to industrialized Western countries. But as a political symbol, the amendments had a major impact. On January 10, 1975, the Soviets informed the United States that they considered the amendments a violation of the 1972 trade agreement. Therefore, Moscow said, it would refuse to put the 1972 agreement into effect. Moscow froze payments on the Lend-Lease debt. Kissinger, in a statement on January 14 (**Document 5.11**), acknowledged that the deal was undone.

Arguments continue over the Jackson-Vanik Amendment's utility in promoting the emigration from the Soviet Union, particularly by Jews. Emigration statistics for Jews, Germans and Armenians (**Document 5.12**) suggest a rough correlation between the overall state of East-West relations and the amount of emigration the Soviets permitted. The peaks in emigration coincide with periods when relations were improving and the Soviets were seeking Western approval for arms control agreements. Troughs, with one exception, coincide with periods of hostility. The exception is the period from 1974–77, following the enactment of the amendment. That decline in emigration has been attributed to Soviet pique at the amendment and the collapse of the trade agreement. Soviet domestic political calculations also doubtless contributed to Moscow's emigration policy, and those internal factors remain only vaguely discernible to outsiders. But the German statistics, in particular, suggest that quiet diplomacy may be as, or even more, effective than coercion in securing Soviet cooperation, since West Germany has never linked trade and emigration. Though the Soviet leaders' motives for opening and closing the emigration gate remain, in the end, known only to themselves, the statistics offer no clear evidence that the Jackson-Vanik Amendment succeeded.

Document 5.1

U.S.-Soviet Grain Agreement of 1983

(Treaties and Other International Acts Series # 10828)

AGREEMENT BETWEEN
THE GOVERNMENT OF THE UNITED STATES OF AMERICA AND
THE GOVERNMENT OF THE UNION OF SOVIET SOCIALIST REPUBLICS
ON THE SUPPLY OF GRAIN

The Government of the United States of America ("USA") and the Government of the Union of Soviet Socialist Republics ("USSR"),

recalling the "Basic Principles of Relations between the United States of America and the Union of Soviet Socialist Republics" of May 29, 1972 and other relevant agreements between them;

desiring to strengthen long-term cooperation between the two countries on the basis of mutual benefit and equality;

mindful of the importance which the production of food, particularly grain, has for the peoples of both countries;

recognizing the need to stabilize trade in grain between the two countries; and

affirming their conviction that cooperation in the field of trade will contribute to overall improvement of relations between the two countries;

have agreed as follows:

ARTICLE I

The Government of the USA and the Government of the USSR hereby enter into an agreement for the purchase and sale of wheat and corn for supply to the USSR. To this end, during the period that this Agreement is in force, except as otherwise agreed by the Parties, the Soviet foreign trade organizations shall purchase from private commercial sources, for shipment in each twelve-month period beginning October 1, 1983, nine million metric tons of wheat and corn grown in the USA; in doing so, the Soviet foreign trade organizations, if interested, may purchase, on account of the said quantity, soybeans and/or soybean meal produced in the USA, in the proportion of one ton of soybeans and/or soybean meal for two tons of grain. In any case, the minimum annual quantities of wheat and corn shall be no less than four million metric tons each.

The Soviet foreign trade organizations may increase the nine million metric ton quantity mentioned above without consultations by as much as three million metric tons of wheat and/or corn for shipment in each twelve-month period beginning October 1, 1983.

The Government of the USA shall employ its good offices to facilitate and encourage such sales by private commercial sources.

Purchases/sales of commodities under this Agreement will be made at the market price prevailing for these products at the time of purchase/sale and in accordance with normal commercial terms.

ARTICLE II

During the term of this Agreement, except as otherwise agreed by the Parties, the Government of the USA shall not exercise any discretionary authority available to it under United States law to control exports of commodities purchased for supply to the USSR in accordance with Article I.

ARTICLE III

In carrying out their obligations under this Agreement, the Soviet foreign trade organizations shall endeavor to space their purchases in the USA and shipments to the USSR as evenly as possible over each twelve-month period.

ARTICLE IV

The Government of the USSR shall assure that, except as the Parties may otherwise agree, all commodities grown in the USA and purchased by Soviet foreign trade organizations under this

111

Agreement shall be supplied for consumption in the USSR.

ARTICLE V

Whenever the Government of the USSR wishes the Soviet foreign trade organizations to be able to purchase more wheat or corn grown in the USA than the amounts specified in Article I, it shall notify the Government of the USA.

Whenever the Government of the USA wishes private commercial sources to be able to sell to the USSR more wheat or corn grown in the USA than the amounts specified in Article I, it shall notify the Government of the USSR.

In both instances, the Parties will consult as soon as possible in order to reach agreement on possible quantities of grain to be supplied to the USSR prior to purchase/sale or conclusion of contracts for the purchase/sale of grain in amounts above those specified in Article I.

ARTICLE VI

The Government of the USA is prepared to use its good offices, as appropriate and within the laws in force in the USA, to be of assistance on questions of the appropriate quality of the grain to be supplied from the USA to the USSR.

FOR THE GOVERNMENT OF THE
UNITED STATES OF AMERICA:

JOHN R. BLOCK.

ARTICLE VII

It is understood that the shipment of commodities from the USA to the USSR under this Agreement shall be in accord with the provisions of the American-Soviet Agreement on Maritime Matters which is in force during the period of shipments hereunder.

ARTICLE VIII

The Parties shall hold consultations concerning the implementation of this Agreement and related matters at intervals of six months, and at any other time at the request of either Party.

ARTICLE IX

This Agreement shall enter into force on execution and shall remain in force until September 30, 1988, unless extended by the Parties for a mutually agreed period.

DONE at Moscow this twenty-fifth day of August, 1983, in duplicate, each in the English and Russian languages, both texts being equally authentic.

FOR THE GOVERNMENT OF THE
UNION OF SOVIET SOCIALIST REPUBLICS:

N. PATOLICHEV.

Document 5.2

Lend Lease Settlement

(Treaties and Other International Acts Series # 7478)

AGREEMENT BETWEEN
THE GOVERNMENT OF THE UNITED STATES OF AMERICA AND
THE GOVERNMENT OF THE UNION OF SOVIET SOCIALIST REPUBLICS
REGARDING SETTLEMENT OF LEND LEASE,
RECIPROCAL AID AND CLAIMS

The Government of the United States of America and the Government of the Union of Soviet Socialist Republics,

considering the need to settle obligations arising out of prosecution of the war against aggression in order to foster mutual confidence and the development of trade and economic relations between the two countries,

desiring to further the spirit of friendship and mutual understanding achieved by the leaders of both countries at the Moscow Summit,

recognizing the benefits of cooperation already received by them in the defeat of their common enemies, and of the aid furnished by each Government to the other in the course of the war, and

desiring to settle all rights and obligations of either Government from or to the other arising out of lend lease and reciprocal aid or otherwise arising out of the prosecution of the war against aggression,

have agreed as follows:

1. This Agreement represents a full and final settlement of all rights, claims, benefits and obligations of either Government from or to the other arising out of or relating to:

(a) the Agreement of June 11, 1942, between the Governments of the United States of America and the Union of Soviet Socialist Republics on principles applying to mutual aid in the prosecution of the war against aggression, including the arrangements between the two Governments preliminary to and replaced by said Agreement,

(b) the Agreement of October 15, 1945, between the Governments of the United States of America and the Union of Soviet Socialist Republics concerning the disposition of lend-lease supplies in inventory or procurement in the United States of America, and

(c) any other matter in respect of the conduct of the war against aggression during the period June 22, 1941 through September 2, 1945.

2. In making this Agreement both Governments have taken full cognizance of the benefits and payments already received by them under the arrangements referred to in Paragraph 1 above. Accordingly, both Governments have agreed that no further benefits will be sought by either Government for any obligation to it arising out of or relating to any matter referred to in said Paragraph 1.

3. (a) The Government of the Union of Soviet Socialist Republics hereby acquires, and shall be deemed to have acquired on September 20, 1945, all such right, title and interest as the Government of the United States of America may have in all lend lease materials transferred by the Government of the United States of America to the Government of the Union of Soviet Socialist Republics, including any article (i) transferred under the Agreement of June 11, 1942, referred to above, (ii) transferred to the Government of the Union of Soviet Socialist Republics under Public Law 11 of the United States of America of March 11, 1941, or transferred under that Public Law to any other government and retransferred prior to September 20, 1945 to the Government of the Union of Soviet Republics, (iii) transferred under the Agreement of October 15, 1945, referred to above, or (iv) otherwise transferred during the period June 22, 1941 through September 20, 1945 in connection with the conduct of the war against aggression.

(b) The Government of the United States of America hereby acquires, and shall be deemed to have acquired on September 20, 1945, all such right, title and interest as the Government of the Union of Soviet Socialist Republics may have in all reciprocal aid materials transferred by the Government of the Union of Soviet Socialist Republics to the

113

Government of the United States of America during the period June 22, 1941 through September 20, 1945.

4. (a) The total net sum due from the Government of the Union of Soviet Socialist Republics to the Government of the United States of America for the settlement of all matters set forth in Paragraph 1 of this Agreement shall be U.S. $722,000,000 payable as provided in subparagraphs (b), (c), and (d) of this Paragraph 4.

(b) (i) Three installments shall be due and payable as follows: $12,000,000 on October 18, 1972, $24,000,000 on July 1, 1973, and $12,000,000 on July 1, 1975. (ii) Subject to subparagraph (c) of this Paragraph 4, after the date ("Notice Date") on which a note from the Government of the United States of America is delivered to the Government of the Union of Soviet Socialist Republics stating that the Government of the United States of America has made available most-favored-nation treatment for the Union of Soviet Socialist Republics no less favorable than that provided in an Agreement Between the Governments of the United States of America and the Union of Soviet Socialist Republics Regarding Trade signed on the date hereof, the balance of $674,000,000 in payment of lend lease accounts shall be paid in equal installments ("Regular Installments") as follows:

(1) If the Notice Date falls on or before May 31, 1974, the first Regular Installment shall be due and payable on July 1, 1974, and subsequent Regular Installments shall be due and payable annually on July 1 of each year thereafter through July 1, 2001, or

(2) If the Notice Date falls on or after June 1, 1974, and (A) If the Notice Date occurs in the period of June 1 through December 1 of any year, the first Regular Installment shall be due and payable not more than 30 days following the Notice Date and subsequent Regular Installments shall be due and payable annually on July 1 of each year thereafter through July 1, 2001; or (B) If the Notice Date occurs in the period of December 2 of any year through May 31 of the following year, the first Regular Installment shall be due and payable on the July 1 next following the Notice Date and subsequent

Regular Installments shall be due and payable annually on July 1 of each year thereafter through July 1, 2001.

(c) In any year, upon written notice to the Government of the United States of America that a deferment of a Regular Installment (except the first and last Regular Installment) next due is necessary in view of its then current and prospective economic conditions, the Government of the Union of Soviet Socialist Republics shall have the right to defer payment of such Regular Installment ("Deferred Regular Installment"). Such right of deferment may be exercised on no more than four occasions. On each such occasion, without regard to whether the Government of the Union of Soviet Socialist Republics defers any subsequent Regular Installments, the Deferred Regular Installment shall be due and payable in equal annual installments on July 1 of each year commencing on the July 1 next following the date the Deferred Regular Installment would have been paid if the Government of the Union of Soviet Socialist Republics had not exercised its right of deferment as to such Regular Installment with the final payment on the Deferred Regular Installment on July 1, 2001, together with interest on the unpaid amount of the Deferred Regular Installment from time to time outstanding at three percent per annum, payable at the same time as the Deferred Regular Installment is due and payable.

(d) The Government of the Union of Soviet Socialist Republics shall have the right to prepay at any time all or any part of its total settlement obligation, provided that no such prepayment may be made at any time when any payment required to be made under this Paragraph 4 has not been paid as of the date on which it became due and payable.

5. Both Governments have agreed that this Agreement covers only rights, claims, benefits and obligations of the two Governments. Further, nothing in this Agreement shall be deemed to terminate the provisions of Article III of the Agreement of June 11, 1942, referred to above.

DONE at Washington in duplicate this eighteenth day of October, 1972, in the English and Russian languages, each text being equally authentic.

FOR THE GOVERNMENT OF THE
UNITED STATES OF AMERICA:

William P. Rogers

FOR THE GOVERNMENT OF THE UNION
OF SOVIET SOCIALIST REPUBLICS:

N.S. Patolichev

Document 5.3

1972 Trade Agreement and Related U.S. Letters

(From *Department of State Bulletin*, November 20, 1972, pp. 595–600.)

AGREEMENT BETWEEN
THE GOVERNMENT OF THE UNITED STATES OF AMERICA AND
THE GOVERNMENT OF THE UNION OF SOVIET SOCIALIST REPUBLICS
REGARDING TRADE

The Government of the United States of America and the Government of the Union of Soviet Socialist Republics,

considering that the peoples of the United States of America and of the Union of Soviet Socialist Republics seek a new era of commercial friendship, an era in which the resources of both countries will contribute to the well-being of the peoples of each and an era in which common commercial interest can point the way to better and lasting understanding,

having agreed at the Moscow Summit that commercial and economic ties are an important and necessary element in the strengthening of their bilateral relations,

noting that favorable conditions exist for the development of trade and economic relations between the two countries to their mutual advantage, desiring to make the maximum progress for the benefit of both countries in accordance with the tenets of the Basic Principles of Relations Between the United States of America and the Union of Soviet Socialist Republics signed in Moscow on May 29, 1972,

believing that agreement on basic questions of economic trade relations between the two countries will best serve the interests of both their peoples,

have agreed as follows:

ARTICLE 1

1. Each Government shall accord unconditionally to products originating in or exported to the other country treatment no less favorable than that accorded to like products originating in or exported to any third country in all matters relating to:

(a) customs duties and charges of any kind imposed on or in connection with importation or exportation including the method of levying such duties and charges;

(b) internal taxation, sale, distribution, storage and use;

(c) charges imposed upon the international transfer of payments for importation or exportation; and

(d) rules and formalities in connection with importation or exportation.

2. In the event either Government applies quantitative restrictions to products originating in or exported to third countries, it shall afford to like products originating in or exported to the other country equitable treatment vis-à-vis that applied in respect of such third countries.

3. Paragraphs 1 and 2 of this Article 1 shall not apply to (i) any privileges which are granted by either Government to neighboring countries with a view toward facilitating frontier traffic, or (ii) any preferences granted by either Government in recognition of Resolution 21 (II) adopted on March 26, 1968 at the Second UNCTAD [United Nations Conference on Trade and Development], or (iii) any action by either Government which is permitted under any multilateral trade agreement to which such Government is a party on the date of signature of this Agreement, if such agreement would permit such action in similar circumstances with respect to like products originating in or exported to a country which is a signatory thereof, or (iv) the exercise by either Government of its rights under Article 3 or 8 of this Agreement.

ARTICLE 2

1. Both Governments will take appropriate measures, in accordance with the laws and regulations then current in each country, to encourage and facilitate the exchange of foods and services between the two countries on the basis of mutual advantage and in accordance with the provisions of this Agreement. In expectation of such joint efforts, both

Governments envision that total bilateral trade in comparison with the period 1969–1971 will at least triple over the three-year period contemplated by this Agreement.

2. Commercial transactions between the United States of America and the Union of Soviet Socialist Republics shall be effected in accordance with the laws and regulations then current in each country with respect to import and export control and financing, as well as on the basis of contracts to be concluded between natural and legal persons of the United States of America and foreign trade organizations of the Union of Soviet Socialist Republics. Both Governments shall facilitate, in accordance with the laws and regulations then current in each country, the conclusion of such contracts, including those on a long-term basis, between natural and legal persons of the United States of America and foreign trade organizations of the Union of Soviet Socialist Republics. It is understood that such contracts will generally be concluded on terms customary in international commercial practice.

3. Both Governments, by mutual agreement, will examine various fields, in which the expansion of commercial and industrial cooperation is desirable, with regard for, in particular, the long-term requirements and resources of each country in raw materials, equipment and technology and, on the basis of such examination, will promote cooperation between interested organizations and enterprises of the two countries with a view toward the realization of projects for the development of natural resources and projects in the manufacturing industries.

4. The Government of the Union of Soviet Socialist Republics expects that, during the period of effectiveness of this Agreement, foreign trade organizations of the Union of Soviet Socialist Republics will place substantial orders in the United States of America for machinery, plant and equipment, agricultural products, industrial products and consumer goods produced in the United States of America.

ARTICLE 3

Each Government may take such measures as it deems appropriate to ensure that the importation of products originating in the other country does not take place in such quantities or under such conditions as to cause, threaten or contribute to disruption of its domestic market. The procedures under which both Governments shall cooperate in carrying out the objectives of this Article are set forth in

Annex 1, which constitutes an integral part of this Agreement.

ARTICLE 4

All currency payments between natural and legal persons of the United States of America and foreign trade and other appropriate organizations of the Union of Soviet Socialist Republics shall be made in United States dollars or any other freely convertible currency mutually agreed upon by such persons and organizations.

ARTICLE 5

1. The Government of the United States of America may establish in Moscow a Commercial Office of the United States of America and the Government of the Union of Soviet Socialist Republics may establish in Washington a Trade Representation of the Union of Soviet Socialist Republics. The Commercial Office and the Trade Representation shall be opened simultaneously on a date and at locations to be agreed upon.

2. The status concerning the functions, privileges, immunities and organization of the Commercial Office and the Trade Representation is set forth in Annexes 2 and 3, respectively, attached to this Agreement, of which they constitute an integral part.

3. The establishment of the Commercial Office and the Trade Representation shall in no way affect the rights of natural or legal persons of the United States of America and of foreign trade organizations of the Union of Soviet Socialist Republics, either in the United States of America or in the Union of Soviet Socialist Republics, to maintain direct relations with each other with a view to the negotiation, execution and fulfillment of trade transactions. To facilitate the maintenance of such direct relations the Commercial Office may provide office facilities at its location to employees or representatives of natural and legal persons of the United States of America, and the Trade Representation may provide office facilities at its location to employees or representatives of foreign trade organizations of the Union of Soviet Socialist Republics, which employees and representatives shall not be officers or members of the administrative, technical or service staff of the Commercial Office or the Trade Representation. Accordingly, the Commercial Office and the Trade Representation, and their respective officers and staff members, shall not participate directly in the negotiation, execution or fulfillment of trade transactions or otherwise carry on trade.

ARTICLE 6

1. In accordance with the laws and regulations then current in each country, natural and legal persons of the United States of America and foreign trade organizations of the Union of Soviet Socialist Republics may open their representations in the Union of Soviet Socialist Republics and the United States of America, respectively. Information concerning the opening of such representations and provision of facilities in connection therewith shall be provided by each Government upon the request of the other Government.

2. Foreign trade organizations of the Union of Soviet Socialist Republics shall not claim or enjoy in the United States of America, and private natural and legal persons of the United States of America shall not claim or enjoy in the Union of Soviet Socialist Republics, immunities from suit or execution of judgment or other liability with respect to commercial transactions.

3. Corporations, stock companies and other industrial or financial commercial organizations, including foreign trade organizations, domiciled and regularly organized in conformity to the laws in force in one of the two countries shall be recognized as having a legal existence in the other country.

ARTICLE 7

1. Both Governments encourage the adoption of arbitration for the settlement of disputes arising out of international commercial transactions concluded between natural and legal persons of the United States of America and foreign trade organizations of the Union of Soviet Socialist Republics, such arbitration to be provided for by agreements in contracts between such persons and organizations, or, if it has not been so provided, to be provided for in separate agreements between them in writing executed in the form required for the contract itself, such agreements:

(a) to provide for arbitration under the Arbitration Rules of the Economic Commission for Europe of January 20, 1966, in which case such agreement should also designate an Appointing Authority in a country other than the United States of America or the Union of Soviet Socialist Republics for the appointment of an arbitrator or arbitrators in accordance with those Rules; and

(b) to specify as the place of arbitration a place in a country other than the United States of America or the Union of Soviet Socialist Republics that is

a party to the 1958 Convention on the Recognition and Enforcement of Foreign Arbitral Awards.

Such persons and organizations, however, may decide upon any other form of arbitration which they mutually prefer and agree best suits their particular needs.

2. Each Government shall ensure that corporations, stock companies, and other industrial or financial commercial organizations, including foreign trade organizations, domiciled and regularly organized in conformity to the laws in force in the other country shall have the right to appear before courts of the former, whether for the purpose of bringing an action or of defending themselves against one, including but not limited to, cases arising out of or relating to transactions contemplated by this Agreement. In all such cases the said corporations, companies and organizations shall enjoy in the other country the same rights which are or may be granted to similar companies of any third country.

ARTICLE 8

The provisions of this Agreement shall not limit the right of either Government to take any action for the protection of its security interests.

ARTICLE 9

1. This Agreement shall enter into force upon the exchange of written notices of acceptance. This Agreement shall remain in force for three years, unless extended by mutual agreement.

2. Both Governments will work through the joint US-USSR Commercial Commission established in accordance with the Communique issued in Moscow on May 26, 1972, in overseeing and facilitating the implementation of this Agreement in accordance with the terms of reference and rules of procedure of the Commission.

3. Prior to the expiration of this Agreement, the joint US-USSR Commercial Commission shall begin consultations regarding extension of this Agreement or preparation of a new agreement to replace this Agreement.

IN WITNESS WHEREOF, the undersigned, duly authorized, have signed this Agreement on behalf of their respective Governments.

DONE at Washington in duplicate this 18th day of October, 1972, in the English and Russian languages, each being equally authentic.

For the Government of the
United States of America:

Peter G. Peterson.

For the Government of the Union
of Soviet Socialist Republics:

N. Patolichev.

Texts of Annexes to Agreement

ANNEX 1 TO THE AGREEMENT BETWEEN THE GOVERNMENT OF THE UNITED STATES OF AMERICA AND THE GOVERNMENT OF THE UNION OF SOVIET SOCIALIST REPUBLICS REGARDING TRADE

PROCEDURE FOR THE IMPLEMENTATION OF ARTICLE 3

1. Both Governments agree to consult promptly at the request of either Government whenever such Government determines that actual or prospective imports of a product originating in the other country under certain conditions or in certain quantities could cause, threaten or contribute to disruption of the market of the requesting country.

2. (a) Consultations shall include a review of the market and trade situation for the product involved and shall be concluded within sixty days of the request unless otherwise agreed during the course of such consultations. Both Governments, in carrying out these consultations, shall take due account of any contracts concluded prior to the request for consultations between natural and legal persons of the United States of America and foreign trade organizations of the Union of Soviet Socialist Republics engaged in trade between the two countries.

(b) Unless a different solution is agreed upon during the consultations, the quantitative import limitations or other conditions stated by the importing country to be necessary to prevent or remedy the market disruption situation in question shall be deemed agreed as between the two Governments.

(c) At the request of the Government of the importing country, if it determines that an emergency situation exists, the limitations or other conditions referred to in its request for consultations shall be put into effect prior to the conclusion of such consultations.

3. (a) In accordance with the laws and regulations then current in each country, each Government shall take appropriate measures to ensure that exports from its country of the products concerned do not exceed the quantities or vary from the conditions established for imports of such products into the other country pursuant to paragraphs 1 and 2 of this Annex 1.

(b) Each Government may take appropriate measures with respect to imports into its country to ensure that imports of products originating in the other country comply with such quantitative limitations or conditions as may be established in accordance with paragraphs 1 and 2 of this Annex 1.

ANNEX 2 TO THE AGREEMENT BETWEEN THE GOVERNMENT OF THE UNITED STATES OF AMERICA AND THE GOVERNMENT OF THE UNION OF SOVIET SOCIALIST REPUBLICS REGARDING TRADE

THE STATUS OF THE COMMERCIAL OFFICE OF THE UNITED STATES OF AMERICA IN THE UNION OF SOVIET SOCIALIST REPUBLICS

ARTICLE 1

The Commercial Office of the United States of America may perform the following functions:

1. Promote the development of trade and economic relations between the United States of America and the Union of Soviet Socialist Republics; and

2. Provide assistance to natural and legal persons of the United States of America in facilitating purchases, sales and other commercial transactions.

ARTICLE 2

1. The Commercial Office shall consist of one principal officer and no more than three deputy officers and a mutually agreed number of staff personnel, provided, however, that the number of officers and staff personnel permitted may be changed by mutual agreement of the two Governments.

2. The Commercial Office, wherever located, shall be an integral part of the embassy of the United

States of America in Moscow. The Government of the Union of Soviet Socialist Republics shall facilitate in accordance with its laws and regulations the acquisition or lease by the Government of the United States of America of suitable premises for the Commercial Office.

3. (a) The Commercial Office, including all of its premises and property, shall enjoy all of the privileges and immunities which are enjoyed by the Embassy of the United States of America in Moscow. The Commercial Office shall have the right to use cipher.

(b) The principal officer of the Commercial Office and his deputies shall enjoy all of the privileges and immunities which are enjoyed by members of the diplomatic staff of the Embassy of the United States of America in Moscow.

(c) Members of the administrative, technical and service staffs of the Commercial Office who are not nationals of the Union of Soviet Socialist Republics shall enjoy all of the privileges and immunities which are enjoyed by corresponding categories of personnel of the Embassy of the United States of America in Moscow.

ANNEX 3 TO THE AGREEMENT BETWEEN THE GOVERNMENT OF THE UNITED STATES OF AMERICA AND THE GOVERNMENT OF THE UNION OF SOVIET SOCIALIST REPUBLICS REGARDING TRADE

THE STATUS OF THE TRADE REPRESENTATION OF THE UNION OF SOVIET SOCIALIST REPUBLICS IN THE UNITED STATES OF AMERICA

ARTICLE 1

The Trade Representation of the Union of Soviet Socialist Republics may perform the following functions:

1. Promote the development of trade and economic relations between the Union of Soviet Socialist Republics and the United States of America; and

2. Represent the interests of the Union of Soviet Socialist Republics in all matters relating to the foreign trade of the Union of Soviet Socialist Republics with the United States of America and provide assistance to foreign trade organizations of the Union of Soviet Socialist Republics in facilitating purchases, sales and other commercial transactions.

ARTICLE 2

1. The Trade Representation shall consist of one principal officer, designated as Trade Representative, and no more than three deputy officers and a mutually agreed number of staff personnel, provided, however, that the number of officers and staff personnel permitted may be changed by mutual agreement of the two Governments.

2. The Trade Representation, wherever located, shall be an integral part of the Embassy of the Union of Soviet Socialist Republics in Washington. The Government of the United States of America shall facilitate in accordance with its laws and regulations the acquisition or lease by the Government of the Union of Soviet Socialist Republics of suitable premises for the Trade Representation.

3. (a) The Trade Representation, including all of its premises and property, shall enjoy all of the privileges and immunities which are enjoyed by the Embassy of the Union of Soviet Socialist Republics in Washington. The Trade Representation shall have the right to use cipher.

(b) The Trade Representative and his deputies shall enjoy all of the privileges and immunities which are enjoyed by members of the diplomatic staff of the Embassy of the Union of Soviet Socialist Republics in Washington.

Members of the administrative, technical and service staffs of the Trade Representation who are not nationals of the United States of America shall enjoy all of the privileges and immunities which are enjoyed by corresponding categories of personnel of the Embassy of the Union of Soviet Socialist Republics in Washington.

Related U.S. Letters

OCTOBER 18, 1972

DEAR MR. MINISTER: I have the honor to refer to our recent discussions relating to Article 3 and Annex 1 of the Agreement Between the Government of the United States of America and the Government of the Union of Soviet Socialist Republics Regarding Trade to be signed today. In accordance with those provisions and discussions, and consistent with current United States laws and regulations concerning exports, it is understood that the United States Government will meet its obligations under paragraph 3(a) of Annex 1 with respect to limitations or conditions established pursuant to a request of the Government of the Union of Soviet Socialist Republics under paragraphs 1 and 2 of Annex 1 by making available to United States exporters information regarding the quantities or conditions stated by the Government of the Union of Soviet Socialist Republics in its request, or as otherwise established following consultations provided for under Annex 1.

I further understand that the Government of the Union of Soviet Socialist Republics will limit or establish conditions on exports of any product from the Union of Soviet Socialist Republics to the United States if requested to do so in accordance with Annex 1.

I would appreciate receiving your confirmation of the foregoing understandings on behalf of the Government of the Union of Soviet Socialist Republics.

Please accept, Mr. Minister, the assurances of my highest consideration.

Sincerely yours,

PETER G. PETERSON

MR. N.S. PATOLICHEV,
Minister of Foreign Trade of the Union of Soviet Socialist Republics.

OCTOBER 18, 1972

DEAR MR. MINISTER: I have the honor to confirm, as was stated by my delegation in the course of the negotiations leading to the conclusion today of the Agreement Between the Government of the United States of America and the Government of the Union of Soviet Socialist Republics Regarding Trade, that while the Trade Representation of the Union of Soviet Socialist Republics in Washington established pursuant to Article 5 of said Agreement, its officers and staff members may engage in appropriate activities to promote trade generally between the two countries for the purposes of said Agreement, as is customary in international practice, United States legislation in force, i.e., Title 22 of the United States Code, Sections 252–254, makes it inappropriate for the Trade Representation, its officers and staff to participate directly in the negotiation, execution or fulfillment of trade transactions or otherwise carry on trade.

I have the further honor to confirm that at such time as the United States of America shall have become a party to the Vienna Convention on Diplomatic Relations, dated April 18, 1961, and its domestic legislation shall have been revised to accord fully with the terms of Articles 29 through 45 of the Convention, regarding diplomatic privileges and immunities, my Government will be prepared to give favorable consideration to amending the Agreement Between the Government of the United States of America and the Government of the Union of Soviet Socialist Republics Regarding Trade by deleting the second and third sentences of paragraph 3 of Article 5, thus permitting officers and members of the administrative, technical and service staffs of the Commercial Office of the United States of America in Moscow and the Trade Representation of the Union of Soviet Socialist Republics in Washinton to participate directly in the negotiation, execution and fulfillment of trade transactions and otherwise carry on trade.

Please accept, Mr. Minister, the assurances of my highest consideration.
Sincerely yours,

PETER G. PETERSON.

OCTOBER 18, 1972

DEAR MR. MINISTER: I have the honor to acknowledge the receipt of your letter of this date, with attachments, which reads as follows:

"Dear Mr. Secretary:

This is in response to your request for information on the procedures established by the Ministry of Foreign Trade for the accreditation of offices of foreign companies including United States companies, and on the facilities made available to such companies once accreditation has been approved.

United States companies will receive treatment no less favorable than that accorded to business entities of any third country in all matters relating to accreditation and business facilitation. Applications by United States firms for accreditation will be handled expeditiously. Any problems arising out of these applications that cannot readily be resolved through the regular procedures shall be resolved through consultation under the Joint US-USSR Commercial Commission at the request of either side.

As you have been advised, the USSR Chamber of Commerce and Industry and the State Committee of the Council of Ministers of the USSR for Science and Technology are establishing a large trade and economic exposition center which will include display pavilions of the various participating countries. The United States has been invited to have such a pavilion. Further, to meet the growing interest of foreign firms in establishing a permanent residence in Moscow, we have decided to construct a large trade center containing offices, hotel and apartment facilities and are asking United States companies to make proposals for and cooperate in the development and building of the trade center. The trade center will be used for, among other things, housing and office facilities for accredited United States companies.

Prior to the availability of these facilities, however, office facilities of an appropriate size in buildings accessible to trade sources will be made available as soon as possible once a United States company is accredited. The facilities to which such firms shall be entitled are explained in the attached information.

It is recognized that from time to time United States businessmen may have problems regarding such facilities which they are unable to resolve through discussions with various foreign trade organizations or other organizations. In such cases officials of my Ministry, as well as those of the State Committee of the Council of Ministers of the USSR for Science and Technology, shall be available through their respective protocol sections for assistance in resolving these problems.

Please accept, Mr. Secretary, the assurances of my highest consideration.
Sincerely yours,

N. PATOLICHEV

Mr. Peter G. Peterson
Secretary of Commerce of the United States of America"

I have the further honor to inform you that I have taken cognizance of the contents of the above letter and its attachments.
Please accept, Mr. Minister, the assurances of my highest consideration.
Sincerely yours,

PETER G. PETERSON

Document 5.4

Presidential Determination Regarding Export-Import Bank Credits to the Soviet Union

(From the *Department of State Bulletin*, November 20, 1972, p. 604.)

TEXT OF PRESIDENTIAL DETERMINATION

THE WHITE HOUSE,
WASHINGTON, OCTOBER 18, 1972

I hereby determine that it is in the national interest for the Export-Import Bank of the United States to guarantee, insure, extend credit and participate in the extension of credit in connection with the purchase or lease of any product or service by, for use in, or for sale or lease to the Union of Soviet Socialist Republics, in accordance with Section 2(b)(2) of the Export-Import Bank Act of 1945, as amended.

Richard Nixon

Document 5.5

Letter from Secretary Kissinger to Senator Jackson

(From the *Congressional Record*, December 13, 1974, p. 39785.)

October 18, 1974

Dear Senator Jackson:

I am writing to you, as the sponsor of the Jackson Amendment, in regard to the Trade Bill (H.R. 10710) which is currently before the Senate and in whose early passage the administration is deeply interested. As you know, Title IV of that bill, as it emerged from the House, is not acceptable to the administration. At the same time, the administration respects the objectives with regard to emigration from the U.S.S.R. that are sought by means of the stipulations in Title IV, even if it cannot accept the means employed. It respects in particular your own leadership in this field.

To advance the purposes we share both with regard to passage of the trade bill and to emigration from the U.S.S.R., and on the basis of discussions that have been conducted with Soviet representatives, I should like on behalf of the administration to inform you that we have been assured that the following criteria and practices will henceforth govern emigration from the U.S.S.R.

First, punitive actions against individuals seeking to emigrate from the U.S.S.R. would be violations of Soviet laws and regulations and will therefore not be permitted by the government of the U.S.S.R. In particular, this applies to various kinds of intimidation or reprisal, such as, for example, the firing of a person from his job, his demotion to tasks beneath his professional qualifications, and his subjection to public or other kinds or recrimination.

Second, no unreasonable or unlawful impediments will be placed in a way of persons desiring to make application for emigration, such as interference with travel or communications necessary to complete an application, the withholding of necessary documentation and other obstacles including kinds frequently employed in the past.

Third, applications for emigration will be processed in order of receipt, including those previously filed, and on a nondiscriminatory basis as regards the place of residence, race, religion, national origin and professional status of the applicant. Concerning professional status, we are informed that there are limitations on emigration under Soviet law in the case of individuals holding certain security clearances, but that such individuals who desire to emigrate will be informed of the date on which they may expect to become eligible for emigration.

Fourth, hardship cases will be processed sympathetically and expeditiously; persons imprisoned who, prior to imprisonment, expressed an interest in emigrating, will be given prompt consideration for emigration upon their release; and sympathetic consideration may be given to the early release of such persons.

Fifth, the collection of the so-called emigration tax on emigrants which was suspended last year will remain suspended.

Sixth, with respect to all the foregoing points, we will be in a position to bring to the attention of the Soviet leadership indications that we may have that these criteria and practices are not being applied. Our representations, which would include but not necessarily be limited to the precise matters enumerated in the foregoing points, will receive sympathetic consideration and response.

Finally, it will be our assumption that with the application of the criteria, practices, and procedures set forth in this letter, the rate of emigration from the U.S.S.R. would begin to rise promptly from the 1973 level and would continue to rise to correspond to the number of applicants. I understand that you and your associates have, in addition, certain understandings incorporated in a letter dated today respecting the foregoing criteria and practices which will henceforth govern emigration from the U.S.S.R. which you wish the President to accept as appropriate guidelines to determine whether the purposes sought through Title IV of the trade bill and further specified in our exchange of correspondence in regard to the emigration practices of non-market economy countries are being fulfilled. You have submitted this letter to me and I wish to advise you on behalf of the President that the understandings in your letter will be among the considerations to be applied by the President in exercising the authority provided for in Sec. 402 of Title IV of the trade bill.

I believe that the contents of this letter represent a good basis, consistent with our shared purposes, for proceeding with an acceptable formulation of Title IV of the trade bill, including procedures for periodic review, so that normal trading relations may go forward for the mutual benefit of the U.S. and the U.S.S.R.

Best regards,

Henry A. Kissinger

Document 5.6

Letter from Senator Jackson to Secretary Kissinger

(From the *Congressional Record*, December 13, 1974, pp. 39785–39786.)

October 18, 1974

Dear Mr. Secretary:

Thank you for your letter of Oct. 18 which I have now had an opportunity to review. Subject to the further understandings and interpretations outlined in this letter, I agree that we have achieved a suitable basis upon which to modify Title IV as passed by the House in circumstances that would substantially promote the objectives of Title IV.

It is our understanding that the punitive actions, intimidation or reprisals that will not be permitted by the government of the U.S.S.R. include the use of punitive conscription against persons seeking to emigrate, or members of their families; and the bringing of criminal actions against persons in circumstances that suggest a relationship between their desire to emigrate and the criminal prosecution against them.

Second, we understand that among the unreasonable impediments that will no longer be placed in the way of persons seeking to emigrate is the requirement that adult applicants receive the permission of their parents or other relatives.

Third, we understand that the special regulations to be applied to persons who have had access to genuinely sensitive classified information will not constitute an unreasonable impediment to emigration. In this connection we would expect such persons to become eligible for emigration within three years of the date on which they last were exposed to sensitive and classified information.

Fourth, we understand that the actual number of emigrants would rise promptly from the 1973 level and would continue to rise to correspond to the number of applicants, and may therefore exceed 60,000 per annum. We would consider a benchmark—a minimum standard of initial compliance—to be the issuance of visas at the rate of 60,000 per annum; and we understand that the President proposes to use the same benchmark as the minimum standard of initial compliance. Until such time as the actual number of emigrants corresponds to the number of applicants the benchmark figure will not include categories of persons whose emigration has been the subject of discussion between Soviet officials and other European governments.

In agreeing to provide discretionary authority to waive the provisions of subsections designated (a) and (b) and Sec. 402 of Title IV as passed by the House, we share your anticipation of good faith in the implementation of the assurances contained in your letter of Oct. 18 and the understandings conveyed by this letter. In particular, with respect to paragraphs three and four of your letter we wish it to be understood that the enumeration of types of punitive action and unreasonable impediments is not and cannot be considered comprehensive or complete and that nothing in this exchange of correspondence shall be construed as permitting types of punitive action or unreasonable impediments not enumerated therein.

Finally, in order adequately to verify compliance with the standard set forth in these letters, we understand that communication by telephone, telegraph and post will be permitted.

Sincerely yours,

Henry M. Jackson

Document 5.7

Letter from Soviet Foreign Minister Gromyko to Secretary Kissinger

(Reprinted in Paula Stern, *Water's Edge; Domestic Politics and the Making of American Foreign Policy*, Westport, Conn.: Greenwood Press, 1979, pp. 168–169. Copyright © 1979 by Paula Stern. Reprinted with permission.)

October 26, 1974

Dear Mr. Secretary of State,

I believe it necessary to draw your attention to the question of the publication in the United States of materials, including the correspondence between you and Senator Jackson, which create a distorted picture of our position as well as of what we told the American side on this matter.

When clarifying the actual state of affairs in response to your request, we underlined that the question as such is entirely within the internal competence of our state. We warned at the time that in this matter we had acted and shall act in strict conformity with our present legislation on that score.

But now silence is being kept about this very matter. At the same time, attempts are being made to ascribe to the elucidations that were furnished by us the nature of some assurances and almost obligations on our part regarding the procedure for the departure of Soviet citizens from the USSR. Some figures are even being quoted as to the supposed number of such citizens, and there is talk about an anticipated increase in that number as compared with previous years.

We resolutely decline such an interpretation. What we said, and you, Mr. Secretary of State, know this well, concerned only and exclusively the real situation concerning the given question. And when we did mention figures—to inform you of the real situation—the point was quite the opposite, namely about the present tendency toward a decrease in the number of persons wishing to leave the USSR and seek permanent residence in other countries.

We believe it important that in this entire matter, considering its principled significance, no ambiguities should remain as regards the position of the Soviet Union.

A. GROMYKO
Minister of Foreign Affairs of the USSR

Document 5.8

The Jackson-Vanik Amendment to the Trade Act of 1974 and Related Clauses

(Public Law 93–618, January 3, 1975)

TITLE IV—TRADE RELATIONS WITH COUNTRIES NOT CURRENTLY RECEIVING NONDISCRIMINATORY TREATMENT

SEC. 401. Exception of the products of certain countries or areas. Except as otherwise provided in this title, the President shall continue to deny nondiscriminatory treatment to the products of any country, the products of which were not eligible for the rates set forth in rate column numbered 1 of the Tariff Schedules of the United States on the date of the enactment of this Act.

SEC. 402. Freedom of emigration in East-West trade.

(a) To assure the continued dedication of the United States to fundamental human rights, and notwithstanding any other provision of law, on or after the date of the enactment of this Act products from any nonmarket economy country shall not be eligible to receive nondiscriminatory treatment (most-favored-nation treatment), such country shall not participate in any program of the Government of the United States which extends credits or credit guarantees or investment guarantees, directly or indirectly, and the President of the United States shall not conclude any commercial agreement with any such country, during the period beginning with the date on which the President determines that such country—

    (1) denies its citizens the right or opportunity to emigrate;

    (2) imposes more than a nominal tax on emigration or on the visas or other documents required for emigration, for any purpose or cause whatsoever; or

    (3) imposes more than a nominal tax, levy, fine, fee, or other charge on any citizen as a consequence of the desire of such citizen to emigrate to the country of his choice, and ending on the date on which the President determines that such country is no longer in violation of paragraph (1), (2), or (3).

(b) After the date of the enactment of this Act, (A) products of a nonmarket economy country may be eligible to receive nondiscriminatory treatment (most-favored-nation treatment), (B) such country may participate in any program of the Government of the United States which extends credits or credit guarantees or investment guarantees, and (C) the President may conclude a commercial agreement with such country, only after the President has submitted to the Congress a report indicating that such country is not in violation of paragraph (1), (2), or (3) of subsection (a). Such report with respect to such country shall include information as to the nature and implementation of emigration laws and policies and restrictions or discrimination applied to or against persons wishing to emigrate. The report required by this subsection shall be submitted initially as provided herein and, with current information, on or before each June 30 and December 31 thereafter so long as such treatment is received, such credits or guarantees are extended, or such agreement is in effect.

(c) (1) During the 18-month period beginning on the date of the enactment of this Act, the President is authorized to waive by Executive order the application of subsection (a) and (b) with respect to any country, if he reports to the Congress that—

    (A) he has determined that such waiver will substantially promote the objectives of this section; and

    (B) he has received assurances that the emigration practices of that country will henceforth lead substantially to the achievement of the objectives of this section.

  (2) During any period subsequent to the 18-month period referred to in paragraph (1), the President is authorized to waive by Executive order the application of subsections (a) and (b) with respect to any country, if the waiver authority granted by this subsection continues to apply to such country pursuant to subsection (d), and if he reports to the Congress that—

    (A) he has determined that such waiver will substantially promote the objectives of this section; and

    (B) he has received assurances that the emigration practices of that country will henceforth lead substantially to the achievement of the objectives of this section.

(3) A waiver with respect to any country shall terminate on the day after the waiver authority granted by this subsection ceases to be effective with respect to such country pursuant to subsection (d). The President may, at any time, terminate by Executive order any waiver granted under this subsection.

(d) (1) If the President determines that the extension of the waiver authority granted by subsection (c) (1) will substantially promote the objectives of this section, he may recommend to the Congress that such authority be extended for a period of 12 months. Any such recommendation shall—

(A) be made not later than 30 days before the expiration of such authority;

(B) be made in a document transmitted to the House of Representatives and the Senate setting forth his reasons for recommending the extension of such authority; and

(C) include, for each country with respect to which a waiver granted under subsection (c) (1) is in effect, a determination that continuation of the waiver applicable to that country will substantially promote the objectives of this section, and a statement setting forth his reasons for such determination.

(2) If the President recommends under paragraph (1) the extension of the waiver authority granted by subsection (c) (1), such authority shall continue in effect with respect to any country for a period of 12 months following the end of the 18-month period referred to in subsection (c) (1), if, before the end of such 18-month period, the House of Representatives and the Senate adopt, by an affirmative vote of a majority of the Members present and voting in each House and under the procedures set forth in section 153, a concurrent resolution approving the extension of such authority, and such resolution does not name such country as being excluded from such authority. Such authority shall cease to be effective with respect to any country named in such concurrent resolution on the date of the adoption of such concurrent resolution. If before the end of such 18-month period, a concurrent resolution approving the extension of such authority is not adopted by

the House and the Senate, but both the House and Senate vote on the question of final passage of such a concurrent resolution and—

(A) both the House and the Senate fail to pass such a concurrent resolution, the authority granted by subsection (c) (1) shall cease to be effective with respect to all countries at the end of such 18-month period;

(B) both the House and the Senate pass such a concurrent resolution which names such country as being excluded from such authority, such authority shall cease to be effective with respect to such country at the end of such 18-month period; or

(C) one House fails to pass such a concurrent resolution and the other House passes such a concurrent resolution which names such country as being excluded from such authority, such authority shall cease to be effective with respect to such country at the end of such 18-month period.

(3) If the President recommends under paragraph (1) the extension of the waiver authority granted by subsection (c) (1), and at the end of the 18-month period referred to in subsection (c) (1) the House of Representatives and the Senate have not adopted a concurrent resolution approving the extension of such authority and subparagraph (A) of paragraph (2) does not apply, such authority shall continue in effect for a period of 60 days following the end of such 18-month period with respect to any country (except for any country with respect to which such authority was not extended by reason of the application of subparagraph (B) or (C) of paragraph (2)), and shall continue in effect for a period of 12 months following the end of such 18-month period with respect to any such country if, before the end of such 60-day period, the House of Representatives and the Senate adopt, by an affirmative vote of a majority of the Members present and voting in each House and under the procedures set forth in section 153, a concurrent resolution approving the extension of such authority, and such resolution does not name such country as being excluded from such authority. Such authority shall cease to be effective with respect to any country named in such

concurrent resolution on the date of the adoption of such concurrent resolution. If before the end of such 60-day period, a concurrent resolution approving the extension of such authority is not adopted by the House and Senate, but both the House and Senate vote on the question of final passage of such a concurrent resolution and—

(A) both the House and the Senate fail to pass such a concurrent resolution, the authority granted by subsection (c) (1) shall cease to be effective with respect to all countries on the date of the vote on the question of final passage by the House which votes last;

(B) both the House and the Senate pass such a concurrent resolution which names such country as being excluded from such authority, such authority shall cease to be effective with respect to such country at the end of such 60-day period; or

(C) one House fails to pass such a concurrent resolution and the other House passes such a concurrent resolution which names such country as being excluded from such authority, such authority shall cease to be effective with respect to such country at the end of such 60-day period.

(4) If the President recommends under paragraph (1) the extension of the waiver authority granted by subsection (c) (1), and at the end of the 60-day period referred to in paragraph (3) the House of Representatives and the Senate have not adopted a concurrent resolution approving the extension of such authority and subparagraph (A) of paragraph (3) does not apply, such authority shall continue in effect until the end of the 12-month period following the end of the 18-month period referred to in subsection (c) (1) with respect to any country (except for any country with respect to which such authority was not extended by reason of the application of subparagraph (B) or (C) of paragraph (2) or subparagraph (B) or (C) of paragraph (3)), unless before the end of the 45-day period following such 60-day period either the House of Representatives or the Senate adopts, by an affirmative vote of a majority of the Members present and voting in that House and under the procedures set forth in section 153, a resolution disapproving the extension of such authority generally or with respect to such country specifically. Such authority

shall cease to be effective with respect to all countries on the date of the adoption by either House before the end of such 45-day period of a resolution disapproving the extension of such authority, and shall cease to be effective with respect to any country on the date of the adoption by either House before the end of such 45-day period of a resolution disapproving the extension of such authority with respect to such country.

(5) If the waiver authority granted by subsection (c) has been extended under paragraph (3) or (4) for any country for the 12-month period referred to in such paragraphs, and the President determines that the further extension of such authority will substantially promote the objectives of this section, he may recommend further extensions of such authority for successive 12-month periods. Any such recommendations shall—

(A) be made not later than 30 days before the expiration of such authority;

(B) be made in a document transmitted to the House of Representatives and the Senate setting forth his reasons for recommending the extension of such authority; and

(C) include, for each country with respect to which a waiver granted under subsection (c) is in effect, a determination that continuation of the waiver applicable to that country will substantially promote the objectives of this section, and a statement setting forth his reasons for such determination.

If the President recommends the further extension of such authority, such authority shall continue in effect until the end of the 12-month period following the end of the previous 12-month extension with respect to any country (except for any country with respect to which such authority has not been extended under this subsection), unless before the end of the 60-day period following such previous 12-month extension, either the House of Representatives or the Senate adopts, by an affirmative vote of a majority of the Members present and voting in that House and under the procedures set forth in section 153, a resolution disapproving the extension of such authority generally or with respect to such country specifically. Such authority shall cease to be effective with respect to all countries on the date of the adoption by either House before the end of such 60-day period of a resolution disapproving the extension of such authority, and shall cease to be effective with respect to any country on the date of the adoption by either House before the end of such 60-day period of a resolution disapproving the extension of such authority with respect to such country.

(e) This section shall not apply to any country the products of which are eligible for the rates set forth in rate column numbered 1 of the Tariff Schedules of the United States on the date of the enactment of this Act.

• • • • •

SEC. 404. Extension of nondiscriminatory treatment.

(a) Subject to the provisions of section 405(c), the President may by proclamation extend nondiscriminatory treatment to the products of a foreign country which has entered into a bilateral commercial agreement referred to in section 405.

(b) The application of nondiscriminatory treatment shall be limited to the period of effectiveness of the obligations of the United States to such country under such bilateral commercial agreement. In addition, in the case of any foreign country receiving nondiscriminatory treatment pursuant to this title which has entered into an agreement with the United States regarding the settlement of lend-lease reciprocal aid and claims, the application of such nondiscriminatory treatment shall be limited to periods during which such country is not in arrears on its obligations under such agreement.

(c) The President may at any time suspend or withdraw any extension of nondiscriminatory treatment to any country pursuant to subsection (a), and thereby cause all products of such country to be dutiable at the rates set forth in rate column numbered 2 of the Tariff Schedules for the United States.

SEC. 405. Authority to enter into commercial agreements.

(a) Subject to the provisions of subsections (b) and (c) of this section, the President may authorize the entry into force of bilateral commercial agreements providing nondiscriminatory treatment to the products of countries heretofore denied such treatment whenever he determines that such agreements

with such countries will promote the purposes of this Act and are in the national interest.

(b) Any such bilateral commercial agreement shall—
(1) be limited to an initial period specified in the agreement which shall be no more than 3 years from the date the agreement enters into force; except that it may be renewable for additional periods, each not to exceed 3 years; if—
(A) a satisfactory balance of concessions in trade and services has been maintained during the life of such agreement, and
(B) the President determines that actual or foreseeable reductions in United States tariffs and nontariff barriers to trade resulting from multilateral negotiations are satisfactorily reciprocated by the other party to the bilateral agreement;
(2) provide that it is subject to suspension or termination at any time for national security reasons, or that the other provisions of such agreement shall not limit the rights of any party to take any action for the protection of its security interests;
(3) include safeguard arrangements (A) providing prompt consultations whenever either actual or prospective imports cause or threaten to cause, or significantly contribute to, market disruption and (B) authorizing the imposition of such import restrictions as may be appropriate to prevent such market disruption;
(4) if the other party to the bilateral agreement is not a party to the Paris Convention for the Protection of Industrial Property, provide rights for United States nationals with respect to patents and trademarks in such country not less than the rights specified in such convention;
(5) if the other party to the bilateral agreement is not a party to the Universal Copyright Convention, provide rights for United States nationals with respect to copyrights in such country not less than the rights specified in such convention;
(6) in the case of an agreement entered into or renewed after the date of the enactment of the Act, provide arrangements for the protection of industrial rights and processes;
(7) provide arrangements for the settlement of commercial differences and disputes;
(8) in the case of an agreement entered into or renewed after the date of the enactment of

this Act, provide arrangements for the promotion of trade, which may include arrangements for the establishment or expansion of trade and tourist promotion offices, for facilitation of activities of governmental commercial officers, participation in trade fairs and exhibits, and the sending of trade missions, and for facilitation of entry, establishment, and travel of commercial representatives;

(9) provide for consultations for the purpose of reviewing the operation of the agreement and relevant aspects of relations between the United States and the other party; and

(10) provide such other arrangements of a commercial nature as will promote the purpose of this Act.

(c) An agreement referred to in subsection (a), and a proclamation referred to in section 404(a) implementing such agreement, shall take effect only if (1) approved by the Congress by the adoption of a concurrent resolution, referred to in section 151, or (2) in the case of an agreement entered into before the date of the enactment of this Act and a proclamation implementing such agreement, a resolution of disapproval referred to in section 152 is not adopted during the 90-day period specified by section 407(c)(2).

SEC. 406. Market disruption.
[See separate section.]

SEC. 407. Procedure for Congressional approval or disapproval of extension of nondiscriminatory treatment and Presidential reports.

(a) Whenever the President issues a proclamation under section 404 extending nondiscriminatory treatment to the products of any foreign country, he shall promptly transmit to the House of Representatives and to the Senate a document setting forth the proclamation and the agreement the proclamation proposes to implement, together with his reasons therefor.

(b) The President shall transmit to the House of Representatives and the Senate a document containing the initial report submitted by him under section 402(b) or 409(b) with respect to a nonmarket economy country. On or before December 31 of each year, the President shall transmit to the House of Representatives and the Senate, a document

containing the report required by section 402(b) or 409(b) as the case may be, to be submitted on or before such December 31.

(c) (1) In the case of a document referred to in subsection (a) (other than a document to which paragraph (2) applies), the proclamation set forth therein may become effective and the agreement set forth therein may enter into force and effect only if the House of Representatives and the Senate adopt, by an affirmative vote of a majority of those present and voting in each House, a concurrent resolution of approval (under the procedures set forth in section 151) of the extension of nondiscriminatory treatment to the products of the country concerned.

(2) In the case of a document referred to in subsection (a) which sets forth an agreement entered into before the date of the enactment of this Act and a proclamation implementing such agreement, such proclamation may become effective and such agreement may enter into force and effect after the close of the 90-day period beginning on the day on which such document is delivered to the House of Representatives and to the Senate, unless during such 90-day period either the House of Representatives or the Senate adopts, by an affirmative vote of a majority of those present and voting in that House, a resolution of disapproval (under the procedures set forth in section 152) of the extension of nondiscriminatory treatment to the products of the country concerned.

(3) In the case of a document referred to in subsection (b) which contains a report submitted by the President under section 402(b) or 409(b) with respect to a nonmarket economy country, if, before the close of the 90-day period beginning on the day on which such document is delivered to the House of Representatives and to the Senate, either the House of Representatives or the Senate adopts, by an affirmative vote of a majority of those present and voting in that House, a resolution of disapproval (under the procedures set forth in section 152) of the report submitted by the President with respect to such country, then, beginning with the day after the date of the adoption of such resolution of disapproval, (A) nondiscriminatory treatment shall not be in force with respect to the products of such country, and the

131

products of such country shall be dutiable at the rates set forth in rate column numbered 2 of the Harmonized Tariff Schedule of the United States, (B) such country may not participate in any program of the Government of the United States which extends credit or credit guarantees or investment guarantees, and (C) no commercial agreement may thereafter be concluded with such country under this title.

Document 5.9

Stevenson Amendment to the Export Import Bank Act

(Public Law 93–646)

SECTION 635e(3)(b)

After January 4, 1975, the [Export-Import] Bank shall not approve any loans or financed guarantees, or combination thereof, in connection with exports to the Union of Soviet Socialist Republics in an aggregate amount in excess of $300,000,000. No such loan or financial guarantee, or combination thereof, shall be for the purchase, lease, or procurement of any product or service for production (including processing and distribution) of fossil fuel energy resources. Not more than $40,000,000 of such aggregate amount shall be for the purchase, lease, or procurement of any product or service which involves research or exploration of fossil fuel energy resources. The President may establish a limitation in excess of $300,000,000 if the President determines that such higher limitation is in the national interest and if the President reports such determination to the Congress together with the reasons therefor, including the amount of such proposed increase which would be available for the export of products and services for research, exploration, and production (including processing and distribution) of fossil fuel energy resources in the Union of Soviet Socialist Republics, and if, after the receipt of such report together with the reasons, the Congress adopts a concurrent resolution approving such determination.

Document 5.10

Byrd Amendment to the Trade Act of 1974

(Public Law 93–618)

SECTION 613. LIMITATION ON CREDIT TO RUSSIA

After the date of enactment of the Trade Act of 1974, no agency of the Government of the United States, other than the Commodity Credit Corporation, shall approve any loans, guarantees, insurance, or any combination thereof, in connection with exports to the Union of Soviet Socialist Republics in an aggregate amount in excess of $300,000,000 without prior congressional approval as provided by law.

Document 5.11

Secretary Kissinger's January 14, 1975 Statement Concerning the Soviet Union's Decision Not to Enact the 1972 Trade Agreement

(From *Department of State Bulletin*, February 3, 1975, pp. 139–140.)

Since the President signed the Trade Act on January 3, we have been in touch with the Soviet Government concerning the steps necessary to bring the 1972 U.S-Soviet Trade Agreement into force.

Article 9 of that agreement provides for an exchange of written notices of acceptance following which the agreement, including reciprocal extension of nondiscriminatory tariff treatment (MFN) [most-favored-nation] would enter into force. In accordance with the recently enacted Trade Act, prior to this exchange of written notices, the President would transmit to the Congress a number of documents, including the 1972 agreement, the proposed written notices, a formal proclamation extending MFN to the U.S.S.R., and a statement of reasons for the 1972 agreement. Either House of Congress would then have had 90 legislative days to veto the agreement.

In addition to these procedures, the President would also take certain steps, pursuant to the Trade Act, to waive the applicability of the Jackson-Vanik amendment. These steps would include a report to the Congress stating that the waiver will substantially promote the objectives of the amendment and that the President has received assurances that the emigration practices of the U.S.S.R. will henceforth lead substantially to the achievement of the objectives of the amendment.

It was our intention to include in the required exchange of written notices with the Soviet Government language, required by the provisions of the Trade Act, that would have made clear that the duration of three years referred to in the 1972 Trade Agreement with the U.S.S.R. was subject to continued legal authority to carry out our obligations.

This caveat was necessitated by the fact that the waiver of the Jackson-Vanik amendment would be applicable only for an initial period of 18 months, with provision for renewal thereafter.

The Soviet Government has now informed us that it cannot accept a trading relationship based on the legislation recently enacted in this country. It considers this legislation as contravening both the 1972 Trade Agreement, which had called for an unconditional elimination of discriminatory trade restrictions, and the principle of noninterference in domestic affairs. The Soviet Government states that it does not intend to accept a trade status that is discriminatory and subject to political conditions and, accordingly, that it will not put into force the 1972 Trade Agreement. Finally, the Soviet Government informed us that if statements were made by the United States, in the terms required by the Trade Act, concerning assurances by the Soviet Government regarding matters it considers within its domestic jurisdiction, such statements would be repudiated by the Soviet Government.

In view of these developments, we have concluded that the 1972 Trade Agreement cannot be brought into force at this time and that the President will therefore not take the steps required for this purpose by the Trade Act. The President does not plan at this time to exercise the waiver authority.

The administration regrets this turn of events. It has regarded and continues to regard an orderly and mutually beneficial trade relationship with the Soviet Union as an important element in the overall improvement of relations. It will, of course, continue to pursue all available avenues for such an improvement, including efforts to obtain legislation that will permit normal trading relationships.

Document 5.12

Soviet Emigration Statistics, 1968–89

Year	Jews*	Germans**	Armenians***
1968	229	0	0
1969	2,979	0	0
1970	1,027	438	0
1971	13,022	886	0
1972	31,681	3,315	75
1973	34,733	4,436	185
1974	20,628	6,345	291
1975	13,221	5,752	455
1976	14,261	9,626	1,779
1977	16,736	9,119	1,390
1978	28,864	8,276	1,123
1979	51,320	6,947	3,581
1980	21,471	6,653	6,109
1981	9,447	3,595	1,905
1982	2,688	1,958	338
1983	1,315	1,447	193
1984	896	913	88
1985	1,140	406	109
1986	914	783	247
1987	8,155	14,488	3,248
1988	19,292	47,572	10,981
1989****	34,105	58,885	3,732

* — Figures compiled jointly by the government of Israel and the State Department.

** — Figures supplied to the State Department by Prof. Sidney Heitman, Colorado State University.

*** — Compiled by the Department of State.

**** — Through August 31. It should be noted that prior to 1988, handfuls of Soviet Pentacostalists emigrated with Israeli visas and were counted among Jewish emigres. Beginning in 1988, the number of Pentacostalists leaving the Soviet Union increased rapidly, and the State Department began compiling separate figures on them. In the first eight months of 1989, the number of Pentacostal emigrants was 7,770.

6

Economic Cooperation and the Helsinki Process

Harry C. Blaney III

The Conference on Security and Cooperation in Europe (CSCE) originated in a proposal made by the Warsaw Pact in 1969. It came to life in the era of Ostpolitik in West Germany under Willy Brandt, the 1971 agreement on Berlin, and détente in the United States, under the leadership of President Nixon and Secretary of State Kissinger to move East-West relations "from confrontation to negotiation." The West saw CSCE as a broad multilateral negotiating process aimed at lessening tensions with the Soviet Union and Eastern Europe and gradually opening up possibilities for strengthening currents of freedom and democracy across the totalitarian East. For the U.S.S.R., CSCE was a means to obtain political acceptance of the status quo in Europe—especially the borders established after World War II.

Lengthy negotiations and discussions—both within the North Atlantic Treaty Organization (NATO) and the Warsaw Pact and between their respective member states—eventually led to initial CSCE consultations. They were decisive in leading to initial CSCE deliberations, but the neutral and nonaligned states of Europe also played a role in launching the CSCE process.

The notion that the CSCE should include economic, technical and scientific issues originally was suggested at a Warsaw Pact foreign ministers' meeting in Prague in October 1969. In December of that year, NATO suggested an even broader agenda that included human rights, information, and environmental issues. Later, NATO added science. The Warsaw Pact accepted this expanded agenda in June 1970.

The process turned into a nearly permanent multilateral negotiation from the outset at Helsinki in July 1973, when 33 European states, the United States and Canada were present, their delegations headed by foreign ministers. At that 1973 meeting, the participants adopted the "Final Recommendations of the Helsinki Consultations," which set the agenda for a long series of formal meetings of the numerous CSCE working groups.

During the 1972–1973 Multilateral Preparatory Talks, the three so-called CSCE "baskets," or issue areas, were created. These baskets were established to incorporate the different priorities, interests and objectives of the diverse set of nations represented. Basket I dealt with "Questions Relating to Security in Europe." Basket II focused on "Cooperation in the Fields of Economics, of Science and Technology, and of the Environment." Basket III dealt with "Cooperation in Humanitarian and Other Fields." Agreement was also reached on an understanding to consider "Follow-Up" activities meant to sustain and further develop the CSCE process.

After nearly two years of negotiations at Geneva, the consultative work culminated in August, 1975 at the Helsinki Summit, when the heads of government of the 34 CSCE nations plus the Vatican adopted the "Final Act." This set forth, in broad terms, agreed provisions and principles to guide East-West relations and to act as a basis for evaluating progress.

The economic provisions of Basket II **(Document 6.1)**, calling for increased East-West economic interaction, promised, on paper at least, to reverse the general thrust of U.S. economic policy toward the Soviet Union. (By the time the Helsinki Summit approved Basket II, the United States had already enacted the Jackson-Vanik Amendment and other bilateral steps that inhibited trade, in addition to maintaining, through COCOM, a restrictive export control regime.) But in practice, Basket II has had little influence on American bilateral economic policies.

American concerns in the Helsinki process have focused mainly on the human rights provisions of Basket III and, increasingly, the security provisions of Basket I. The major Soviet objectives lay in the Basket I security issues, although the Soviets also hoped that progress in Basket II issues would legitimize an open approach to East-West trade, improve cooperation in science and technology, and—to a much lesser degree until very recently—promote collaboration on environmental issues. In general, however, neither superpower has made implementation of Basket II a high priority.

The Basket II provisions covered commercial exchanges, business contacts and facilities, economic and commercial information, marketing, industrial cooperation, trade, arbitration, and science and technology. The preamble to the operative economic sections stipulated that such activities would reinforce peace and security in Europe and would promote economic progress. The parties agreed to "intensify" such cooperation "irrespective" of their dissimilar systems. They also inserted a section underlining the importance of reciprocity and calling for equality among the participating nations. They agreed that the level of economic relations between the participating countries had not reached its potential and resolved to promote "the expansion of their mutual trade in goods and services, and to ensure conditions favorable to such development."

This statement was an implicit criticism, on the part of the Eastern countries, of political barriers that held down the level of trade between the blocs. The document also raised the question of most-favored nation tariff status and stated that the countries recognized the beneficial trade effects which it can yield. This was as far as consensus reached, however, at a time when the Soviet-American trade agreement had just collapsed because of Soviet anger at the Jackson-Vanik and Stevenson amendments.

The Basket II provisions also considered the long-term development of trade in the context of monetary and financial questions. They urged the Soviet Union to develop a more open, convertible currency system. They recognized the need of Eastern Bloc nations for credits and for access to Western financial institutions and loans.

The West charged that state controls in the East undercut initiatives by Western businessmen to gain access to contacts and information needed for developing commercial ties. The participating countries undertook to "reduce or progressively eliminate all kinds of obstacles to the development of trade..." They called for the creation of favorable conditions for the participation of companies in the development of East-West trade. And they recommended improving exchanges of information, particularly on trade and regulations. This was an indirect allusion to the murky information that many communist nations provided about their trade patterns and associated regulations.

In the years immediately after the Helsinki Summit, détente gave way to disillusionment. In that context, the CSCE review process, which commenced with a meeting held in Belgrade in 1977–1978, achieved only limited advances in the economic and trade field. During the post-Helsinki period, follow-up on Basket II issues was largely given to the Trade Committee of the United Nations' Economic Commission for Europe (ECE). But the ECE proved unable, in the end, to make significant progress. It provided a forum where both Western countries and members of the Soviet bloc's Council for Mutual Economic Assistance (CMEA) could talk about economic issues and make some minor progress on areas such as limiting transboundary air pollution.

Only slow improvement occurred in the problem areas cited in Basket II, most of it only in the latter half of the 1980s. Over time, East bloc nations developed their own statistical capability. They increasingly realized the importance foreign investment and trade could play in their economies. With this insight, they also better understood that they needed foreign credits from Western banks who insisted on accurate information. They turned to the United Nations' ECE to help them develop better data about economic activities and transparency of information about trade and financial flows.

In 1982, however, a report published by the U.S. Congress's CSCE Commission found major shortcomings in the Soviet bloc's compliance with Basket II. The commission cited lack of progress in the areas of economic and marketing information, facilitation of business contacts, access to industrial and commercial end-users, and free scientific exchange. The Soviets, in particular, were cited for the elimination of direct international telephone dialing service and the sudden, arbitrary, and exorbitant increases in the cost of business activities in Moscow. Far from improving, the commission charged, Soviet statistics had grown worse. There was no Soviet report, for instance, on the 1981 grain harvest.

Before the Soviet invasion of Afghanistan, the United States and other countries entered into discussions with the Soviet Union on 11 different economic subject areas. Hungary and Romania were accorded MFN treatment by Washington. Trade between East and West had grown tenfold from the levels it had fallen to at the depth of the Cold War. This reflected not so much the success of provisions in the Final Act, as a willingness on the part of some participating countries to seek advantage in economic cooperation under the general rubric of détente. But Afghanistan reversed that positive trend.

Following Belgrade, there was a second review conference in Madrid from September 1980 to July 1983, largely focused on human rights issues. It was held in the shadow of Afghanistan and the crackdown in Poland on supporters of Solidarity seeking

138

greater democracy and better working conditions. The United States used the Madrid forum to highlight publicly the U.S.S.R.'s many human rights violations.

Not surprisingly, Madrid yielded no follow-up meeting specifically on Basket II economic issues, although a seminar on economic, scientific, and cultural cooperation in the Mediterranean was approved. The Madrid meeting did, however, come to an agreement on the right of workers to organize and incorporated this principle into the CSCE documentation. It is a tenet which has been repeatedly violated by various signing states before and after they acceded to it in Madrid.

The follow-up meeting in Vienna from November, 1986 to January, 1989, was a milestone in the CSCE economic process. In effect, the meeting confirmed that CSCE was an ongoing process which had an indefinite ending date.

The major Basket II outcome of the Vienna meeting was an agreement to hold a conference on economic issues at Bonn in the spring of 1990. **(Document 6.2)** The main proponent of the meeting on the Western side was the Federal Republic of Germany,—specifically, its Foreign Minister, Hans-Dietrich Genscher. West Germany has always been one of the most enthusiastic Western advocates of trade with the East. The United States was skeptical, but in light of radical changes occurring in the Soviet Union and the series of Soviet-American summit meetings and agreements, it was difficult for America to be the sole holdout against the urging of a vital and determined ally.

In light of the accomplishments recorded in the human rights and security areas since 1975, Basket II seems thus far the least productive of the areas of activity covered in the Final Act. From the outset, the CSCE governments agreed only to broad principles and only politically binding language. Each participating nation had a distinct set of interests in East-West trade and did not want to be bound by any specific CSCE obligations or limits. Western European countries had already established strong trading and economic ties with individual countries in the Eastern Bloc, and they did not want to air those relationships. Nor did they want to debate them with the United States, since America often disagreed with Europe on the benefits of East-West trade. The Soviets, meanwhile, until recently remained preoccupied with their security and political objectives, and did not press very hard to advance Basket II economic objectives. The Eastern Europeans had their own reasons for passivity. They were either wary of

foreign—especially Western—involvement in their economies or they were largely focused on specific bilateral and private agreements.

Many of these factors have changed during the recent period of reform in the Soviet Union and Eastern Europe. Bonn is likely to see a very different atmosphere than existed in earlier CSCE fora.

Soviet objectives in the new CSCE Basket II arena are part-and-parcel of the larger Soviet policy of modernization and economic reform. General Secretary Mikhail Gorbachev has stated on a number of occasions that perestroika requires a deeper and more effective integration of modern science and technology into the productive process at all levels. While giving lip service to developing their indigenous technological base, Soviet experts acknowledge privately that the only way for their country to succeed in this is to utilize fully foreign technology and goods.

To this end, the Soviets see the Bonn conference as another mechanism to obtain a broad international consensus favoring improved trade and other economic benefits. Moreover, in 1975, the Soviets refused to acknowledge that their own antiquated economic system and backward infrastructure were the main barriers to their integration into the modern world's trading system. Now, they not only openly acknowledge the problem, but are fully engaged in the process of opening up their economy to the world.

The CSCE economic process serves the Soviets by enshrining trade as a normal and acceptable element in relations between capitalist and non-capitalist nations. It dovetails with decisions to permit a much wider range of access to international trade and hard currency by Soviet economic entities than at any time since the New Economic Policy era of the 1920s. The Soviets, belatedly, have truly tried to carry out many of the CSCE objectives in the Gorbachev era. For instance, within broad lines of governmental regulation, many individual Soviet enterprises can now buy and sell in the foreign market.

Joint ventures, specifically sanctioned by Basket II, have become a key element in the Soviet modernization strategy. This system was designed to obtain foreign—especially Western—know-how, technology and management expertise as cheaply as possible for the Soviet economy. Some East European governments, in the decade after the Helsinki Summit, used this concept effectively and widely. On the Western side, many businessmen, long wary of doing business with communists, may now look to the CSCE as a source of public and official approval for those activities. The agreement on the

Bonn meeting signaled that East-West economic cooperation was again a feasible course for Western countries.

Basket II seems ready to become a major forum for ongoing multilateral discussions of the broad issues and principles involved in East-West economic relations. It has moved from a set of general statements made more than a decade ago to a continuing program for fostering closer East-West economic ties.

Document 6.1

Excerpts from the Helsinki Final Act

(From *Department of State Bulletin*, September 1, 1975, pp. 323–338.)

The Conference on Security and Co-operation in Europe, which opened at Helsinki on 3 July 1973 and continued at Geneva from 18 September 1973 to 21 July 1975, was concluded at Helsinki on 1 August 1975 by the High Representatives of Austria, Belgium, Bulgaria, Canada, Cyprus, Czechoslovakia, Denmark, Finland, France, the German Democratic Republic, the Federal Republic of Germany, Greece, the Holy See, Hungary, Iceland, Ireland, Italy, Liechtenstein, Luxembourg, Malta, Monaco, the Netherlands, Norway, Poland, Portugal, Romania, San Marino, Spain, Sweden, Switzerland, Turkey, the Union of Soviet Socialist Republics, the United Kingdom, the United States of America and Yugoslavia.

During the opening and closing stages of the Conference the participants were addressed by the Secretary-General of the United Nations as their guest of honour. The Director-General of UNESCO and the Executive Secretary of the United Nations Economic Commission for Europe addressed the Conference during its second stage.

During the meetings of the second stage of the Conference, contributions were received, and statements heard, from the following non-participating Mediterranean States on various agenda items: the Democratic and Popular Republic of Algeria, the Arab Republic of Egypt, Israel, the Kingdom of Morocco, the Syrian Arab Republic, Tunisia.

Motivated by the political will, in the interest of peoples, to improve and intensify their relations and to contribute in Europe to peace, security, justice and co-operation as well as to rapprochement among themselves and with the other States of the world,

Determined, in consequence, to give full effect to the results of the Conference and to assure, among their States and throughout Europe, the benefits deriving from those results and thus to broaden, deepen and make continuing and lasting the process of détente,

The High Representatives of the participating States have solemnly adopted the following:

• • • • • •

CO-OPERATION IN THE FIELD OF ECONOMICS, OF SCIENCE AND TECHNOLOGY AND OF THE ENVIRONMENT

The participating States,

convinced that their efforts to develop co-operation in the fields of trade, industry, science and technology, the environment and other areas of economic activity contribute to the reinforcement of peace and security in Europe and in the world as a whole,

recognizing that co-operation in these fields would promote economic and social progress and the improvement of the conditions of life,

aware of the diversity of their economic and social systems,

reaffirming their will to intensify such co-operation between one another, irrespective of their systems,

recognizing that such co-operation, with due regard for the different levels of economic development, can be developed, on the basis of equality and mutual satisfaction of the partners, and of reciprocity permitting, as a whole, an equitable distribution of advantages and obligations of comparable scale, with respect for bilateral and multilateral agreements,

taking into account the interests of the developing countries throughout the world, including those among the participating countries as long as they are developing from the economic point of view; reaffirming their will to co-operate for the achievement of the aims and objectives established by the appropriate bodies of the United Nations in the pertinent documents concerning development, it being understood that each participating State maintains the positions it has taken on them; giving special attention to the least developed countries,

convinced that the growing world-wide economic interdependence calls for increasing common and effective efforts towards the solution of major world economic problems such as food, energy, commodities, monetary and financial problems, and therefore emphasizes the need for promoting stable and equitable international economic relations, thus contributing to the continuous and diversified economic development of all countries,

having taken into account the work already undertaken by relevant international organizations and wishing to take advantage of the possibilities offered by these organizations, in particular by the United Nations Economic Commission for Europe, for giving effect to the provisions of the final documents of the Conference,

considering that the guidelines and concrete recommendations contained in the following texts are aimed at promoting further development of their mutual economic relations, and convinced that their co-operation in this field should take place in full respect for the principles guiding relations among participating States as set forth in the relevant document,

have adopted the following:

1. Commercial Exchanges

General provisions

The participating States,

conscious of the growing role of international trade as one of the most important factors in economic growth and social progress,

recognizing that trade represents an essential sector of their co-operation, and bearing in mind that the provisions contained in the above preamble apply in particular to this sector,

considering that the volume and structure of trade among the participating States do not in all cases correspond to the possibilities created by the current level of their economic, scientific and technological development,

are resolved to promote, on the basis of the modalities of their economic co-operation, the expansion of their mutual trade in goods and services, and to ensure conditions favourable to such development;

recognize the beneficial effects which can result for the development of trade from the application of most favoured nation treatment;

will encourage the expansion of trade on as broad a multilateral basis as possible, thereby endeavouring to utilize the various economic and commercial possibilities;

recognize the importance of bilateral and multilateral intergovernmental and other agreements for the long-term development of trade;

note the importance of monetary and financial questions for the development of international trade, and will endeavour to deal with them with a view to contributing to the continuous expansion of trade;

will endeavour to reduce or progressively eliminate all kinds of obstacles to the development of trade;

will foster a steady growth of trade while avoiding as far as possible abrupt fluctuations in their trade;

consider that their trade in various products should be conducted in such a way as not to cause or threaten to cause serious injury—and should the situation arise, market disruption—in domestic markets for these products and in particular to the detriment of domestic producers of like or directly competitive products; as regards the concept of market disruption, it is understood that it should not be invoked in a way inconsistent with the relevant provisions of their international agreements; if they resort to safeguard measures, they will do so in conformity with their commitments in this field arising from international agreements to which they are parties and will take account of the interests of the parties directly concerned;

will give due attention to measures for the promotion of trade and the diversification of its structure;

note that the growth and diversification of trade would contribute to widening the possibilities of choice of products;

consider it appropriate to create favourable conditions for the participation of firms, organizations and enterprises in the development of trade.

Business contacts and facilities

The participating States,

Conscious of the importance of the contribution which an improvement of business contacts, and the accompanying growth of confidence in business relationships, could make to the development of commercial and economic relations,

will take measures further to improve conditions for the expansion of contacts between representatives of official bodies, of the different organizations, enterprises, firms and banks concerned with foreign trade, in particular, where useful, between sellers and users of products and services, for the purpose of studying commercial possibilities, concluding contracts, ensuring their implementation and providing after-sales services;

will encourage organizations, enterprises and firms concerned with foreign trade to take measures to accelerate the conduct of business negotiations;

will further take measures aimed at improving working conditions of representatives of foreign organizations, enterprises, firms and banks concerned with external trade, particularly as follows:

- by providing the necessary information, including information on legislation and procedures relating to the establishment and operation of permanent representation by the above mentioned bodies;
- by examining as favourably as possible requests for the establishment of permanent representation and of offices for this purpose, including, where appropriate, the opening of joint offices by two or more firms;
- by encouraging the provision, on conditions as favourable as possible and equal for all representatives of the above-mentioned bodies, of hotel accommodation, means of communication, and of other facilities normally required by them, as well as of suitable business and residential premises for purposes of permanent representation;

recognize the importance of such measures to encourage greater participation by small and medium sized firms in trade between participating States.

Economic and commercial information

The participating States,

conscious of the growing role of economic and commercial information in the development of international trade,

considering that economic information should be of such a nature as to allow adequate market analysis and to permit the preparation of medium and long term forecasts, thus contributing to the establishment of a continuing flow of trade and a better utilization of commercial possibilities,

expressing their readiness to improve the quality and increase the quantity and supply of economic and relevant administrative information,

considering that the value of statistical information on the international level depends to a considerable extent on the possibility of its comparability,

will promote the publication and dissemination of economic and commercial information at regular intervals and as quickly as possible, in particular:

- statistics concerning production, national income, budget, consumption and productivity;
- foreign trade statistics drawn up on the basis of comparable classification including breakdown by product with indication of volume and value, as well as country of origin or destination;
- laws and regulations concerning foreign trade;
- information allowing forecasts of development of the economy to assist in trade promotion, for example, information on the general orientation of national economic plans and programmes;
- other information to help businessmen in commercial contacts, for example, periodic directories, lists, and where possible, organizational charts of firms and organizations concerned with foreign trade;

will in addition to the above encourage the development of the exchange of economic and commercial information through, where appropriate, joint commissions for economic, scientific and technical co-operation, national and joint chambers of commerce, and other suitable bodies;

will support a study, in the framework of the United Nations Economic Commission for Europe, of the possibilities of creating a multilateral system of notification of laws and regulations concerning foreign trade and changes therein;

will encourage international work on the harmonization of statistical nomenclatures, notably in the United Nations Economic Commission for Europe.

Marketing

The participating States,

recognizing the importance of adapting production to the requirements of foreign markets in order to ensure the expansion of international trade,

conscious of the need of exporters to be as fully familiar as possible with and take account of the requirements of potential users,

will encourage organizations, enterprises and firms concerned with foreign trade to develop further the knowledge and techniques required for effective marketing;

will encourage the improvement of conditions for the implementation of measures to promote trade and to satisfy the needs of users in respect of imported products, in particular through market research and advertising measures as well as, where useful, the establishment of supply facilities, the furnishing of spare parts, the functioning of after sales services, and the training of the necessary local technical personnel;

will encourage international co-operation in the field of trade promotion, including marketing, and the work undertaken on these subjects within the international bodies, in particular the United Nations Economic Commission for Europe.

2. Industrial co-operation and projects of common interest

Industrial co-operation

The participating States,

considering that industrial co-operation being motivated by economic considerations, can

143

- create lasting ties thus strengthening long-term overall economic co-operation,
- contribute to economic growth as well as to the expansion and diversification of international trade and to a wider utilization of modern technology,
- lead to the mutually advantageous utilization of economic complementarities through better use of all factors of production, and
- accelerate the industrial development of all those who take part in such co-operation,

propose to encourage the development of industrial co-operation between the competent organizations, enterprises and firms of their countries;

consider that industrial co-operation may be facilitated by means of intergovernmental and other bilateral and multilateral agreements between the interested parties;

note that in promoting industrial co-operation they should bear in mind the economic structures and the development levels of their countries;

note that industrial co-operation is implemented by means of contracts concluded between competent organizations, enterprises and firms on the basis of economic considerations;

express their willingness to promote measures designed to create favourable conditions for industrial co-operation;

recognize that industrial co-operation covers a number of forms of economic relations going beyond the framework of conventional trade, and that in concluding contracts on industrial co-operation the partners will determine jointly the appropriate forms and conditions of co-operation, taking into account their mutual interests and capabilities;

recognize further that, if it is in their mutual interest, concrete forms such as the following may be useful for the development of industrial co-operation: joint production and sale, specialization in production and sale, construction, adaptation and modernization of industrial plants, co-operation for the setting up of complete industrial installations with a view to thus obtaining part of the resultant products, mixed companies, exchanges of ''know-how,'' of technical information, of patents and of licences, and joint industrial research within the framework of specific co-operation projects;

recognize that new forms of industrial co-operation can be applied with a view to meeting specific needs;

note the importance of economic, commercial, technical and administrative information such as to ensure the development of industrial co-operation;

consider it desirable:

- to improve the quality and the quantity of information relevant to industrial co-operation, in particular the laws and regulations, including those relating to foreign exchange, general orientation of national economic plans and programmes as well as programme priorities and economic conditions of the market; and
- to disseminate as quickly as possible published documentation thereon;

will encourage all forms of exchange of information and communication of experience relevant to industrial co-operation, including through contacts between potential partners and, where appropriate, through joint commissions for economic, industrial, scientific and technical co-operation, national and joint chambers of commerce, and other suitable bodies;

consider it desirable, with a view to expanding industrial co-operation, to encourage the exploration of co-operation possibilities and the implementation of co-operation projects and will take measures to this end, *inter alia*, by facilitating and increasing all forms of business contacts between competent organizations, enterprises and firms and between their respective qualified personnel;

note that the provisions adopted by the Conference relating to business contacts in the economic and commercial fields also apply to foreign organizations, enterprises and firms engaged in industrial co-operation, taking into account the specific conditions of this co-operation, and will endeavour to ensure, in particular, the existence of appropriate working conditions for personnel engaged in the implementation of co-operation projects;

consider it desirable that proposals for industrial co-operation projects should be sufficiently specific and should contain the necessary economic and technical data, in particular preliminary estimates of the cost of the project, information on the form of co-operation envisaged, and market possibilities, to enable potential partners to proceed with initial studies and to arrive at decisions in the shortest possible time;

will encourage the parties concerned with industrial co-operation to take measures to accelerate the conduct of negotiations for the conclusion of co-operation contracts;

recommend further the continued examination—for example within the framework of the United Nations Economic Commission for Europe—of means of improving the provision of information to those concerned on general conditions of industrial co-operation and guidance on the preparation of contracts in this field;

consider it desirable to further improve conditions for the implementation of industrial co-operation projects, in particular with respect to:

- the protection of the interests of the partners in industrial co-operation projects, including the legal protection of the various kinds of property involved;
- the consideration, in ways that are compatible with their economic systems, of the needs and possibilities of industrial co-operation within the framework of economic policy and particularly in national economic plans and programmes;

consider it desirable that the partners, when concluding industrial co-operation contracts, should devote due attention to provisions concerning the extension of the necessary mutual assistance and the provision of the necessary information during the implementation of these contracts, in particular with a view to attaining the required technical level and quality of the products resulting from such co-operation projects.

Projects of common interest

The participating States,

considering that their economic potential and their natural resources permit, through common efforts, long-term co-operation in the implementation, including at the regional or sub-regional level, of major projects of common interest, and that these may contribute to the speeding-up of the economic development of the countries participating therein,

considering it desirable that the competent organizations, enterprises and firms of all countries should be given the possibility of indicating their interest in participating in such projects, and, in case of agreement, of taking part in their implementation,

noting that the provisions adopted by the Conference relating to industrial cooperation are also applicable to projects of common interest,

regard it as necessary to encourage, where appropriate, the investigation by competent and interested organizations, enterprises and firms of the possibilities for the carrying out of projects of common interest in the fields of energy resources and of the exploitation of raw materials, as well as of transport and communications;

regard it as desirable that organizations, enterprises and firms exploring the possibilities of taking part in projects of common interest exchange with their potential partners, through the appropriate channels, the requisite economic, legal, financial and technical information pertaining to these projects;

consider that the fields of energy resources, in particular, petroleum, natural gas and coal, and the extraction and processing of mineral raw materials, in particular, iron ore and bauxite, are suitable ones for strengthening long-term economic co-operation and for the development of trade which could result;

consider that possibilities for projects of common interest with a view to long-term economic co-operation also exist in the following fields:

- exchanges of electrical energy within Europe with a view to utilizing the capacity of the electrical power stations as rationally as possible;
- co-operation in research for new sources of energy and, in particular, in the field of nuclear energy;
- development of road networks and co-operation aimed at establishing a coherent navigable network in Europe;
- co-operation in research and the perfecting of equipment for multimodal transport operations and for the handling of containers;

recommend that the States interested in projects of common interest should consider under what conditions it would be possible to establish them, and if they so desire, create the necessary conditions for their actual implementation.

3. Provisions concerning trade and industrial co-operation

Harmonization of standards

The participating States,

recognizing the development of international harmonization of standards and technical regulations and of international co-operation in the field of certification as an important means of eliminating technical obstacles to international trade and industrial co-operation, thereby facilitating their development and increasing productivity,

reaffirm their interest to achieve the widest possible international harmonization of standards and technical regulations;

express their readiness to promote international agreements and other appropriate arrangements on acceptance of certificates of conformity with standards and technical regulations;

consider it desirable to increase international co-operation on standardization, in particular by supporting the activities of intergovernmental and other appropriate organizations in this field.

Arbitration

The participating States,

considering that the prompt and equitable

settlement of disputes which may arise from commercial transactions relating to goods and services and contracts for industrial co-operation would contribute to expanding and facilitating trade and co-operation,

considering that arbitration is an appropriate means of settling such disputes,

recommend, where appropriate, to organizations, enterprises and firms in their countries, to include arbitration clauses in commercial contracts and industrial co-operation contracts, or in special agreements;

recommend that the provisions on arbitration should provide for arbitration under a mutually acceptable set of arbitration rules, and permit arbitration in a third country, taking into account existing intergovernmental and other agreements in this field.

Specific bilateral arrangements

The participating States,

conscious of the need to facilitate trade and to promote the application of new forms of industrial co-operation,

will consider favourably the conclusion, in appropriate cases, of specific bilateral agreements concerning various problems of mutual interest in the fields of commercial exchanges and industrial co-operation, in particular with a view to avoiding double taxation and to facilitating the transfer of profits and the return of the value of the assets invested.

4. Science and technology

The participating States,

convinced that scientific and technological co-operation constitutes an important contribution to the strengthening of security and co-operation among them, in that it assists the effective solution of problems of common interest and the improvement of the conditions of human life,

considering that in developing such co-operation, it is important to promote the sharing of information and experience, facilitating the study and transfer of scientific and technological achievements, as well as the access to such achievements on a mutually advantageous basis and in fields of co-operation agreed between interested parties,

considering that it is for the potential partners, i.e. the competent organizations, institutions, enterprises, scientists and technologists of the participating States to determine the opportunities for

mutually beneficial co-operation and to develop its details,

affirming that such co-operation can be developed and implemented bilaterally and multilaterally at the governmental and non-governmental levels, for example, through intergovernmental and other agreements, international programmes, co-operative projects and commercial channels, while utilizing also various forms of contacts, including direct and individual contacts,

aware of the need to take measures further to improve scientific and technological co-operation between them,

Possibilities for improving co-operation

Recognize that possibilities exist for further improving scientific and technological co-operation, and to this end, express their intention to remove obstacles to such co-operation, in particular through:

- the improvement of opportunities for the exchange and dissemination of scientific and technological information among the parties interested in scientific and technological research and co-operation including information related to the organization and implementation of such co-operation;
- the expeditious implementation and improvement in organization, including programmes, of international visits of scientists and specialists in connexion with exchanges, conferences and co-operation;
- the wider use of commercial channels and activities for applied scientific and technological research and for the transfer of achievements obtained in this field while providing information on and protection of intellectual and industrial property rights;

Fields of co-operation

Consider that possibilities to expand co-operation exist within the areas given below as examples, noting that it is for potential partners in the participating countries to identify and develop projects and arrangements of mutual interest and benefit:

Agriculture

Research into new methods and technologies for increasing the productivity of crop cultivation and animal husbandry; the application of chemistry to agriculture; the design, construction and utilization of agricultural machinery; technologies of irrigation and other agricultural land improvement works;

Energy

New technologies of production, transport and distribution of energy aimed at improving the use of existing fuels and sources of hydroenergy, as well as research in the field of new energy sources, including nuclear, solar and geothermal energy;

New technologies, rational use of resources

Research on new technologies and equipment designed in particular to reduce energy consumption and to minimize or eliminate waste;

Transport technology

Research on the means of transport and the technology applied to the development and operation of international, national and urban transport networks including container transport as well as transport safety;

Physics

Study of problems in high energy physics and plasma physics; research in the field of theoretical and experimental nuclear physics;

Chemistry

Research on problems in electrochemistry and the chemistry of polymers, of natural products, and of metals and alloys, as well as the development of improved chemical technology, especially materials processing; practical application of the latest achievements of chemistry to industry, construction and other sectors of the economy;

Meteorology and hydrology

Meteorological and hydrological research, including methods of collection, evaluation and transmission of data and their utilization for weather forecasting and hydrology forecasting;

Oceanography

Oceanographic research, including the study of air/sea interactions;

Seismological research

Study and forecasting of earthquakes and associated geological changes; development and research of technology of seism-resisting constructions;

Research on glaciology, permafrost and problems of life under conditions of cold

Research on glaciology and permafrost; transportation and construction technologies; human adaptation to climatic extremes and changes in the living conditions of indigenous populations;

Computer, communication and information technologies

Development of computers as well as of telecommunications and information systems; technology associated with computers and telecommunications, including their use for management systems, for production processes, for automation, for the study of economic problems, in scientific research and for the collection, processing and dissemination of information;

Space research

Space exploration and the study of the earth's natural resources and the natural environment by remote sensing in particular with the assistance of satellites and rocket-probes;

Medicine and public health

Research on cardiovascular, tumour and virus diseases, molecular biology, neurophysiology; development and testing of new drugs; study of contemporary problems of pediatrics, gerontology and the organization and techniques of medical services;

Environmental research

Research on specific scientific and technological problems related to human environment.

Forms and methods of co-operation

Express their view that scientific and technological co-operation should, in particular, employ the following forms and methods:

- exchange and circulation of books, periodicals and other scientific and technological publications and papers among interested organizations, scientific and technological institutions, enterprises and scientists and technologists, as well as participation in international programmes for the abstracting and indexing of publications;
- exchanges and visits as well as other direct contacts and communications among scientists and technologists, on the basis of mutual agreement and other arrangements, for such purposes as consultations, lecturing and conducting research, including the use of laboratories, scientific libraries, and other documentation centres in connexion therewith;
- holding of international and national conferences, symposia, seminars, courses and other meetings of a scientific and technological character, which would include the participation of foreign scientists and technologists;
- joint preparation and implementation of programmes and projects of mutual interest on

the basis of consultation and agreement among all parties concerned, including, where possible and appropriate, exchanges of experience and research results, and correlation of research programmes, between scientific and technological research institutions and organizations;

- use of commercial channels and methods for identifying and transferring technological and scientific developments, including the conclusion of mutually beneficial co-operation arrangements between firms and enterprises in fields agreed upon between them and for carrying out, where appropriate, joint research and development programmes and projects;

consider it desirable that periodic exchanges of views and information take place on scientific policy, in particular on general problems of orientation and administration of research and the question of a better use of large-scale scientific and experimental equipment on a co-operative basis;

recommend that, in developing co-operation in the field of science and technology, full use be made of existing practices of bilateral and multilateral co-operation, including that of a regional or subregional character, together with the forms and methods of co-operation described in this document;

recommend further that more effective utilization by made of the possibilities and capabilities of existing international organizations, intergovernmental and non-governmental, concerned with science and technology, for improving exchanges of information and experience, as well as for developing other forms of co-operation in fields of common interest, for example:

- in the United Nations Economic Commission for Europe, study of possibilities for expanding multilateral co-operation, taking into account models for projects and research used in various international organizations; and for sponsoring conferences, symposia, and study and working groups such as those which would bring together younger scientists and technologists with eminent specialists in their field;
- through their participation in particular international scientific and technological co-operation programmes, including those of UNESCO and other international organizations, pursuit of continuing progress towards the objectives of such programmes, notably those of UNISIST [World Science Information System] with particular respect to information policy guidance, technical advice, information contributions and data processing.

5. Environment

The participating States,

affirming that the protection and improvement of the environment, as well as the protection of nature and the rational utilization of its resources in the interests of present and future generations, is one of the tasks of major importance to the well-being of peoples and the economic development of all countries and that many environmental problems, particularly in Europe, can be solved effectively only through close international co-operation,

acknowledging that each of the participating States, in accordance with the principles of international law, ought to ensure, in a spirit of cooperation, that activities carried out on its territory do not cause degradation of the environment in another State or in areas lying beyond the limits of national jurisdiction,

considering that the success of any environmental policy presupposes that all population groups and social forces, aware of their responsibilities, help to protect and improve the environment, which necessitates continued and thorough educative action, particularly with regard to youth,

affirming that experience has shown that economic development and technological progress must be compatible with the protection of the environment and the preservation of historical and cultural values; that damage to the environment is best avoided by preventive measures; and that the ecological balance must be preserved in the exploitation and management of natural resources,

Aims of co-operation

Agree to the following aims of co-operation, in particular:

- to study, with a view to their solution, those environmental problems which, by their nature, are of a multilateral, bilateral, regional or subregional dimension; as well as to encourage the development of an interdisciplinary approach to environmental problems;
- to increase the effectiveness of national and international measures for the protection of the environment, by the comparison and, if appropriate, the harmonization of methods of gathering and analyzing facts, by improving the knowledge of pollution phenomena and rational utilization of natural resources, by the exchange of information, by the harmonization of definitions and the adoption, as far as possible, of a common terminology in the field of the environment;

- to take the necessary measures to bring environmental policies closer together and, where appropriate and possible, to harmonize them;
- to encourage, where possible and appropriate, national and international efforts by their interested organizations, enterprises and firms in the development, production and improvement of equipment designed for monitoring, protecting and enhancing the environment.

Fields of co-operation

To attain these aims, the participating States will make use of every suitable opportunity to co-operate in the field of environment and, in particular, within the areas described below as examples:

Control of air pollution

Desulphurization of fossil fuels and exhaust gases; pollution control of heavy metals, particles, aerosols, nitrogen oxides, in particular those emitted by transport, power stations, and other industrial plants; systems and methods of observation and control of air pollution and its effects, including long-range transport of air pollutants;

Water pollution control and fresh water utilization

Prevention and control of water pollution, in particular of transboundary rivers and international lakes; techniques for the improvement of the quality of water and further development of ways and means for industrial and municipal sewage effluent purification; methods of assessment of fresh water resources and the improvement of their utilization, in particular by developing methods of production which are less polluting and lead to less consumption of fresh water;

Protection of the marine environment

Protection of the marine environment of participating States, and especially the Mediterranean Sea, from pollutants emanating from land-based sources and those from ships and other vessels, notably the harmful substances listed in Annexes I and II to the London Convention on the Prevention of Marine Pollution by the Dumping of Wastes and Other Matters; problems of maintaining marine ecological balances and food chains, in particular such problems as may arise from the exploration and exploitation of biological and mineral resources of the seas and the sea-bed;

Land utilization and soils

Problems associated with more effective use of lands, including land amelioration, reclamation and recultivation; control of soil pollution, water and air erosion, as well as other forms of soil degradation; maintaining and increasing the productivity of soils with due regard for the possible negative effects of the application of chemical fertilizers and pesticides;

Nature conservation and nature reserves

Protection of nature and nature reserves; conservation and maintenance of existing genetic resources, especially rare animal and plant species; conservation of natural ecological systems; establishment of nature reserves and other protected landscapes and areas including their use for research, tourism, recreation and other purposes;

Improvement of environmental conditions in areas of human settlement

Environmental conditions associated with transport, housing, working areas, urban development and planning, water supply and sewage disposal systems; assessment of harmful effects of noise and noise control methods; collection, treatment and utilization of wastes, including the recovery and recycling of materials; research on substitutes for non-biodegradable substances;

Fundamental research, monitoring, forecasting and assessment of environmental changes

Study of changes in climate, landscapes and ecological balances under the impact of both natural factors and human activities; forecasting of possible genetic changes in flora and fauna as a result of environmental pollution; harmonization of statistical data, development of scientific concepts and systems of monitoring networks, standardized methods of observation, measurement and assessment of changes in the biosphere; assessment of the effects of environmental pollution levels and degradation of the environment upon human health; study and development of criteria and standards for various environmental pollutants and regulation regarding production and use of various products;

Legal and administrative measures

Legal and administrative measures for the protection of the environment including procedures for establishing environmental impact assessments.

Forms and methods of co-operation

The participating States declare that problems relating to the protection and improvement of the environment will be solved on both a bilateral and a multilateral, including regional and sub-regional, basis, making full use of existing patterns and forms of co-operation. They will develop co-operation in the field of the environment in particular by taking into consideration the Stockholm Declaration on the Human Environment, relevant resolutions of the United Nations General Assembly and the United Nations Economic Commission for Europe Prague symposium on environmental problems.

The participating States are resolved that co-operation in the field of the environment will be implemented in particular through:

- exchanges of scientific and technical information, documentation and research results, including information on the means of determining the possible effects on the environment of technical and economic activities;
- organization of conferences, symposia and meetings of experts;
- exchanges of scientists, specialists and trainees;
- joint preparation and implementation of programmes and projects for the study and solution of various problems of environmental protection;
- harmonization, where appropriate and necessary, of environmental protection standards and norms, in particular with the object of avoiding possible difficulties in trade which may arise from efforts to resolve ecological problems of production processes and which relate to the achievement of certain environmental qualities in manufactured products;
- consultations on various aspects of environmental protection, as agreed upon among countries concerned, especially in connexion with problems which could have international consequences.

The participating States will further develop such co-operation by:

- promoting the progressive development, codification and implementation of international law as one means of preserving and enhancing the human environment, including principles and practices, as accepted by them, relating to pollution and other environmental damage caused by activities within the jurisdiction or control of their States affecting other countries and regions;
- supporting and promoting the implementation of relevant international Conventions to which they are parties, in particular those designed to prevent and combat marine and fresh water pollution, recommending States to ratify Conventions which have already been signed, as well as considering possibilities of accepting other appropriate Conventions to which they are not parties at present;

- advocating the inclusion, where appropriate and possible, of the various areas of co-operation into the programmes of work of the United Nations Economic Commission for Europe, supporting such co-operation within the framework of the Commission and of the United Nations Environment Programme, and taking into account the work of other competent international organizations of which they are members;
- making wider use, in all types of co-operation, of information already available from national and international sources, including internationally agreed criteria, and utilizing the possibilities and capabilities of various competent international organizations.

The participating States agree on the following recommendations on specific measures:

- to develop through international co-operation an extensive programme for the monitoring and evaluation of the long-range transport of air pollutants, starting with sulphur dioxide and with possible extension to other pollutants, and to this end to take into account basic elements of a co-operation programme which were identified by the experts who met in Oslo in December 1974 at the invitation of the Norwegian Institute of Air Research;
- to advocate that within the framework of the United Nations Economic Commission for Europe a study be carried out of procedures and relevant experience relating to the activities of Governments in developing the capabilities of their countries to predict adequately environmental consequences of economic activities and technological development.

6. Co-operation in other areas

Development of Transport

The participating States,

considering that the improvement of the conditions of transport constitutes one of the factors essential to the development of co-operation among them,

considering that it is necessary to encourage the development of transport and the solution of existing problems by employing appropriate national and international means,

taking into account the work being carried out on these subjects by existing international organizations, especially by the Inland Transport Committee of the United Nations Economic Commission for Europe, note that the speed of technical progress in the various fields of transport makes desirable a development of co-operation and an increase in exchanges of information among them;

declare themselves in favour of a simplification and a harmonization of administrative formalities in the field of international transport, in particular at frontiers;

consider it desirable to promote, while allowing for their particular national circumstances in this sector, the harmonization of administrative and technical provisions concerning safety in road, rail, river, air and sea transport;

express their intention to encourage the development of international inland transport of passengers and goods as well as the possibilities of adequate participation in such transport on the basis of reciprocal advantage;

declare themselves in favour, with due respect for their rights and international commitments, of the elimination of disparities arising from the legal provisions applied to traffic on inland waterways which are subject to international conventions and, in particular, of the disparity in the application of those provisions; and to this end invite the member States of the Central Commission for the Navigation of the Rhine, of the Danube Commission and of other bodies to develop the work and studies now being carried out, in particular within the United Nations Economic Commission for Europe;

express their willingness, with a view to improving international rail transport and with due respect for their rights and international commitments, to work towards the elimination of difficulties arising from disparities in existing international legal provisions governing the reciprocal railway transport of passengers and goods between their territories;

express the desire for intensification of the work being carried out by existing international organizations in the field of transport, especially that of the Inland Transport Committee of the United Nations Economic Commission for Europe, and express their intention to contribute thereto by their efforts;

consider that examination by the participating States of the possibility of their accession to the different conventions or to membership of international organizations specializing in transport matters, as well as their efforts to implement conventions when ratified, could contribute to the strengthening of their co-operation in this field.

Promotion of tourism

The participating States,

aware of the contribution made by international tourism to the development of mutual understanding among peoples, to increased knowledge of other countries' achievements in various fields, as well as to economic, social and cultural progress,

recognizing the interrelationship between the development of tourism and measures taken in other areas of economic activity,

express their intention to encourage increased tourism on both an individual and group basis in particular by:

- encouraging the improvement of the tourist infrastructure and co-operation in this field;
- encouraging the carrying out of joint tourist projects including technical co-operation, particularly where this is suggested by territorial proximity and the convergence of tourist interests;
- dealing in a positive spirit with questions connected with the allocation of financial means for tourist travel abroad, having regard to their economic possibilities, as well as with those connected with the formalities required for such travel, taking into account other provisions on tourism adopted by the Conference;
- facilitating the activities of foreign travel agencies and passenger transport companies in the promotion of international tourism;
- encouraging tourism outside the high season;
- examining the possibilities of exchanging specialists and students in the field of tourism, with a view to improving their qualifications;
- promoting conferences and symposia on the planning and development of tourism;

consider it desirable to carry out in the appropriate international framework, and with the co-operation of the relevant national bodies, detailed studies on tourism, in particular:

- a comparative study on the status and activities of travel agencies as well as on ways and means of achieving better co-operation among them;
- a study of the problems raised by the seasonal concentration of vacations, with the ultimate objective of encouraging tourism outside peak periods;
- studies of the problems arising in areas where tourism has injured the environment;

consider also that interested parties might wish to study the following questions:

- uniformity of hotel classification; and

• tourist routes comprising two or more countries;

will endeavour, where possible, to ensure that the development of tourism does not injure the environment and the artistic, historic and cultural heritage in their respective countries;

will pursue their co-operation in the field of tourism bilaterally and multilaterally with a view to attaining the above objectives.

Economic and social aspects of migrant labour

The participating States,

considering that the movements of migrant workers in Europe have reached substantial proportions, and that they constitute an important economic, social and human factor for host countries as well as for countries of origin,

recognizing that workers' migrations have also given rise to a number of economic, social, human and other problems in both the receiving countries and the countries of origin,

taking due account of the activities of the competent international organizations, more particularly the International Labour Organization, in this area,

are of the opinion that the problems arising bilaterally from the migration of workers in Europe as well as between the participating States should be dealt with by the parties directly concerned, in order to resolve these problems in their mutual interest, in the light of the concern of each State involved to take due account of the requirements resulting from its socio-economic situation, having regard to the obligation of each State to comply with the bilateral and multilateral agreements to which it is party, and with the following aims in view:

to encourage the efforts of the countries of origin directed towards increasing the possibilities of employment for their nationals in their own territories, in particular by developing economic co-operation appropriate for this purpose and suitable for the host countries and the countries of origin concerned;

to ensure, through collaboration between the host country and the country of origin, the conditions under which the orderly movement of workers might take place, while at the same time protecting their personal and social welfare and, if appropriate, to organize the recruitment of migrant workers and the provision of elementary language and vocational training;

to ensure equality of rights between migrant workers and nationals of the host countries with regard to conditions of employment and work and to social security, and to endeavour to ensure that migrant workers may enjoy satisfactory living conditions, especially housing conditions;

to endeavour to ensure, as far as possible, that migrant workers may enjoy the same opportunities as nationals of the host countries of finding other suitable employment in the event of unemployment;

to regard with favour the provision of vocational training to migrant workers and, as far as possible, free instruction in the language of the host country, in the framework of their employment;

to confirm the right of migrant workers to receive, as far as possible, regular information in their own language, covering both their country of origin and the host country;

to ensure that the children of migrant workers established in the host country have access to the education usually given there, under the same conditions as the children of that country and, furthermore, to permit them to receive supplementary education in their own language, national culture, history and geography;

to bear in mind that migrant workers, particularly those who have acquired qualifications, can by returning to their countries after a certain period of time help to remedy any deficiency of skilled labour in their country of origin;

to facilitate, as far as possible, the reuniting of migrant workers with their families;

to regard with favour the efforts of the countries of origin to attract the savings of migrant workers, with a view to increasing, within the framework of their economic development, appropriate opportunities for employment, thereby facilitating the reintegration of these workers on their return home.

Training of personnel

The participating States,

Conscious of the importance of the training and advanced training of professional staff and technicians for the economic development of every country,

declare themselves willing to encourage co-operation in this field notably by promoting exchange of information on the subject of institutions, programmes and methods of training and advanced training open to professional staff and technicians in the various sectors of economic activity and especially in those of management, public planning, agriculture and commercial and banking techniques;

consider that it is desirable to develop, under mutually acceptable conditions, exchanges of professional staff and technicians, particularly through training activities, of which it would be left to the competent and interested bodies in the participating States to discuss the modalities—duration, financing, education and qualification levels of potential participants;

declare themselves in favour of examining through appropriate channels, the possibilities of co-operating on the organization and carrying out of vocational training on the job, more particularly in professions involving modern techniques.

(Signed at Helsinki on August 1, 1975)

Document 6.2

Excerpts from the Concluding Document of the CSCE Follow-Up Meeting in Vienna

(From *Department of State Bulletin*, March 1989, pp. 21–40.)

The representatives of the participating States of the Conference on Security and Co-operation in Europe (CSCE), Austria, Belgium, Bulgaria, Canada, Cyprus, Czechoslovakia, Denmark, Finland, France, the German Democratic Republic, the Federal Republic of Germany, Greece, the Holy See, Hungary, Iceland, Ireland, Italy, Liechtenstein, Luxembourg, Malta, Monaco, the Netherlands, Norway, Poland, Portugal, Romania, San Marino, Spain, Sweden, Switzerland, Turkey, the Union of Soviet Socialist Republics, the United Kingdom, the United States of America and Yugoslavia met in Vienna from 4 November 1986 to 19 January 1989 in accordance with the provisions of the Final Act relating to the Follow-up to the Conference, as well as on the basis of the other relevant CSCE documents.

The participants were addressed on 4 November 1986 by the Austrian Federal Chancellor.

Opening statements were made by all Heads of Delegations among whom were Ministers and Deputy Ministers of many participating States. Some Ministers of Foreign Affairs addressed the Meeting also at later stages.

The participants were addressed by a representative of the Secretary-General of the United Nations. Contributions were made by representatives of the United Nations Economic Commission for Europe (ECE) and UNESCO (UN Educational, Scientific & Cultural Organization).

Contributions were also made by the following non-participating Mediterranean States: Algeria, Egypt, Israel, Lebanon, Libya, Morocco, Syria and Tunisia.

The representatives of the participating States reaffirmed their commitment to the CSCE process and underlined its essential role in increasing confidence, in opening up new ways for cooperation, in promoting respect for human rights and fundamental freedoms and thus strengthening international security.

The participating States welcomed the favourable developments in the international situation since the conclusion of the Madrid Meeting in 1983 and expressed their satisfaction that the CSCE process has contributed to these developments. Noting the intensification of political dialogue among them and the important progress in negotiations on military security and disarmament, they agreed that renewed efforts should be undertaken to consolidate these positive trends and to achieve a substantial further improvement of their mutual relations. Accordingly, they reaffirmed their resolve to implement fully, unilaterally, bilaterally and multilaterally all the provisions of the Final Act and of the other CSCE documents.

As provided for in the agenda of the Vienna Meeting, the representatives of the participating States held a thorough exchange of views both on the implementation of the provisions of the Final Act, and the Madrid Concluding Document and of the tasks defined by the Conference, as well as, in the context of the questions dealt with by the latter, on the deepening of their mutual relations, the improvements of security and the development of cooperation in Europe and the development of the process of détente in the future.

During this exchange of views the participating States examined thoroughly and in detail the implementation of the Final Act and of the Madrid Concluding Document. Different and at times contradictory opinions were expressed about the extent of the realization of these commitments. While encouraging developments were noted in many areas, the participants criticized the continuing serious deficiencies in the implementation of these documents.

An open and frank discussion was held about the application of and respect for the principles of the Final Act. Concern was expressed about serious violations of a number of these principles. In particular, questions relating to respect for human rights and fundamental freedoms were the focus of intensive and controversial discussion. The participating States agreed that full respect for the principles, in all their aspects, is essential for the improvement of their mutual relations.

The implementation of the provisions of the Final Act concerning confidence-building measures, co-operation in the field of economics, of science and technology and of environment, concerning questions relating to security and cooperation in the Mediterranean as well as concerning cooperation in humanitarian and other fields was discussed. The implementation of the provisions of the Madrid Concluding Document and of other CSCE documents was also discussed. It was considered that the numerous possibilities offered by the Final Act had not been sufficiently utilized.

The participating States also expressed concern about the spread of terrorism and condemned it unreservedly.

The discussion reflected the broader context of the CSCE process and confirmed the importance of taking into account its world dimension in implementing the provisions of the Final Act.

In their deliberations the representatives of the participating States took into account the results of

- the Stockholm Conference on Confidence and Security-Building Measures and Disarmament in Europe;
- the Athens Meeting of Experts in order to pursue the examination and elaboration of a generally acceptable method for the peaceful settlement of disputes aimed at complementing existing methods;
- the Venice Seminar on Economic, Scientific and Cultural Co-operation in the Mediterranean;
- the Ottawa Meeting of Experts on Questions concerning Respect, in their States, for Human Rights and Fundamental Freedoms, in all their Aspects, as embodied in the Final Act;
- the Budapest "Cultural Forum";
- the Bern Meeting of Experts on Human Contacts.

The participating States moreover noted that the tenth anniversary of the signing of the Final Act had been commemorated at Helsinki on 1 August 1985.

The participating States reaffirmed their commitment to the continuation of the CSCE process as agreed to in the chapter on the Follow-up to the Conference contained in the Final Act.

• • • • • •

Co-operation in the Field of Economics, of Science and Technology and of the Environment

The participating States reaffirm their willingness to further their co-operation in the fields of economics, of science and technology and of the environment, and to promote stable and equitable international economic relations in the interest of all States. They express their readiness to intensify the dialogue in the competent fora with a view to facilitating appropriate solutions for key interrelated economic issues such as money, finance, debt and

trade. In this connection they stress the importance of policies aimed at promoting structural adjustments, stimulating the growth of national economies and creating an international economic environment conducive to development.

The participating States recognize the important role of the United Nations Economic Commission for Europe (ECE) in fostering regional economic co-operation and in contributing to the implementation of the provisions of the Final Act and subsequent CSCE documents. They express their readiness to make further use of the existing framework, resources and experience of the ECE in areas which are of significance for the implementation of recommendations of the CSCE.

Trade and Industrial Cooperation

1. In order to make better use of their economic potential, and to foster the expansion of their commercial exchanges, the participating States will make further efforts to promote favourable conditions for trade and industrial co-operation, taking into account all the relevant provisions of the Final Act and the Madrid Concluding Document.

2. The participating States recognize the importance of favourable business conditions for the development of trade between them. They will facilitate direct contacts between business people, potential buyers and end-users, including on-site contacts relevant to the business intended or being transacted. They will take measures to improve working conditions for business people regarding, among other things, accreditation, accommodation, communications and recruitment and management of personnel. They will also take measures to avoid unjustifiable delays in visa procedures and customs clearance. Further, they recognize the opportunities offered by trade fairs and exhibitions for developing commercial contacts and achieving concrete business results.

3. The participating States will continue their efforts further to reduce or progressively eliminate obstacles of all kinds to trade, thus contributing to the expansion and diversification of their commercial relations. They express their support for the work done in this field in appropriate international fora.

4. The participating States will encourage forms of trade compatible with the efficient conduct of international business relations and will also encourage business partners to decide independently upon their trading patterns. As to compensation transactions in all their forms, they recommend that proposals of this kind be addressed at the beginning of negotiations and, when agreed upon, dealt

with in a flexible way, especially regarding the choice of products. In this connection the special concerns of small and medium-sized enterprises should be taken into account. The participating States recognize the valuable role of the ECE in dealing with questions related to compensation transactions.

5. The participating States recognize that, within their respective economies, increased autonomy for enterprises can help achieve a better response to market needs and thus contribute to the development of trade and co-operation among them.

6. In order to facilitate the identification of market opportunities, the participating States will further promote the publication and availability of comprehensive, comparable and timely economic and commercial information. They will publish up-to-date macroeconomic information and statistics, and envisage making balance of payments figures available. They will also provide the United Nations trade data-bank, COMTRADE, with detailed data in a format relevant to the efficient conduct of foreign trade. They will encourage co-operation between their statistical services and within the framework of the ECE in order, *inter alia*, to facilitate the identification of disparities in foreign trade statistics and to improve the international comparability of such statistics. Furthermore, they consider it useful to increase the publication and exchange of statistics on such topics as demography, public health, agriculture, the environment and energy.

7. Noting the growing importance of services in their mutual economic relations, the participating States will examine, in appropriate bodies, developments in this area and prospects for improved access to the services' market.

8. Affirming the importance of industrial co-operation in their long-term economic relations, the participating States will promote measures designed to create favourable conditions for the development of such co-operation. They will therefore examine, within the competent fora, the improvement of the legal, administrative and economic framework for industrial co-operation. Furthermore, they will exchange contacts between potential partners, develop exchanges of appropriate information and promote the participation of small and medium-sized enterprises in industrial co-operation.

9. The participating States recognize that productive, competitive and profit-earning joint ventures can play a role in mutually beneficial industrial co-operation. They will improve the legal, administrative and financial conditions for investment in, and operation of, joint ventures. They will also promote the exchange of all information relevant to the establishment of joint ventures, including all necessary technical information, as well as information on management, labour conditions, accounting and taxation, repatriation of profits and the protection of investments, production conditions and access to domestic supplies and markets.

10. The participating States stress the importance of their standardization policies and practices, and of related activities for the facilitation of international trade, especially regarding products subject to compulsory certification. Accordingly, they will consider mutual recognition of their national testing and certification procedures and practices, and promote co-operation among relevant national bodies and within international organizations including the ECE.

11. The participating States recognize the growing importance of effective marketing in the development of trade and industrial co-operation, in the production and promotion of new products and in meeting the needs of the consumer. Given the growth of marketing opportunities, they will seek to improve the conditions for firms and organizations engaging in research into domestic or foreign markets and in other marketing activities.

12. The participating States affirm the usefulness for all enterprises, and especially for small and medium-sized ones, of flexible and mutually agreed arbitration provisions for ensuring the equitable settlement of disputes in international trade and industrial co-operation. Bearing in mind the relevant provisions of the Final Act and the Madrid Concluding Document they attach particular importance to freedom in the choice of arbitrators, including the presiding arbitrator, and of the country of arbitration. They recommend that consideration be given to the adoption of the Model Law on international commercial arbitration of the United Nations Commission on International Trade Law (UNCITRAL). In addition, they recognize the value of agreements on co-operation in the field of commercial arbitration between Chambers of Commerce and other arbitration bodies.

13. The participating States agree to convene a Conference on Economic Co-operation in Europe. This Conference will take place in Bonn from 19 March to 11 April 1990. The aim of the Conference is to provide new impulses for economic relations between participating States, in particular by improving business conditions for commercial exchanges and industrial co-operation, and by considering new possibilities for, and ways of, economic co-operation. The Conference will be attended by representatives of the participating States

and of the business community. The agenda, timetable and other organizations' modalities are set out in Annex V. The next Follow-up Meeting, to be held in Helsinki, commencing on 24 March 1992, will assess the results achieved at the Conference.

Science and Technology

14. The participating States emphasize the important role of science and technology in their overall economic and social development, bearing in mind particularly those sciences and technologies which are of direct relevance to improving the quality of life.

15. Recognizing the importance of scientific and technological co-operation the participating States will develop further mutually advantageous co-operation in the fields already set forth in the Final Act, and will examine possibilities for co-operation in new areas of growing importance and common interest. Furthermore, they express their intention to improve conditions for such co-operation by fostering the exchange of information on, and experience with, scientific and technological achievements, having in mind especially the interests of the countries of the region which are developing from the economic point of view.

16. The participating States also reaffirm the role of general intergovernmental agreements as well as of bilateral agreements involving universities, scientific and technological institutions and industry, in developing mutually beneficial exchanges. Underlining the importance of freedom of communication and exchange of views for progress in science and technology, they will promote and support direct and individual contacts between scientists, specialists and interested business people. Recalling the conclusions reached at the Hamburg Scientific Forum, they will respect human rights and fundamental freedoms, which represent one of the foundations for a significant improvement in international scientific co-operation at all levels. They will also endeavour to create conditions enabling interested partners to develop appropriate joint research programmes and projects on the basis of reciprocity and mutual advantage and, when appropriate, on a commercial basis.

17. Given the depletion of natural resources, including non-renewable sources of energy, the participating States will promote co-operation in the rational use of such resources, and in the use of alternative sources of energy, including thermonuclear fusion.

18. Taking note of the progress made in, and the new opportunities offered by, research and development in biotechnology, the participating States consider it desirable to enhance the exchange of information on laws and regulations relating to the safety aspects of genetic engineering. They will therefore facilitate consultation and exchange of information on safety guidelines. In this context they emphasize the importance of ethical principles when dealing with genetic engineering and its application.

19. The participating States will develop their co-operation in medical and related sciences by intensifying research and the exchange of information on drug abuse and on new or increasingly wide-spread diseases. They will co-operate in particular in combating the spread of AIDS (acquired immune deficiency syndrome), taking into account the global AIDS Strategy of the World Health Organization (WHO). They will also co-operate in research concerning the long-term consequences of radiation.

20. The participating States recognize the importance of scientific research, of environmentally sound technologies and, in particular, of improved international cooperation in these fields, for the monitoring, prevention and reduction of pollution. They will therefore promote, *inter alia*, within the relevant international fora, exchange of information on, and experience with, these technologies. In this respect they will also promote, on a commercial basis, exchanges in the fields of pollution-abatement technologies, technologies and products with less or no emission of ozone-depleting substances, processing and combustion techniques, new methods of waste treatment, including recycling and disposal, and low- and non-waste technologies.

21. The participating States will exchange appropriate information in specific fields of engineering industries and automation. They will do this on the basis of mutual advantage for potential partners, who will decide independently on the areas of co-operation and with due respect for bilateral and multilateral agreements. To this end they will, *inter alia*, develop statistics in fields of engineering industries of commercial importance.

22. In the context of their scientific and technological co-operation, the participating States will consider the possibility of encouraging the development and use of alternatives to animal experimentation, including for product testing.

23. In the important field of nuclear energy, the participating States recognize that, while individual States should assume full responsibility for the safety of their own nuclear facilities, nuclear safety requires closer international co-operation, especially within the International Atomic Energy Agency (IAEA). They note that it is essential to maintain the

highest possible safety standards in the management and operation of nuclear facilities. They therefore support the work done within the IAEA in developing basic safety principles, and urge all States to use the revised Nuclear Safety Standards—NUSS codes—as a basis for regulating nuclear safety practices. They also recall the need further to improve the efficiency of the existing system of nuclear liability.

Environment

24. Recognizing the need for preventive action, the participating States will strengthen their co-operation and intensify efforts aimed at protecting and improving the environment, bearing in mind the need to maintain and restore the ecological balance in air, water and soil. They will do this by, *inter alia*, developing their internal legislation and international commitments, and by applying the best available means, taking into account levels of development as well as economic and technical constraints. They underline the importance of the Regional Strategy for Environmental Protection and Rational Use of Natural Resources in ECE Member Countries Covering the Period up to the Year 2000 and Beyond. They welcome, and will take due account of the report of the World Commission on Environment and Development and the Environmental Perspective to the Year 2000 and Beyond, as well as the work already undertaken within the competent international fora, in particular within the framework of the 1979 Convention on Long-Range Transboundary Air Pollution (hereafter called ''the Convention'').

25. The participating States are convinced of the need for timely and effective reductions of sulphur emissions or their transboundary fluxes. They call upon contracting parties and signatories to the Convention to become parties to the Protocol on the reduction of sulphur emissions or their transboundary fluxes by at least 30 per cent. They recommend that further steps to reduce sulphur emissions, in line with the objectives of the Protocol, be taken by those States which are not parties to the Protocol, and that those States where this goal is already accomplished continue to control their emissions. Recalling that the said Protocol provides for reductions of sulphur emissions at the latest by 1993, they will work within the framework of the convention for the elaboration at an early date of an arrangement for further reductions of sulphur emissions beyond the level established by the Protocol.

26. The participating States consider that control and reduction of nitrogen oxide emissions, or their transboundary fluxes, deserve high priority in their pollution abatement programmes. They welcome the elaboration and adoption of a protocol on control of nitrogen oxide emissions.

27. Furthermore, they recognize the need to develop, within the framework of the Convention, arrangements to reduce emissions of other relevant air pollutants such as hydrocarbons and those producing photochemical oxidants. They will strengthen their co-operation accordingly, including by collecting and processing the necessary information.

28. The participating States agree to strengthen and develop the Cooperative Programme for the Monitoring and Evaluation of the Long-Range Transmission of Air Pollutants in Europe (EMEP), *inter alia*, through extending and improving the system of monitoring stations, providing EMEP with the necessary information regarding emissions of pollutants, furthering developing comparable methods of measurement and expanding coverage to include other relevant air pollutants, in particular nitrogen oxidants. They also recommend that those countries which have not yet done so should become parties to the Protocol on the Long-Term Financing of EMEP.

29. The participating States will make every effort to become parties, as soon as possible, to the Vienna Convention for the Protection of the Ozone Layer and to the Montreal Protocol on Substances that Deplete the Ozone Layer. Further, they will foster national action and international co-operation on the control and reduction of the emission of ozone-depleting substances.

30. The participating States agree that further national and international research efforts should be made regarding the global warming phenomenon, and the role played therein by emissions of carbon dioxide and trace gases in order to provide a scientific basis for mitigative action.

31. In order to protect and improve freshwater resources and to reduce significantly the pollution of seas and coastal areas, transboundary watercourses and international lakes from all sources of pollution, the participating States will develop and intensify national efforts as well as bilateral and multilateral co-operation. They recommend the elaboration of a framework convention or specific conventions to improve the protection of transboundary watercourses and international lakes. They will reduce significantly discharges of toxic, persistent and potentially hazardous substances. Furthermore, they will devote special attention to the development of appropriate alternatives to sea disposal in

order to decrease progressively and substantially the dumping of harmful wastes and the incineration of noxious liquid wastes at sea, with a view to the early termination of such methods.

32. The participating States recognize the need to improve international co-operation on the trans-boundary movement of hazardous wastes. Taking into account the valuable work done in other international fora, they will encourage the elaboration of international agreements, including a global convention on the control of transboundary movements of hazardous wastes.

33. The participating States will seek closer co-operation and greater exchange of information on the problems associated with potentially hazardous chemicals, including assessment of the risks to health and the environment. They will explore possibilities for closer harmonization of their legislation and regulations of the handling of these chemicals.

34. The participating States will strengthen international co-operation on natural resources and flora and fauna. They will promote early accession to, and effective implementation of, relevant agreements. They will also develop further effective measures to combat soil degradation and to protect flora, fauna and their habitats on the basis of the Declaration on this subject adopted by the ECE. They will intensify their exchanges of views and experience on ways and means of achieving a more rational use of natural resources.

35. The participating States acknowledge the importance of the contribution of persons and organizations dedicated to the protection and improvement of the environment, and will allow them to express their concerns. They will promote greater public awareness and understanding of environmental issues and will co-operate in the field of environmental education, *inter alia*, through exchanges of experience and results of research studies, development of educational programmes and ecological training.

36. The participating States will co-operate bilaterally and multilaterally with a view to improving and co-ordinating their arrangements for prevention, early warning, exchange of information and mutual assistance in cases of industrial accidents likely to cause transboundary damage to the environment. They will also initiate the examination of key elements related to the transboundary character of industrial accidents, such as clean up, restoration and liability.

37. The participating States agree to convene a Meeting on the protection of the environment. This Meeting will take place in Sofia from 16 October to 3 November 1989. The aim of the Meeting is to elaborate recommendations on principles and guidelines for further measures and co-operation in new and important areas of environmental protection. The agenda, timetable and other organizational modalities are set out in Annex VI. The next Follow-up Meeting, to be held in Helsinki, commencing on 24 March 1992, will assess the results achieved at the meeting.

Co-operation in Other Areas

38. The participating States recognize the important role of transport in economic and social development and the overall consequences of increased activity in the transport sector, including problems related to the environment. They will therefore encourage the elaboration of measures for achieving an economically more efficient transport system, taking into account the relative merits of different modes of transport and their potential effects on human health, safety and the environment. In this connection they will, through bilateral and multilateral means, give particular attention to questions concerning multimodal transport networks, combined transport, transit flows and the simplification of transport formalities and, in particular, of transport documents. They also welcome the work done by the ECE in this context.

39. The participating States underline the economic importance of tourism and its contribution to the mutual understanding of peoples. They therefore favour the development of co-operation in this field and will facilitate normal contacts between tourists and the local population. To this end they will endeavour to improve the infrastructure for tourism, *inter alia*, by diversifying accommodation and by developing facilities for low-budget and youth tourism, including small-scale private accommodation. They will also consider in a positive spirit the progressive phasing out for foreign tourists of minimum exchange requirements where they apply, allow the reconversion of legally acquired local currency and, furthermore, encourage non-discriminatory pricing for all foreign tourists irrespective of their nationality. They will also reduce arrival and departure procedures to the necessary minimum. The participating States will create conditions conducive to the establishment of joint projects in the field of tourism, including joint ventures and personnel training programmes.

40. The participating States emphasize the need for effective implementation of the provisions of the Final Act and the Madrid Concluding Document relating to migrant workers and their families in

Europe. They invite host countries and countries of origin to make efforts to improve further the economic, social, cultural and other conditions of life for migrant workers and their families legally residing in the host countries. They recommend that host countries and countries of origin should promote their bilateral co-operation in relevant fields with a view to facilitating the reintegration of migrant workers and their families returning to their country of origin.

41. The participating States will, in accordance with their relevant commitments undertaken in the Final Act and the Madrid Concluding Document, consider favourable applications for family reunification as well as family contacts and visits involving migrant workers from other participating States legally residing in the host countries.

42. The participating States will ensure that migrant workers from other participating States and their families can freely enjoy and maintain their national culture and have access to the culture of the host country.

43. Aiming at ensuring effective equality of opportunity between the children of migrant workers and the children of their own nationals regarding access to all forms and levels of education, the participating States affirm their readiness to take measures needed for the better use and improvement of educational opportunities. Furthermore, they will encourage or facilitate, where reasonable demand exists, supplementary teaching in their mother tongue for the children of migrant workers.

44. The participating States recognize that issues of migrant workers have their human dimension.

45. The participating States acknowledge that the impact of economic and technological change is being acutely felt in the work place. They underline their readiness to encourage co-operation in the field of vocational training policy through increased exchange of information and experience, with the aim of enhancing the educational standards, professional knowledge, skills and adaptability of personnel involved in industry and commerce.

46. The participating States recognize the importance of facilitating the integration of young people into professional life. They will therefore continue their efforts to ensure the necessary conditions for the education and vocational training of young people and to promote youth employment opportunities in various sectors of the economy. They will continue their efforts to create conditions for developing the level of scientific and cultural knowledge of their citizens, especially young people, and for facilitating their access to achievements in the areas of natural and social sciences, as well as culture.

• • • • • •

ANNEX V

Conference on Economic Co-operation in Europe

I. AGENDA
  1. Formal opening. Address by a representative of the host country.
  2. Statements by delegations of the participating States.
  3. Contributions by the Economic Commission for Europe (ECE) and the International Chamber of Commerce (ICC).
  4. Consideration of the following items:
      A. Development and diversification of economic relations through practical measures regarding:
          (a) Business contacts
          (b) Working conditions for businesspeople
          (c) Economic and commercial information
          (d) Role of small and medium-sized enterprises
          (e) Marketing and product promotion
      B. Industrial co-operation: Requirements for the establishment and operation, on a mutually advantageous basis, of joint ventures and other forms of industrial co-operation such as co-production, specialization and licensing:
          (a) Economic conditions and legal administrative aspects
          (b) Investment-related matters
      C. Co-operation in specific areas:
          (a) Energy and raw material saving techniques
          (b) Equipment for environmental protection
          (c) Techniques aimed at improving the quality of life
          (d) Agro-industry and food processing, including natural food production
          (e) Machinery for the production of durable and non-durable consumer goods
          (f) Urban development and town planning.

D. Monetary and financial aspects of commercial exchanges and industrial co-operation, such as:

(a) Currency convertibility and pricing and their effects on international competition

(b) Financial instruments and other support facilities offered by the financial services sector.

5. Concluding discussion and summing up.

6. Formal closure.

II. ORGANIZATIONAL FRAMEWORK AND OTHER MODALITIES

1. The Conference will be attended by delegations, which may include businesspeople and representatives of relevant organizations and institutions, from the participating States. At the concluding Plenary meetings, in the fourth week, delegations may also include leading members of the business community and of relevant organizations and institutions. The Conference will open on 19 March 1990 at 3 p.m., in Bonn. It will close on 11 April 1990.

2. The ECE and the ICC are invited to attend the Conference.

3. All Plenary meetings will be open. Unless otherwise agreed, all meetings of Subsidiary Working Bodies will be open.

4. Agenda items 1, 5 and 6 will be dealt with in the Plenary. Agenda item 4 will be dealt with in the Plenary and in Subsidiary Working Bodies (SWBs), in a balanced and structured way. Contributions under Agenda items 2 and 3 may be made both in the Plenary and in the SWBs.

5. Subsidiary Working Bodies A, B, C and D will be set up and will deal with Agenda item 4, in the following manner:

SWB A: Development and diversification of economic relations through practical measures regarding:
- Business contacts
- Working conditions for businesspeople
- Economic and commercial information
- Role of small and medium-sized enterprises

SWB B: Industrial co-operation: Requirements for the establishment and operation, on a mutually advantageous basis, of joint ventures and other forms of industrial co-operation such as co-production, specialization and licensing:

- Economic conditions and legal and administrative aspects
- Investment-related matters
- Marketing and product promotion

SWB C: Co-operation in specific areas:
- Energy and raw material saving techniques
- Equipment for environmental protection
- Techniques aimed at improving the quality of life
- Agro-industry and food processing, including natural food production
- Machinery for the production of durable and non-durable consumer goods
- Urban development and town planning

SWB D: Monetary and financial aspects of commercial exchanges and industrial co-operation, such as:
- Currency convertibility and pricing, and their effects on international competition
- Financial instruments and other support facilities offered by the financial services sector.

6. The Plenary will decide upon working methods which may be required to deal with the specific topics of Agenda item 4 and with Agenda item 5.

7. Sessions of the Plenary and of the Subsidiary Working Bodies will be held according to the attached work programme.

8. The Chair at the opening and closing Plenary sessions will be taken by a representative of the host country. After the opening session, the Chair will be taken in daily rotation, in French alphabetical order, starting with a representative of Austria.

9. The Chair at the opening meetings of the SWBs will be taken by a representative of the host country. Selection of the next Chairman will be by lot. The Chair will then be taken in daily rotation among the representatives of the participating States in French alphabetical order.

10. In conformity with paragraph 74 of the Final Recommendations of the Helsinki Consultations, the Government of the Federal Republic of Germany will designate an Executive Secretary. This designation will be subject to approval by the participating States.

11. The other rules of procedure, the working methods and the scale of distribution of expenses of the CSCE will, *mutatis mutandis,* be applied to the Conference.

(The follow-up meeting of the Conference on Security and Cooperation in Europe was held in Vienna from November 4, 1986 to January 17, 1989.)

7

Controlling Information

Joan Kloepfer

Recent efforts by the United States to prevent the transfer of technology to unfriendly countries have focused increasingly on the desire to control the transfer of information or technical "know-how." Traditionally, information associated with the development and production of most new technologies has been readily available in this country. It forms the basis upon which new discoveries are made and helps the U.S. to maintain its lead in the technological race. At the same time, however, some U.S. government officials have come to view the very accessibility of this material as a significant security risk. It permits Soviets and others to take advantage of our open society to learn the latest developments in science and technology without having to undergo their own lengthy process of research and development. A difficult dilemma is thus presented for our policymakers: Can we control the transfer of information to our adversaries without causing irreparable harm to our own technological base?

In the last decade or so, Congress, the President, and various departments and agencies have taken steps to control the dissemination of technical information. New provisions were added to the security classification rules. Amendments were made to the Export Administration Act, the Atomic Energy Act and the Invention Secrecy Act. A National Security Decision Directive was issued to protect information retrievable through databases. A Library Awareness Program was instituted to monitor foreign access to technical information in our nation's libraries. Prepublication review clauses began to appear in government contracts with university researchers.

This trend toward greater controls on the exchange of information has caused concern among such diverse groups as the American Physical Society, the American Library Association, and the Information Industry Association. While few would dispute the need for some kind of limitation on the flow of advanced technical data from the U.S. to East bloc countries, scientists and academics have grown increasingly alarmed at what they perceive to be mounting encroachments on intellectual freedom and restrictions on the exchange of ideas in this country.

The focus on controlling the flow of information goes back to 1976. In that year, the Defense Science Board Task Force on Export of U.S. Technology of the Department of Defense issued a report in which it analyzed the effectiveness of the then-current U.S. export control restrictions and identified those technology transfer mechanisms that required the most attention. Called the Bucy Report after task force chairman J. Fred Bucy, it recommended that control over the transfer of design and manufacturing know-how, rather than over product sales, be accorded primary emphasis in the U.S. export control regime. In addition to turnkey factories, joint ventures, and licenses involving extensive teaching effort, the list of information transfer mechanisms that the task force felt should be carefully monitored included scientific exchanges.

Technical Data Controls

In an effort to implement the Bucy Report's recommendations, Congress added new provisions to the Export Administration Act of 1979, which were designed to control the export of "technical data." The concomitant Export Administration Regulations (EAR) define "technical data" as "information of any kind that can be used, or adapted for use, in the design, production, manufacture, utilization, or reconstruction of articles or materials. The data may take a tangible form, such as a model, prototype, blueprint, or an operating manual; or they may take an intangible form such as technical service. All software is technical data." The term "export" as it applies to technical data is defined to include an actual transmission of data abroad as well as release of data in the U.S. to foreign nationals. Among the vehicles listed in the regulations for the export of technical data are oral exchanges of information. In this case, materials to be regulated are contained in the Commodity Control List and the Militarily Critical Technologies List.

In addition to these regulations, which are administered by the Commerce Department, the International Traffic in Arms Regulations (ITAR), which are administered by the State Department under the Arms Export Control Act of 1976, also govern the export of certain types of technical data. The materials to be regulated under ITAR are contained in the U.S. Munitions List, which includes certain dual-use technologies.

The Department of Defense assists the Departments of Commerce and State in maintaining the Commodity Control List and the U.S. Munitions List, and thus plays a major role in determining which data is subject to export controls. In 1984, Congress gave DoD authority to implement controls on the dissemination of unclassified information domestically as well. The Defense Authorization Act for that fiscal year contained a new provision granting the Secretary of Defense the right to "withhold from public disclosure any technical data with military or space application in the possession of, or under the control of the Department of Defense, if such data may not be exported lawfully outside the United States without an approval, authorization or license under the Export Administration Act or the Arms Export Control Act." **(Document 7.1)** In accordance with this authority, the Department of Defense issued new regulations in November 1984 governing the disclosure of such data, which permit DoD to deny requests for technical data submitted under the Freedom of Information Act. NASA and the Department of Energy are currently seeking similar authority.

The Export Administration Regulations allow unclassified technical data to be exported under two types of general licenses, depending upon the type of data involved. General License GTDA (Technical Data Available to All Destinations) covers data that is already publicly available. As its name suggests, it may be exported anywhere. Data governed by General License GTDR (Technical Data under Restriction) may not be exported to certain countries. In practice, a general license is tantamount to an exemption from the licensing process, as it is granted more or less automatically and requires no license application. The export of data not covered by these two types of general licenses may require specific permission in the form of a validated export license.

Restrictions on Scientists

To many multinational firms, which are accustomed to protecting proprietary information from competitors, export restrictions on the flow of data are a nuisance in that they inhibit internal corporate communication. To scientists, however, they represent a far greater threat. Highly technical scientific papers and international conferences have frequently been subjected to restrictions under either the Export Administration Regulations or the International Traffic in Arms Regulations by agents of the Departments of Commerce, State, and Defense. Sometimes, conference attendees are required to sign letters agreeing not to divulge information from the conference to foreigners from certain countries. Similarly, users of the new San Francisco/Moscow Teleport, a direct computer-linked electronic mail service between the U.S. and the U.S.S.R., are asked to sign agreements saying that they will follow export control laws.

Periodically, government officials have invoked export control regulations to prevent papers from being delivered altogether. A dramatic example of this occurred in 1982, when over 150 papers scheduled to be presented at a symposium of the Society of Photo-Optical Instrumentation Engineers were withdrawn due to government pressure at the last minute. Since then, a number of other such incidents have occurred in different circumstances and with various effects. Foreigners have been banned from participating in certain conference sessions and even in one celebrated case from attending a university course that involved the presentation of restricted technical information. Examples like these are causing concern among some scientists and engineers who appreciate the importance of foreign input in the development of new technologies. In 1985, the presidents of twelve leading scientific and engineering societies, including the American Association for the Advancement of Science and the American Chemical Society, declared in a letter to Defense Secretary Weinberger their refusal to sponsor closed or restricted access meetings.

Classification

In addition to export control regulations, there are other rules governing the dissemination of information. The most fundamental of these are the security classification rules, which were broadened by the Reagan Administration through Executive Order 12356 of April 2, 1982. **(Document 7.2)** In addition to expanding significantly the scope of information to be classified, this order provides for the reclassification of previously declassified information and discontinues the past practice of automatically declassifying information after a certain period of time.

In a move to safeguard information which had been reviewed for classification and which had been determined to be unclassifiable under applicable law, the Department of Energy instituted new regulations in April 1985 designed to identify and protect from dissemination "Unclassified Controlled Nuclear Information." A 1981 amendment to the Atomic Energy Act of 1954 provided the authority for these regulations. **(Document 7.3)** An oft-cited example of an effort to restrict unclassified data related to nuclear weapons production occurred in 1979, when the U.S. Government tried to prevent *The Progressive* magazine from publishing an article on the workings of hydrogen bombs, which was written entirely with the help of readily-available unclassified material.

Under the Invention Secrecy Act of 1951, which Congress amended in 1988, the Commerce Department's Patent and Trademark Office may also prevent the dissemination of technical information through its authority to place patent applications under secrecy orders. **(Document 7.4)** Patent applications contain detailed information that describes how a specific invention can be developed or practiced. Because applications are published when a patent is issued, the Patent Commissioner may be instructed by the Secretary of Energy or by the Secretary of Defense or by another defense agency head to withhold a patent by issuing a secrecy order so as to prevent that information from becoming public.

In a 1987 report, a panel of the Committee on Science, Engineering, and Public Policy of the National Academy of Sciences expressed its concern that increased application of secrecy orders may be detrimental to the process of innovation in this country. In the opinion of the panel, this would "undermine the benefits of the patent system, increase the duplication of R & D activities, and result in important innovations being withheld from commercial markets."

Databases and Libraries

Among the more controversial measures designed to protect unclassified information deemed sensitive was National Security Decision Directive 145 (NSDD 145), issued by the White House on September 17, 1984. **(Document 7.5)** Entitled "National Policy on Telecommunications and Automated Information Systems Security," the directive aimed at preventing the unwanted exploitation of information accessible through databases. Although the directive specifically applied only to government

systems, it stated that "in cases where implementation of security measures to non-governmental systems would be in the national security interest, the private sector shall be encouraged, advised, and where appropriate, assisted in undertaking the application of such measures." Operators of private commercial and scientific databases subsequently received visits from agents of the F.B.I., the C.I.A., and the National Security Agency inquiring about the types of information they carried and whether they might be able to monitor or limit customers' access to that information. At this point, Congress saw fit to intervene. The Computer Security Act of 1987, which was signed into law in January 1988, effectively removed the security of civilian public and private databases from the jurisdiction of the military. Whereas NSDD 145 had given the Department of Defense and the National Security Agency authority to protect sensitive information in all federal computer systems, the Computer Security Act limited this authority to classified information in DoD's own systems. It then entrusted security for all remaining civilian systems to the National Bureau of Standards in the Commerce Department and relegated NSA to an advisory role. Despite these changes, NSDD 145 has not yet been repealed or revised, a fact that is causing some concern among congressional supporters of the Computer Security Act.

Databases are seen to warrant special attention because of the relative ease with which a user can piece together bits of information. Therefore, despite the fact that the information may be publicly available elsewhere, the fact that it is contained in a database makes it a potential threat to national security. The case of NTIS is instructive here. The National Technical Information Service is government-operated and provides its subscribers with unclassified information resulting from government-sponsored research. Although this information consists of openly published material, and therefore qualifies for a general export license, the Commerce Department determined in 1980 that Soviet subscriptions to NTIS represented a significant transfer of technology and therefore directed that these be suspended. Recently, the FBI has interpreted this policy to include barring access to the service by Soviets and others at library facilities within the U.S.

In fact, the need to prevent unfriendly foreigners from using NTIS was cited as one justification for the FBI's Library Awareness Program. Under this program, FBI agents contacted librarians at specialized facilities or members of their staffs and asked them to report on researchers with "foreign-sounding names" who might be involved in hostile intelligence-gathering efforts. Most of the librarians involved were indignant at the intrusion and refused to cooperate. The FBI has apparently halted these controversial visits in the face of congressional hearings and general public criticism. Although the Bureau has been reluctant to discuss the affair in any detail, the privately-funded National Security Archive filed and won a Freedom of Information Act lawsuit. The information thus obtained failed, however, to shed much light on the program's justification.

Recent trends in technical data control policy have affected the academic community in a variety of ways ranging from attempts to restrict the research activities of foreign scholars to prepublication review requirements contained in government-sponsored research contracts. With regard to exchange students and visiting scholars, the institutions involved have generally objected to government demands that they police these people. Prepublication review requirements have not been particularly well-received either. The contractor in this case must promise not to disclose any information obtained during the conduct of his research without prior approval from the department or agency providing the funding, even if that research derived entirely from unclassified sources. Many universities argue that this amounts to censorship and refuse to agree to contracts containing such restrictions.

In 1982, the National Academy of Sciences Panel on Scientific Communication and National Security concluded that "the vast majority of university research, whether basic or applied, should be subject to no limitations on access or communications." This influential report laid the basis for two new declarations of policy in 1985. One of them was contained in the Export Administration Amendments Act of that year, which stated, "It is the policy of the United States to sustain vigorous scientific enterprise. To do so involves sustaining the ability of scientists and other scholars freely to communicate research findings, in accordance with applicable provisions of law, by means of publication, teaching, conferences, and other forms of scholarly exchange." A few months later, President Reagan signed National Security Decision Directive 189 (NSDD 189) of September 21, 1985. **(Document 7.6)** It ruled that "no restrictions may be placed upon the conduct or reporting of federally funded fundamental research that has not received national security classification, except as provided in applicable U.S. statutes." The "applicable provisions of law" and "applicable U.S. statutes" mentioned in these statements include the above-cited Arms Export Control Act of 1976, the Atomic Energy Act of 1954, the Invention Secrecy Act of 1951, the 1984 Department of Defense Authorization Act, and, of course, the Export Administration Act of 1979. As the authority embodied in these laws to control the dissemination of unclassified information remains unaltered and continues to be applied, the new declarations do not represent a significant change in policy.

With the present emphasis in the United States on international economic competitiveness, this issue will likely take on an economic as well as a security dimension. As our position in the international trading community erodes, future measures aimed at controlling information will increasingly seek justification on economic rather than on national security grounds, but with similar effects on scientific communication.

166

Document 7.1

Excerpt from 1984 Defense Authorization Act

(Title 10 U.S. Code)

Section 130. Authority to withhold from public disclosure certain technical data

(a) Notwithstanding any other provision of law, the Secretary of Defense may withhold from public disclosure any technical data with military or space application in the possession of, or under the control of, the Department of Defense, if such data may not be exported lawfully outside the United States without an approval, authorization, or license under the Export Administration Act of 1979 (50 U.S.C. App. 2401-2420) or the Arms Export Control Act (22 U.S.C. 2751 et seq.). However, technical data may not be withheld under this section if regulations promulgated under either such Act authorize the export of such data pursuant to a general, unrestricted license or exemption in such regulations.

(b) (1) Within 90 days after September 24, 1983, the Secretary of Defense shall propose regulations to implement this section. Such regulations shall be published in the Federal Register for a period of no less than 30 days for public comment before promulgation. Such regulations shall address, where appropriate, releases of technical data to allies of the United States and to qualified United States contractors, including United States contractors that are small business concerns, for use in performing United States Government contracts.

(2) In this section, the term "technical data with military or space application" means any blueprints, drawings, plans, instructions, computer software and documentation, or other technical information that can be used, or be adapted for use, to design, engineer, produce, manufacture, operate, repair, overhaul, or reproduce any military or space equipment or technology concerning such equipment.

Document 7.2

Excerpts from Executive Order 12356 of April 2, 1982

(From *Federal Register*, Volume 47, Number 66, Tuesday, April 6, 1982.)

National Security Information

This Order prescribes a uniform system for classifying, declassifying, and safeguarding national security information. It recognizes that it is essential that the public be informed concerning the activities of its Government, but that the interests of the United States and its citizens require that certain information concerning the national defense and foreign relations be protected against unauthorized disclosure. Information may not be classified under this Order unless its disclosure reasonably could be expected to cause damage to the national security.

NOW, by the authority vested in me as President by the Constitution and laws of the United States of America, it is hereby ordered as follows:

Part 1

Original Classification

Section 1.1 Classification Levels

(a) National security information (hereinafter ''classified information'') shall be classified at one of the following three levels:

(1) ''Top Secret'' shall be applied to information, the unauthorized disclosure of which reasonably could be expected to cause exceptionally grave damage to the national security.

(2) ''Secret'' shall be applied to information, the unauthorized disclosure of which reasonably could be expected to cause serious damage to the national security.

(3) ''Confidential'' shall be applied to information, the unauthorized disclosure of which reasonably could be expected to cause damage to the national security.

(b) Except as otherwise provided by statute, no other terms shall be used to identify classified information.

(c) If there is a reasonable doubt about the need to classify information, it shall be safeguarded as if it were classified pending a determination by an original classification authority, who shall make this determination within thirty (30) days. If there is reasonable doubt about the appropriate level of classification, it shall be safeguarded at the higher level of classification pending a determination by an original classification authority, who shall make this determination within thirty (30) days.

Section 1.2 Classification Authority

(a) Top Secret. The authority to classify information originally as Top Secret may be exercised only by:

(1) the President;

(2) agency heads and officials designated by the President in the *Federal Register*; and

(3) officials delegated this authority pursuant to Section 1.2(d)

(b) Secret. The authority to classify information originally as Secret may be exercised only by:

(1) agency heads and officials designated by the President in the *Federal Register*;

(2) officials with original Top Secret classification authority; and

(3) officials delegated such authority pursuant to Section 1.2(d).

(c) Confidential. The authority to classify information originally as Confidential may be exercised only by:

(1) agency heads and officials designated by the President in the *Federal Register*;

(2) officials with original Top Secret or Secret classification authority; and

(3) officials delegated such authority pursuant to Section 1.2(d)

(d) Delegation of Original Classification Authority.

(1) Delegations of original classification authority shall be limited to the minimum required to

administer this Order. Agency heads are responsible for ensuring that designated subordinate officials have a demonstrable and continuing need to exercise this authority.

(2) Original Top Secret classification authority may be delegated only by the President; an agency head or official designated pursuant to Section 1.2(a)(2); and the senior official designated under Section 5.3(a)(1), provided that official has been delegated original Top Secret classification authority by the agency head.

(3) Original Secret classification authority may be delegated only by the President; an agency head or official designated pursuant to Sections 1.2(a)(2) and 1.2(b)(1); an official with original Top Secret classification authority; and the senior official designated under Section 5.3(a)(1), provided that official has been delegated original Secret classification authority by the agency head.

(4) Original Confidential classification authority may be delegated only by the President; an agency head or official designated pursuant to Sections 1.2(a)(2), 1.2(b)(b)(1) and 1.2(c)(1); an official with original Top Secret classification authority; and the senior official designated under Section 5.3(a)(1), provided that official has been delegated original classification authority by the agency head.

(5) Each delegation of original classification authority shall be in writing and the authority shall not be redelegated except as provided in this Order. It shall identify the official delegated the authority by name or position title. Delegated classification authority includes the authority to classify information at the level granted and lower levels of classification.

(e) Exceptional Cases. When an employee, contractor, licensee, or grantee of an agency that does not have original classification authority originates information believed by that person to require classification, the information shall be protected in a manner consistent with this Order and its implementing directives. The information shall be transmitted promptly as provided under this Order or its implementing directives to the agency that has appropriate subject matter interest and classification authority with respect to this information. That agency shall decide within thirty (30) days whether to classify this information. If it is not clear which agency has classification responsibility for this information, it shall be sent to the Director of the Information Security Oversight Office. The Director

shall determine the agency having primary subject matter interest and forward the information, with appropriate recommendations, to that agency for a classification determination.

Section 1.3 Classification Categories

(a) Information shall be considered for classification if it concerns:

(1) military plans, weapons, or operations;

(2) the vulnerabilities or capabilities of systems, installations, projects, or plans relating to the national security;

(3) foreign government information;

(4) intelligence activities (including special activities), or intelligence sources or methods;

(5) foreign relations or foreign activities of the United States;

(6) scientific, technological, or economic matters relating to the national security;

(7) United States Government programs for safeguarding nuclear materials or facilities;

(8) cryptology;

(9) a confidential source; or

(10) other categories of information that are related to the national security and that require protection against unauthorized disclosure as determined by the President or by agency heads or other officials who have been delegated original classification authority by the President. Any determination made under this subsection shall be reported promptly to the Director of the Information Security Oversight Office.

(b) Information that is determined to concern one or more of the categories in Section 1.3(e) shall be classified when an original classification authority also determines that its unauthorized disclosure, either by itself or in the context of other information, reasonably could be expected to cause damage to the national security.

(c) Unauthorized disclosure of foreign government information, the identity of a confidential foreign source, or intelligence sources or methods is presumed to cause damage to the national security.

(d) Information classified in accordance with Section 1.3 shall not be declassified automatically as a result of any unofficial publication or inadvertent or unauthorized disclosure in the United States or abroad of identical or similar information.

Section 1.4 Duration of Classification

(a) Information shall be classified as long as required by national security considerations. When it can be determined, a specific date or event for declassification shall be set by the original classification authority at the time the information is originally classified.

(b) Automatic declassification determinations under predecessor orders shall remain valid unless the classification is extended by an authorized official of the originating agency. These extensions may be by individual documents or categories of information. The agency shall be responsible for notifying holders of the information of such extensions.

(c) Information classified under predecessor orders and marked for declassification review shall remain classified until reviewed for declassification under the provisions of this Order.

Section 1.6 Limitations on Classification

(a) In no case shall information be classified in order to conceal violations of law, inefficiency, or administrative error; to prevent embarrassment to a person, organization, or agency; to restrain competition; or to prevent or delay the release of information that does not require protection in the interest of national security.

(b) Basic scientific research information not clearly related to the national security may not be classified.

(c) The President or an agency head or official designated under Sections 1.2(a)(2), 1.2(b)(1), or 1.2(c)(1) may reclassify information previously declassified and disclosed if it is determined in writing that (1) the information requires protection in the interest of national security; and (2) the information may reasonably be recovered. These reclassification actions shall be reported promptly to the Director of the Information Security Oversight Office.

(d) Information may be classified or reclassified after an agency has received a request for it under the Freedom of Information Act (5 U.S.C. 552) or the Privacy Act of 1974 (5 U.S.C. 552a) or the mandatory review provisions of this Order (Section 3.4) if

such classification meets the requirements of this Order and is accomplished personally and on a document-by-document basis by the agency head, the deputy agency head, the senior agency official designated under Section 5.3(a)(1), or an official with original Top Secret classification authority.

Part 2

Derivative Classification

Section 2.1 Use of Derivative Classification

(a) Derivative classification is (1) the determination that information is in substance the same as information currently classified, and (2) the application of the same classification markings. Persons who only reproduce, extract, or summarize classified information, or who only apply classification markings derived from source material or as directed by a classification guide, need not possess original classification authority.

(b) Persons who apply derivative classification markings shall:

(1) observe and respect original classification decisions; and

(2) carry forward to any newly created documents any assigned authorized markings. The declassification date or event that provides the longest period of classification shall be used for documents classified on the basis of multiple sources.

Part 3

Declassification and Downgrading

Section 3.1 Declassification Authority

(a) Information shall be declassified or downgraded as soon as national security considerations permit. Agencies shall coordinate their review of classified information with other agencies that have a direct interest in the subject matter. Information that continues to meet the classification requirements prescribed by Section 1.3 despite the passage of time will continue to be protected in accordance with this Order.

(b) Information shall be declassified or downgraded by the official who authorized the original classification, if that official is still serving in the same position; the originator's successor; a supervisory official of either; or officials delegated such authority in writing by the agency head or the senior agency official designated pursuant to Section 5.3(a)(1).

(c) If the Director of the Information Security Oversight Office determines that information is classified in violation of this Order, the director may require the information to be declassified by the agency that originated the classification. Any such decision by the Director may be appealed to the National Security Council. The information shall remain classified, pending a prompt decision on the appeal.

(d) The provisions of this Section shall also apply to agencies that, under the terms of this Order, do not have original classification authority, but that had such authority under predecessor orders.

Section 3.3 Systematic Review for Declassification

(a) The Archivist of the United States shall, in accordance with procedures and timeframes prescribed in the Information Security Oversight Office's directives implementing this Order, systematically review for declassification or downgrading (1) classified records accessioned into the National Archives of the United States, and (2) classified presidential papers or records under the Archivist's control. Such information shall be reviewed by the Archivist for declassification or downgrading in accordance with systematic review guidelines that shall be provided by the head of the agency that originated the information, or in the case of foreign government information, by the Director of the Information Security Oversight Office in consultation with interested agency heads.

(b) Agency heads may conduct internal systematic review programs for classified information originated by their agencies contained in records determined by the Archivist to be permanently valuable but that have not been accessioned into the National Archives of the United States.

(c) After consultation with affected agencies, the Secretary of Defense may establish special procedures for systematic review for declassification of classified cryptologic information, and the Director of Central Intelligence may establish special procedures for systematic review for declassification of classified information pertaining to intelligence activities (including special activities), or intelligence sources or methods.

Section 3.4 Mandatory Review for Declassification

(a) Except as provided in Section 3.4(b), all information classified under this Order or predecessor orders shall be subject to a review for declassification by the originating agency, if:

(1) the request is made by a United States citizen or permanent resident alien, a federal agency, or a State or local government; and

(2) the request describes the document or material containing the information with sufficient specificity to enable the agency to locate it with a reasonable amount of effort.

(b) Information originated by a President, the White House Staff, by committees, commissions, or boards appointed by the President, or others specifically providing advice and counsel to a President or acting on behalf of a President is exempted from the provisions of Section 3.4(a). The Archivist of the United States shall have the authority to review, downgrade and declassify information under the control of the Administrator of General Services or the Archivist pursuant to sections 2107, 2107 note, or 2203 of title 44, United States Code. Review procedures developed by the Archivist shall provide for consultation with agencies having primary subject matter interest and shall be consistent with the provisions of applicable laws or lawful agreements that pertain to the respective presidential papers or records. Any decision by the Archivist may be appealed to the Director of the Information Security Oversight Office. Agencies with primary subject matter interest shall be notified promptly of the Director's decision on such appeals and may further appeal to the National Security Council. The information shall remain classified pending a prompt decision on the appeal.

(c) Agencies conducting a mandatory review for declassification shall declassify information no longer requiring protection under this Order. They shall release this information unless withholding is otherwise authorized under applicable law.

(d) Agency heads shall develop procedures to process requests for the mandatory review of classified information. These procedures shall apply to information classified under this or predecessor orders. They shall also provide a means for administratively appealing a denial of a mandatory review request.

(e) The Secretary of Defense shall develop special procedures for the review of cryptologic information, and the Director of Central Intelligence shall develop special procedures for the review of information pertaining to intelligence activities (including special activities), or intelligence sources or methods, after consultation with affected agencies. The Archivist shall develop special procedures for the review of information accessioned into the National Archives of the United States.

(f) In response to a request for information under the Freedom of Information Act, the Privacy Act of 1974, or the mandatory review provisions of this Order:

(1) An agency shall refuse to confirm or deny the existence or non-existence of requested information whenever the fact of its existence or non-existence is itself classifiable under this Order.

(2) When an agency receives any request for documents in its custody that were classified by another agency, it shall refer copies of the request and the requested documents to the originating agency for processing, and may, after consultation with the originating agency, inform the requester of the referral. In cases is which the originating agency determines in writing that a response under Section 3.4(f)(1) is required, the referring agency shall respond to the requester in accordance with that Section.

Part 4

Safeguarding

Section 4.1 General Restrictions on Access

(a) A person is eligible for access to classified information provided that a determination of trustworthiness has been made by agency heads or designated officials and provided that such access is essential to the accomplishment of lawful and authorized Government purposes.

(b) Controls shall be established by each agency to ensure that classified information is used, processed, stored, reproduced, transmitted, and destroyed only under conditions that will provide adequate protection and prevent access by unauthorized persons.

(c) Classified information shall not be disseminated outside the executive branch except under conditions that ensure that the information will be given protection equivalent to that afforded within the executive branch.

(d) Except as provided by directives issued by the President through the National Security Council, classified information originating in one agency may

not be disseminated outside any other agency to which it has been made available without the consent of the originating agency. For purposes of this Section, the Department of Defense shall be considered one agency.

Section 4.2 Special Access Programs

(a) Agency heads designated pursuant to Section 1.2(a) may create special access programs to control access, distribution, and protection of particularly sensitive information classified pursuant to this Order or predecessor orders. Such programs may be created or continued only at the written direction of these agency heads. For special access programs pertaining to intelligence activities (including special activities but not including military operational, strategic and tactical programs), or intelligence sources or methods, this function will be exercised by the Director of Central Intelligence.

(b) Each agency head shall establish and maintain a system of accounting for special access programs. The Director of the Information Security Oversight Office, consistent with the provisions of Section 5.2(b)(4), shall have non-delegable access to all such accountings.

Section 4.3 Access by Historical Researchers and Former Presidential Appointees

(a) The requirement in Section 4.1(a) that access to classified information may be granted only as is essential to the accomplishment of authorized and lawful Government purposes may be waived as provided in Section 4.3(b) for persons who:

(1) are engaged in historical research projects, or

(2) previously have occupied policy-making positions to which they were appointed by the President.

(b) Waivers under Section 4.3(a) may be granted only if the originating agency:

(1) determines in writing that access is consistent with the interest of national security;

(2) takes appropriate steps to protect classified information from unauthorized disclosure or compromise, and ensures that the information is safeguarded in a manner consistent with this Order; and

(3) limits the access granted to former presidential appointees to items that the person originated,

reviewed, signed, or received while serving as a presidential appointee.

Part 5

Implementation and Review

Section 5.1 Policy Direction

(a) The National Security Council shall provide overall policy direction for the information security program.

(b) The Administrator of General Services shall be responsible for implementing and monitoring the program established pursuant to this Order. The Administrator shall delegate the implementation and monitorship functions of this program to the Director of the Information Security Oversight Office.

Part 6

General Provisions

Section 6.1 Definitions

(a) "Agency" has the meaning provided at 5 U.S.C. 552(e).

(b) "Information" means any information or material, regardless of its physical form or characteristics, that is owned by, produced by or for, or is under the control of the United States Government.

(c) "National security information" means information that has been determined pursuant to this Order or any predecessor order to require protection against unauthorized disclosure and that is so designated.

(d) "Foreign government information" means:

(1) information provided by a foreign government or governments, an international organization of governments, or any element thereof with the expectation, expressed or implied, that the information, the source of the information, or both, are to be held in confidence; or

(2) information produced by the United States pursuant to or as a result of a joint arrangement with a foreign government or governments or an international organization of governments, or any element thereof, requiring that the information, the arrangement, or both, are to be held in confidence.

(e) "National security" means the national defense or foreign relations of the United States.

(f) "Confidential source" means any individual or organization that has provided, or that may reasonably be expected to provide, information to the United States on matters pertaining to the national security with the expectation, expressed or implied, that the information or relationship, or both, be held in confidence.

(g) "Original classification" means an initial determination that information requires, in the interest of national security, protection against unauthorized disclosure, together with a classification designation signifying the level of protection required.

Section 6.2 General

(a) Nothing in this Order shall supersede any requirement made by or under the Atomic Energy Act of 1954, as amended. "Restricted Data" and "Formerly Restricted Data" shall be handled, protected, classified, downgraded, and declassified in conformity with the provisions of the Atomic Energy Act of 1954, as amended, and regulations issued under that Act.

(b) The Attorney General, upon request by the head of an agency or the Director of the Information Security Oversight Office, shall render an interpretation of this Order with respect to any question arising in the course of its administration.

(c) Nothing in this Order limits the protection afforded any information by other provisions of law.

(d) Executive Order No. 12056 of June 28, 1978, as amended, is revoked as of the effective date of this Order.

(e) This Order shall become effective on August 1, 1982.

THE WHITE HOUSE

Document 7.3

Excerpts from 1981 Amendment to the Atomic Energy Act

(Title 42 U.S. Code Annotated)

Section 2168. Dissemination of unclassified information

(a) Dissemination prohibited; rules and regulations; determinations of Secretary prerequisite to issuance of prohibiting regulations or orders; criteria

(1) In addition to any other authority or requirement regarding protection from dissemination of information, and subject to section 552(b)(3) of Title 5, the Secretary of Energy (hereinafter in this section referred to as the "Secretary"), with respect to atomic energy defense programs, shall prescribe such regulations, after notice and opportunity for public comment thereon, or issue such orders as may be necessary to prohibit the unauthorized dissemination of unclassified information pertaining to—

(A) the design of production facilities or utilization facilities;

(B) security measures (including security plans, procedures, and equipment) for the physical protection of (i) production or utilization facilities, (ii) nuclear material contained in such facilities, or (iii) nuclear material in transit; or

(C) the design, manufacture, or utilization of any atomic weapon or component if the design, manufacture, or utilization of such weapon or component was contained in any information declassified or removed from the Restricted Data category by the Secretary (or the head of the predecessor agency of the Department of Energy) pursuant to section 2162 of this title.

(2) The Secretary may prescribe regulations or issue orders under paragraph (1) to prohibit the dissemination of any information described in such paragraph only if and to the extent that the Secretary determines that the unauthorized dissemination of such information could reasonably be expected to have a significant adverse effect on the health and safety of the public or the common defense and security by significantly increasing the likelihood of (A) illegal production of nuclear weapons, or (B) theft, diversion, or sabotage of nuclear materials, equipment, or facilities.

(3) In making a determination under paragraph (2), the Secretary may consider what the likelihood of an illegal production, theft, diversion, or sabotage referred to in such paragraph would be if the information proposed to be prohibited from dissemination under this section were at no time available for dissemination.

(4) The Secretary shall exercise his authority under this subsection to prohibit the dissemination of any information described in paragraph (1) of this subsection—

(A) so as to apply the minimum restrictions needed to protect the health and safety of the public or the common defense and security; and

(B) upon a determination that the unauthorized dissemination of such information could reasonably be expected to result in a significant adverse effect on the health and safety of the public or the common defense and security by significantly increasing the likelihood of (i) illegal production of nuclear weapons, or (ii) theft, diversion, or sabotage of nuclear materials, equipment, or facilities.

(5) Nothing in this section shall be construed to authorize the Secretary to authorize the withholding of information from the appropriate committees of the Congress.

• • • • • •

(e) Quarterly reports for interested persons; contents

The Secretary shall prepare on a quarterly basis a report to be made available upon the request of any interested person, detailing the Secretary's application during that period of each regulation or order prescribed or issued under this section. In particular, such report shall—

(1) identify any information protected from disclosure pursuant to such regulation or order;

(2) specifically state the Secretary's justification for determining that unauthorized dissemination of the information protected from disclosure under such regulation or order could reasonably be expected to have a significant adverse effect on the

health and safety of the public or the common defense and security by significantly increasing the likelihood of illegal production of nuclear weapons, or theft, diversion, or sabotage of nuclear materials, equipment, or facilities, as specified under subsection (a) of this section; and

(3) provide justification that the Secretary has applied such regulation or order so as to protect from disclosure only the minimum amount of information necessary to protect the health and safety of the public or the common defense and security.

Document 7.4

Authority of the Patent and Trademark Office to Impose Secrecy Orders on Patent Applications

(Title 35 U.S. Code Annotated)

Section 181. Secrecy of certain inventions and withholding of patent

Whenever publication or disclosure by the grant of a patent on an invention in which the Government has a property interest might, in the opinion of the head of the interested Government agency, be detrimental to the national security, the Commissioner upon being so notified shall order that the invention be kept secret and shall withhold the grant of a patent therefor under the conditions set forth hereinafter.

Whenever the publication or disclosure of an invention by the granting of a patent, in which the Government does not have a property interest, might in the opinion of the Commissioner, be detrimental to the national security, he shall make the application for patent in which such invention is disclosed available for inspection to the Atomic Energy Commission*, the Secretary of Defense, and the chief officer of any other department or agency of the Government designated by the President as a defense agency of the United States.

Each individual to whom the application is disclosed shall sign a dated acknowledgment thereof, which acknowledgment shall be entered in the file of the application. If, in the opinion of the Atomic Energy Commission, the Secretary of a Defense Department, or the chief officer of another department or agency so designated, the publication or disclosure of the invention by the granting of a patent therefor would be detrimental to the national security, the Atomic Energy Commission, the Secretary of a Defense Department, or such other chief officer shall notify the Commissioner and the Commissioner shall order that the invention be kept secret and shall withhold the grant of a patent for such period as the national interest requires, and notify the applicant thereof. Upon proper showing by the head of the department or agency who caused the secrecy order to be issued that the examination of the application might jeopardize the national interest, the Commissioner shall thereupon maintain the application in a sealed condition and notify the applicant thereof. The owner of an application which has been placed under a secrecy order shall

have a right to appeal from the order to the Secretary of Commerce under rules prescribed by him.

An invention shall not be ordered kept secret and the grant of a patent withheld for a period of more than one year. The Commissioner shall renew the order at the end thereof, or at the end of any renewal period, for additional periods of one year upon notification by the head of the department or the chief officer of the agency who caused the order to be issued that an affirmative determination has been made that the national interest continues so to require. An order in effect, or issued, during a time when the United States is at war, shall remain in effect for the duration of hostilities and one year following cessation of hostilities. An order in effect, or issued, during a national emergency declared by the President shall remain in effect for the duration of the national emergency and six months thereafter. The Commissioner may rescind any order upon notification by the heads of the departments and the chief officers of the agencies who caused the order to be issued that the publication or disclosure of the invention is no longer deemed detrimental to the national security.

Section 182. Abandonment of invention for unauthorized disclosure

The invention disclosed in an application for patent subject to an order made pursuant to section 181 of this title may be held abandoned upon its being established by the Commissioner that in violation of said order the invention has been published or disclosed or that an application for a patent therefor has been filed in a foreign country by the inventor, his successors, assigns, or legal representatives, or anyone in privity with him or them, without the consent of the Commissioner. The abandonment shall be held to have occurred as of the time of violation. The consent of the Commissioner shall not be given without the concurrence of the heads of the departments and the chief officers of the agencies who caused the order to be issued. A holding of abandonment shall constitute forfeiture by the applicant, his successors, assigns, or legal representatives, or anyone in privity with him or them, of all claims against the United States based upon such invention.

Section 183. Right to compensation

An applicant, his successors, assigns, or legal representatives, whose patent is withheld as herein provided, shall have the right, beginning at the date the applicant is notified that, except for such order, his application is otherwise in condition for allowance, or February 1, 1952, whichever is later, and ending six years after a patent is issued thereon, to apply to the head of any department or agency who caused the order to be issued for compensation for the damage caused by the order of secrecy and/or for the use of the invention by the Government, resulting from his disclosure. The right to compensation for use shall begin on the date of the first use of the invention by the Government. The head of the department or agency is authorized, upon the presentation of a claim, to enter into an agreement with the applicant, his successors, assigns, or legal representatives, in full settlement for the damage and/or use. This settlement agreement shall be conclusive for all purposes notwithstanding any other provision of law to the contrary. If full settlement of the claim cannot be effected, the head of the department or agency may award and pay to such applicant, his successors, assigns, or legal representatives, a sum not exceeding 75 per centum of the sum which the head of the department or agency considers just compensation for the damage and/or use. A claimant may bring suit against the United States in the United States Claims Court or in the District Court of the United States for the district in which such claimant is a resident for an amount which when added to the award shall constitute just compensation for the damage and/or use of the invention by the Government. The owner of any patent issued upon an application that was subject to a secrecy order issued pursuant to section 181 of this title, who did not apply for compensation as above provided, shall have the right, after the date of issuance of such patent, to bring suit in the United States Claims Court for just compensation for the damage caused by reason of the order of secrecy and/or use by the Government of the invention resulting from his disclosure. The right to compensation for use shall begin on the date of the first use of the invention by the Government. In a suit under the provisions of this section the United States may avail itself of all defenses it may plead in an action under section 1498 of title 28. This section shall not confer a right of action on anyone or his successors, assigns, or legal representatives who, while in the full-time employment or service of the United States, discovered, invented, or developed the invention on which the claim is based.

Section 184. Filing of application in foreign country

Except when authorized by a license obtained from the Commissioner a person shall not file or cause or authorize to be filed in any foreign country prior to six months after filing in the United States an application for patent or for the registration of a utility model, industrial design, or model in respect of an invention made in this country. A license shall not be granted with respect to an invention subject to an order issued by the Commissioner pursuant to section 181 of this title without the concurrence of the head of the departments and the chief officers of the agencies who caused the order to be issued. The license may be granted retroactively where an application has been filed abroad through error and without deceptive intent and the application does not disclose an invention within the scope of section 181 of this title.

The term ''application'' when used in this chapter includes applications and any modifications, amendments, or supplements thereto, or divisions thereof.

The scope of a license shall permit subsequent modifications, amendments, and supplements containing additional subject matter if the application upon which the request for the license is based is not, or was not, required to be made available for inspection under section 181 of this title and if such modifications, amendments, and supplements do not change the general nature of the invention in a manner which would require such application to be made available for inspection under such section 181. In any case in which a license is not, or was not, required in order to file an application in any foreign country, such subsequent modifications amendments, and supplements may be made, without a license, to the application filed in the foreign country if the United States application was not required to be made available for inspection under section 181 and if such modifications, amendments, and supplements do not, or did not, change the general nature of the invention in a manner which would require the United States application to have been made available for inspection under such section 181.

Section 185. Patent barred for filing without license

Notwithstanding any other provisions of law any person, and his successors, assigns, or legal representatives, shall not receive a United States patent for an invention if that person, or his successors, assigns, or legal representatives shall, without procuring the license prescribed in section 184 of this title, have made, or consented to or assisted another's making, application in a foreign country for a patent or for the registration of a utility model, industrial design, or model in respect of the invention. A United States patent issued to such person, his successors, assigns, or legal representatives shall be invalid, unless the failure to procure such license was through error and without deceptive intent, and the patent does not disclose subject matter within the scope of section 181 of this title.

Section 186. Penalty

Whoever, during the period or periods of time an invention has been ordered to be kept secret and the grant of a patent thereon withheld pursuant to section 181 of this title, shall, with knowledge of such order and without due authorization, willfully publish or disclose or authorize or cause to be published or disclosed the invention, or material information with respect thereto, or whoever willfully, in violation of the provisions of section 184 of this title, shall file or cause or authorize to be filed in any foreign country an application for patent or for the registration of a utility model, industrial design, or model in respect of any invention made in the United States, shall, upon conviction, be fined not more than $10,000 or imprisoned for not more than two years, or both.

Sections 187. Nonapplicability to certain persons

The prohibitions and penalties of this chapter shall not apply to any officer or agent of the United States acting within the scope of his authority, nor to any person acting upon his written instructions or permission.

Section 188. Rules and regulations, delegation of power

The Atomic Energy Commission, the Secretary of a defense department, the chief officer of any other department or agency of the Government designated by the President as a defense agency of the United States, and the Secretary of Commerce, may separately issue rules and regulations to enable the respective department or agency to carry out the provisions of this chapter, and may delegate any power conferred by this chapter.

[*The Atomic Energy Commission was abolished and succeeded by the Energy Research and Development Administration, which was in turn succeeded by the Department of Energy.]

Document 7.5

National Security Decision Directive 145 (Unclassified Version)

(The White House, September 17, 1984)

NATIONAL POLICY ON TELECOMMUNICATIONS
AND AUTOMATED INFORMATION SYSTEMS SECURITY

Recent advances in microelectronics technology have stimulated an unprecedented growth in the supply of telecommunications and information processing services within the government and throughout the private sector. As new technologies have been applied, traditional distinctions between telecommunications and automated information systems have begun to disappear. Although this trend promises greatly improved efficiency and effectiveness, it also poses significant security challenges. Telecommunications and automated information processing systems are highly susceptible to interception, unauthorized electronic access, and related forms of technical exploitation, as well as other dimensions of the hostile intelligence threat. The technology to exploit these electronic systems is widespread and is used extensively by foreign nations and can be employed, as well, by terrorist groups and criminal elements. Government systems as well as those which process the private or proprietary information of U.S. persons and businesses can become targets for foreign exploitation.

Within the government these systems process and communicate classified national security information and other sensitive information concerning the vital interests of the United States. Such information, even if unclassified in isolation, often can reveal highly classified and other sensitive information when taken in aggregate. The compromise of this information, especially to hostile intelligence services, does serious damage to the United States and its national security interests. A comprehensive and coordinated approach must be taken to protect the government's telecommunications and automated information systems against current and projected threats. This approach must include mechanisms for formulating policy, for overseeing systems security resources programs, and for coordinating and executing technical activities.

This Directive: Provides initial objectives, policies, and an organizational structure to guide the conduct of national activities directed toward safeguarding systems which process or communicate sensitive information from hostile exploitation; establishes a mechanism for policy development; and assigns responsibilities for implementation. It is intended to assure full participation and cooperation among the various existing centers of technical expertise throughout the Executive Branch, to promote a coherent and coordinated defense against the hostile intelligence threat to these systems, and to foster an appropriate partnership between government and the private sector in attaining these goals. This Directive specifically recognizes the special requirements for protection of intelligence sources and methods. It is intended that the mechanisms established by this Directive will initially focus on those automated information systems which are connected to telecommunications transmission systems.

1. Objectives. Security is a vital element of the operational effectiveness of the national security activities of the government and of military combat readiness. Assuring the security of telecommunications and automated information systems which process and communicate classified national security information, and other sensitive government national security information, and offering assistance in the protection of certain private sector information are key national responsibilities. I, therefore, direct that the government's capabilities for securing telecommunications and automated information systems against technical exploitation threats be maintained or improved to provide for:

a. A reliable and continuing capability to assess threats and vulnerabilities, and to implement appropriate, effective countermeasures.
b. A superior technical base within the government to achieve this security, and support for a superior technical base within the private sector in areas which complement and enhance government capabilities.

179

c. A more effective application of government resources and encouragement of private sector security initiatives.

d. Support and enhancement of other policy objectives for national telecommunications and automated information systems.

2. Policies. In support of these objectives, the following policies are established:

a. Systems which generate, store, process, transfer or communicate classified information in electrical form shall be secured by such means as are necessary to prevent compromise or exploitation.

b. Systems handling other sensitive, but unclassified, government or government-derived information, the loss of which could adversely affect the national security interest, shall be protected in proportion to the threat of exploitation and the associated potential damage to the national security.

c. The government shall encourage, advise, and, where appropriate, assist the private sector to: identify systems which handle sensitive non-government information, the loss of which could adversely affect the national security; determine the threat to, and vulnerability of, these systems; and formulate strategies and measures for providing protection in proportion to the threat of exploitation and the associated potential damage. Information and advice from the perspective of the private sector will be sought with respect to implementation of this policy. In cases where implementation of security measures to non-governmental systems would be in the national security interest, the private sector shall be encouraged, advised, and, where appropriate, assisted in undertaking the application of such measures.

d. Efforts and programs begun under PD-24 which support these policies shall be continued.

3. Implementation. This Directive establishes a senior level steering group; an interagency group at the operating level; an executive agent and a national manager to implement these objectives and policies.

4. Systems Security Steering Group.

a. A Systems Security Steering Group consisting of the Secretary of State, the Secretary of the Treasury, the Secretary of Defense, the Attorney General, the Director of the Office of Management and Budget, the Director of Central Intelligence, and chaired by the Assistant to the President for National Security Affairs is established. The Steering Group shall:

(1) Oversee this Directive and ensure its implementation. It shall provide guidance to the Executive Agent and through him to the National Manager with respect to the activities undertaken to implement this Directive.

(2) Monitor the activities of the operating level National Telecommunications and Information Systems Security Committee and provide guidance for its activities in accordance with the objectives and policies contained in this Directive.

(3) Review and evaluate the security status of those telecommunications and automated information systems that handle classified or sensitive government or government-derived information with respect to established objectives and priorities, and report findings and recommendations through the National Security Council to the President.

(4) Review consolidated resources program and budget proposals for telecommunications systems security, including the COMSEC Resources Program, for the US Government and provide recommendations to OMB for the normal budget review process.

(5) Review in aggregate the program and budget proposals for the security of automated information systems of the departments and agencies of the government.

(6) Review and approve matters referred to it by the Executive Agent in fulfilling the responsibilities outlined in paragraph 6 below.

(7) On matters pertaining to the protection of intelligence sources and methods be guided by the policies of the Director of Central Intelligence.

(8) Interact with the Steering Group on National Security Telecommunications to ensure that the objectives and policies of this Directive and NSDD-97, National Security Telecommunications Policy, are addressed in a coordinated manner.

(9) Recommend for Presidential approval additions or revisions to this Directive as national interests may require.

(10) Identify categories of sensitive non-government information, the loss of which could adversely affect the national security interest, and recommend steps to protect such information.

b. The National Manager for Telecommunications and Information Systems Security shall function as executive secretary to the Steering Group.

5. The National Telecommunications and Information Systems Security Committee.

a. The National Telecommunications and Information Systems Security Committee (NTISSC) is established to operate under the direction of the Steering Group to consider technical matters and develop operative policies as necessary to implement the provisions of this Directive. The Committee shall be chaired by the Assistant Secretary of Defense (Command, Control, Communications and Intelligence) and shall be composed of a voting representative of each member of the Steering Group and of each of the following:

The Secretary of Commerce
The Secretary of Transportation
The Secretary of Energy
Chairman, Joint Chiefs of Staff
Administrator, General Services Administration
Director, Federal Bureau of Investigation
Director, Federal Emergency Management Agency
The Chief of Staff, United States Army
The Chief of Naval Operations
The Chief of Staff, United States Air Force
Commandant, United States Marine Corps
Director, Defense Intelligence Agency
Director, National Security Agency
Manager, National Communications System

b. The Committee shall:

(1) Develop such specific operating policies, objectives, and priorities as may be required to implement this Directive.

(2) Provide telecommunication and automated information systems security guidance to the departments and agencies of the government.

(3) Submit annually to the Steering Group an evaluation of the status of national telecommunications and automated information systems security with respect to established objectives and priorities.

(4) Identify systems which handle sensitive, non-government information, the loss and exploitation of which could adversely affect the national security interest, for the purpose of encouraging, advising and, where appropriate, assisting the private sector in applying security measures.

(5) Approve the release of sensitive systems technical security material, information, and techniques to foreign governments or international organizations with the concurrence of the Director of Central Intelligence for those activities which he manages.

(6) Establish and maintain a national system for promulgating the operating policies, directives, and guidance which may be issued pursuant to this Directive.

(7) Establish permanent and temporary subcommittees as necessary to discharge its responsibilities.

(8) Make recommendations to the Steering Group on Committee membership and establish criteria and procedures for permanent observers from other departments or agencies affected by specific matters under deliberation, who may attend meetings upon invitation of the Chairman.

(9) Interact with the National Communications System Committee of Principals established by Executive Order 12472 to ensure the coordinated execution of assigned responsibilities.

c. The Committee shall have two subcommittees, one focusing on telecommunications security and one focusing on automated information systems security. The two subcommittees shall interact closely and any recommendations concerning implementation of protective measures shall combine and coordinate both areas where appropriate, while considering any differences in the level of maturity of the technologies to support such implementation. However, the level of maturity of one technology shall not impede implementation in other areas which are deemed feasible and important.

  d. The Committee shall have a permanent secretariat composed of personnel of the National Security Agency and such other personnel from departments and agencies represented on the Committee as are requested by the Chairman. The National Security Agency shall provide facilities and support as required. Other departments and agencies shall provide facilities and support as requested by the Chairman.

6. The Executive Agent of the Government for Telecommunications and Information Systems Security. The Secretary of Defense is the Executive Agent of the Government for Communications Security; under authority of Executive Order 12333. By authority of this Directive he shall serve an expanded role as Executive Agent of the Government for Telecommunications and Automated Information Systems Security and shall be responsible for implementing, under his signature, the policies developed by the NTISSC. In this capacity he shall act in accordance with policies and procedures established by the Steering Group and the NTISSC to:

  a. Ensure the development, in conjunction with NTISSC member departments and agencies, of plans and programs to fulfill the objectives of this Directive, including the development of necessary security architectures.
  b. Procure for and provide to departments and agencies of the government and, where appropriate, to private institutions (including government contractors) and foreign governments, technical security material, other technical assistance, and other related services of common concern, as required to accomplish the objectives of this Directive.
  c. Approve and provide minimum security standards and doctrine, consistent with provisions of the Directive.
  d. Conduct, approve, or endorse research and development of techniques and equipment for telecommunications and automated information systems security for national security information.
  e. Operate, or coordinate the efforts of, government technical centers related to telecommunications and automated information systems security.
  f. Review and assess for the Steering Group the proposed telecommunications systems security programs and budgets for the departments and agencies of the government for each fiscal year and recommend alternatives, where appropriate. The views of all affected departments and agencies shall be fully expressed to the Steering Group.
  g. Review for the Steering Group the aggregated automated information systems security program and budget recommendations of the departments and agencies of the US Government for each fiscal year.

7. The National Manager for Telecommunications Security and Automated Information Systems Security. The Director, National Security Agency is designated the National Manager for Telecommunications and Automated Information Systems Security and is responsible to the Secretary of Defense as Executive Agent for carrying out the foregoing responsibilities. In fulfilling these responsibilities the National Manager shall have authority in the name of the Executive Agent to:

  a. Examine government telecommunications systems and automated information systems and evaluate their vulnerability to hostile interception and exploitation. Any such activities, including those involving monitoring of official telecommunications, shall be conducted in strict compliance with law, Executive Orders and applicable Presidential Directives. No monitoring shall be performed without advising the heads of the agencies, departments, or services concerned.
  b. Act as the government focal point for cryptography, telecommunications systems security, and automated information systems security.
  c. Conduct, approve, or endorse research and development of techniques and equipment for telecommunications and automated information systems security for national security information.
  d. Review and approve all standards, techniques, systems and equipments for telecommunications and automated information systems security.
  e. Conduct foreign communications security liaison, including agreements with foreign

governments and with international and private organizations for telecommunications and automated information systems security, except for those foreign intelligence relationships conducted for intelligence purposes by the Director of Central Intelligence. Agreements shall be coordinated with affected departments and agencies.

f. Operate such printing and fabrication facilities as may be required to perform critical functions related to the provision of cryptographic and other technical security material or services.

g. Assess the overall security posture and disseminate information on hostile threats to telecommunications and automated information systems security.

h. Operate a central technical center to evaluate and certify the security of telecommunications systems and automated information systems.

i. Prescribe the minimum standards, methods and procedures for protecting cryptographic and other sensitive technical security material, techniques, and information.

j. Review and assess annually the telecommunications systems security programs and budgets of the departments and agencies of the government, and recommend alternatives, where appropriate, for the Executive Agent and the Steering Group.

k. Review annually the aggregated automated information systems security program and budget recommendations of the departments and agencies of the U.S. Government for the Executive Agent and the Steering Group.

l. Request from the heads of departments and agencies such information and technical support as may be needed to discharge the responsibilities assigned herein.

m. Enter into agreements for the procurement of technical security material and other equipment, and their provision to government agencies and, where appropriate, to private organizations, including government contractors, and foreign governments.

8. The Heads of Federal Departments and Agencies shall:

a. Be responsible for achieving and maintaining a secure posture for telecommunications and automated information systems within their departments or agencies.

b. Ensure that the policies, standards and doctrines issued pursuant to this Directive are implemented within their departments or agencies.

c. Provide to the Systems Security Steering Group, the NTISSC, Executive Agent, and the National Manager, as appropriate, such information as may be required to discharge responsibilities assigned herein, consistent with relevant law, Executive Order, and Presidential Directives.

9. Additional Responsibilities.

a. The Secretary of Commerce, through the Director, National Bureau of Standards, shall issue for public use such information in automated information systems as the Steering Group may approve. The Manager, National Communications System, through the Administrator, General Services Administration, shall develop and issue for public use such information in telecommunications systems as the National Manager may approve. Such standards, while legally applicable only to Federal Departments and Agencies, shall be structured to facilitate their adoption as voluntary American National Standards as a means of encouraging their use by the private sector.

b. The Director, Office of Management and Budget shall:

   (1) Specify data to be provided during the annual budget review by the departments and agencies on programs and budgets relating to telecommunications systems security and automated information systems security of the departments and agencies of the government.

   (2) Consolidate and provide such data to the National Manager via the Executive Agent.

   (3) Review for consistency with this Directive, and amend as appropriate, OMB Circular A-71 (Transmittal Memorandum No. 1), OMB Circular A-76, as amended, and other OMB policies and regulations which may pertain to the subject matter herein.

10. Nothing in this Directive:

a. Alters the existing authorities of the Director of Central Intelligence, including his responsibility to act as Executive Agent of the Government for technical security countermeasures (TSCM).

b. Provides the NTISSC, the Executive Agent, or the National Manager authority to examine the facilities of other departments and agencies without approval of the head of such department or agency, nor to request or collect information concerning their operation for any purpose not provided for herein.

c. Amends or contravenes the provisions of existing law, Executive Orders, or Presidential Directives which pertain to the privacy aspects or financial management of automated information systems or to the administrative requirements for safeguarding such resources against fraud, abuse, and waste.

d. Is intended to establish additional review processes for the procurement of automated information processing systems.

11. For the purposes of this Directive, the following terms shall have the meanings indicated:

a. Telecommunications means the preparation, transmission, communication or related processing of information by electrical, electromagnetic, electromechanical, or electro-optical means.

b. Automated Information Systems means systems which create, prepare, or manipulate information in electronic form for purposes other than telecommunication, and includes computers, word processing systems, other electronic information handling systems, and associated equipment.

c. Telecommunications and Automated Information Systems Security means protection afforded to telecommunications and automated information systems, in order to prevent exploitation through interception, unauthorized electronic access, or related technical intelligence threats, and to ensure authenticity. Such protection results from the application of security measures (including cryptosecurity, transmission security, emission security, and computer security) to systems which generate, store, process, transfer, or communicate information of use to an adversary, and also includes the physical protection of sensitive technical security material and sensitive technical security information.

d. Technical security material means equipment, components, devices, and associated documentation or other media which pertain to cryptography, or to the securing of telecommunications and automated information systems.

12. The functions of the Interagency Group for Telecommunications Protection and the National Communications Security Committee (NCSC) as established under the authority of the Interagency Group or the NCSC, which have not been superseded by this Directive, shall remain in effect until modified or rescinded by the Steering Group or the NTISSC, respectively.

3. Except for ongoing telecommunications protection activities mandated by and pursuant to PD/NSC-24, that Directive is hereby superseded and cancelled.

Document 7.6

National Security Decision Directive 189

(The White House, September 21, 1985)

NATIONAL POLICY ON THE TRANSFER OF SCIENTIFIC, TECHNICAL AND ENGINEERING INFORMATION

I. PURPOSE

This directive establishes national policy for controlling the flow of science, technology, and engineering information produced in federally-funded fundamental research at colleges, universities, and laboratories. Fundamental research is defined as follows:

" 'Fundamental research' means basic and applied research in science and engineering, the results of which ordinarily are published and shared broadly within the scientific community, as distinguished from proprietary research and from industrial development, design, production, and product utilization, the results of which ordinarily are restricted for proprietary or national security reasons."

II. BACKGROUND

The acquisition of advanced technology from the United States by Eastern Bloc nations for the purpose of enhancing their military capabilities poses a significant threat to our national security. Intelligence studies indicate a small but significant target of the Eastern Bloc intelligence gathering effort is science and engineering research performed at universities and federal laboratories. At the same time, our leadership position in science and technology is an essential element in our economic and physical security. The strength of American science requires a research environment conducive to creativity, an environment in which the free exchange of ideas is a vital component.

In 1982, the Department of Defense and National Science Foundation sponsored a National Academy of Sciences study of the need for controls on scientific information. This study was chaired by Dr. Dale Corson, President Emeritus of Cornell University. It concluded that, while there has been a significant transfer of U.S. technology to the Soviet Union, the transfer has occurred through many routes with universities and open scientific communication of fundamental research being a minor contributor. Yet as the emerging government-university-industry partnership in research activities continues to grow, a more significant problem may well develop.

III. POLICY

It is the policy of this Administration that, to the maximum extent possible, the products of fundamental research remain unrestricted. It is also the policy of this Administration that, where the national security requires control, the mechanism for control of information generated during federally-funded fundamental research in science, technology and engineering at colleges, universities and laboratories is classification. Each federal government agency is responsible for: a) determining whether classification is appropriate prior to the award of a research grant, contract, or cooperative agreement and, if so, controlling the research results through standard classification procedures; b) periodically reviewing all research grants, contracts, or cooperative agreements for potential classification. No restrictions may be placed upon the conduct or reporting of federally-funded fundamental research that has not received national security classification, except as provided in applicable U.S. Statutes.

8

Up from Autarky

Sarah C. Carey

When Mikhail Gorbachev came to power in 1985 and began developing his policy of *perestroika*, or economic reform, he inherited a system that came as close to autarky as any large, developed economy in the world. The Soviet Union maintained a non-convertible currency. It gave a few state organizations under the jurisdiction of the Ministry of Foreign Trade monopoly powers over foreign trade and, with minor exceptions, it barred investment by Western capital. The state's policy, unchanged since Stalin's time, was to rely on the capitalist world for as little as possible.

It was also a system in trouble. Growth had stagnated. World oil prices were falling rapidly, and oil was the major generator of hard, or convertible, currency for the Soviet economy. Without hard currency, the Soviets could not begin to import the technology they needed to modernize their industries.

Devising a new Soviet policy toward the world economy required more than eighteen months. A broad restructuring of foreign trade was announced in late 1986 and early 1987. This included the leadership's declaration of intent to become a full participant in the international bodies that establish policy for trade and finance (the GATT, the World Bank, the IFC, etc.). It also included reorganization of the old Ministry of Foreign Trade as the Ministry of Foreign Economic Relations and the creation of the Commission on Foreign Economic Relations, an umbrella policy-making and regulatory organization that reports directly to the Council of Ministers.

The former Ministry's monopoly over foreign trade was dissolved, with authorization to trade given initially to twenty ministries and seventy enterprises. This decentralization increased gradually until April 1, 1989, when all enterprises and producing cooperatives were authorized to import and export on their own or through trading companies. Similar decentralization occurred in regard to the Soviet banking system; GOSBANK became a central or regulatory bank, the former Bank for Foreign Trade was reorganized and a series of new banks created, each of which now has the opportunity to become involved in foreign trade transactions.

These reforms, directed primarily at the foreign trade sector, coincided with major reforms of the domestic economy. During the same period of time, state enterprises were given greater decision-making authority, were put on *khozraschet* (self-financing) and were permitted to retain a larger percentage of their hard currency earnings (thereby encouraging exports). New private companies were created, known as cooperatives, (now reaching more than 75,000 in number) which have also become active in foreign trade. Equally important, the USSR began a far-reaching reform of its legal system, fundamentally altering commercial rights and relationships in ways that encourage foreign investment. These efforts included reform of the patent and copyright laws, redefinition of concepts of property and ownership and a new system of insuring international investments in the USSR.

Joint Ventures

Most importantly, from the standpoint of Western companies seeking a foothold in the Soviet market, a pair of decrees **(Documents 8.1 and 8.2)** issued on January 13, 1987 laid out new rules permitting joint ventures between Soviet and foreign enterprises. Prior to these, there had been a limited number of industrial cooperation agreements with foreign firms, involving a small amount of investment. But the joint venture decrees led to the first major Western investments in the Soviet economy since the 1920s. By late 1989, the Soviets had recorded almost 1000 joint venture agreements, roughly 12 percent of which involved American firms. Many more were under negotiation.

The original joint venture decrees established some major principles. The governance of each joint venture would be defined by its charter and would permit significant Western involvement—up to 49% ownership and broad representation, unanimous or ''blocking votes'' and the right to name the Vice

Chairman of the Board of Directors and the Deputy General Director. Joint ventures were to be registered with the USSR Ministry of Finance and approved by the Council of Ministers.

The January 1987 decrees also established the right of the joint venture to develop its own business plan, to set the prices for its products and to engage directly in foreign trade. These and many other activities ordinarily controlled by various Soviet regulatory bodies were left to the discretion of the joint venture's board of directors. Further, the transfer of technology to the joint venture and quality control assurances were to be negotiated by the parties to the joint venture, alleviating the concerns of the Western partners that their products would not meet corporate standards. Taxation of the joint venture's profits was set at 30% with a withholding tax on repatriated profits of 20%. An automatic two-year tax holiday was granted, with the possibility of negotiating further holidays. Negotiators soon learned that the tax on profits could be avoided if the joint venture reinvested its earnings or enlarged the various "funds" authorized by the charter, with the Western partner being compensated for its investments via various charges for technology, training, etc., instead of through the distribution of profits.

The initial decree has been modified on a number of occasions, with almost all of the modifications reflecting a highly flexible attitude on the part of the Soviets and a responsiveness to the complaints of foreigners. Decree 1074 of September 1987 **(Document 8.3)** granted joint ventures the right to obtain parts on the Soviet market directly, without having to go through foreign trade organizations (FTOs). It also reduced the approval level for the creation of a joint venture from the Council of Ministers to the ministry or other organization with supervisory jurisdiction over the Soviet party. It further permitted the Western partner to utilize ruble profits (for joint ventures producing for the domestic market) to purchase goods on the Soviet market for export that otherwise could only be purchased with hard currency.

Decree 1405 of December 1988 **(Document 8.4)** liberalized the foreign trade and joint venture rules still further. As noted above, it gave every Soviet enterprise, including cooperatives, the right to engage directly in foreign trade. It authorized the establishment of currency auctions in which Soviet enterprises could bid, in rubles, for hard currency surpluses of other enterprises or reserves put up for sale by the central bank. This promised to be a first step toward a convertible ruble, but to date that

promise has not been realized. The first auction in November 1989 resulted in a 10:1 exchange rate in favor of the dollar, but was not open to foreign or joint venture participants. The December 1988 decree also allowed cooperatives to form joint ventures on an equal footing with state enterprises. And, it did away with the 1987 requirements that the joint venture's chief executive and Board Chairman be Soviet citizens and that the Soviet partners own a minimum of 51 percent of the new company.

In addition, Decree 1405 granted further tax concessions regarding the withholding tax on the repatriated profits of foreign joint venture partners. This applies only if the joint venture is producing certain products or if the joint venture is located in the Soviet Far East. It also gave joint ventures sole discretion over questions of hiring and firing and the remuneration of their Soviet employees, as well as over decisions related to insurance and accounting. The latter is particularly significant, reflecting a Soviet commitment to move toward international standards of accounting.

These changes have created a greater interest on the part of U.S. companies in joint ventures and have stimulated tremendous activity by Soviet organizations seeking to become involved in foreign trade for the first time. Many Soviet business organizations, concerned about the current upheaval and change in the Soviet economy, seem to feel that the best security blanket for the future is a Western partner.

Ministries' Role

Meanwhile, the industrial ministries' role in the game has been diminishing. The ministry of the future is destined to play less of a role in day-to-day operations and more of a regulatory or policy-making role. Some ministries have already weakened considerably. Others, such as GOSAGROPROM, the state agro-industrial complex, have been eliminated altogether. Increasingly, decision-making responsibility regarding industrial development is decentralized. This coincides with the domestic reorganization of relations between Moscow and the regions, giving republic and local governments greater taxing and other authority. These developments have been a mixed blessing for foreign businessmen, who found it easier to deal with centralized ministries that could meet their requirements for land, buildings, apartments, raw materials and other items. Now Western companies must deal with a broad range of organizations scattered through the USSR.

Decree 203 of March 7, 1989 **(Document 8.5)** marked the only instance in recent foreign trade regulations where opportunities appeared to be narrowed rather than expanded. One of the decree's major goals was to limit the involvement of joint ventures in middleman operations, unless those operations are necessary to meet the hard currency needs of the joint venture. Some of the early joint ventures, for instance, had imported computers, ostensibly to help them develop software for both the Soviet and export markets. Instead, they had turned around and sold the computers on the Soviet internal market for greatly increased prices. The decree cautioned joint ventures not to engage in the purchase and sale of finished goods without special permission.

In a move affecting all exporters (not just joint ventures), the decree established a list **(Document 8.6)** of goods which may be imported or exported only with the specific permission of interested ministries, as well as a list of goods which cannot be exported at all. In some cases, the items on the list surprised no one. No one expected the Soviet Union, for instance, to allow the unrestricted export of raw or cut diamonds. In other cases, it appeared that certain ministries were unreasonably seeking to reassert themselves. Why, for instance, should the Ministry of Foreign Economic Relations control the right to export waste products from steel production?

The place of the joint venture in the larger context of Soviet foreign trade is still evolving. When the original joint venture decrees were issued in January 1987, the only way in which many Soviet organizations could participate directly in foreign trade was through a joint venture. That, of course, changed with the December, 1988 decree. A decree in May 1989 **(Document 8.7)** provided that with the proper permission, any Soviet organization may buy foreign securities and form foreign corporations. These measures make it possible for Soviet enterprises to get involved directly in foreign markets without going through specially privileged Soviet organizations or joint ventures. However, the joint venture—in the USSR as elsewhere—remains one of the few avenues for ensuring the continued involvement of a Western partner. There are indications that the whole concept of a joint venture may soon be superseded by generic legislation which will make stock-issuing companies possible with and without foreign ownership.

More Reforms

The Soviets have a range of additional reforms under discussion that promise to further liberalize foreign trade and investment. These include the creation of free economic zones, where additional tax, customs, and financial incentives will be available to foreign investors; the right to enter into long-term leases of land, buildings and other assets; and the possible creation of a gold-backed or product-backed ruble. Other reforms, such as broader stock ownership, that are being discussed largely in the context of the domestic economy, may also be available to foreigners.

The most important steps toward breaking down the barriers to trade with the outside world would be to replace price subsidies with market pricing and to make the ruble fully convertible. The Soviets are fully committed to this course of action and are trying to design the best strategy for effecting it. They are also preparing the way for such reforms by creating the legal infrastructure capable of handling open trade and investment with the West. Mikhail Gorbachev, in his letter to the heads of the major Western economic powers **(Document 8.8)**, has stated that the Soviets want to continue the process of integrating their economy with the world's. As long as that remains the case, Soviet foreign trade and joint venture legislation is likely to become more open, moving ever further away from autarky.

Document 8.1

On the Establishment in the Territory of the U.S.S.R. and Operation of Joint Ventures with the Participation of Soviet Organizations and Firms from Capitalist and Developing Countries

(Decree of the U.S.S.R. Council of Ministers, January 13, 1987)

For the purpose of further development of trade, economic, scientific and technical cooperation with capitalist and developing countries on a stable and mutually beneficial basis, the USSR Council of Ministers hereby decrees:

I. General Provisions

1. Joint ventures with the participation of Soviet organizations and firms of capitalist and developing countries (hereinafter "joint ventures") shall be established in the territory of the USSR with the authorization of the USSR Council of Ministers and on the basis of agreements concluded by partners therein.

Joint ventures shall be governed in their activities by the Decree of the Presidium of the USSR Supreme Soviet of January 13, 1987, "On Questions Concerning the Establishment in the Territory of the USSR and Operation of Joint Ventures, International Amalgamations and Organizations with the Participation of Soviet and Foreign Organizations, Firms and Management Bodies," by this Decree and other legislative acts of the Union of Soviet Socialist Republics and Union Republics with exceptions provided for by interstate and intergovernmental agreements, which the USSR is a party to.

2. Proposals in respect of the establishment of joint ventures with feasibility studies and draft foundation documents annexed thereto shall be submitted by Soviet organizations concerned to Ministries and government agencies, under which they operate. Ministries and government agencies of the Union Republics shall submit such proposals to the Councils of Ministers of their Republics.

The aforesaid Ministries and government agencies of the USSR and the Councils of Ministers of Union Republics shall agree upon the proposals with the USSR State Planning Committee, the USSR Ministry of Finance and other Ministries and government agencies concerned.

The agreed proposals for the establishment of joint ventures shall be submitted to the USSR Council of Ministers.

3. Ministries and government agencies, within the system of which Soviet partners in joint ventures

operate, shall set up joint ventures with the purpose to satisfy more fully domestic requirements for certain types of manufactured products, raw materials and foodstuffs, to attract advanced foreign equipment and technologies, management expertise, additional material and financial resources to the USSR national economy, to expand the national export sector and to reduce superfluous imports.

II. Partners in, Property and Rights of Joint Ventures

4. One or more Soviet enterprises (amalgamations and other organizations) which are legal entities, and one or more foreign firms (companies, corporations and other organizations) which are legal entities may be partners in a joint venture.

5. The share of the Soviet side in the authorized fund of a joint venture shall be not less than 51 per cent.

6. Joint ventures are legal entities under Soviet law. They may, in their own name, contract, acquire proprietary and non-proprietary personal rights, undertake obligations, sue and be sued in courts of justice and in arbitration tribunals. Joint ventures shall have independent balance and operate on the basis of full cost accounting, self-support and self-financing.

7. A joint venture shall have a charter approved by its partners. The charter shall specify the nature of the joint venture, the objectives of its operation, its legal address, the list of partners, the amount of the authorized fund, the shares of partners therein, the procedure for raising the authorized fund (including foreign currency contents), the structure, composition and competence of the venture's management bodies, the decision-making procedure, the range of issues to be unanimously settled, and the joint venture liquidation procedure. The charter may incorporate other provisions related to the specific character of a joint venture's operations unless these are contrary to Soviet law.

8. The period of operation of a joint venture shall be specified by its partners in an agreement on the establishment thereof or in the joint venture's charter (hereinafter "foundation documents").

9. As soon as the foundation documents come into force, joint ventures established in the territory of the USSR shall be registered with the USSR Ministry of Finance and acquire the rights of a legal entity at the time of registration. A notification on the establishment of joint ventures shall be published in the press.

10. The authorized fund of a joint venture is formed from contributions made by the partners. It can be replenished by using profits derived from business operation of the joint venture and, if necessary, through additional contributions by the partners.

11. Contributions to the authorized fund of a joint venture may include buildings, structures, equipment and other assets, rights to use land, water and other natural resources, buildings, structures and equipment, as well as other proprietary rights (including those to work inventions and use know-how), money assets in the currencies of the partners' countries and in freely convertible currencies.

12. The contribution of the Soviet partner to the authorized fund of a joint venture is evaluated in rubles on the basis of agreed prices with due regard to world market prices. The contribution of the foreign partner is evaluated in the same manner, with the value of the contribution being converted to rubles at the official exchange rate of the USSR State Bank as of the date of signing the joint venture agreement or as of any other date agreed by the partners. In the absence of world market prices the value of contributed property is agreed by the partners.

13. Equipment, materials and other property imported into the USSR by foreign partners in a joint venture as their contribution to the authorized fund of the venture are exempt from custom duties.

14. The property of a joint venture is subject to compulsory insurance with USSR insurance agencies.

15. A joint venture is entitled under Soviet legislation to own, use and dispose of its property in accordance with the objectives of its activities and the purpose of the property. The property of a joint venture shall not be requisitioned or confiscated in the administrative order.

The property rights of a joint venture shall be protected under Soviet legislation protecting state-owned Soviet organizations. Execution can be applied to the property of a joint venture only by a decision of bodies empowered under USSR legislation to hear disputes involving joint ventures.

16. Partners in a joint venture shall have the right to assign, by common consent, their shares in the joint venture fully or partially to third parties. In each particular case the assignment is effected with an endorsement of the State Foreign Economic Commission of the USSR Council of Ministers. Soviet partners have the priority right to acquire shares of foreign partners.

If a joint venture is reorganized its rights and obligations shall pass to the assignees.

17. Industrial property rights, belonging to joint ventures are protected by the Soviet law, including protection in the form of patents. The procedure for the assignment of industrial property rights to a joint venture by partners therein and by a joint venture to partners therein, as well as for commercial working of those rights and their protection abroad is defined by the foundation documents.

18. A joint venture shall be liable on its obligations in all of its property.

The Soviet State and the partners in a joint venture shall not be liable on its obligations, nor shall a joint venture be liable on the obligations of the Soviet State and of the partners in the venture.

Affiliates of a joint venture established in the territory of the USSR, which are legal entities, shall not be liable on the obligations of joint ventures, nor shall joint ventures be liable on the obligations of such affiliates.

19. Joint ventures established in the territory of the USSR may set up affiliates and representation offices provided their foundation documents stipulate their right to do so.

Affiliates of joint ventures set up with the participation of Soviet organizations in other countries shall be established in the territory of the USSR in accordance with the rules which apply to the establishment of joint ventures.

20. Disputes between a joint venture and Soviet state-owned cooperative and other public organizations, disputes among joint ventures, and disputes among partners in a joint venture over matters related to its activities shall be settled according to legislation of the USSR either by the USSR courts or, by common consent of both sides, by an arbitration tribunal.

III. Operation of Joint Ventures

21. The governing body of a joint venture is a board consisting of persons appointed by the partners. Its decision-making procedure is defined by the foundation documents.

The operational activities of a joint venture are governed by a management consisting of Soviet and foreign citizens.

The Chairman of the Board and the Director-General shall be citizens of the USSR.

22. A joint venture shall enter into relations with central state authorities of the USSR and of the Union Republics through authorities superior to the Soviet partner in the joint venture. Its contacts with local government authorities and other Soviet organizations shall be direct.

23. A joint venture is independent in developing and approving its business operation programmes. State bodies of the USSR shall not fix any mandatory plans for a joint venture nor shall they guarantee a market for its products.

24. A joint venture is entitled to transact independently in export and import operations necessary for its business activities, including export and import operations in the markets of CMEA member-countries.

The aforementioned export and import operations may also be effected through Soviet foreign trade organizations or marketing networks of foreign partners under contractual arrangements.

Shipping into and out of the USSR by a joint venture of goods and other property is effected under licences issued according to legislation of the USSR.

A joint venture is entitled to maintain correspondence, as well as telegraph, teletype and telephone communications with organizations in other countries.

25. All foreign currency expenditures of a joint venture, including transfer of profits and other sums due to foreign partners and specialists shall be covered by proceeds from sales of the joint venture's products on foreign markets.

26. Sales of products of a joint venture on the Soviet market and supplies to the joint venture from this market of equipment, raw and other materials, components, fuel, energy and other produce shall be effected through respective Soviet foreign trade organizations and paid in rubles on the basis of contractual prices with due regard to world market prices.

27. If necessary, a joint venture may use credits on commercial terms:
- in foreign currency—from the USSR Bank for Foreign Trade or, with its consent from foreign banks and firms;
- in rubles—from the USSR State Bank or the USSR Bank for Foreign Trade.

28. The USSR State Bank or the USSR Bank for Foreign Trade shall be authorized to check if credits extended to a joint venture are used for specified purposes, are secured and repaid in due time.

29. Monetary assets of a joint venture shall be deposited on its ruble account or currency account with the USSR State Bank and the USSR Bank for Foreign Trade respectively and shall be used for the purposes of the joint venture's operations. The money on the accounts of the joint venture shall bear interest:
- in foreign currency—depending on the world money market rates;
- in rubles—on terms and according to the procedure specified by the USSR State Bank.

Exchange rates fluctuations regarding foreign currency accounts of joint ventures and their operations in foreign currencies shall be carried over to their profit-and-loss accounts.

30. A joint venture shall form a reserve fund and other funds necessary for its operation and for the social needs of its personnel.

Deductions from profits shall be added to the reserve fund until the latter totals 25 per cent of the authorized fund of the joint venture. The amount of annual deductions to the reserve fund shall be defined by the foundation documents.

31. The profits of a joint venture, less the amounts to be appropriated by the USSR national budget and sums allocated to form and replenish the joint venture's funds shall be distributed among the partners in proportion to each partner's share in the authorized fund.

32. Foreign partners in a joint venture are guaranteed that amounts due to them as their share in distributed profits of the joint venture are transferable abroad in foreign currency.

33. Joint ventures shall make depreciation payments under regulations applying to state-owned Soviet organizations unless a different system is stipulated by the foundation documents. The sums thus accumulated shall remain at the joint venture's disposal.

34. The design and construction of joint venture's facilities, including those intended for social needs, shall be effected through contractual arrangements and paid for with the joint venture's own or loan money. Prior to approval, designs shall be agreed upon under the procedure established by the USSR State Building Committee. Orders from joint ventures shall receive priority both as regards limits on construction/assembly work to be carried out by Soviet construction/assembly organizations and as regards material resources required for the construction.

35. Cargoes of joint ventures shall be transported under the procedure established for Soviet organizations.

IV. Taxation of Joint Ventures

36. Joint ventures shall pay taxes at the rate of 30 per cent of their profit remaining after deductions

to their reserve and other funds intended for the development of production, science and technology. Sums paid in taxes shall be appropriated to the USSR national budget.

Joint ventures shall be exempt from taxes on their profits during the two initial years of their operation.

The USSR Ministry of Finance shall be authorized to reduce the tax rate or to completely exempt from tax individual payers.

37. The assessment of the profit tax shall be effected by a joint venture.

The amounts of the advance tax payment for a current year shall be declared by a joint venture on the basis of its financial plans for a current year. The assessment of the final tax amount on the profit, actually made during the expired financial year, shall be effected by a joint venture not later than March 15 of the year following the year under review.

38. Financial authorities are empowered to verify tax calculations prepared by joint ventures.

Overpaid taxes for the expired year can either be set off against current tax payments, or refunded to the payer at the latter's request.

39. The amount of the profit tax declared for the current year shall be transferred to the budget by equal installments not later than 15 days before the end of each quarter. The final amount shall be paid not later than April 1 of the year following the year under review.

Delayed payments shall be charged at the rate of 0.05 percent for every day of delay.

Collection of the sums of the tax not paid in time shall be carried out in accordance with the procedure described in regard to foreign legal persons by the Rules on Collection of Delayed Taxes and Non-tax Payments, endorsed by the Decree of the Presidium of the USSR Supreme Soviet of January 26, 1981 (Vedomosti Verkhovnogo Soveta SSSR, 1981, N.5, Art. 122).

40. A joint venture has the right to appeal against actions of financial authorities in regard to tax collection. An appeal is lodged with the financial authority which verifies the tax calculation. Each case shall be decided within one month from the day of the ruling.

The lodging of an appeal does not defer paying the tax.

41. Unless otherwise provided for by a treaty between the USSR and a respective foreign state, the part of the profit due to a foreign partner in a joint venture shall be taxed, if transferred abroad, at the rate of 20 per cent.

42. The aforementioned taxation procedure is applied to income made by joint ventures established in the territory of the USSR and by USSR affiliates of joint ventures set up with the participation of Soviet organizations in other countries, as a result of their operations both in the territory of the USSR, on its continental shelf, in the USSR economic zone, and in the territory of other countries.

43. Regulations regarding the taxation of joint ventures shall be issued by the USSR Ministry of Finance.

V. Supervision of Joint Ventures' Operations

44. In order to enable partners in a joint venture to exercise their supervision rights, the foundation documents shall stipulate a procedure for providing partners with information related to the operation of the joint venture, the state of its property, its profits and losses.

A joint venture may set up an auditing service to be formed in a manner defined by the foundation documents.

45. Joint ventures shall be held responsible under Soviet law for complying with the accounting and bookkeeping procedure and for the correctness thereof.

Joint ventures shall not submit any accounting or business information to the state or other authorities of foreign countries.

46. The auditing of finance, business and commercial activities of joint ventures shall be carried out for a consideration by the Soviet auditing organization operating on a self-supporting basis.

VI. Personnel of Joint Ventures

47. The personnel of joint ventures shall consist mainly of Soviet citizens. The management of a joint venture shall conclude collective agreements with a trade union organization formed at the enterprise. The contents of these agreements including provisions for the social needs of the personnel are defined by Soviet legislation and by the foundation documents.

48. The pay, routine of work and recreation, social security and social insurance of Soviet employees of joint ventures shall be regulated by Soviet legislation. This legislation shall also apply to foreign citizens employed at joint ventures, except for matters of pay, leaves, and pensions which are stipulated by a contract signed with each foreign employee.

The USSR State Committee for Labour and Social Affairs and the All-Union Central Council of Trade Unions shall be authorized to adopt special rules for the application of Soviet social insurance legislation to foreign employees of joint ventures.

49. A joint venture shall make contributions to the USSR national budget for state-sponsored social insurance of Soviet and foreign employees, as well as payments for pensions for Soviet employees in accordance with rates established for state-owned Soviet organizations. Contributions to cover foreign employees' pensions shall be transferred to respective funds in the countries of their permanent residence (in these countries' currencies).

50. The pay of foreign employees of a joint venture is subject to income tax at the rate and in accordance with the procedure set up by the Decree of the Presidium of the USSR Supreme Soviet of May 12, 1976 ''On the Income Tax Levied on Foreign Legal and Physical Persons'' (Vedomosti Verkhovnogo Soveta SSSR, 1978, No. 20, Art. 313). The unutilized portion of foreign employees' pay may be transferred abroad in foreign currency.

VII. Liquidation of Joint Ventures

51. A joint venture may be liquidated in cases and in the manner stipulated by the foundation documents, and also by a decision of the USSR Council of Ministers if the activities thereof are not consistent with the objectives defined by these documents. A notification of a liquidation of a joint venture shall be published in the press.

52. In the case of liquidation of a joint venture or upon withdrawal from it, the foreign partner shall have the right to return his contribution in money or in kind pro rata to the residual balance value of this contribution at the moment of liquidation of the joint venture, after discharging his obligations to the Soviet partners and third parties.

53. The liquidation of a joint venture shall be registered with the USSR Ministry of Finance.

Chairman of the USSR Council of Ministers
N. RYZHKOV

Manager of Operations of the USSR Council of Ministers
M. SMIRTIUKOV

Document 8.2

On Questions Concerning the Establishment in the Territory of the USSR and Operation of Joint Ventures, International Amalgamations and Organizations with the Participation of Soviet and Foreign Organizations, Firms and Management Bodies

(Decree of the Presidium of the USSR Supreme Soviet of January 13, 1987)

The Presidium of the USSR Supreme Soviet decrees:

1. Joint ventures established in the territory of the USSR with participation of Soviet and foreign organizations, firms and management bodies shall pay tax on profit at the rate and in the order provided for by the USSR Council of Ministers. Tax shall be appropriated to the USSR national budget.

Joint ventures shall be exempt from tax on profit for the two initial years of their operation.

The USSR Ministry of Finance shall be authorized to reduce the tax rate or to completely exempt from tax individual payers.

2. Collection of the sums of the tax not paid in time shall be carried out conformable to the procedure prescribed in regard of foreign legal persons by the Rules on Collection of Delayed Taxes and Non-tax Payments, endorsed by the Decree of the Presidium of the USSR Supreme Soviet of January 26, 1981. (Vedomosti Verkhovnogo Soveta SSSR, 1981, No. 5, Art. 122.)

3. Unless otherwise provided for by a treaty between the USSR and respective foreign state, the part of the profit due to a foreign partner in a joint venture shall be taxed, if transferred abroad, at the rate stipulated by the USSR Council of Ministers.

4. Land, entrails of the earth, water resources, and forests may be made available for use to joint ventures as for payment as well as free of charge.

5. Disputes of joint ventures, international amalgamations and organizations with Soviet state-owned, cooperative and other public organizations, their disputes among themselves, as well as disputes among partners in a joint venture, international amalgamation or organization over matters related to their activity shall be considered by the USSR courts or, upon agreement of the parties, by an arbitration tribunal, and in cases stipulated by the USSR legislation—by tribunals of state arbitration.

In this connection Article 9 of the USSR Law of November 30, 1979 "On State Arbitration in the USSR" (Vedomosti Verkhovnogo Soveta SSSR, 1979, No. 49, Art. 844) shall be amended to include after the words "and organizations" the words "joint ventures, international amalgamations and organizations of the USSR and other CMEA member-countries."

Chairman of the Presidium
of the USSR Supreme Soviet
A. GROMYKO

Secretary of the Presidium
of the USSR Supreme Soviet
T. MENTESHASHVILI

Document 8.3

On Additional Measures to Improve the Country's External Economic Activity in the New Conditions of Economic Management

(Excerpts from the Decree of the C.P.S.U. Central Committee and the USSR Council of Ministers as published by *Ekonomicheskaya Gazeta*, No. 41, October, 1987.)

On the Improvement of Work on the Establishment and Operation of Joint Ventures, International Amalgamations and Organizations, and on the Expansion of Direct Ties with Enterprises and Organizations in Socialist Countries

It is deemed necessary to simplify the existing procedures for taking decisions on the establishment of joint ventures, international amalgamations and organizations. USSR ministries and departments and the Council of Ministers of the Union republics are granted the right to independently take such decisions.

With a view to developing production and organizing cooperation, associations, enterprises and organizations, irrespective of the existence of agreements and protocols on direct ties, are permitted to sign contracts for single shipments of products, samples of articles, instruments, fittings, tools and secondary resources released in the process of the production of materials, machines and equipment, as well as contracts for the provision of services...

On the Further Development of Cooperation with Firms in the Capitalist and Developing Countries and Improvement of the Work on the Establishment and Operation of Joint Ventures and Lines of Production

With the aims of consistently realizing the CPSU's strategical course on using the advantages presented by the world division of labour, of consolidating the USSR's positions in international trade and applying the achievements of world science and technology in the national economy it is considered necessary to substantially invigorate the activity of the USSR's ministries, departments, enterprises and organizations in developing cooperation with the capitalist and developing countries.

The ministries and departments of the USSR and the Councils of Ministers of Union republics are granted the right to independently take decisions on setting up on Soviet territory joint ventures together with firms in the capitalist and developing countries.

It is established that a joint venture by agreement with Soviet enterprises and organizations shall determine the kind of currency to be paid in settlements for products realized and goods purchased as well as the procedure for realizing its products on the Soviet market and for shipping goods from this market.

By agreement between the participants in a joint venture their contributions to the authorized fund may be assessed in both Soviet and foreign currency.

It is considered expedient to appreciably expand the country's cooperation with the capitalist and developing countries' firms abroad in the fields of science and technology, trade, finance, services, tourism and advertising and with this purpose in mind to practise the establishment of joint research and design organizations, engineering, sales and advertising firms, joint servicing and repair of exported machinery, sending of skilled specialists and workers, purchase of shares, bonds and other securities, their issue and floatation.

On the Further Development of Economic Methods for Managing the Country's External Economic Ties

The CPSU Central Committee and the USSR Council of Ministers consider it necessary to ensure further improvement in the planning of the country's foreign economic ties as an integral component of the entire system of macroeconomic planning, to increase the effect of planning on the USSR's active participation in the international division of labour, promotion of socialist economic integration, effective change in the Soviet Union's export and import pattern, development of the initiative of associations, enterprises and organizations for expanding the export of competitive products, reduce irrational imports. To this end the USSR State Planning Committee, the USSR State Committee for Material and Technical Supply, USSR ministries and departments and the Councils of Ministers of Union republics are entrusted to ensure, through the system of government orders and limits, absolute fulfilment of the Soviet Union's international obligations arising from:

- the results of state plan coordination between the USSR and other socialist countries and the targets of the Comprehensive Programme of the CMEA Member-Countries' Scientific and Technological Progress until the Year 2000;
- trade and payment agreements between the USSR and India, Finland and other countries;
- agreements on economic and technical cooperation between the USSR and other countries.

The USSR State Planning Committee and the USSR State Committee for Material and Technical Supply are instructed to fully take into account in their draft plans and material balance-sheets the results of the agreements reached by USSR ministries and departments on export shipments to the capitalist countries, with the aim of obtaining the greatest possible increase in exports for freely convertible currency. The Councils of Ministers of Union republics shall be guided by this provision in respect to republican ministries and departments.

In conformity with the USSR Law on State Enterprise (Association), it is established, with a view to using favourable changes in the world market situation and developing direct contacts and other effective forms of economic cooperation, that enterprises (associations) have the right to export machinery and other products made over and above the government order and obligations under economic contracts.

With the object of consolidating the plan principles of the foreign economic activity of USSR ministries and departments, the Councils of Ministers of Union republics, associations, enterprises and organizations it is established that within the framework of their plans, in the sections on foreign economic ties, provision shall be made, pursuant to the targets of the state economic and social development plan, for measures and assignments to develop the export base, increase the output of products competitive on foreign markets, promote socialist economic integration including realization of the Comprehensive Programme of the CMEA Member-Countries' Scientific and Technological Progress, ensure thrifty expenditure of currency resources, deepen international cooperation in production and ensure the activity of joint ventures, international amalgamations and organizations.

The standing bodies of the USSR Council of Ministers are instructed to exercise methodological guidance and control as concerns the drawing up and realization of the said sections of the plan.

It is established that the output of joint ventures abroad as far as the portion purchased by the USSR is concerned, as well as the products obtained by way of processing raw materials and semifinished goods on a give-and-take basis are taken into account in the production and realization plans Soviet associations, enterprises and organizations and also in the export and import plans in the manner established by the USSR State Planning Committee.

With a view to raising the interest of foreign partners in setting up joint ventures on Soviet territory it is recognized possible to exempt these ventures from taxes on their profits during the first two years of their operation.

To simplify the procedure for using the currency funds of USSR associations, enterprises, organizations, ministries and departments and the Councils of Ministers of Union republics they are permitted to purchase products with their currency funds without first agreeing the matter through the appropriate foreign trade associations of the USSR Ministry of Foreign Trade, USSR State Committee for Foreign Economic Relations, Councils of Ministers of Union republics, USSR sectoral ministries and departments, foreign trade firms of associations, enterprises and organizations. Such purchases shall be made as a matter of top priority and considered when assessing results of the foreign trade organizations' plans.

The established procedure under which the said funds are spent on the import of machines, equipment, materials and other goods needed for the technical re-equipment, modernization and expansion of production and conduct of research and development, experimental and design work and other activities, and as concerns the funds in transferable rubles, to purchase goods for the work collectives, should be strictly followed.

The USSR ministries and departments, the Councils of Ministers of Union republics, associations, enterprises and organizations shall be responsible for the rational and thrifty expenditure of the currency funds at their disposal.

The State Foreign Economic Commission of the USSR Council of Ministers is instructed to work out and approve the procedure for organizing and carrying out systematic analysis and control over the effective expenditure of the said funds.

With a view to stimulating export shipments, the USSR Bank for Foreign Trade is permitted to grant associations, enterprises and organizations credit facilities in foreign currency to:

- set up and develop lines of export production for a period up to eight years, with these credit facilities being repaid from the proceeds of their exports;
- ensure their current activity, for a period up to two years;

• secure their future earnings, with due regard for the contracts signed on export goods.

With the aim of developing the socialist initiative of associations, enterprises and organizations and extending their economic autonomy it is considered possible for them and also USSR ministries and departments to combine their currency funds, transfer them to other enterprises, ministries, departments and banks on mutually advantageous terms, including the payment of appropriate interest, as well as invest them abroad with the consent of USSR ministries and departments.

The USSR Bank for Foreign Trade by agreement with the USSR Ministry of Finance is instructed, within a period of two months, to approve the procedure for the above-enumerated use of currency resources...

The CPSU Central Committee and the USSR Council of Ministers are confident that the above measures, when implemented, will ensure an appreciable rise in the initiative of associations, enterprises and organizations, USSR ministries and departments and the Councils of Ministers of Union republics ensuring the greatest possible increase in the effectiveness of the USSR's external economic ties in the interest of the country's accelerated social and economic development.

Document 8.4

Excerpts from "On Further Development of the Foreign Economic Activity of State, Cooperative, and Other Public Enterprises, Amalgamations, and Organizations."

(Resolution of the USSR Council of Ministers as published in *Ekonomicheskaya Gazeta* No. 51, Dec., 1988.)

The Council of Ministers of the USSR postulates that the foreign economic activity of state, cooperative and other public enterprises, amalgamations, and organizations is an integral part of their economic life, an active component of our ongoing work on radical economic reform, on strengthening the economy of the country and on raising its international authority, and on emerging on the modern level of technology and the organization of production.

The XIXth all-Union Conference of the CPSU acknowledged the expedience of restructuring the system of foreign economic relations in the framework of the current five-year plan. This is called for by the fact that, despite the creation of the organizational-legal and economic conditions, there are as yet no substantial achievements in foreign economic activity, particularly in the development of exports and the rationalization of its structure. Imports, as before, are mainly used for the resolution of current problems. The principle of currency self-sufficiency works weakly. We have yet to overcome the efforts of ministries and departments, and of the councils of ministers of the union republics, to solve their problems with resources they have not earned themselves. There is not enough socialist economic initiative by the economic leaders, and they do not give the necessary implementation to the measures adopted to stimulate foreign economic activity.

With the goals of a real broadening of the sphere of foreign economic ties, of actively including in this work enterprises, productive cooperatives, and other organizations, of further simplifying the procedure for organizing foreign economic ties, of realizing them in conditions of full hard currency self-sufficiency, of the consistent use of monetary-product relations, the Council of Ministers of the USSR resolves:

1. To consider as one of the most important tasks of national, republic, branch, and local organs of administration the provision of the organizational and economic conditions for the active inclusion of enterprises, amalgamations, productive cooperatives and other organizations in the various forms of foreign economic activity on the principles of currency self-sufficiency and the development of socialist economic initiative.

Attaching priority significance to the development of cooperation with socialist countries, to steadily create the conditions for active participation of the USSR in the formation of a unified market of the CMEA member countries on the basis of more thorough integration, the widespread inclusion of enterprises, amalgamations, and organizations in foreign economic activity and the expansion of their self-sufficiency in those questions, the use of commodity-money relations, and the joint action of national markets.

Legal and Organizational Questions of Foreign Economic Activity

2. To acknowledge the necessity of fundamentally democratizing the right to engage directly in export-import operations (including the markets of capitalist and developing countries).

To establish that from 1 April, 1989, the right to directly conduct export-import operations is held by all enterprises, amalgamations, productive cooperatives and other organizations whose production (works or services) is competitive on the foreign market. Their export-import operations are conducted on the basis of currency self-sufficiency, the results enter as an organic part into the totals of the economic activity, and affect the formulation of the economic stimulus funds and the currency funds.

Enterprises, amalgamations, productive cooperatives and other organizations can engage in export-import operations directly, creating for this, given the necessity, self-financing foreign trade firms, or on an agreed basis through other foreign trade organizations, being guided by the achievement of the most favorable conditions for exporting and importing, currency self-sufficiency and self-financing, and proceeding from the understanding that the state will not be responsible for their debts. The rules of currency assignment, established for enterprises, amalgamations, productive cooperatives and other organizations will not change in connection with the type of foreign economic organization they use to export their product (goods or services).

The Ministry of Foreign Economic Relations, the Ministry of Finance and the Chamber of Trade and Industry of the USSR will, within one month, work out and present to the Council of Ministers a suggestion for a registration system for enterprises, amalgamations, productive cooperatives and other organizations engaging in export-import operations.

The State Foreign Economic Commission of the Council of Ministers is given the right, through the representation of the Ministry of Foreign Economic Relations of the USSR and the councils of ministers of the union republics to suspend the engagement in export-import operations of enterprises, amalgamations, productive cooperatives and other organizations in cases where there is unfair competition or where their activity harms the interests of the state.

3. For the purposes of creating conditions for raising the effectiveness of the sale of Soviet goods and services on the foreign market, for doing away with unjustified competition among Soviet exporters, for reducing marketing costs and also for optimizing purchases abroad, it is considered appropriate to form on a voluntary basis various types of foreign economic organizations, including interdepartmental amalgamations, consortia, associations, stock companies, trading houses, and other organizations with the participation of the producers of the goods and services, of foreign economic amalgamations, and also, where necessary, of banks, sales-supply, and other organizations. The rules of currency accounting established for the participants in such organizations, are unchanged. The relations between participants in such organizations are structured in accordance with existing legislation and their charter documents.

The aforementioned foreign economic organizations with participation of foreign partners are formed in the same way as joint ventures.

The charters of foreign economic organizations formed in accordance with this section are affirmed (accepted) by agreement with the Ministry of Foreign Economic Relations of the USSR.

4. To establish that enterprises, amalgamations, productive cooperatives and other organizations may export things they produce with the exception of particular types which will be listed by the Council of Ministers of the USSR.

Enterprises, amalgamations and other organizations may import for their needs, using their own or borrowed means, raw materials, manufactured items, machines and equipment, spare parts and other goods and services necessary for technical refitting, reconstruction, expansion of production, protection of the environment, scientific and technical research, experimental design work, and other goals envisioned by existing legislation. Productive cooperatives import in accordance with the Law of the USSR on Cooperatives, using their own or borrowed funds.

The Council of Ministers will determine the list of items forbidden to import.

Using their own hard currency resources, they may also, in the established manner, send on business trips specialists and other workers for participation in negotiations on scientific-technical, production and commercial questions, in international exhibitions and fairs, for markets, for the exchange of experience, for training, and for other purposes in accordance with effective legislation.

State enterprises, amalgamations and organizations may expend, according to the decision of labor collectives, resources in transferable rubles and the currencies of the CMEA countries, and up to 10 percent (15 percent for enterprises, amalgamations and organizations in the Far Eastern Economic Zone) of their resources in other forms of currency, including hard currency, to acquire consumer goods, medicines and medical technology, and for strengthening the material-technical base of the social-cultural sphere.

The Ministry of Trade of the USSR and the State Committee on Prices will determine the order and conditions of the sale of consumer goods purchased with currency funds.

5. The Ministry of Foreign Economic Relations of the USSR with the approval of the State Foreign Economic Commission of the Council of Ministers of the USSR will introduce, for determined periods, licensing and quotas of exports and imports for particular goods, types of services, countries or groups of countries in those cases when this is demanded by the state of payment relations, and other economic and political conditions.

6. With the goal of meeting general state interests in the conduct of foreign economic relations, of expanding and perfecting the means of realizing the foreign economic policy of the USSR, the Ministry of Foreign Economic Relations of the USSR, the State Committee on Prices, the State Committee on Statistics, GOSPLAN, the Ministry of Finance, the State Committee on Standards, and the Main Directorate of State Customs Control are to develop suggestions for a new customs tariff for the USSR and

present it to the Council of Ministers by 1 January, 1990. They are to proceed from the possible use of the tariff in the formation of prices for imported goods, the regulation of demand and supply in the internal market of the country, and also as a basis for conducting international trade negotiations, including with GATT and the EEC;

- they are to develop and assure the phased introduction, beginning 1 January 1989, of a system of measures for operational, non-tariff regulation of foreign economic relations, anticipating, in part, the introduction of corresponding customs rules and the use of instruments of non-tariff regulation. In developing this system, they are to take into account the international obligations of the USSR, the possibility of its use for current regulation of the foreign economic ties of the USSR, including for the goals of their balanced development and the achievement of favorable results in international trade negotiations;
- they are to accelerate the processing of customs statistics, including the calculation of cooperation based on direct ties, border and coastal trade, meaning to provide for its introduction before 1990.

7. The Ministry of Foreign Economic Relations of the USSR and the Ministry of Justice of the USSR, with the participation of interested national ministries and agencies and of the councils of ministers of the union republics are to continue the perfection of the legal base of the foreign economic relations of the USSR—first of all of new forms of cooperation. During the years 1988–90, there must be developed legislation on stock companies, on rules of competition, on the defense of the consumer's interest, on the regime of currency operations, on the economic activity of Soviet enterprises and organizations abroad, and on other foreign economic questions. They are to complete this work as a preparation for the 1990 draft national law on foreign trade and other forms of foreign economic activity.

8. The Council plans to continue the policy line of consistent development and strengthening of the principle of currency self-sufficiency of enterprises, amalgamations and organizations, of the branches of the national economy and territorial complexes, and raising the efficiency of their foreign economic activity.

GOSPLAN and the Ministry of Finance are to develop and present to the Council proposals for

switching, beginning 1 January 1991, to full currency self-sufficiency of the separate branches of the national economy of the USSR, the union republics, and the territorial complexes, first of all the Far Eastern Economic Zone. They are to examine in this the procedure for forming in the branches of the national economy and the union republics their centralized currency funds for the resolution of social-economic tasks common to the branches or the region.

The Council acknowledges the necessity of moving, beginning 1 January, 1991, toward the establishment of stable norms for the five-year plan period governing the state's share of the foreign currency proceeds of enterprises, amalgamations, productive cooperatives, and other organizations, earned by exporting goods or services they produce.

In practical activity, it is necessary to be governed strictly by stable norms.

GOSPLAN and the Ministry of Finance, together with national ministries and agencies and the councils of ministers of the union republics, are to develop and present to the Council proposals for the establishment in the 13th five-year plan of the indicated norms for the ministries and agencies of the USSR and the councils of ministers of the union republics.

The ministries and agencies of the USSR and the councils of ministers of the union republics are to establish for their subordinate enterprises, amalgamations and organizations norms for the state share of proceeds in foreign currency, differentiated by the necessity of accounting for the specifics of their work. In this, the indicated organs must provide for the allocation to the state in accordance with the norms established for them.

The Development of Economic Methods of Administration and Stimulus

10. To strengthen the role of foreign economic relations and the union of centralized planning with the development of initiative and the economic self-sufficiency of enterprises, amalgamations, and organizations, intending to provide on this basis for the increase of currency income and the economical expenditure of foreign currency, national ministries and agencies and the councils of ministers of the union republics are to operate on the basis that the satisfaction of their import demands must depend on their direct activity in the development of exports.

12. With the goal of expanding the participation of the USSR in the world division of labor, deepening

integrating processes, particularly new forms of cooperation, of raising the realism of the appraisal of the effectiveness of exports and imports, the switch to a new currency conversion rate is foreseen, beginning 1 January 1991, for use in accounting on foreign economic operations.

GOSBANK, the Ministry of Finance, GOSPLAN and the Vnesheconombank are to develop for presentation to the Council by the end of 1989 concrete proposals on the size, manner of establishing, and use of the currency exchange rate.

The Ministry of Finance, GOSPLAN, the State Committee on Labor and Social Questions and the V.Ts.S.P.S., in preparing proposals for the taxation of profits (income) of state, cooperative and public amalgamations, enterprises, and organizations, are to work on the basis of accounting for the differentiated rates of taxation of the economic results of their export-import activity.

13. The Council acknowledges the necessity of simplifying the existing system of accounting in the conduct of export-import activity by state enterprises, amalgamations and organizations, gradually turning away from the use in the evaluation of factual contract prices in Soviet rubles of different currency exchange rates.

Before the switch to accounting with the use of the new currency rate, (the Council resolves) to employ, beginning 1 January 1990, a 100 percent increment to the exchange rate relationship of freely convertible currency to the ruble.

16. For the development of socialist initiative in enterprises, amalgamations, productive cooperatives and other organizations, the expansion of their ability to attract currency resources for the solution of the social-economic tasks of the labor collectives, there will be introduced an exchange of resources of currency funds, the selling and buying of these resources for Soviet rubles at agreed prices in currency auctions, organized by the Vnesheconombank of the USSR.

GOSBANK, together with the Ministry of Finance, Vnesheconombank, and GOSPLAN, are to work out a system for the sale and purchase of foreign currency at the aforementioned auctions, using for these purposes the resources of the currency funds of exporters in all kinds of currency, as well as resources in transferable rubles from central sources.

17. Vnesheconombank may give out to enterprises, amalgamations, productive cooperatives and other organizations bank credits of up to five million rubles in foreign currency, to be amortized by use of all the currency proceeds from export of goods or services produced as a result of the investment of the borrowed funds. GOSPLAN will, each year, establish limits on the resources allocated for these purposes.

22. Enterprises, amalgamations and organizations furnishing production for export will allocate part of their currency fund resources to their subcontractors. The size of these shares will be determined by agreement, taking into account the contributions to the production of the export good.

Currency resources are transferred to the subcontractors' accounts in the Vnesheconombank after payment by the foreign purchaser.

Questions of the Organization and Activity of Joint Ventures, International Amalgamations and Organizations.

31. In the interests of energizing the work of creating on the territory of the USSR joint ventures with the participation of organizations and firms from foreign countries, it is ordered that:

- The share of Soviet and foreign participants in the equity fund of a joint enterprise will be determined by agreement between them.
- A foreign citizen can be the chairman or general director of a joint venture.
- Fundamental questions about the activity of a joint venture will be decided at a meeting of the board on the basis of unanimity of all the members.
- Questions of hiring and firing, of the form and scale of labor pay, and also of the material encouragement of the workers of the joint venture in Soviet rubles will be decided by the joint venture.
- Goods brought into the Soviet Union by the joint venture for the needs of production development may be subject to minimum duties or free of duty.
- Foreign workers in joint ventures may use Soviet rubles to pay for living quarters and other services with the exception of cases foreseen by decisions of the Council of Ministers of the USSR.

In the interests of stimulating the creation of joint ventures in the Far Eastern Economic Region, it is deemed necessary to free those ventures from the payment of taxes on profits for the first three years from the moment the declared profit is received.

The Ministry of Finance of the USSR is commissioned to reduce by up to 10 percent the tax on profits of joint ventures created in the Far Eastern Economic Region.

Within three months it is to develop and affirm rules for determining the taxable income of joint ventures, taking into account the practice of foreign states.

32. It is deemed appropriate to accord to the Ministry of Finance of the USSR the right not to subject to taxes for a determined period a part of the profit accruing to the foreign partner in a joint venture where it is transferred abroad or to reduce the rate of the indicated tax if another arrangement is not provided for in an agreement between the USSR and the corresponding government. This right is subject to use primarily in the production by joint ventures of consumer goods, medicines and medical technology, scientific production having important national economic significance, and also to joint ventures in the Far Eastern Economic Region.

33. The transfer of shares in a joint venture, the insurance of risks of a joint venture, as well as revisions in its financial-economic activity are done by agreement by the parties.

34. The Main Customs Administration, together with the Ministry of Foreign Economic Relations, will provide customs privileges to the foreign personnel of joint ventures.

35. State enterprises, amalgamations, and organizations are accorded the right to take decisions on the creation of joint ventures, international amalgamations, organizations with foreign organizations and firms with the consent of higher administrative organs.

Productive cooperatives create joint ventures with foreign firms and organizations with the consent of the council of ministers of the appropriate union republic which has no oblast division, of the council of ministers of an autonomous republic, or of the krai, oblast, Moscow or Leningrad soviet executive committee, according to the location of the cooperative, with the consent of the ministry or agency in whose enterprise the cooperative was formed.

New construction or major remodeling of existing buildings when a joint venture is created requires the consent of the territorial organ of administration.

In the remaining cases, the Soviet partners in joint ventures, international amalgamations and organizations will present to the territorial organs of administration the corresponding information.

Separate Questions of Foreign Economic Activity

37. The Ministry of Foreign Economic Relations, GOSPLAN, the Ministry of Finance, the Customs Administration, and the Ministry of Justice, along with other interested agencies, are to prepare and introduce to the Council in the first quarter of 1989 proposals for the creation in the USSR, and first of all in the Far Eastern Economic Region, of "zones of joint enterprise," with a concentration in them of joint ventures with foreign participation and on the possible status and location of these zones.

38. GOSBANK, the Vnesheconombank, and the Ministry of Finance are to work out and present to the Council of Ministers in the first quarter of 1989 concrete proposals for the phased development of partial convertibility of the Soviet ruble into foreign currency.

39. GOSPLAN, the Ministry of Finance, GOSBANK and the Vnesheconombank are to present to the Council of Ministers in the first quarter of 1989 proposals for perfecting the plan of the combined currency target (balance of payments of the USSR).

• • •

40. The provisions of this resolution relating to productive cooperatives apply as well to all cooperatives conducting productive activity, and their allies (amalgamations).

41. Ministries and agencies of the USSR are to make the necessary changes in their rules to accommodate this resolution.

The Ministry of Foreign Economic Relations and the Ministry of Justice are to prepare, with the participation of GOSPLAN, GOSSNAB, the Ministry of Finance, GOSBANK, the Vnesheconombank, and other interested ministries and agencies, and present within two months to the Council of Ministers proposals for the introduction of legislation implementing the changes flowing from this resolution.

Document 8.5

On Measures for State Regulation of Foreign Economic Relations

(Decree of the USSR Council of Ministers, March 7, 1989, No. 203, as published in *Ekonomicheskaya Gazeta*, No. 13, March 1989)

With a view to assuring effective management of foreign economic relations and combining the broad economic independence of participants in foreign economic ties with state regulation of this activity, the USSR Council of Ministers decrees:

1. In accordance with the Decree of the USSR Council of Ministers of December 2, 1988, no. 1405, On the Further Development of the External Economic Activity of State, Cooperative and Other Public Enterprises, Associations and Organizations, the following system of state regulation of foreign economic relations shall be established in the USSR, including:

- registration of participants in external economic ties;
- declaration of goods and other property moved across the USSR state border;
- procedure for exporting and importing individual goods for national purposes;
- measures for effective regulation of external economic ties.

The above system shall apply to all forms of foreign economic relations, including direct production, scientific and technological ties, coastal and border trade, commodity exchange operations, and to all participants in external economic ties.

The above system shall apply to all forms of foreign economic relations, including direct production, scientific and technological ties, coastal and border trade, commodity exchange operations, and to all participants in external economic ties.

Registration of Participants in External Economic Relations

2. All those willing to use the right granted to them to have a direct outlet to the foreign market must register themselves with the USSR Ministry of Foreign Economic Relations, including registration through the offices of its plenipotentiaries in the localities.

Registration shall include: submission of the registration card filled out in due form; the giving of the registration number; the entry in the official State Register of Participants in External Economic Ties; the issue of the Registration Certificate.

The USSR Ministry of Foreign Economic Relations shall:

- have its plenipotentiary in autonomous republics, territories and regions;
- accomplish registration with the use of modern computing machines; set up a single data bank on the registered sections of external economic ties.

Registration shall be made not later than 30 days from the date of receiving the application. The USSR Ministry of Foreign Economic Relations shall immediately inform the executive committees of the relevant territorial and regional Soviets of People's Deputies, the Councils of Ministers of Union and autonomous republics, ministries and departments of the USSR about the registration.

Ministries and departments, the Councils of Ministers of Union and autonomous republics, the executive committees of local Soviets of People's Deputies shall give every possible assistance to the USSR Ministry of Foreign Economic Relations and its plenipotentiaries in the localities.

Participants in external economic ties, which were granted the right to deal directly on foreign markets prior to the adoption of the present Decree, shall register themselves on general grounds.

The USSR Ministry of Finance, while registering joint ventures, international amalgamations and organizations set up on Soviet territory in accordance with the established procedure, shall see to it that they are also registered with the USSR Ministry of Foreign Economic Relations as participants in external economic ties.

Participants in external economic ties shall be responsible for the authenticity of information supplied at the time of registration and for any subsequent changes altering that information.

3. The USSR Ministry of Foreign Economic Relations shall be granted the right:

- to apply to ministries and departments, the Councils of Ministers of Union and autonomous republics, the executive committees of local Soviets of People's Deputies, banks and participants in external economic ties, if and when necessary, for affirmation of the authenticity of information given in registration cards;

• to collect from participants in external economic ties payment in the amounts fixed by the USSR Ministry of Foreign Economic Relations by agreement with the USSR Ministry of Finance to compensate for registration expenses.

Declaration of Goods and Other Property Moved Across the USSR State Border

4. It is established that after April 1, 1989 onward, goods and other property moved across the USSR state border shall be declared by submitting a correctly completed cargo customs declaration form to USSR state customs control bodies.

The declaration shall be made by participants in external economic ties independently or on a contractual basis through the All-Union Foreign Economic Association Sojuzvneshtrans of the USSR Ministry of Foreign Economic Relations or any other organizations indicated by USSR state customs control bodies.

Goods and other property moved across the USSR state border without presentation of a cargo customs declaration or with a violation of the established declaration procedure shall not be allowed to leave or enter the USSR. A statement in the customs declaration of deliberately false information shall entail responsibility before the law.

5. USSR state customs control bodies shall collect payment for customs procedures, including payments in the currency of settlement with the partner, in the amounts fixed by the Main Customs Administration under the USSR Council of Ministers by agreement with the USSR Ministry of Finance.

The Main Customs Administration under the USSR Council of Ministers shall be allowed to use these resources in the established manner for development of the state customs service and the social needs of its work collectives.

6. It is established that the information contained in the cargo customs declaration shall be the official initial data for state statistics in the area of foreign economic relations.

The USSR State Committee for Statistics, the USSR Ministry of Foreign Economic Relations and the Main Customs Administration under the USSR Council of Ministers shall assure the introduction in the USSR in 1989–1990 of a system of gathering, processing and the publication of state statistics for foreign economic relations in a form adequate to meet today's demands for the completeness, authenticity, publicity and international comparability of these statistics.

Procedure for Exporting and Importing Individual Goods for National Purposes

7. To approve the annexed lists of products (work, services) which in 1989 and 1990 will be exported and imported by enterprises, associations, production cooperatives and other Soviet organizations on licences issued by appropriate ministries and departments of the USSR and the Councils of Ministers of Union republics.

It is established that this procedure shall also be used in all transactions of purchase and sale of the given products (work, services) with foreign firms and organizations on Soviet territory.

The State Foreign Economic Commission of the USSR Council of Ministers shall be allowed to make individual alterations in the approved lists of products (work, services).

8. Joint ventures, international amalgamations and organizations on Soviet territory may only export their own products (work, services) and import products (work, services) necessary for their own needs. For intermediary operations permission shall be needed from the USSR Ministry of Foreign Economic Relations.

Production cooperatives and their unions (associations) may only export products (work, services) independently produced by them. They shall have no right to engage in buying goods with the object of their resale for export, in importing goods for their subsequent resale on the USSR's home market and mediation in external economic transactions as a form of activity.

Other participants in external economic ties, too, shall not engage in buying goods with the aim of their resale for export and in importing goods for their subsequent resale on the USSR's home market, unless it is envisaged otherwise in the regulations in force.

Measures for Effective Regulation of External Economic Ties

9. With a view to the balanced development of external economic ties and improvement of instruments implementing the country's foreign economic policy, measures shall, in special cases, be taken to effectively regulate external economic ties such as export and import restrictions, suspension of operations being undertaken by participants in the external economic ties.

Export and import restrictions shall be imposed for definite periods of time on individual goods (work, services), countries and groups of countries, whenever this is required by the state of payment relations, other economic and political conditions and, in particular, for:

- regulating the supply and demand on the USSR's home market;
- discharging the USSR's international obligations relating to export and import regulation;
- achieving mutually advantageous understanding at international trade talks;
- taking retaliatory measures against discriminatory actions on the part of foreign states and/or their alliances.

The above export and import restrictions shall be imposed by the State Foreign Economic Commission of the USSR Council of Ministers by representation of the USSR Ministry of Foreign Economic Relations in conjunction with competent government agencies in the form of quantitative or value import or export quotas. All transactions carried out within the framework of such quotas shall be subject to licensing.

Quotas shall not be applicable to the import into the USSR of goods on account of Soviet imports and for projects under construction on Soviet territory.

The provisions of the present paragraph shall not be applicable to the export of products made by joint ventures, international amalgamations and organizations set up on Soviet territory or to imports for their own needs.

10. The State Foreign Economic Commission of the USSR Council of Ministers by representation of the USSR Ministry of Foreign Economic Relations and the Councils of Ministers of Union republics shall suspend transactions carried out by participants in external economic ties whenever there is unfair competition or their activity is detrimental to the interests of the state.

Decisions to suspend transactions shall be taken whenever there are cases of:

- violation of Soviet legislation on measures for effective regulation of the USSR's external economic ties, failure to observe the provisions of the USSR's international agreements, as well as violation of the legislation of foreign countries, which has entailed economic or political damage to the USSR;
- execution of foreign economic transactions with the violation of statutory legal competence, as well as unsanctioned commodity-exchange (barter) operations;
- repeated failure to effect obligatory export shipments with the simultaneous export of similar goods in other forms;
- exports from the USSR at unjustifiably low prices or imports into the USSR at excessive prices;
- repeated exportation or importation of low-quality goods;
- communication of deliberately false information in advertisements, customs, currency-and-financial and registration documents;
- other violations of Soviet legislation.

Foreign economic transactions may be suspended by banning a specific transaction or by suspending all such transactions of the infringer for a period up to one year.

The infringer may also be given a warning without suspending his external economic activity or his export-import operations shall be made subject to licensing for a period up to six months.

Decision on suspension may be altered or cancelled, provided the reasons for it have been eliminated.

The provisions of the present Paragraph shall also be applicable to foreign firms and organizations which have committed such violations on Soviet territory.

Document 8.6

Soviet Export Control List, 1989–1990

(Approved by the Council of Ministers, March 7, 1989. The controlled product is followed by the state body which may license* its export.)

List of products (work, services), exportable in 1989 and 1990 by
enterprises, associations, production cooperatives and other Soviet organizations
under licences issued by relevant ministries and departments of the USSR and by the Councils of
Ministers of Union Republics

1. Crude oil, natural gas, gas condensate, oil products (petrol, kerosene, rocket fuel, diesel fuel, mazout, hard paraffin, lubricating oils)—USSR Ministry of Foreign Economic Relations

2. Coal (fuel and coking coal, including anthracite and furnace charge)—USSR Ministry of Foreign Economic Relations

3. Ores and ferrous metal concentrates, pig iron, rolled ferrous metals, steel pipes, ferroalloys, vanadium pentoxide, ferrous metal scrap and waste—USSR Ministry of Foreign Economic Relations

4. Ores, non-ferrous metal concentrates and industrial products, precious metal ores and concentrates, non-ferrous metals, including secondary ones, their alloys, powders, oxides salts, solutions, semi-finished products, rolled stock, non-ferrous metal scrap and waste—USSR Ministry of Foreign Economic Relations

5. Rare and rare-earth metals, their compounds and semiconductor materials—USSR Ministry of Foreign Economic Relations

6. Industrial products of precious metals—USSR Central Diamond and Gold Board (Glavalmazzoloto)

7. Apatite concentrate, ammonia, mineral fertilizers, sulphur, sulphuric acid, boron-containing raw materials and products thereof, acetic acid, acetic anhydride, cyclohexane, cyclohexanone, methanol, caprolactam, polyurethanes—USSR Ministry of the Fertilizer Industry

8. Benzene (except coal benzene)—USSR Ministry of Foreign Economic Relations

9. Phenol, styrenes, soot (industrial carbon), synthetic rubber—USSR Ministry of the Petrochemical Industry

10. Polyethylene, polypropylene, polystyrene, polyvinyl chloride resin, ion-exchange resins, plasticizers, dimethyl terephthalate, acrylonitrile, ethylene glycol, dye-stuffs and semi-finished products for their manufacture, textile chemical threads and fibres, plastic pipes, ethyl alcohol (or grain alcohol)—USSR Ministry of the Chemical Industry

11. Timber and pulp-and-paper products (except low-grade wood and timber-processing waste)—USSR Ministry of the Timber Industry

12. Mackle-paper—USSR State Committee for Material and Technical Supply, Councils of Ministers of Union republics

13. Cement—USSR Ministry of the Building Materials Industry

14. Semiprecious crude stones and articles thereof, collection materials and palaeontologic samples—USSR Ministry of Geology, USSR Academy of Sciences (according to relevant nomenclature)

15. Cotton (except low-grade), flax fibre, natural wool, furs and raw peltry grain (including cereals, flour, fodder concentrates, oil seeds, vegetable oils, food animal fats (including butter), sugar, meat and meat products, milk and dairy products—USSR Ministry of Foreign Economic Relations

16. Fish and fish products (except fresh water fish other than sturgeon)—USSR Ministry of Fisheries

17. Fresh water fish, except sturgeon—Councils of Ministers of Union republics

18. Liqueur and vodka—USSR State Committee for Agriculture and Related Industries

19. Wine—Councils of Ministers of Union republics

20. Wild animals and birds—Councils of Ministers of Union republics

21. Wild flora—Councils of Ministers of Union republics

22. Medicines (including medicinal herbs and plants)—Councils of Ministers of Union republics

23. Products of Tibetan medicine—Councils of Ministers of Union republics

24. Medical equipment—USSR Ministry of Public Health

25. Soviet inventions and other results of R & D—USSR State Committee for Science and Technology

26. Theatrical, concert and other artistic activity—USSR Ministry of Culture

27. Placement of funds in foreign currency in the form of credits, loans, deposits and so on—Vnesheconombank of the USSR

28. Medicines—USSR Ministry of Public Health

29. Chemical plant-protecting substances—USSR Ministry of the Fertilizer Industry

30. Printed matter and services for publication in the USSR—USSR State Committee for Publishing, Printing and Bookselling

31. Cinema, video and audio production—USSR State Committee for Cinematography, USSR State Committee for Television and Radio, USSR State Committee for Publishing, Printing and Bookselling, USSR Ministry of Culture, Councils of Ministers of Union republics (according to relevant nomenclature)

32. Services for the construction of projects on Soviet territory with the invitation of foreign firms at the expense of centralized sources—USSR Ministry of Foreign Economic Relations

33. Invitation of foreign manpower—USSR State Committee for Labour and Social Affairs

*The USSR Ministry of Culture and the Vnesheconombank of the USSR shall issue licences without permission of the USSR Ministry of Foreign Economic Relations.

NOTE: Enterprises, associations, production cooperatives and other Soviet organizations shall not export armaments, ammunition, war materials or special complementary articles for their manufacture, explosives; nuclear materials (including materials in the form of heat-generating assemblies), technologies, equipment, installations, special non-nuclear materials and the related services, sources of ionizing radiation; precious metals, alloys and articles thereof; precious stones and articles thereof; individual types of products and technologies which are or may be used for manufacturing armaments and war materials (the nomenclature shall be brought to the notice of manufacturers in the established manner); poisons; narcotics and psychotropic substances, devices for opium and hashish smoking; works of art, antiquities and other articles of significant artistic, historical, scientific and other cultural value, historical and cultural monuments; other products and services whose export is prohibited, unless otherwise provided for by legislation.

Document 8.7

Concerning the Development of the Economic Activity of Soviet Organizations Abroad

(Excerpts from USSR Council of Ministers Decree No. 412, May 18, 1989.)

The USSR Council of Ministers notes that in practice the foreign economic activity of Soviet organizations has not yet attained the necessary development. The provision of technical assistance of the USSR to foreign governments is not linked with the subsequent participation of Soviet organizations in their management and operation and in the acquisition of income. The few foreign stock companies in which Soviet organizations participate as a rule operate outside the sphere of production and are little known in foreign business circles. Directed investments in enterprises abroad and operations with securities are not utilized to a sufficient extent.

For the purposes of securing the foreign economic interests of the USSR, strengthening the position of the country in the world economy, and improving and developing the economic activity of Soviet organizations abroad the USSR Council of Ministers decrees:

1. It is established that the economic activity of Soviet organizations abroad must be directed towards:
   - actively promoting Soviet goods, especially industrial goods, on foreign markets;
   - ensuring the stable and efficient supply of the country with the necessary resources through imports, including through their directed production in foreign countries;
   - obtaining supplementary income from foreign economic activity, including by means of operations with securities;
   - mastering new forms of cooperation, in particular in the field of economic cooperation, investment, and finance and utilizing advanced foreign technology and experience in management;
   - promoting the deepening of socialist economic integration on the level of its economic links;
   - strengthening contacts with business and public circles in foreign countries.

2. Developing the economic activity of Soviet organizations abroad by means of:
   - establishing enterprises there with Soviet participation in their capital and management (hereinafter called: "foreign enterprises");
   - investing in income-producing assets (securities) of other enterprises and in operations on security and commodity markets (hereinafter called: "securities operations").

3. It is established that Soviet state enterprises, associations and organizations and also consortiums, stock companies, trading houses, associations for business cooperation with foreign countries, and other associations that are organized with their participation and are registered as participants in foreign economic relations (hereinafter called: "the Soviet partners") may establish foreign enterprises and conduct securities operations.

Procedures for the Participation of Soviet Partners in Foreign Enterprises

4. It is established that:
   - foreign enterprises shall be established by Soviet state enterprises, associations, and organizations with the consent of the superior ministry, agency of the USSR, councils of ministers of the union republics, taking into account the recommendations of the USSR Ministry of Foreign Economic Relations and the USSR Ministry of Foreign Affairs and by stock companies, associations, consortiums, trading houses, and also state enterprises, associations, and organizations not included in the system of ministries and agencies with the consent of the USSR Ministry of Foreign Economic Relations and taking into account the recommendations of the USSR Ministry of Foreign Affairs;
   - production cooperatives (their leagues) and other public organizations may establish foreign enterprises after registration as participants in foreign economic relations in accordance with the field of such registration with the consent of the USSR Ministry of Foreign Economic Relations and taking into account the recommendations of the USSR Ministry of Foreign Affairs;
   - the foreign enterprises that are established shall be registered by the Soviet partners in a special register that will be kept by the USSR Finance Ministry;

- securities operations shall be carried out by the Soviet partners through the USSR Bank for Foreign Economic Relations, Soviet banks abroad, or independently with subsequent reporting of their content to the USSR Finance Ministry and the USSR Ministry of Foreign Economic Relations.

5. It is recommended that the Soviet partners establish foreign enterprises by means of setting up new ones or obtaining the shares of existing enterprises and also on the basis of facilities set up in the course of the economic and technical assistance of the USSR to foreign countries.

6. Economic relations between the Soviet partners and foreign enterprises shall be governed by contracts.

7. It is established that:
- in determining the programs of economic activity of foreign enterprises the Soviet partners shall bring to the attention of their representatives in the executive bodies of these enterprises the recommended volume of general commercial turnover, breaking out the volume of sales of Soviet export goods and services and the anticipated amount of foreign currency to be transferred to the USSR;
- Soviet employees of foreign enterprises may receive bonuses and other supplementary payments in foreign currency that are credited to the personnel of these enterprises in accordance with local regulations. The USSR Finance Ministry and the USSR State Committee for Labor and Social Problems shall determine the procedures and maximum amounts of bonuses and other supplemental payments that may be received.
- Soviet personnel of foreign enterprises shall be covered by the schedule of work and rest (length of workday, leaves, non-working days and holidays), standards for travel and other business expenses, and also other conditions of work established for these enterprises;
- when Soviet employees of foreign enterprises are sent on business trips to the USSR their salaries are maintained at 100 per cent of their base salary in foreign currency;

The USSR Finance Ministry and the USSR State Committee for Labor and Social Problems with the participation of the interested ministries and agencies shall within two months:
- establish procedures for the utilization by the Soviet partners of the difference between the

salaries and other payments received by the Soviet employees of foreign enterprises and their official base salaries and also procedures for reimbursing the expenses for maintaining Soviet personnel who cannot be included in the indicated enterprises;
- provide that the earnings level of Soviet personnel of foreign enterprises be determined by the management of the foreign enterprises while the level of official base salaries is determined by the Soviet partners of these enterprises;
- develop progressive norms for the withholding amounts that are transferred to the social security and insurance funds in the USSR from the incomes received by the Soviet employees of foreign enterprises in the country where they are stationed after deduction of local taxes.

8. Supervision over the effective utilization of the Soviet contribution to the capital of foreign enterprises shall be exercised by their Soviet partners. The Soviet representatives in the executive bodies of the foreign enterprises shall present annual reports on the operation of the enterprises to their Soviet partners.

The forms for such reporting shall be established by the Soviet partners with the consent of the State Committee of the USSR for Statistics and the USSR Finance Ministry.

9. It is recommended that the Soviet partners of various foreign enterprises combine their efforts to resolve economic problems and form multi-branch foreign enterprises, associations, and joint management bodies of the holding company type in the common interest.

Financing, Incentives, and Provision of Personnel for Foreign Economic Activity

10. The establishment and activity of foreign enterprises are financed as a rule through the internal resources of the Soviet partners, the centralized hard currency holdings of their superior administrative bodies, and also through borrowed funds, while securities operations are financed through the internal resources of the Soviet partners and through borrowed funds.

Borrowed funds for these purposes are generated from the assets of hard currency holdings of the interested Soviet economic organizations, credits from the USSR Bank for Foreign Economic Relations, and, under its license, also from foreign banks, including Soviet banking institutions abroad.

The use of local currency held in the accounts of Soviet organizations by the Soviet partners for the establishment and support of the current activity of foreign enterprises, and also for conducting securities operations is considered appropriate.

11. It is established that the dividends received from the activity of foreign enterprises and also the income from securities operations that is transferred to the USSR be reflected in a ruble equivalent in the general results of the economic activity of the Soviet partners. The total amounts of these dividends and incomes in foreign currency shall be credited fully to the hard currency funds of the Soviet partners in the event that the foreign enterprise is formed from their internal resources or partially (in accordance with the established norms for allocations to their hard currency funds) if the foreign enterprise is formed from an allocation of hard currency from centralized sources. In this regard the Soviet partners pay taxes into the state budget and make use of tax preferences in the established manner.

12. Soviet partners are required to staff foreign enterprises with highly qualified Soviet specialists, including foreign economic personnel appropriate for the field of the enterprise who have a command of the foreign languages needed for work in these enterprises.

The tours of duty of Soviet employees in foreign enterprises shall be determined by the Soviet partners based on production requirements.

13. The USSR Ministry of Foreign Economic Relations, the USSR Finance Ministry, and the USSR Ministry of Foreign Affairs shall ensure the training, retraining, and upgrading of Soviet specialists at the All-Union Academy of Foreign Trade, Moscow Finance Institute, and Moscow State Institute of International Relations for carrying out securities operations and also for work in foreign enterprises.

14. The USSR Ministry of Foreign Economic Relations together with the USSR Finance Ministry, . USSR Bank for Foreign Economic Relations, and the USSR Chamber of Commerce and Industry shall generalize and analyze the experience of the economic activity of Soviet organizations abroad, providing the Soviet partners with the necessary consultations, including those provided on a contractual basis.

15. The USSR Ministry of Foreign Economic Relations and the USSR Ministry of Justice with the participation of the interested ministries and agencies of the USSR shall present proposals for amendments to existing legislation arising from this decree to the USSR Council of Ministers within two months.

Chairman of the
USSR Council of Ministers N. RYZHKOV

Administrator of Affairs of the
USSR Council of Ministers M. SMIRTYUKOV

[seal: Administration of Affairs of the
USSR Council of Ministers General Department]

Document 8.8

Excerpts from President Mikhail Gorbachev's Letter to the Leaders of the Major Industrial Countries Meeting in Paris in July, 1989

(The letter was addressed to President Francois Mitterrand of France. It is reprinted here from *Soviet American Trade*, August 1989, pp. 6–8.)

Mr. President:

In addressing myself to you in your capacity as president of the fifteenth annual economic conference of the leaders of the seven countries which takes place in Paris on July 15 and 16, and through you to the other participants in this meeting, I wish to share some ideas on the key problems of the world economy which exert their influence on all countries, without exception.

Interdependence, while helpful in surmounting the division of the world, at the same time augments considerably the risk of a clash of interests, of an explosion of contradictions.

Traditionally, in order to resolve the economic contradictions between states, it was sufficient to find an equilibrium on the basis of strictly national interests. Today, however, such an equilibrium will be precarious if it is based on other than the universal interests of humanity.

The attainment of a true equilibrium, assuring a stable character to interdependence, can only be the fruit of complimentary actions. An objective process, the formation of a coherent world economy, implies that the world economic partnership be placed on a qualitatively new level.

We are observing with interest the efforts of the seven most developed states in the Western world, with a view toward focusing on coordination in macroeconomic policy. We reckon that it is possible, with coordination, to make the processes of the world economy more predictable. This is an important premise for guaranteeing international economic security.

Acting on the question of economic security, we have foremost in our minds the formation of stable, deideologized, mutually advantageous bases for co-creation and co-development.

Just as do other countries, the Soviet Union seeks to resolve these problems while adapting its national economy to a new structure of the international division of labor, which is in gestation. Our *perestroika* is inseparable from a policy aimed at full and complete participation in the world economy. This orientation, ingrained in the new political thinking, is determined equally by our direct economic interest. But, quite obviously, the rest of the world cannot help but gain from the opening to the world economy of such a market as the USSR. Of course, mutual advantage implies mutual responsibility and respect of the rights of all participants in international economic relations.

There remain in the domain of these relations quite a few contradictions. The zone of converging and common interests of the states is sufficiently large and can serve as a base for interaction. The proof of this is notably furnished by the positive changes in the bilateral economic links between the Soviet Union and many Western countries, by the agreements established in Vienna in the matter of ''basket two'' of European cooperation, and by the establishment of ties between the EEC and CMEA.

Meanwhile, multilateral, East-West cooperation on global economic problems is manifestly failing to keep pace with the development of bilateral and regional ties. This state of affairs cannot be justified, given the weight of our states in the world economy and the responsibility they bear for its rational functioning and efficiency for the good of each nation and the world community in general.

The Soviet Union is for free and constructive interaction, aimed at the solution of problems through common efforts. We see points of convergence and complimentarity in the approaches of the parties to global problems, in particular the settlement of indebtedness of the Third World. It doesn't matter who gets the credit for the best initiative. What is important is that there exists a real possibility to contribute together to the efficiency of practical measures in the sphere of debt settlement.

We are in favor of collective assistance for development, of coordination of actions by creditors and debtors, of donors and recipients, and in favor of multilateral aid. These can become one of the considerable material guarantees for the participation, with equal rights and responsibilities, of the countries on the road to development in the world economy.

Another problem we all face is linked to the tendencies toward integration, which are acquiring more and more vigor in diverse regions of the world. We would like to see development in the sense of a universal partnership. Today, life itself is destroying—progressively, and with great difficulty, but nevertheless, destroying—the old obstacles raised artificially between different economic systems. It's good that each system conserves its characteristic traits, that they have borrowed much from one another, that they use similar tools of management.

It is becoming urgent that we find methodologies of harmonization of economic processes, an acceptable methodology for all countries and universal usage. In the future, it will also be possible to research procedures for achieving a docking, on a global scale, of the different mechanisms for macroeconomic coordination.

We are ready to engage in a constructive dialog on these questions. As a beginning, we can establish contacts among professionals in diverse domains—e.g., at the level of government experts. The important thing is to find a common economic language, to proceed to a reciprocal exchange of information, to develop indicators of the base of economic development, for the regulation of credit links and of aid to the Third World, and statistics as a point of departure for collaboration.

I hope that these reflections will be useful for the participants of the summit meeting in Paris and that the results of that meeting will help in the search for an equilibrium of national, regional and universal economic interests.

With respect,
M. Gorbachev

9

Soviet Foreign Economic Relations, 1970–95

Kevin L. Tritle

Despite substantial growth in trade since 1970, the USSR remains a relatively small player in the world economy. Energy and arms sales dominate its export sector. Weakening world energy prices in the early 1980s and Mikhail Gorbachev's ambitious modernization program, however, have hammered home the need for Moscow to take measures to broaden its export base and make better use of its imports. To this end, Moscow has restructured its foreign trade apparatus and embarked on new forms of economic cooperation, such as joint ventures on Soviet soil. The benefits from these changes are not likely to be realized for a number of years, forcing Moscow to continue to rely on energy sales. Should the Soviets be unable to maintain their energy exports, total exports are likely to fall, leaving Moscow the choice of borrowing more heavily or letting imports fall.

The Soviet Union entered the 1970s with a relatively small level of foreign trade compared with the trade-per-capita of the developed Western countries **(Figure 9.1)**. In fact, the value of two-way trade with the world totaled less than $25 billion in 1970, accounting for 5 percent of total global commerce **(Figure 9.2)**. And of this trade, more than 60 percent was with the Council for Mutual Economic Assistance (CMEA) countries, Bulgaria, Czechoslovakia, East Germany, Hungary, Poland, Romania, Mongolia, and Cuba **(Figure 9.3)**. In contrast, two-way trade with the developed Western countries was just over $5 billion in 1970, and was virtually nonexistent with most of the non-Communist countries of the Third World.

Although the direction of trade was rather narrow at the beginning of the 1970s, the commodity composition of Moscow's exports to the world showed greater diversity **(Table 9.4)**. The Soviet's top export earner was machinery and equipment, comprising about one-fifth of Soviet exports. Exports of base metals and manufactures, crude oil and refined petroleum products, consumer goods, and arms, each made up 8–15 percent of Soviet sales abroad. Wood and chemical exports, together,

accounted for another 10 percent. Moscow's imports in 1970 were a bit more focused, with purchases of machinery and equipment, and consumer goods—mostly agriculture products—each comprising more than one third of total Soviet purchases.

Export Growth

From this relatively small trading base, the USSR's global commerce grew dramatically during the decade. Exports averaged 20 percent annual growth, due mainly to Moscow's ability to take advantage of rising world oil prices. Indeed, Moscow's oil revenues went from $1.5 billion in 1970 to $22.2 billion by 1979, with the volume of sales rising by two-thirds **(Figure 9.5)**. Similar circumstances enabled gas revenues to climb from less than $100 million in 1970 to $3.2 billion by the end of the decade.

These energy sales were the driving force in Moscow's seven-fold increase in exports to the West during the 1970s. Energy deliveries were also the linchpin of Moscow's trade with its CMEA allies and would have climbed to an even higher share of exports to these countries except for the CMEA pricing formula which kept Soviet oil prices charged to allies from rising as fast as the world price of oil. Through 1974, prices in intra-CMEA oil trade were set at five-year intervals, based on the average of world oil prices during the preceding five-year period. Beginning in 1976, the oil pricing formula was changed to allow oil prices to change annually according to average world oil prices during the previous five years.

On the other hand, oil deliveries played a smaller role in Moscow's rapid increase in exports to Third World countries. Here, Moscow's aggressive arms marketing policies, combined with an expanding economic aid program helped boost the sale of Soviet manufactured goods to the Less-Developed Countries four-fold during the 1970s. Moscow's economic aid program focused on large heavy industrial projects in the public sector and the development of natural resources. The credits for these projects were often provided on very favorable terms, but were tied to the purchase of Soviet machinery and equipment.

Import Boom

Flush with "petro" dollars, and faced with a domestic economic structure that failed to satisfy growing technological and agricultural requirements, Moscow boosted imports 400 percent during the 1970s. Topping the Soviet shopping list were purchases of machinery and equipment. Eastern Europe supplied about three-fourths of these type of goods during the 1970s, which were composed mostly of industrial machinery and transport equipment. The Developed West, however, became an increasingly important source for high technology items not available from Eastern Europe, with Western equipment imports climbing from $1 billion in 1970 to $7 billion yearly in 1978–79.

Moscow also turned to world markets for large amounts of agricultural products in this period. In fact, the West played a larger role than CMEA in meeting Moscow's agricultural import needs, supplying 50 percent of Soviet purchases in the 1970s. Disregarding the grossly overpriced sugar purchases from Cuba, for as much as eight times the world price, the West's share was two-thirds. The flow of Third World raw materials and industrial consumer goods into the Soviet Union also increased steadily during the 1970s, some of which was payment for earlier Soviet economic aid.

Hard Currency Balance

The Soviet Union perennially exported more than it imported from other Communist countries and the Third World during the 1970s, giving Moscow an overall balance of trade surplus in all but a few years. However, hard currency imports from the West exceeded exports to those countries by $17 billion during the 1970s, forcing Moscow to finance this trade deficit, as well as other hard currency expenditures, by other means **(Table 9.6)**. Earnings from the sale of arms and other Soviet manufactured goods to the Third World generated some $1 billion to $5 billion annually in hard currency which helped to pay for some goods from the industrialized West. Moreover, Moscow's gold sales, which rose from negligible amounts in 1970 to more than $2.5 billion in 1978, generated $1.5 billion yearly on average in the second half of the 1970s. Tourism, interest earnings, transit fees and other miscellaneous hard

currency revenues rose from about $800 million in 1970 to $1.5 billion in 1979, also providing some support.

Nonetheless, Moscow had to look to foreign financial markets to close the gap between its hard currency receipts and outlays. Soviet hard currency debt rose from $1.7 billion at the end of 1971 to $12.5 billion at yearend 1975, growing at an average annual rate of 65 percent for the period **(Table 9.7)**. A determined campaign to curb the rapid rise in debt reduced the rate at which debt was being accrued, but the overall size of the debt continued to rise throughout the second half of the decade. By 1979, Moscow's hard currency debt to the West stood at $21.3 billion.

Moscow's trade with the world continued to grow in the early 1980s, albeit at a much slower pace than in the 1970s. As in the late 1970s, energy sales were the backbone of Moscow's export program. Already making up two-fifths of Soviet exports by 1980, the share of oil and gas sales rose to one-half in 1981–84. For regions such as the West, energy's share was closer to three-quarters.

Oil continued to represent the lion's share of these energy exports. Even though world oil prices began falling in 1982, Moscow was able to boost the value of oil sales to the West during the early 1980s by increasing oil deliveries. And despite Moscow's 10 percent cut in the volume of oil deliveries to Eastern Europe starting in 1982, rising CMEA oil prices enabled the Soviets to boost the value of oil exports to these countries.

Natural gas sales, which made up just 2 percent of Soviet exports during the 1970s, took off in the early 1980s. From a level of $3.2 billion in 1979, gas exports topped $9 billion in 1984, representing 10 percent of Soviet foreign sales that year. Much of the growth in gas exports can be explained by the completion of gas export pipelines during the period, combined with the signing of sizable gas supply contracts with France, Italy, West Germany, Austria, and most of the East European countries.

Energy sales also played a larger role in Moscow's exports to the Third World in the early 1980s, particularly oil deliveries to India, which typically made up two-thirds of the $1.3 billion to $1.9 billion in total exports to New Delhi. Nevertheless, arms remained Moscow's best sellers in the Third World. Faced with strong Middle Eastern demand and willing to provide sophisticated equipment, often on favorable terms, Moscow was able to boost military sales by 40 percent between 1980 and 1984. Moscow also continued to have success in securing about $1 billion a year in sales of Soviet capital goods to Third

World development projects, mostly in the Middle East. Sales of other Soviet goods to the Third World actually fell in the early 1980s as Moscow's own demand increased and many less developed countries looked to Western suppliers for consumer goods.

Commensurate with the slowdown in exports, Moscow's imports from the world grew at only 4 percent, on average, in 1980–84. This was down sharply from the 20 percent average annual growth rate recorded in the 1970s. As in the 1970s, however, Moscow's imports continued to be dominated by machinery and equipment, and agricultural products. Eastern Europe continued to be the largest supplier of the first category. Dissatisfaction with the benefits of imported Western technology as well as Western trade sanctions implemented following the imposition of martial law in Poland and the invasion of Afghanistan, helped slow down the growth in machinery and equipment imports from the West. The West remained an important source for agricultural products because of perennially poor Soviet grain harvests in the early 1980s.

Although the CMEA countries and the developed West remained the Soviet Union's top suppliers in 1980–84, imports from the Third World became increasingly noteworthy. For example, the United States' grain embargo in 1980 enabled the Third World to boost its grain sales to the Soviet Union from less than $230 million in 1979 to $1.2 billion in 1980. And between 1980 and 1984 Moscow purchased almost $6 billion of Argentinian grain. Moscow also began large-scale acceptance of oil in lieu of cash payment for arms, reselling virtually all of this oil to third countries **(Table 9.8)**. Worth less than $1 billion in 1980, Soviet imports of mostly Middle Eastern crude oil topped $3 billion in 1984, constituting one-third of Moscow's purchases from the Third World.

The Soviets' trade surpluses with the world averaged more than $10 billion yearly in 1980–84. However, much of these surpluses resulted from Moscow's willingness to allow many of its Third World allies to run up substantial trade deficits in exchange for non-economic perks such as political support at various political forums and access to military bases. Indeed, Moscow allowed Cuba, Vietnam, Mongolia, North Korea, Laos, and Cambodia, to run up a combined tab for civilian goods of about $12 billion in 1980–84. Moreover, Afghanistan, Nicaragua, Ethiopia, South Yemen, Angola, and Mozambique will likely never pay for most of the $3 billion in non-military goods that Moscow provided them on credit over the same period. Adding in the supply of military goods to these Third World

allies for which Moscow will likely never be paid, the economic value to Moscow of its trade surpluses becomes even less.

Moscow's decision to trim the growth in imports from the West resulted in a slight trade surplus with this group of countries during the first part of the 1980s. Hard currency debt, as a result, grew much more slowly for 1980–84 than during the previous decade. Indeed gross debt in 1984 of $22.2 billion was only about $1 billion higher than the debt in 1979, while net debt actually declined somewhat to just $10.7 billion.

Oil Problems

The U.S.S.R. recorded its first drop in exports in more than 25 years in 1985 as domestic oil production problems forced Moscow to cut oil exports by more than 300,000 b/d at a loss of more than $4 billion in revenues. Moscow's decision to let deliveries to the West bear the brunt of the decline reduced the value of total exports to the developed West to pre-1980 levels. Oil deliveries to CMEA countries remained unscathed, and combined with a higher CMEA oil price than the year before, allowed Moscow to register an increase in export revenues to this group of countries. While Moscow's oil deliveries to the Third World also remained constant, overall Soviet exports to the Third World fell in 1985 because of a 20 percent drop in arms sales.

The value of energy sales continued to dictate the level of total Soviet exports in 1986–87. The collapse of world oil prices in 1986 more than offset Moscow's 400,000 b/d rebound in oil exports, causing total oil revenues to fall for the second year in a row. Receiving a price almost one-half lower than the year before, oil revenues from the West declined almost $5 billion in 1986, reducing total exports to this group of countries for the second year running. A rebound in oil revenues in 1987 of some $3.4 billion—a result of both higher prices and volumes—coincided with an increase in total exports of some $3.9 billion to the West.

Moscow continued to benefit from higher-than-world oil prices in 1986–87 in its trade with CMEA. Indeed, the combination of increased oil deliveries to Romania, larger gas deliveries and machinery exports to Eastern Europe, and oil prices some 50–100 percent higher than world levels enabled Moscow to export record amounts of Soviet goods to CMEA countries in both years.

Moscow was able to more than offset a $1 billion decline in oil exports to the Third World in 1986 by selling a record amount of arms that year. In fact, arms sales generated three-quarters of total Soviet sales to the less-developed countries that year. Moscow's ability to keep arms sales high in 1987, combined with higher world oil prices led to record Soviet exports to the Third World that year.

As opposed to the past, Moscow was not able to generate much hard currency from its Third World sales. Many of Moscow's traditional cash customers, such as Iraq and Libya, were also hit hard by falling oil prices, requiring the Soviets to provide favorable financing to make sales. Other customers already receiving Soviet goods on credit could not meet their payment obligations, prompting Moscow to reschedule their debts. Therefore, despite record arms exports in 1986–87, actual cash earnings from such sales were much less.

Overall, Soviet imports grew at an average annual rate of 6 percent in 1985–87. All of the increase, however, can be explained by higher imports from Eastern Europe, probably a response, in part, to Soviet demands at the CMEA Economic Summit in 1984 and other CMEA forums, that Eastern Europe boost exports and undertake a number of projects more to the benefit of the Soviet Union. Indeed, both imports of machinery and equipment and consumer goods rose significantly from Eastern Europe during this period.

In contrast to increased imports from Eastern Europe, imports from the West in 1985–87 averaged about $2.3 billion less than the previous three-year average of $26.4 billion. The reduced need for imported grain because of good Soviet harvests explains most of the cuts from the West. Soviet combined grain purchases from the United States, Canada, Australia, and Western Europe dropped from $5.3 billion in 1984 to $1.8 billion in 1987. Although the dollar value of other imports from the industrialized West remained stable for the period, the slide of the U.S. dollar vis-à-vis many other Western currencies resulted in a significant drop in "real" purchases.

The dollar value of imports from the Third World remained relatively unchanged from 1984 to 1985, but dropped 25 percent in 1986 as grain purchases from Argentina fell by more than $1 billion. Despite a small rebound in grain imports and other agricultural purchases in 1987, total imports from the less-developed countries remained depressed, in part because of oil pricing disputes with Libya which caused oil imports from that country to fall.

While overall trade surpluses continued in the mid-1980s, Moscow ran a trade deficit with the West of almost $1 billion in 1985. And the collapse in world oil prices the next year contributed largely to

the almost $4 billion deficit with this group of countries. Moscow responded to the deficits by selling record amounts of gold and stepping up borrowing from the West. Gross debt climbed to almost $42 billion in 1987, as Moscow was forced not only to borrow to cover the trade deficits with the West, but also to meet debt service obligations. It must be noted, however, that Moscow remained a relatively prudent borrower during these hectic times, with much of the climb in the dollar value of gross debt attributable to the decline of the U.S. dollar vis-à-vis those currencies in which the Soviets were borrowing.

Financial Institutions

The Soviets began expanding their use of Western financial markets, and sought to beef up ties with some multilateral economic institutions. For example, in August 1986, the Soviet Foreign Trade Bank agreed to invest $3.2 million in a yen-dominated bond issue, marking the first entry of the U.S.S.R. into the international bond market. And in 1988, the Soviets issued their own sovereign bonds in the Swiss and German markets. The Soviets have also begun an aggressive pursuit of closer ties with some multilateral economic institutions such as the General Agreement on Tariffs and Trade (GATT). Moscow has touched base with the International Monetary Fund (IMF), but did not pursue membership with this organization.

While many of Moscow's foreign economic overtures have focused on improving commercial relations with the West, a reevaluation by Moscow of its economic ties—both military and commercial—with virtually every region in the world is underway. In Eastern Europe, Moscow is trying to rejuvenate a trading system which suffers from pricing problems, excessive centralization of trade decisions, and the inconvertibility of the Soviet ruble among these countries. The vast amounts of economic and military assistance that Moscow sends annually to the Communist less-developed countries is coming under closer scrutiny, especially now that Gorbachev has made the improvement of the Soviet economy a high priority. Elsewhere in the Third World, a more business-like approach, relatively free of political and ideological trappings is becoming more prevalent.

Moscow's foreign economic initiatives to date have not produced any visible improvement in the Soviets' trade picture. Preliminary examination of Soviet trade statistics for 1988 indicates that energy and other raw material sales continued to make up the bulk of Soviet exports. Imports continued to be dominated by purchases of machinery and equipment and agricultural products, with the latter rising somewhat because of higher grain requirements.

Although Soviet moves such as the decentralization of trade, and the formation of joint ventures could provide some boost to exports of manufactured goods in the late 1990s, longstanding problems of inappropriate and inferior technology, poor marketing skills, and inadequate after-sales service will likely stymie the growth of these exports until then. Energy exports are also not likely to grow significantly in the 1990s, and in fact, could very well fall during the next decade should Moscow's domestic oil production begin to decline. How quickly the value of energy exports falls depends, in part, on prevailing world oil prices and Western demand for Soviet natural gas.

A more stringent credit policy towards the Communist Less Developed Countries and other Third World nations could have a telling effect on Soviet export levels to those countries. Moscow's unwillingness in the future to underwrite Cuba's and Vietnam's economies alone, could drop total exports by as much as 5 percent. Tighter Soviet credit, combined with increased competition and relatively moderate growth in Third World arms demand could also portend a fall in Soviet arms deliveries. Finally, Moscow's domestic needs and the Third World's inability to pay for Soviet project assistance, could reduce machinery and equipment sales abroad.

Exports to Eastern Europe are also likely to fall somewhat over the next couple of years as CMEA energy prices fall. Indeed, lower CMEA energy prices in 1988 were behind the first decline in Soviet exports to this region in over 20 years. Projected low energy prices over the next few years, in accordance with the CMEA pricing formula, combined with Soviet quality concerns could very well cause imports from Eastern Europe to also fall.

Therefore, barring a large jump in energy prices or renewed hostility involving one of Moscow's arms customers, total exports could fall. Unless Moscow is willing to depart from its traditionally conservative borrowing practices, imports, too, will decline. Such a trade downturn would prove most inopportune for a leadership seeking to invigorate its domestic economy and play a bigger role in the world economy.

Figure 9.1
Trade-per-capita: OECD Average vs USSR

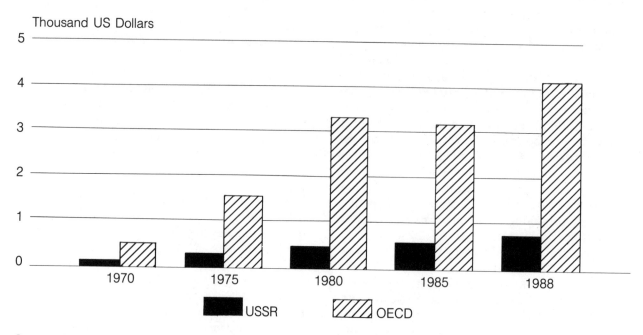

Source: *Handbook of Economic Statistics, 1988.* Central Intelligence Agency

Figure 9.2
USSR: Trade with the World

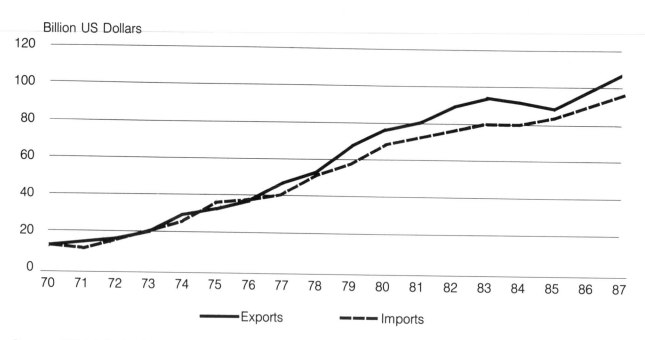

Source: Official Soviet foreign trade statistics published in *Vneshnyaya Torgovlya, USSR.*

Figure 9.3
USSR: Total Trade Turnover by Region, 1970–87

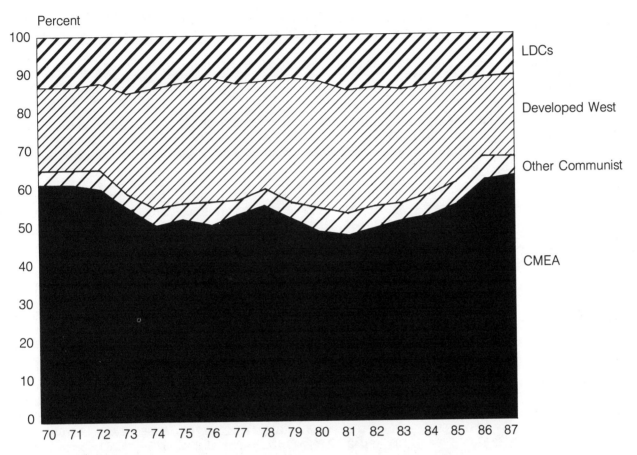

Source: Official Soviet foreign trade statistics published in *Vneshnyaya Torgovlya, USSR.*

Table 9.4
USSR: Commodity Composition of Trade*

	1970	1975	1977	1979	1980	(Millions US$) 1981	1982	1983	1984	1985	1986	1987
Total Exports	12,787	33,407	45,227	64,912	76,437	79,380	87,168	91,652	91,495	87,196	97,053	107,664
Machinery & Equipment	2,656	6,026	8,268	11,051	11,662	10,271	10,468	10,635	10,510	11,214	13,520	15,440
Base Metals & Manufactures	1,978	3,813	2,819	3,113	3,551	3,511	3,645	3,682	3,534	3,616	4,440	4,771
Crude oil & Refined products	1,429	8,212	12,784	22,211	27,851	30,029	35,028	38,092	38,001	33,843	31,898	36,066
Consumer Goods	1,310	2,378	2,307	2,805	2,679	2,733	2,573	2,597	2,583	2,574	3,214	3,688
Arms	1,050	2,534	4,843	6,127	6,153	7,432	9,325	9,300	8,576	6,912	9,698	10,477
Wood & Wood Products	831	1,916	2,300	2,666	3,093	2,632	2,471	2,587	2,575	2,638	3,289	3,502
Chemicals	334	949	979	1,498	2,025	2,275	2,203	2,307	2,707	2,836	2,770	2,979
Natural Gas	52	640	1,391	3,196	5,679	7,571	8,148	8,509	9,180	9,234	10,512	10,103
Unspecified	2,059	3,863	8,105	10,694	12,002	11,517	13,228	13,618	13,478	12,969	17,693	20,211
Other	1,048	3,076	1,431	1,551	1,742	1,409	79	325	351	1,360	19	427
Total Imports	11,720	37,072	40,926	57,958	68,472	73,158	77,847	80,445	80,409	83,315	88,873	95,971
Machinery & Equipment	4,166	12,574	15,594	22,018	23,198	22,106	26,766	30,709	29,451	30,941	36,145	39,746
Consumer Goods	3,975	13,110	13,294	18,538	24,136	28,609	27,449	24,976	26,900	26,710	25,449	26,120
Agriculture Products	2,303	9,110	9,133	13,565	17,437	20,914	19,340	17,713	18,719	17,546	14,780	15,339
Grain	135	2,673	1,392	3,448	5,114	7,257	6,120	5,147	6,816	5,950	2,868	2,463
Base Metals & Manufactures	691	3,595	2,482	4,499	4,653	4,594	5,359	4,948	4,656	4,897	5,263	5,480
Chemicals	493	1,447	1,467	2,224	3,275	3,211	3,028	3,216	3,256	3,744	3,990	4,516
Crude oil & Refined products	25	552	580	937	918	1,214	1,952	2,742	3,108	2,734	2,870	2,554
Other	2,370	5,794	7,509	9,742	12,292	13,424	13,293	13,854	13,038	14,289	15,156	17,555

*Derived from official Soviet trade statistics published in *Vneshnyaya Torgovlya, USSR.*

Figure 9.5
Soviet Oil Exports: Value, Volume, and Prices

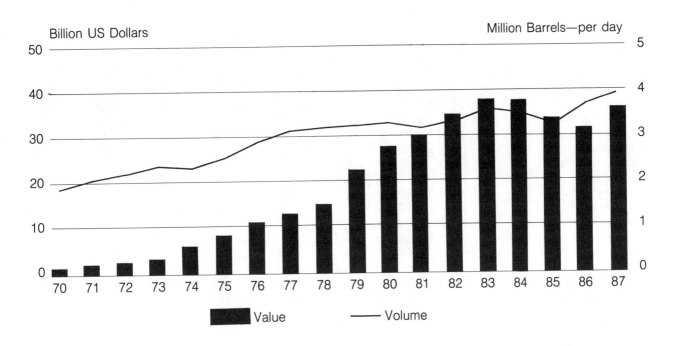

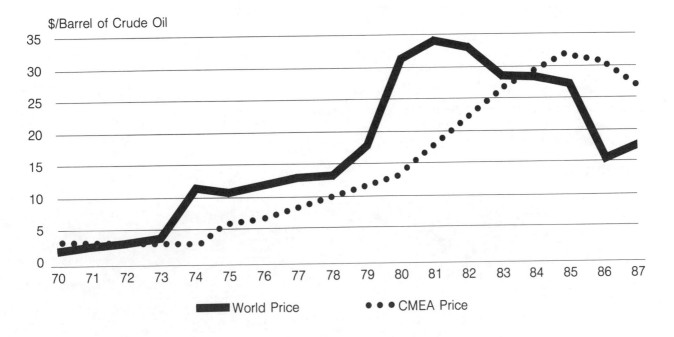

Sources: Value data from *Vneshnyaya Torgovlya, USSR.*
Volume and world price data from *International Energy Statistical Review*, CIA.
CMEA price data estimated using CMEA pricing formulas.

Table 9.6
USSR: Hard Currency Balance of Payments(a)

					(Millions US$)			
	1970	1975	1980	1983	1984	1985	1986	1987(b)
Trade Balance	−306	−4,804	1,814	4,712	4,727	519	2,013	5,999
Exports	2,405	9,453	27,874	32,429	32,173	26,400	25,111	28,908
Developed West	1,982	7,001	21,309	23,354	23,447	19,734	16,522	20,032
Third World(c)	423	2,452	6,565	9,075	8,726	6,666	8,589	8,876
Imports	2,711	14,257	26,060	27,717	27,446	25,881	23,098	22,909
Developed West	2,374	12,199	21,338	21,747	21,383	20,104	19,275	18,877
Third World	337	2,058	4,722	5,970	6,063	5,777	3,823	4,032
Net interest	−80	−521	−1,219	−1,040	−1,163	−1,482	−1,740	−2,235
Other invisibles(d)	500	760	890	1,100	1,100	1,100	1,100	1,100
Current account balance	114	−4,565	1,485	4,772	4,664	137	1,373	4,864
Change in gross debt(e)	290	6,786	−1,072	116	224	6,803	7,175	5,000
Change in assets(f)	25	−163	−35	277	−664	1,787	1,635	0
Estimated exchange rate effect on debts and assets	NA	−22	−411	−1,070	−688	3,248	3,322	3,500
Net credits to the Third World	NA	715	950	3,200	2,700	1,700	4,100	4,800
Gold sales	0	725	1,580	750	1,000	1,800	4,000	3,500
Capital account balance	265	6,981	4	−1,541	−124	1,868	2,118	200
Errors and omissions(g)	−379	−2,416	−1,489	−3,213	−4,540	−2,005	−3,491	−5,064

(a) Estimated
(b) Preliminary
(c) Including military exports to the Third World
(d) Including estimated net receipts from tourism, transportation, and official transfers.
(e) Including additions to short-term debt
(f) Net change in assets held in Western commercial banks.
(g) Including hard currency aid to and trade with other Communist countries, trade credits to finance exports to developed countries, and other nonspecified hard currency expenditures, as well as, errors and omissions in other line items of the accounts.

Source: *Handbook of Economic Statistics, 1988,* Central Intelligence Agency.

Table 9.7
USSR: Estimated Hard Currency Debt to the West

(Millions US$)

	1975	1976	1977	1978	1979	1980	1981	1982	1984	1985	1986	1987(a)
Gross debt	12,502	17,648	17,953	20,797	21,332	20,540	22,517	21,877	22,216	29,021	36,004	41,642
Commercial debt	8,205	11,391	9,825	10,976	11,557	11,045	14,392	12,785	13,160	19,501	25,921	31,083
Commercial bank debt	7,463	10,295	8,405	9,362	10,221	9,973	13,587	12,050	12,433	18,584	24,743	29,709
Promissory notes	742	1,096	1,420	1,614	1,336	1,072	805	735	727	917	1178	1,374
Government-backed debt	4,297	6,257	8,128	9,821	9,775	9,495	8,125	9,092	9,056	9,520	10,083	10,559
Assets held in Western banks	3,780	4,791	5,134	6,829	9,997	9,962	9,796	11,918	11,531	13,318	14,913	14,386
Net debt	8,722	12,857	12,819	13,968	11,335	10,578	12,721	9,959	10,685	15,703	21,091	27,256

(a) Preliminary estimate.

Source: *Handbook of Economic Statistics, 1988*, Central Intelligence Agency.

Table 9.8
USSR: Oil Imports, 1970–87[1]

	1970	1975	1976	1977	1978	1979	(Millions US$) 1980	1981	1982	1983	1984	1985	1986	1987
Total	92	151	144	141	188	156	97	116	183	274	320	289	333	323
Algeria	10	20	0	0	0	0	1	1	0	0	15	29	68	26
Egypt	40	4	3	0	0	0	0	0	0	0	0	0	0	0
Iran	0	0	0	0	0	0	0	45	18	44	25	15	0	4
Iraq	0	106	116	92	128	76	36	0	2	46	77	65	92	52
Libya	0	0	0	21	31	59	34	34	119	118	125	96	92	52
Saudia Arabia	0	0	0	0	0	0	0	0	0	21	38	48	58	0
Other[2]	42	21	25	28	29	21	26	36	44	45	40	36	52	47

(1) Quantities for 1970–76, 1986–87 are from *Vneshnyaya Torgovlya, USSR.*
   Quantities for other years were estimated on the basis of Soviet foreign trade value data and collateral trade data.
(2) Includes some imports of refined oil products from the Developed West.

Table 9.9
USSR: Top 15 Trading Partners*

(Millions US$)

	1970	1975	1980	1985	1987
East Germany	3,657	7,817	14,168	18,314	23,272
Czechoslovakia	2,435	5,436	11,063	16,155	21,621
Poland	2,609	6,746	12,323	14,558	20,337
Bulgaria	2,016	5,547	10,933	15,014	20,269
Hungary	1,643	4,550	8,837	11,362	15,295
Cuba	1,160	3,598	6,569	9,621	11,942
West Germany	604	3,860	8,901	8,514	7,832
Romania	1,020	2,121	4,298	5,111	7,721
Yugoslavia	577	2,167	5,929	7,307	6,280
Finland	589	2,440	5,988	5,987	5,914
Italy	523	1,983	4,673	4,556	5,516
France	458	1,802	5,779	4,535	4,121
Japan	724	2,672	4,193	3,860	4,110
India	405	953	2,679	3,701	3,442
United Kingdom	712	1,334	2,790	2,283	3,334

* Total trade turnover. Ranking based on 1987 trade position.

Source: Official Soviet foreign trade statistics published in *Vneshnyaya Torgovlya, USSR.*